Schriftenreihe der HHL Leipzig Graduate School of Management

HHL LEIPZIG GRADUATE SCHOOL OF MANAGEMENT

Reihe herausgegeben von
Stephan Stubner, Leipzig, Deutschland

In dieser Schriftenreihe werden aktuelle Forschungsergebnisse aus dem Bereich Unternehmensführung präsentiert. Die einzelnen Beiträge spiegeln die wissenschaftliche Ausrichtung der HHL in Forschung und Lehre wider. Sie zeichnen sich vor allem durch eine ganzheitliche, integrative Perspektive aus und sind durch den Anspruch geprägt, Theorie und Praxis zu verbinden sowie in besonderem Maße internationale Aspekte einzubeziehen.

Weitere Bände in der Reihe http://www.springer.com/series/12648

Maximilian Schosser

Big Data to Improve Strategic Network Planning in Airlines

With a foreword by Prof. Dr. Iris Hausladen

Springer Gabler

Maximilian Schosser
HHL Leipzig Graduate School of Management
Heinz-Nixdorf Chair of IT-based Logistics
Leipzig, Germany

Dissertation HHL Leipzig Graduate School of Management, 2019

Schriftenreihe der HHL Leipzig Graduate School of Management
ISBN 978-3-658-27581-5 ISBN 978-3-658-27582-2 (eBook)
https://doi.org/10.1007/978-3-658-27582-2

Springer Gabler

This Springer Gabler imprint is published by the registered company Springer Fachmedien Wiesbaden GmbH part of Springer Nature.
The registered company address is: Abraham-Lincoln-Str. 46, 65189 Wiesbaden, Germany

For my wife Karin who filled the days of my PhD studies with pure joy.

For my mother Jutta who taught me the most important trait as a researcher – curiosity.

For my father Rudolf whose perfectionist mind helped with great suggestions for this thesis.

Foreword

Big data not just evolved as a popular buzzword over time but is meanwhile seen as a high potential field for improving business processes and decisions taken by responsible persons in different industry sectors, such as airlines.

Nevertheless, available advantages of big data have not yet been adequately measured from an economic perspective and have very often not yet been exploited at all or to a reasonable level. Additionally, corresponding theoretical concepts and scientific developments focusing on the area of network planning in airlines are currently more or less missing. Those challenging deficits make the topic considered by Mr. Schosser highly relevant both from a theoretical as well as a practical perspective.

Thus, the main objective of the thesis consists in closing both the scientific research gap and providing a solution to practitioners focusing on the assessment of big data opportunities in the network planning context of airlines.

The author provides with the step-by-step, theoretically and empirically based development of the framework, its elements and procedures in the present doctoral thesis an outstanding analytical as well as conceptual personal contribution. The framework is from a content-related point of view to be honored as a pioneering achievement and the dissertation contains a lot of new findings that represent a starting point for further work predominantly in the research and practice field of big data evaluation focused on airline network planning that can be transferred to further use cases respectively fields of applications.

The book, which is based on a dissertation at the HHL Leipzig Graduate School of Management, is aimed equally at readers from science and practice, dealing with (big) data collection, economic evaluation of big data as well as big data analytics.

Leipzig, May 2019 *Prof. Dr. Iris Hausladen*

Preface

The idea for this PhD thesis was born during a consulting project at a European airline, where different departments were at completely different maturity stages of using Big Data. While at some departments network planning was done the old-fashioned way, with legacy IT-systems, data and processes, other departments had already implemented a much more agile way of integrating Big Data.

The network planning department was frequently approached by data providers with concrete offers, but there was no method to evaluate the impact of the data for airline network planning, and most of the offers were turned down for this reason. At the same time, there was no research available to answer this question. The main objective of this PhD thesis is hence to alleviate the lack of evaluation methods and provide a concise answer/approach/framework of how Big Data can create value for individual network planning steps.

The target audience of this thesis comprises airline network planners of all seniority levels and fellow researchers working on Big Data applications for the transportation industry, on network optimization problems or on commercial topics in airlines. I tried to find a middle ground between content of pure scientific interest (e.g., chapters 2 and 3), and presenting relevant findings for practitioners (chapters 4, 5 and 6).

Finally, I want to thank everyone who contributed to this PhD thesis, in particular my thesis advisor Prof. Dr. Iris Hausladen, who provided guidance and challenge whenever necessary. Further, I want to thank all interview partners of our airline case study group, who need to stay anonymous due to non-disclosure agreements. Philipp Behrends, Karin Garcia and Rudolf Schosser made an invaluable contribution by reviewing and commenting on various drafts of this thesis. My thanks go also to all staff and students of HHL Leipzig Graduate School of Management who made my time there so enjoyable. Finally, I want to thank Maximilian Rothkopf for helping to shape the idea and David Speiser for his support of my PhD project. My PhD thesis would not have been possible without the financial support during my educational leave granted by the Zurich Office of McKinsey & Company.

Berlin, May 2019 *Maximilian Schosser*

Contents

List of Figures

List of Tables

List of Abbreviations

ACL	-	Airport Coordination Limited
ACMI	-	Aircraft, Crew, Maintenance and Insurance
ADS-B	-	Automatic Dependent Surveillance Broadcast
API	-	Application Programming Interface
ASK	-	Available Seat Kilometers
AWB	-	Air Waybill
BD	-	Big Data
BDA	-	Big Data Analytics
BDO	-	Big Data Opportunity
BI&A	-	Business Intelligence & Analytics
BT	-	Block Time
CAR	-	Cargo Airline
CASS	-	Cargo Accounts Settlement System
CCO	-	Chief Commercial Officer
CEO	-	Chief Executive Officer
COO	-	Chief Operations Officer
DOC	-	Direct Operating Cost
e.g.	-	For example (Latin: exempli gratia)
EASA	-	European Aviation Safety Agency
e-AWB	-	Electronic Air Waybill
EBIT	-	Earnings Before Interest and Tax
et al.	-	Et alii
etc.	-	Et cetera
EU	-	European Union
FDI	-	Foreign Direct Investment
FSC	-	Full-Service Carrier
FTE	-	Full-Time Equivalent
GB	-	Gigabyte
GDP	-	Gross Domestic Product
GDS	-	Global Distribution System
GPS	-	Global Positioning System
HS	-	Hub-And-Spoke
i.e.	-	That is (Latin: id est)

IAG	-	International Airlines Group
IATA	-	International Air Transport Association
ICAO	-	International Civil Aviation Organization
IMF	-	International Monetary Fund
IOC	-	Indirect Operating Cost
IP	-	Internet Protocol
IS	-	Information Systems
IT	-	Information Technology
KPI	-	Key Performance Indicator
LCC	-	Low-Cost Carrier
LoRaWAN	-	Low Range Wide Area Network
MCT	-	Minimum Connection Time
MIDT	-	Marketing Information Data Tape
MIT	-	Massachusetts Institute of Technology
NLP	-	Natural Language Processing
NP	-	Network Planning
NPV	-	Net Present Value
OAG	-	Official Airline Guide
O&D	-	Origin & Destination
OECD	-	Organisation for Economic Co-operation and Development
OR	-	Operations Research
p.	-	Page
P&RM	-	Pricing & Revenue Management
pp.	-	Pages
PP	-	Point-To-Point
QSI	-	Quality Of Service Index
RBV	-	Resource-Based View
RFID	-	Radio-Frequency Identification
RQ	-	Research Question
RR	-	Random Radial
RSK	-	Revenue Seat Kilometers
RTK	-	Revenue Ton Kilometers
SCA	-	Scheduled Charter Airline
SCM	-	Supply Chain Management

SRS	-	Schedule Reference Service
TAT	-	Turn-Around Time
TB	-	Terabyte
UK	-	United Kingdom
US	-	United States
USD	-	United States Dollar
VHB	-	German Academic Association for Business Research
VM	-	Virtual Machine
WTO	-	World Trade Organization

1 Introduction

1.1 Problem and research gap definition

1.1.1 Practical problem

Big data has become one of the most prominent buzzwords of the modern corporate world, which is a remarkably fast feat for a new phenomenon. It became fashionable at the onset of the 2010s, fueled by popular articles in the Harvard Business Review (McAfee & Brynjolfsson, 2012) and the MIT Sloan Management Review (Davenport, Barth, & Bean, 2012). Its broad scope makes it directly or indirectly crucial for all industries, and as early as 2011, Manyika et al. (2011, p. 1) estimated a global big data (BD) value generation potential of more than 1 trillion US Dollar (USD).

Since airlines had been producing vast amounts of data even before the term big data was coined, its potential value in the industry was noticed early on (Noyes, 2014). In a recent survey, more than 60% of aviation executives named big data as a top priority for their company (Hodgson & Waldmeir, 2018). The airline business is receptive to a wide range of big data applications: the single customer view enables hyper-personalized customer experience and marketing activities (Chen et al., 2017; Hodgson & Waldmeir, 2018; Noyes, 2014); higher granularity of customer insights can be utilized for customized pricing and revenue management (Boin et al., 2017); real-time information on transfer passengers and irregular situations can help reduce delays and smoothen flight operations (Bowcott & Dichter, 2014; Chen et al., 2017); finally, predictive maintenance can reduce unplanned aircraft groundings and lower maintenance cost (Bradbury, 2018; Chen et al., 2017).

Although airlines are at the forefront of big data adoption, not all business processes and departments in the industry participate at the same speed. Bertram (2017) proposes various big data applications for network planning (NP), including mobile location data and real-time flight radar data.

M. Schosser, *Big Data to Improve Strategic Network Planning in Airlines*,
Schriftenreihe der HHL Leipzig Graduate School of Management,
https://doi.org/10.1007/978-3-658-27582-2_1

However, most NP departments in airlines have not yet adopted any big data application in their NP process.

Investment in big data opportunities (BDOs) require the creation of a sound business plan with clearly defined costs and benefits (Bertram, 2017). The airline business is a low-margin industry that is very reluctant to make large exploratory investments to prove use cases with an uncertain probability of success (Hodgson & Waldmeir, 2018). Airline network planners currently struggle to estimate the benefit potential of BDOs in prioritizing and formulating reliable business cases. This book addresses this practical problem by consolidating and structuring potential BDOs for airline NP. Subsequently, it develops a benefit evaluation methodology based on NP-specific performance metrics.

1.1.2 Scientific research gap

Big data has experienced a rapid increase in popularity in the scientific research community. Akoka, Comyn-Wattiau, and Laoufi (2017, p. 110) and Govindan et al. (2018, p. 344) found a significant increase in the number of studies on big data, especially since 2014[1]. Historically, computer science and engineering are the major research domains investigating big data, while business and management science has been catching up only recently (Govindan et al., 2018, p. 346). While the scientific discussion on big data is maturing, there is still no unanimous definition pertaining to its characteristics (Mauro, Greco, & Grimaldi, 2015, p. 103).

Although a holistic big data value chain has been proposed by Gandomi and Haider (2015, p. 141), little research has been conducted on the sources and types of big data (Akoka et al., 2017, p. 111). While information systems architecture and big data analytics techniques are under

[1] Govindan et al. (2018) found an 8-fold increase of academic publications with big data in title, abstract or full-text between 2014 and 2017.

academic focus, big data sources are mostly treated as input factors and not as key value contributors.

Furthermore, there is little research on big data which is specifically targeted at the airline industry. Authors concentrate on individual use cases, including predictive maintenance (Badea, Zamfiroiu, & Boncea, 2018), air traffic optimization (Ayhan et al., 2013), and marketing and flight operations (Chen et al., 2017). There is no scholarly contribution on the use of big data for airline NP yet.

This study aims to bridge this gap in two ways. First, it shifts the attention from big data architecture and analytics towards the opportunities evolving from specific big data sources. Even the most advanced infrastructure and analytic tools cannot create value if they use meaningless data. Second, the study provides a perspective on big data applications for airline NP, and thus complements research on other domains of application in airlines.

1.2 Objective of the study and research questions

The objectives of this study aim to close the scientific research gap laid out in the previous section and address the practical problem discussed previously in order to evaluate big data opportunities for airline NP. As the first step, the most recent research on big data and on NP in airlines needs to be assessed. Based on the existing body of literature, a clear definition of big data in the context of airline NP must be developed to build a solid foundation to find solutions to the practical problem.

A deep understanding of NP processes, tools, and data types in practice must be created before applications for BDOs in airline NP can be developed. The current state of these processes, tools and data types can then be contrasted with the theoretical concepts of strategic airline NP.

Based on the status quo of airline NP, the information requirements of airline network planners can be identified. BDOs should address these information needs to create value for airline NP. The definition of concrete

BDOs and the qualitative evaluation of their applicability and usefulness for airline NP is the most crucial objective of this study.

Finally, the development of a cost and benefit evaluation scheme for BDOs in airline NP should address the practical problem described in the previous section. This requires the determination of relevant key performance indicators to measure the contribution of big data opportunities in terms of financial value.

The research objectives can be condensed into four specific research questions, which are presented in Figure 1.1. All research questions are of an explanatory nature since the research phenomenon has not yet been discussed in literature.

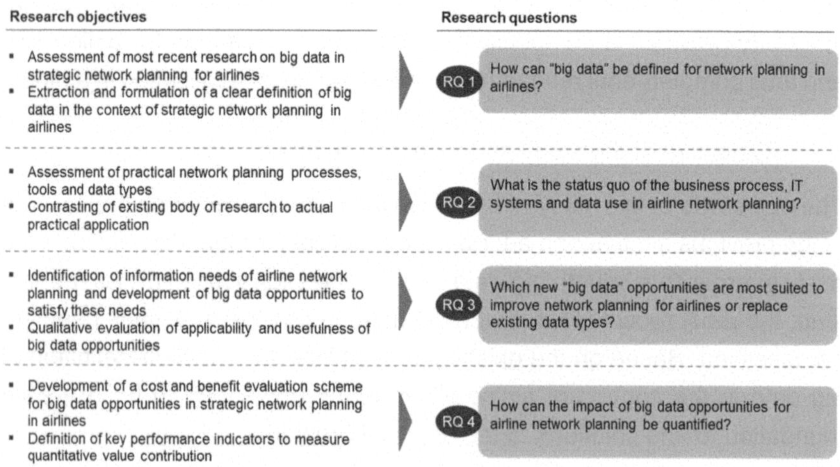

Figure 1.1 – Research objectives and research questions[2]

[2] Source: Own illustration.

2 Methodology

The choice of the research methodology does not depend only on the characteristics of the research topic or the individual preferences of the researcher. It should also be underpinned by a sound philosophical research paradigm and must be suitable to answer the research questions and fulfil the objectives defined in the previous chapter. Sub-chapter 2 presents the paradigm that drives the research. Detailed descriptions of the literature review process (sub-chapter 2.2) and of the multi-stage comparative case study (sub-chapter 2.3) introduce the major techniques employed for the rest of this study.

Figure 2.1 summarizes the logical development of the research methodology, as described before.

Step in methodology development	*Outcome for this thesis*	*Relevant section*
Research questions & objectives	▪ 4 research questions to address practical problem	▪ 1.1
Research paradigm	▪ Pragmatic view	▪ 2.1
Research approach	▪ Qualitative-dominant research approach	▪ 2.1
Research design	▪ Explanatory sequential qualitative study	▪ 2.1
Choice of methods & techniques	▪ Structured literature review ▪ Comparative case study	▪ 2.2 ▪ 2.3

Figure 2.1 – Overview of research methodology development[3]

[3] Source: Own illustration.

M. Schosser, *Big Data to Improve Strategic Network Planning in Airlines*, Schriftenreihe der HHL Leipzig Graduate School of Management,
https://doi.org/10.1007/978-3-658-27582-2_2

2.1 Development of research design

This study adopts the pragmatic view as the research paradigm. Pragmatism incorporates elements of both post-positivism and constructivism by accepting the co-existence of subjective, inter-subjective, and objective reality (Antwi & Hamza, 2015, p. 223). Research problems in management sciences, especially emerging phenomena, are rarely ever completely quantifiable or solely based on human interactions (Wynn & Williams, 2012, p. 789). Hence, pragmatists emphasize on the consequences of actions that cause real-world problems, which are addressed in practical research (Creswell, 2013, p. 6).

The four research questions defined in chapter 1 are clearly derived from a practical problem – the vagueness of BDO benefits for airline NP. The objective is not only to understand the causal effects of big data, manifested in the expected economic impact, but also to analyze the current processes and beliefs followed by airline network planners. Furthermore, the recency of big data calls for a holistic investigation, as there may not be sufficient material available to answer the research questions empirically. The combination of (1) the practical research focus, (2) an emergent research topic, and (3) the complexity of the four research questions require the adoption of a pragmatist perspective for this research project.

Pragmatists advocate for an appropriate mix of qualitative and quantitative methods, which best suits the research objectives (Creswell, 2013, p. 213). Table 2.1 summarizes the relevant decision-making criteria for qualitative, quantitative, or mixed-method approaches.

Table 2.1 – Decision-making criteria for research approach[4]

Criteria	Quantitative approach	Qualitative approach	Mixed methods approach
Research questions	Confirmatory	Exploratory	Both
Purpose	Theory testing	Theory building	Solving practical problems
Context	▪ High-quality data available / possible to collect (including sufficiently large N) ▪ Comparable research objects ▪ Experimental set-up possible	▪ No previous research on topic ▪ No or insufficient data available ▪ Research objects not comparable	▪ Quantitative and qualitative data available ▪ Emergent research topic

Applying these decision-making criteria, a qualitative-dominant approach with quantitative elements appears most appropriate for this study. While research question (RQ) 1 and RQ 2 are purely exploratory, RQ 3 and RQ 4 have a confirmatory element complementing the explanatory character of the questions. The motivation behind conducting this study originates from a practical problem, which should be analyzed and solved from a scientific perspective. Theory building or testing is not a research objective of this study. Furthermore, "big data" is an emerging research topic that is increasingly garnering interest in the fields of science and practice. The absent large-scale implementation of big data in airline NP impedes a purely quantitative study. However, airlines are sufficiently comparable, in that the research would benefit from a small-scale quantitative element in order to evaluate the usefulness and potential of big data. Furthermore, a sequential research setup is the most appropriate, since the research questions need to be answered consecutively.

[4] Own illustration based on Creswell (2013, pp. 157–211).

After selecting a general research design, the most appropriate research methods need to be determined. Yin (2017, p. 8) proposed three decision-making criteria for this: the nature of the research question, the need for behavioral control, and the focus on present or past events (see Table 2.2). Since none of the research questions require behavioral control and all of them focus on contemporary events, experiments and historic studies can be ruled out. This leaves literature review, case study, and survey as potential research methods. All these methods are suited for a qualitative-dominant research design and can contribute towards answering the research questions.

Table 2.2 – Comparison of research methods[5]

Research method	Qualitative/quantitative	Form of research question	Requires behavioral control of events?	Focuses on contemporary events?
Experiment	Quantitative	How, why?	Yes	Yes
Survey	Quantitative	Who, what, where, how many, how much?	No	Yes
Literature analysis	Qualitative	How, why, who, what, where, how many, how much?	No	Yes/No
Historic study	Qualitative	How, why?	No	No
Case Study	Qualitative	How, why?	No	Yes

RQ 1 is "How can 'big data' be defined for network planning in airlines?" considering the existing research and theories. A structured analysis of the literature is the most suited research method for this, as both recent and historic literature can be explored. Although RQ 2 and RQ 3 start with "what" and "which" respectively, both questions have an exploratory character calling for a predominantly qualitative method. For this purpose, a

[5] Own illustration following Yin (2017, p. 8).

qualitative comparative case study, featuring a quantitative small-scale survey, seems to be the best suited to answer the questions. The case study is also extended to finally answer RQ 4 in the final research phase.

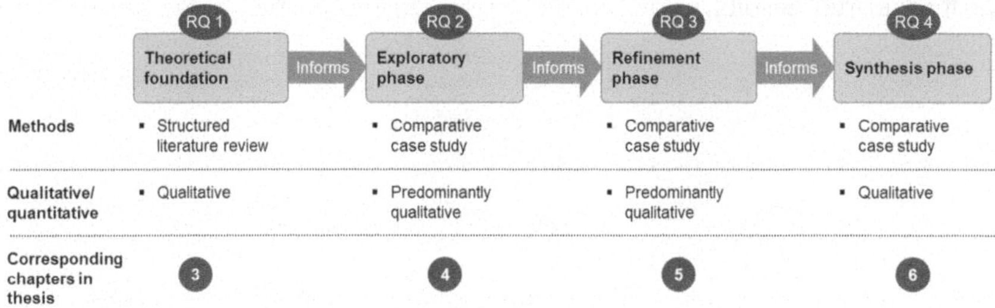

Figure 2.2 – Four-phase research design[6]

Figure 2.2 schematizes the four phases of the research design. The detailed methodology, including the chosen techniques, are presented in the following sub-chapters. The set-up and execution of the structured literature review is explained in section 2.2. Section 2.3 is dedicated to explaining the case study set-up, including the data collection and survey design methodology. Chapters 3–6 of this study present the theories and findings from each respective research question (see Figure 2.2).

Ensuring high research quality is a key objective of the research design phase. Cooper and Schindler (2000, p. 211) identify "validity" and "reliability" as key quality measures for research in management. Reliability is a measure to "ensure consistent results" (Cooper & Schindler, 2000, p. 215) within and across research projects. Validity indicates the correct measurement and analysis of the intended phenomena. Accordingly, Yin (2017, p. 41) proposed reliability and three validity aspects as measures for research quality, namely construct validity, internal validity, and external validity. Construct validity describes the ability of a research method or, more

[6] Source: Own illustration.

specifically, a research construct such as a survey to analyze the right research subject. Internal validity minimizes systematic errors and biases in the research process, whereas external validity ensures the generalizability of research results.

	Quality criteria			
	Reliability	**Construct validity**	**Internal validity**	**External validity**
Description	The degree to which a research method delivers consistent research results	The degree to which a research method analyzes what it claims, to be analyzing	The degree to which a research method minimizes systematic errors and biases	The degree to which a research method produces generalizable results
Tactics for literature review	▪ Thorough documentation of the search process	▪ Appropriate keyword choice	▪ Clear screening and evaluation logic	▪ Choice of relevant databases ▪ Diligent forward/ backward search
Tactics for comparative case study	▪ Case study protocol ▪ Case study database ▪ Standardized questionnaire	▪ Multiple sources of evidence ▪ Chain of evidence ▪ Review of draft reports by key informants	▪ Pattern matching ▪ Explanation building ▪ Alternative explanations ▪ Logical models ▪ Selection of appropriate score system	▪ Clear replication logic in case studies ▪ Theoretical case sampling ▪ Minimization of non-response rate

Figure 2.3 – Tactics to ensure the quality criteria for selected research methods[7]

The structured literature review process proposed by Vom Brocke et al. (2009, p. 2211–2212) aims to ensure that these quality measures are met, arguing that literature reviews should be considered a self-contained research method and thus should be subject to the very same quality measures. Similarly, Yin (2017, p. 41) has recommended tactics for designing rigorous case studies, following the aforementioned research quality criteria. For surveys (which are part of the comparative case study), Creswell (2013, p. 155) and Cooper and Schindler (2000, p. 216) have suggested various tactics to guarantee reliability and validity in the research process. Figure 2.3 summarizes the proposed tactics to meet the

[7] Own illustration following Yin (2017, p. 41), Creswell (2013, pp. 155–157), Cooper and Schindler (2000, pp. 215–218), and Vom Brocke et al. (2009, p. 2212).

discussed quality criteria. The tactics are implemented in the research design and will be further described in the sections dedicated to them.

2.2 Literature review

In order to build on established scientific theories and highlight the purpose of a research project, the literature review is the fundamental starting point to connect the research to the existing body of knowledge by uncovering relevant research gaps (Vom Brocke et al., 2009, p. 2206).

2.2.1 Design of a structured literature review process

Paré et al. (2015, pp. 185–189) identified nine literature review archetypes based on the research objective and the dominant research methods of a project[8]. According to this classification, a realist review is most suited for this study, since the research questions are already defined, and the overall research strategy follows a qualitative approach with quantitative elements. A realist review should follow an iterative and purposive search strategy and include both conceptual and empirical works. The studies can be down-selected based on pre-defined formal criteria (e.g., journal quality or publication date) or qualitative criteria (e.g., abstract reviews).

The structured literature review process proposed by Vom Brocke et al. (2009) includes most of the realist review criteria and is specifically intended for multidisciplinary research, with strong rooting in the information systems (IS) research domain.

The starting point of a structured literature review is the identification of relevant search terms and knowledge containers to assure external validity. In an academic context, this means selecting the appropriate publica-

[8] Please refer to Appendix 1 for a complete overview of the typology of literature review.

tions and databases that pertain to the relevant literature. To define appropriate search terms, Vom Brocke et al. (2009, p. 2214) proposed a structured decomposition of titles or research questions as well as the inclusion of intended theories and research paradigms. This step is crucial to guarantee construct validity, i.e., to ensure that the search delivers the intended results. These activities comprise Step 1 in Figure 2.4 and are presented in detail in the next section.

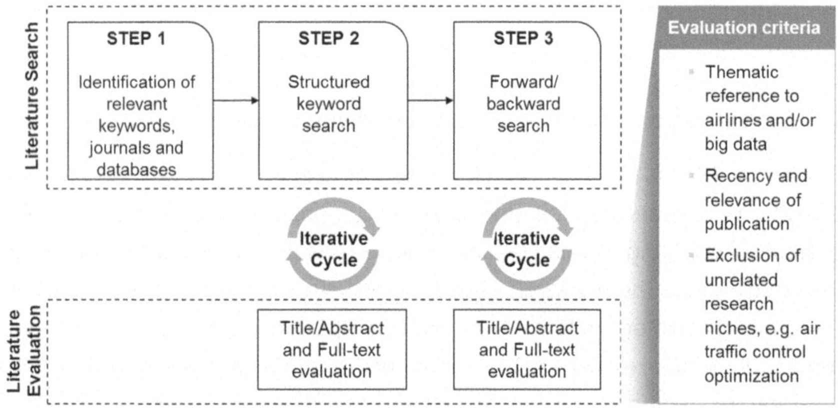

Figure 2.4 – Structured literature review process[9]

Step 2 entails the actual keyword search in the selected databases and publications. The results are evaluated through a three-step approach. First, the title is evaluated to exclude literature on completely unrelated research fields (e.g., medicine) or in languages other than English, German, or Spanish. The second iteration is a qualitative abstract screening to exclude thematically irrelevant contributions (e.g., literature on air traffic control optimization). The full-text evaluation is the last iteration to confirm or refute the actual relevance of the contribution (e.g., non-content editorials

9 Own illustration following Vom Brocke et al. (2009).

or book reviews). These steps need to be followed strictly for all individual searches to ensure internal validity of the literature review.

Finally, Step 3 aims to identify additional literature based on a forward/backward search, using the most relevant contributions identified in Step 2. The evaluation iterations in Step 3 are similar to those of Step 2.

2.2.2 *Identification of keywords, databases, and journals*

The title of this study can be deconstructed as three major elements. "Big data" describes the phenomenon that is the primary research subject. The phenomenon is examined for a specific industry, namely "airlines," and for a specific business process, the "strategic network planning." The two guiding theories for this research are the resource-based view of the firm and network theory[10], which have also been included in the keywords. Synonyms and adjacent search terms complement the extracted keyword in each area (see Table 2.3).

Table 2.3 – Keyword extraction for the literature review[11]

Extracted keyword	Source	Type	Synonyms and related search terms
"big data"	Title	Primary research subject	"data management" "business intelligence" "business analytics"
"airline"	Title	Industry	"aviation" "logistics" "transportation"
"strategic network planning"	Title	Process	"strategic planning" "network planning"
"resource-based view"	Theoretic concept	Theory	"RBV"
"network theory"	Theoretic concept	Theory	-

[10] Compare sub-chapter 3 for a detailed discussion on theory selection.

[11] Source: Own illustration.

The combination of the four keyword categories results in 15 different search queries when synonyms and related search terms are included using the Boolean string "OR"[12]. Appendix 4 displays the aforementioned combinations.

For the identification of the relevant journals and databases, the primary research domains for this study must be identified first. The research domains of VHB-JOURQUAL 3 ranking (VHB, 2015), curated by the German Academic Association for Business Research (VHB), are evaluated with a scoring model based on the relative search results for each of the extracted keywords (see Appendix 3 for the detailed scoring results).

Logistics, operations research (OR), strategic management, and information systems are the most relevant domains for this research. General management science, international management, marketing, organization science, production management, and technology, innovation & entrepreneurship are other domains of medium importance.

The combination of three platforms, EbscoHost, Elsevier, and SpringerLINK, provides full-text access to the 39 most important journals[13] in the relevant research domains (see **Appendix 5** for a graphical summary). Google Scholar complements the three access points as a meta-search engine, as it also includes scientific reports, conference papers, and books that are not accessible via the scientific databases.

---

[12] Example: The complete Boolean Phrase for combination 4 would read as ["big data" OR "data management" OR "business intelligence" OR "business analytics"] AND ["airline" OR "aviation" OR "logistics" OR "transportation"] AND ["strategic network planning" OR "strategic planning" OR "network planning"] AND ["resource-based view" OR "RBV" OR "network theory"].

[13] Based on VHB-JOURQUAL 3 ranking VHB (2015): Journals ranked A+ from all the relevant research domains plus journals ranked A from logistics, operations research, strategic management and information systems. Appendix 4 provides a complete list of the 39 journals.

2.2.3 Results of the structured keyword search

During the initial search, the parameters were set to a full-text search and limited to academic articles, conference proceedings, and books[14]. For the initial search with one keyword only (combinations 1a to 1d in Appendix 2), the search terms for object (big data), industry (airline), and theories (resource-based view OR network theory) resulted in at least 10,000 hits at each access point, while the keyword chosen for the relevant process (strategic network planning) produced less than 1000 hits at all access points. Therefore, the keyword selection for processes was extended with the two decompositions “strategic planning” and “network planning.”

The initial round of the structured literature search followed the keyword combination scheme presented in Appendix 2 and entailed 15 individual searches. The search was commenced with the full combination of all relevant keywords (4a) to identify the most relevant literature first. Subsequently, the search terms were relaxed by combining only three (3a–3d) or two keywords (2a–2f). Finally, the single keyword search was repeated (1a–1d). The titles and abstracts of the first 400 results of each search were screened to identify the relevant works. Duplicates were only counted in the first appearance. The detailed search results are listed in **Appendix 6**.

In total, 610 relevant studies were identified for the full-text evaluation, out of which 207 passed the full-text review and were used for forward/backward search. The main factor for rejection of a study was focus on different research topics (158), such as air traffic control or communication network planning. Other major reasons for rejection were lack of originality of research content (86) and non-scientific research publications (71). The forward/backward search was conducted iteratively during the full-text review

[14] In Google Scholar, patents and citations were excluded.

process and yielded 136 additional publications. The relevant body of literature for the theoretical aspect of this study consequently comprises 343 publications, as depicted in Figure 2.5.

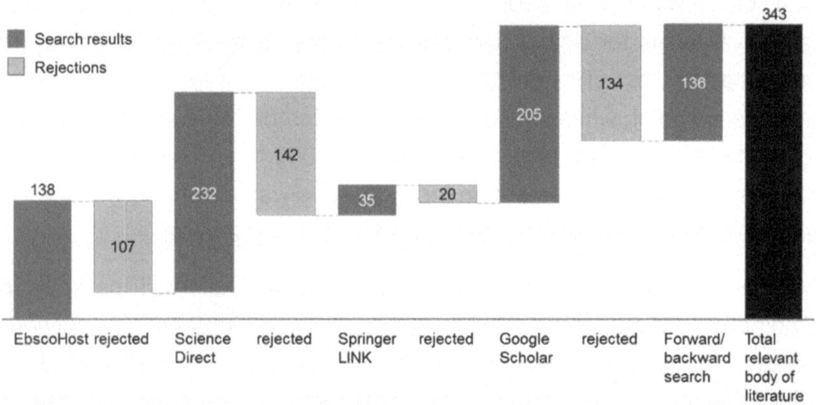

Figure 2.5 – Build-up of a relevant body of literature[15]

Out of the 343 publications, 290 are articles from peer-reviewed academic journals. Among these, 83 articles have been published in unranked publications, such as industry-specific journals and published conference proceedings. Appendix 7 summarizes the most frequent publications for each VHB ranking category. Thus, most of the publications are from information systems, operations research, and strategic management research domains. The 53 remaining sources are mostly books (31), book chapters (11), and research reports (4).

[15] Source: Own illustration.

2.2.4 Description of the research gap

Only two useful contributions could be determined from the combination of all keywords (combination code 4a in Appendix 6). However, these two are general textbooks (Bazargan, 2016; Shaw, 2016) that do not discuss airlines, network planning, big data, and any of the theories in the same context but in different chapters of the books.

The keyword combination 3a of airlines, big data, and strategic network planning is either researched from an air traffic control perspective (Ayhan et al., 2013) or network planning is only considered a potential application of airline big data (Chen et al., 2017; Larsen, 2013). In fact, there is no academic contribution that has explicitly analyzed the role of big data in airline network planning.

Combination 3b (airlines, big data, and resource-based view or network theory) yields research that focuses on the role of big data in the resource-based view, where airlines serve as general examples (e.g., Erevelles, Fukawa, & Swayne, 2016). In turn, network theory-centered publications mention big data as a potential means to improve network optimization in airlines (e.g., Akartunalı et al., 2013). None of the identified publications elaborate the examples to an extent that can broaden the understanding of big data opportunities in airlines.

The combination of big data, strategic network planning, and resource-based view or network theory (combination 3c) yields useful studies on the strategic impact of big data from a resource-based perspective (e.g., Grover et al., 2018)[16]. However, these contributions are industry-agnostic and do not consider airline-specific network planning.

[16] The resulting literature is discussed in detail in section 3.7.3.

Combination 3d, yields by far the most search results from all the third-degree keyword searches[17]. A rich body of literature exists on airline network planning, most of which originates from operations research (see subchapter 3.5 for a detailed discussion). However, most of the studies focus on optimization methods and not on used data.

Research that stem from the lower-degree keyword searches (1a–d and 2a–f) emphasize on specific aspects of big data, airlines, strategic network planning, and the theoretical foundations. All of the analyzed studies lack an integrated perspective of big data in strategic network planning for airlines, which presents a significant gap that this study aims to bridge.

2.3 Comparative case study

The actual case study design follows the method proposed by Eisenhardt (1989, p. 533), depicted in Table 2.4.

Table 2.4 – The case study method adopted from Eisenhardt (1989)

Step	Activity	Corresponding sections and chapters
Getting started	Definition of research questions Selection of research method Selection of case study type	1.2 2 2.3.1
Selecting cases	Theoretical sampling	2.3.2
Crafting Instruments & Protocols	Data collection and analysis techniques	0
Entering the field	Data collection	Chapter 4 and 5
Analyzing data	Within case analysis Cross-case analysis	Chapter 4, 5, and 6
Shaping hypothesis	Replication of logic	Chapter 4, 5, and 6[18]
Enfolding literature	Comparison with supporting & conflicting literature	Chapter 3 and 7
Reaching closure	Distillation of newly generated knowledge	Chapter 8

[17] 2'453 compared to less than 1'000 for all other 3rd-degree combinations (see Appendix 6).

[18] Hypothesis on RQs developed within the respective chapter.

The first step "Getting started" also includes the work required before determining the case study design, which has been explained in the previous sections of this chapter. This section starts with the selection of the case study type (section 2.3.1), explains the theoretical case sampling (section 2.3.2), and presents the data collection and analysis techniques (section 2.3.3). Section 2.3.4 reviews the research quality criteria for the case study research.

2.3.1 Selection of the case study type

The first step in the actual case study design is determining the most appropriate case study type. Eisenhardt and Graebner (2007, p. 27) have proposed two generic case study types, namely single case studies and multiple case studies. While single case studies are the most suited to describe the existence of a specific phenomenon, multiple case studies have more explanatory power as they enable the researcher to compare the same phenomenon within multiple settings. Baxter and Jack (2008, p. 550) compared the design choice with the set-up of an experimental research design. If the purpose is to discover a phenomenon, a single experiment or case study is sufficient. If the properties of the phenomenon need to be analyzed, multiple experiments – or multiple cases – are required. Yin (2017, p. 47) has also stated that although multiple case studies have more explanatory power, resource constraints can sometimes favor a single case study setup.

The multiple or comparative case study method is the most appropriate design for this study for three reasons. First, the phenomenon "big data" already exists and is widely used for other airline functions, such as pricing and revenue management (P&RM). Thus, this research aims not to discover a completely new phenomenon but explain its application and usefulness in network planning. Second, the NP process in airlines differs widely depending on the chosen business model. A single case study would thus limit the generalizability of results to other airlines and thereby reduce external validity. Third, multiple airlines showed keen interest in participating in this study, so the availability of cases was not a limiting factor.

2.3.2 Case sampling

The case study guidelines developed by Eisenhardt and Graebner (2007) and refined by Yin (2017) were followed when selecting cases among the interested airlines and other research partners. These other research partners included potential providers of big data and system developers for airline NP software. While the airlines form the "core" comparative case study, data providers and system developers contribute with a different and very specific perspective on the "data source" topic.

Airline case sampling

Theoretical sampling is the most appropriate sampling approach for multiple case studies, as it ensures generalizability and thus the external validity of the research (Eisenhardt & Graebner, 2007, p. 27; Yin, 2017, p. 43). Eisenhardt (1989, p. 537) recommends defining relevant selection criteria that allow the systematic comparison of a researched phenomenon across cases.

For the airline cases, four relevant selection criteria were identified. Business model is the most frequently used classification criterion in airline management literature (Wittmer & Bieger, 2011, p. 31), and it will also be used as the primary classification criterion in this study. However, other influencing factors, such as fleet size, network type and route structure have a considerable influence on the structure of the network process (Goedeking, 2010, vii) and thus on the BDOs needed for its improvement. For each selection criterion, three to four possible specifications were defined (see Table 2.5).

Table 2.5 – Specification criteria for case study airlines[19]

Criterion	Specifications
Business model	▪ Full-service carrier (FSC) ▪ Low-cost carriers (LCC) ▪ Scheduled-charter airline (SCA) ▪ Cargo airline (CAR)
Fleet size	▪ Large (> 100 aircraft) ▪ Mid-sized (30–100 aircraft) ▪ Small (< 30 aircraft)
Network type	▪ Multi-hub ▪ Single-hub ▪ Point-to-point
Route structure	▪ Mostly long-haul ▪ Mostly short-haul ▪ Mixed

Four different business models are considered for the case sampling (Sterzenbach, Conrady, & Fichert, 2013, p. 225). Full-service or legacy carriers (FSCs) are mostly developed from former state-owned airlines, and they target a wide spectrum of passengers. They usually offer a premium product and additional services, such as a frequent flyer program. Low-cost carrier (LCCs) are the alternative draft to this model, which offers a product with the bare minimum ("no frills"). Scheduled charter airlines (SCAs) or "leisure carriers" focus on touristic routes and sell large seat contingents to travel operators. Cargo airlines (CARs) focus on transporting freight only. The business models are discussed in full details in Section 3.2.3.

Fleet size serves as a proxy for airline size, since that data is more easily available than financial data or passenger data[20]. It is distinguished in three levels, ranging from small (< 30 airplanes) to large (> 100 airplanes). Traditionally, network types are distinguished in hub-and-spoke (HS) and

[19] Source: Own illustration.

[20] Financial data for privately owned airlines is not published often; passenger data is available consistently only for IATA member airlines.

point-to-point (PP) models. However, with increased merger and acquisition activity in the airline domain, many airlines have developed multi-hub models, leveraging the hubs of the merged airlines (Burghouwt, 2007). Thus, point-to-point, single-hub, and multi-hub network types are distinguished. Route structures can be systemized by the route type. Some airlines serve predominantly long-haul routes (over 4,500 km), while others serve predominantly short-haul routes (under 4,500 km), and some have a mixed route structure.

Each criterion specification should be represented multiple times in the case study group. Table 2.6 collates information on the nine participating airlines, which have been anonymized for this study. All airlines are based in Europe and participated in all the interview rounds. This ensures validity not only across the case sample but also in time throughout the research project (Yin, 2017, p. 43).

Table 2.6 – Airline case study participant overview[21]

Airline	Business model	Fleet size[22]	Network type	Route type
FSC 1	Full-Service Carrier	Large	Multi-hub	Mixed
FSC 2	Full-Service Carrier	Medium	Single-hub	Mixed
LCC 1	Low-Cost Carrier	Medium	Point-to-point	Short-haul
LCC 2	Low-Cost Carrier	Large	Point-to-point	Short-haul
SCA 1	Scheduled Charter Airline	Medium	Point-to-point	Mixed
SCA 2	Scheduled Charter Airline	Small	Point-to-point	Short-haul
CAR 1	Cargo Airline	Small	Single-hub	Long-haul
CAR 2	Cargo Airline	Small	Multi-hub	Long-haul
CAR 3	Cargo Airline	Small	Single-hub	Long-haul

In addition to the nine airlines, a large system development company and ten potential data providers agreed to support the research project and

[21] Source: Own illustration.

[22] Assessed on October 4, 2016 with data from airfleets.net (2016).

complement the data collected in the comparative case study. They are not part of the actual case study group but serve as tri-angulation partners who help define the feasibility of potential big data opportunities.

2.3.3 Data collection and analysis techniques

The data collection process is structured as three phases, in compliance with the research process presented in

Figure 2.1: the first phase aims to assess the status quo of NP in airlines; the second phase intends to discover and qualitatively evaluate potential BDOs; and the last phase aims to develop an estimation methodology for the financial impact of investment in big data.

A double tri-angulation principle is followed throughout the study. This principle is particularly suited for research concepts with small sample sizes that do not allow for statistical significance testing (Berg, 2004, p. 51). The first triangulation calls for multiple data collection techniques, whereas the second triangulation applies to the sources.

Data from the participating airlines is collected through interviews, surveys, and internal documents to satisfy the first tri-angulation dimension. Representatives of system developers and data providers are also included in the interview process to establish a tri-angulation of sources. Figure 2.6 schematizes the double tri-angulation principle.

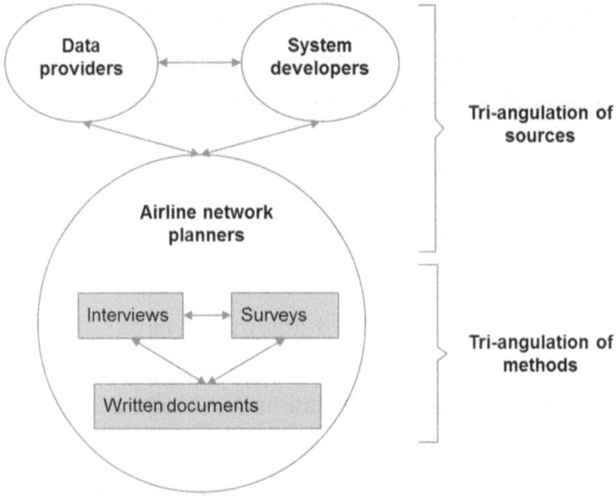

Figure 2.6 – Double tri-angulation approach[23]

Exploratory phase – status-quo assessment

The initial data collection in the status-quo assessment is partly exploratory and partly explanatory. Since NP processes and potential organizational set-ups are well-researched (refer to sub-chapter 3.5), a semi-standardized questionnaire has been developed to assess these topics. In contrast, the use of data for airline NP is not well described in literature, which requires an exploratory set-up (Creswell, 2013, p. 211). In an exploratory set-up, non-standardized questions are used to extract common themes via coding the interview transcript, which can then be used to conduct a second standardized interview to ensure holistic coverage and comparability across the case study participants (Berg, 2004, p. 105). The status quo assessment starts with non-standardized questions on the use of current data sources in NP to extract data types by coding, which are then reiterated to the interviewees in the form of a standardized online survey. Figure

[23] Source: Own illustration. following Berg (2004).

2.7 summarizes the data collection and analysis process of the status quo assessment phase, whose results are presented in chapter 4.

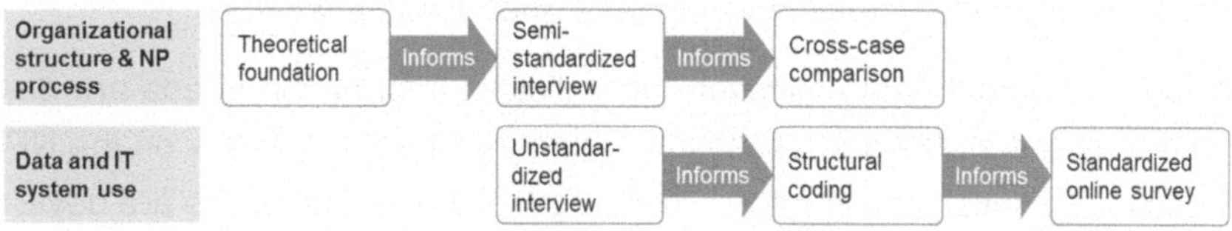

Figure 2.7 – Data collection and analysis techniques of status-quo assessment[24]

A structural coding technique is used for the analysis of the non-standardized questions for the assessment of current data and information technology (IT) system use. Structural coding is especially useful if a set of potential outcomes is analyzed across a group of multiple participants (Saldaña, 2016, p. 98). The coding object are data sources, and the initial set of codes is derived from the data sources referenced in airline network planning literature (section 1). In addition, there is an open code – "new" – for all data sources mentioned by airline network planners, which have not been derived from literature.

There might be the case that an airline has not mentioned a data type in response to the open question, even though it is being used. In order to capture the complete picture of the data sources and IT systems used, the first interview is complemented with a structured questionnaire that constitutes all coded items, including the data types labelled as "new." The structured questionnaire includes three questions per data source. The first question entails a simple confirmation on whether a specific data type is used (yes/no). The second and third questions evaluate the usefulness and reliability of a data source. Berg (2004, pp. 105–108) recommends the use of four-point rating scales for the measurement of usefulness. A classical Likert scale is not appropriate here, as the questionnaire does not

[24] Source: Own illustration.

capture personal attitudes towards an item but intends to rate them objectively. The questionnaire for the status quo interviews is attached in Appendix 8 and the subsequent survey in Appendix 9.

Refinement phase – qualitative big data opportunity evaluation

Before the actual data collection, nine distinct information needs are derived from the status quo assessment and the literature review on the NP process. To satisfy these information needs, 23 potential BDOs are developed from three different sources, namely the initial status quo interviews, a press review, and the analyzed body of literature.

These 23 BDOs are then presented and explained to the airline network planners in the case study group. After the presentation, a standardized online survey (see Appendix 10) asked for the perceived benefit potential for the airline-specific NP. To increase granularity in the responses, a six-point scale was chosen (Berg, 2004, pp. 105–108).

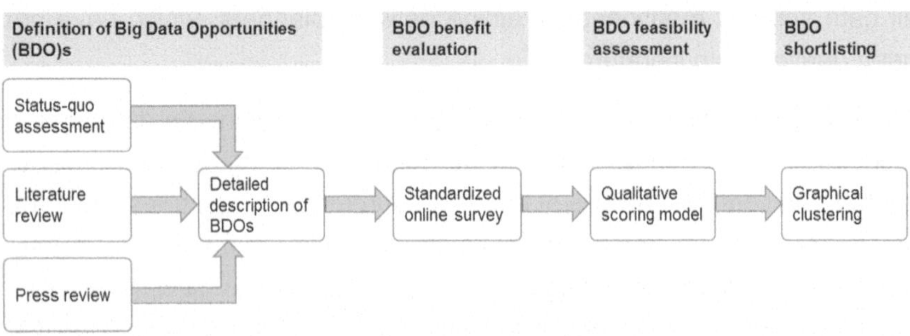

Figure 2.8 – Data collection and analysis techniques of BDO evaluation[25]

In addition, a feasibility scoring scheme is developed based on the existing literature (see section 5.3.4). The individual dimension scores are aggre-

[25] Source: Own illustration.

gated for each BDO in order to calculate a total feasibility score. The average perceived benefit potential and the total feasibility score of each BDO are then plotted on a two-dimensional matrix. The 12 BDOs among these with the highest benefit potential and feasibility ratio are selected for further analysis.

Synthesis phase – Quantification methodology for BDO benefits

The last interview round was related to the key performance indicators (KPIs), information on which was collected through the semi-standardized interviews in the exploratory phase. The airline network planners were asked to evaluate the impact of each of the 12 shortlisted BDOs on the primary and secondary KPIs of their airline. Similar to the initial benefit evaluation in the refinement phase, a six-point assessment scale was chosen. The results of the structured interview were then used to inform the development of the business case scheme to quantify the financial benefits of the shortlisted BDOs.

2.3.4 Research quality assurance

In accordance with the data quality criteria derived from the literature in sub-chapter 2, displayed in Figure 2.3, specific tactics have been deployed to ensure the reliability and validity of the comparative case study.

A case study database, which includes the case study protocol, has been created to ensure research reliability. This database contains all the interview transcripts as well as the associated analyses[26]. The interview transcripts and the report summaries were sent to the interviewees for verification to ensure construct validity. Furthermore, specific sections of the interviews were verified with system developers and data providers to triangulate information.

[26] Due to data confidentiality, the complete transcripts cannot be appended to this thesis, as the doctoral thesis will be publicly available. The anonymized case reports can be requested from the author.

The theoretical sampling of the comparative case study has a positive influence on both internal and external validity. The comparison of different cases enabled pattern matching, helping identify potential biases. Logical models derived from the literature could also be tested with multiple cases, since all sampling criteria were present in at least two cases. The research design applied the same logic to all cases to ensure external validity. This means that all interview protocols were standardized across cases as well as across supporting sources.

3 Theoretical foundation

3.1 Development of a theoretical concept

When following a qualitative research design, as developed in chapter 2, it is vital to ground the research on a relevant overarching theory (Creswell, 2013, p. 63). The research topic "big data to improve strategic network planning in airlines" is situated on the intersection of four different research domains – information systems, logistics, operations research, and strategic management. The overarching theory needs to be applicable to all domains to facilitate the creation of an overarching theoretical concept, although additional technical theories can be used to explain certain phenomena or research objects (Wynn & Williams, 2012, p. 798).

There is no literature on the prevalence of certain theories across the four relevant research domains, but Defee et al. (2010) studied the use of over 80 theories, clustered in 13 theory groups, in the logistics research domain. They found that competition theory, microeconomic theory, and system theory are the most frequently used groups of theories. Each of these groups comprises several specific theories, from which only the two most frequently used theories are considered in this study.

Figure 3.1 compares the search results of the combinations of the considered theories herein with research domains and research topics. It identifies the most appropriate specific theories for this study. It is hereby assumed that a large number of search results within each domain or topic indicates whether a theory is widely used and well established.

The most widely cited theories, across research domains and topics, are the resource-based view, game theory, and network theory. These theories are all well-established in the three research domains (Logistics, OR, and IS) and two research topics (big data and airlines) being studied. However, the resource-based view (RBV) is the only theory which has a strong influence on strategic management research, and network theory is the only well-established theory for strategic NP.

M. Schosser, *Big Data to Improve Strategic Network Planning in Airlines*,
Schriftenreihe der HHL Leipzig Graduate School of Management,
https://doi.org/10.1007/978-3-658-27582-2_3

Group of theories	Candidate theory	Applicability to research domains: Logistics (LOG)	Operations research (OR)	Strategic management (SM)	Information systems (IS)	Applicability to research objects: Big Data	Airlines	Strategic network planning
Competitive	Resource-based view	very common	common	very common	common	established	very common	sporadic
	Market-based view	sporadic	negligible	very common	sporadic	sporadic	negligible	negligible
Micro-economic	Transaction costs	sporadic	sporadic	sporadic	sporadic	negligible	sporadic	sporadic
	Game theory	very common	established	sporadic	very common	very common	very common	sporadic
Systems	General systems theory	sporadic	common	negligible	sporadic	negligible	sporadic	sporadic
	Network theory	common	very common	sporadic	very common	very common	very common	very common

Legend: very common, common, established, sporadic, negligible

Figure 3.1 – Evaluation of the candidate theories[27]

Since RBV is well-established across all relevant research domains, it is used as an overarching theory to develop the theoretical concept. Network theory is used to specifically underpin strategic NP. Figure 3.2 schematizes the theoretical concept and the resulting structure of this chapter. The sections in this chapter serve two purposes. They either define the research constructs, which are essential for the practical research presented in chapters 4 to 6, or they provide the theoretical background on theories and research objects.

Sub-chapters 3.2 and 3.6 define and describe the research objects “airlines” and “big data” respectively. After an introduction to network theory in sub-chapter 3.3, the third research object “strategic network planning” is

[27] Own illustration; the selection of candidate theories based on Defee et al. (2010); the circles reflect a relative number of search results from EBSCOhost search combining each theory with research area and research topics, e.g. (“resource-based view” AND “logistics”). Absolute search results in title and abstract have been recorded and standardized for each research domain/topic. A full circle represents >70% of the highest search result, an empty circle <10% of the highest search result.

established in sub-chapters 3.4 (airline networks) and 3.5 (network planning). Sub-chapter 3.7 finally integrates the research objects within the theoretical framework developed in the first sub-chapter of this chapter.

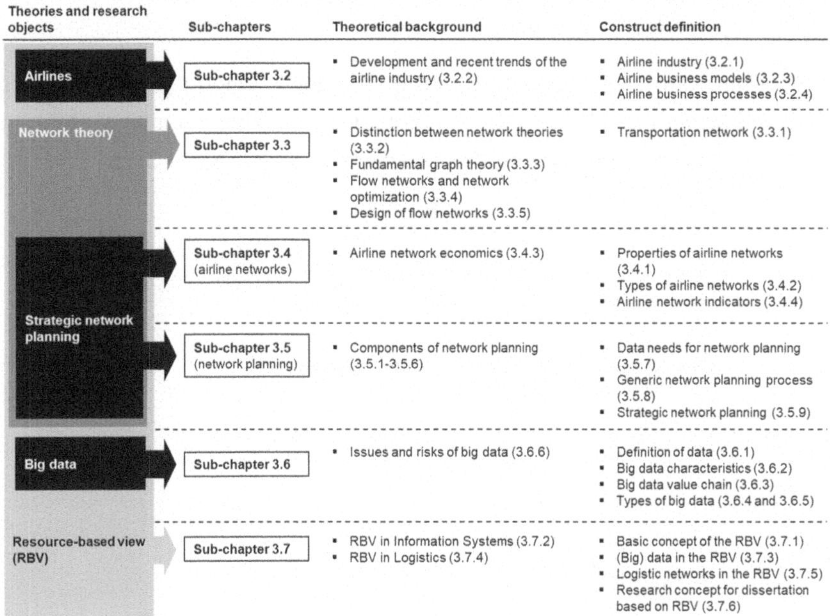

Figure 3.2 – Structure and purpose of the theoretical foundation chapter[28]

3.2 Airlines and their business models

This sub-chapter defines the research topic, airlines, for clarity in the further course of this study. Section 3.2.1 delimits the airline industry within the wider sphere of aviation systems. Developments and recent trends in

[28] Source: Own illustration.

the airline industry are summarized in section 3.2.2. The last sections present different business models followed by airlines (3.2.3) and the most important business processes (3.2.4).

3.2.1 The airline industry

Airlines are one group of actors in the broader aviation system. Wittmer and Vespermann (2011, pp. 39–40) have described the aviation system as a classic economic demand and supply system (see Figure 3.3).

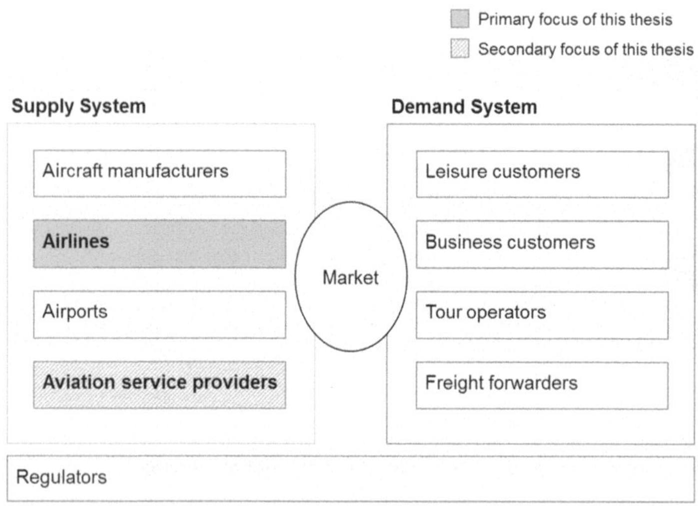

Figure 3.3 – The aviation system from a supply-demand perspective[29]

The supply side of the system contains the aircraft manufacturers, airlines, airports, and aviation service providers. Aircraft manufacturers produce the movable transportation assets, whereas airports provide the immobile infrastructure assets. The broader industry of aircraft manufacturing is also referred to as the aerospace industry, comprising end-manufacturers, such

[29] Source: Own illustration. adapted from Wittmer and Vespermann (2011, p. 40).

as Airbus and Boeing, as well as numerous component suppliers (Wensveen, 2015, p. 18). Airlines use mobile and immobile assets to offer a transportation service for passengers or goods. Wensveen (2015, p. 164) defined airlines as "certified and scheduled air carriers" in contrast to uncertified general aviation actors. Companies operating in the general aviation field do not offer scheduled flights (e.g., pure charter carriers) or are not certified for commercial transportation services (e.g., flying schools). The supply system is facilitated by a multitude of aviation service providers[30], who enable it to function properly.

The aviation demand system mostly comprises individual passengers, who can be categorized as individual leisure customers or business customers (Wittmer & Vespermann, 2011, p. 40). Tour operators typically block large capacity contingents on scheduled flights, which are then sold on their own economic responsibility. In the air cargo industry, most demand stems from freight forwarders, which bundle logistic services from different transportation modes, such as shipping, air cargo, and trucking, for the actual end-customer. Both these systems are controlled by official regulators, who define the associated security standards, traffic, and passenger rights (Wittmer & Vespermann, 2011, p. 41).

The main task of NP is spatial and temporal asset allocation, which is a core competence of airlines (Sterzenbach et al., 2013, p. 301), which henceforth are the primary research focus. Since NP is a very complex process, it relies on multiple data and system providers to cover the need for information. These providers are part of the aviation service providers, which are the secondary focus of this study.

[30] Examples: air traffic control, aviation system providers, aviation data providers, ground handling, catering, maintenance providers, aircraft leasing companies.

3.2.2 *Development and recent trends in the airline industry*

Historically, the development of the airline industry has been heavily influenced by technological progress and changes in regulation. Most authors such as Doganis (2010, pp. 25–63) and Gillen (2006, pp. 367–369) distinguish between a regulated and a deregulated era.

Until 1978, all major aviation markets were heavily regulated. All routes needed governmental approval in specifying the permitted frequency, seat capacity, and even the ticket price, which was calculated based on the distance and service components (Doganis, 2010, p. 36). This led to the creation of linear networks, which are economically inferior to the point-to-point or hub-and-spoke networks (see section 3.4.2 for a detailed discussion) in a free market.

The deregulation of the air transport system started with the Airline Deregulation Act in the United States in 1978 which was completely implemented in 1985 (Gillen & Morrison, 2005, p. 162). This deregulation had a severe impact on the airline business models and networks. The "open sky" policies[31] allowed the establishment of more efficient network types, namely the point-to-point and hub-and-spoke networks (see section 3.4.2). The abolition of pre-defined fares led to a sharp decrease in airfare, hence increasing cost pressure on the airlines (Doganis, 2010, p. 47). This sparked both the consolidation of legacy carriers and the development of new business models, most notably of the low-cost carriers (Gillen, 2006, pp. 370–372).

As cross-border mergers had failed to deliver the expected synergies in the past (Schosser & Wittmer, 2015), airlines sought alternative means of closer cooperation in the form of strategic alliances to leverage network effects and revenue synergies (Gillen, 2006, p. 371). As of 2016, the three

[31] Airlines can connect whichever airport pair they wish to, without regulatory approval; however, limited airport slots hinder the unlimited choice of connections.

major alliances (Star Alliance, Oneworld, and Skyteam) control over 60% of the total available passenger airline capacity (Statista, 2018).

3.2.3 Airline business models

Business models are used as the most common classification factors for airlines, since they constitute the "fundamental differences [...], i.e. the service level offered, the regional reach, and the main function of an airline" (Wittmer & Bieger, 2011, p. 31). Therefore, this study also adopts airline business models as the main classification criterion.

Scholars have distinguished up to six different business models for airlines, and a continuous space of "hybrid" business models. Prior to the deregulation, airline business models could be categorized as four archetypes (Sterzenbach et al., 2013, p. 225): first, legacy or full-service carriers (FSCs), which served a broad, regulated network and targeted all passenger types. The second archetype was leisure or scheduled charter airlines (SCAs), which served point-to-point flights to holiday destinations, thus mainly targeting tourists. Third, regional carriers predominantly served business customers on low-volume routes. Finally, cargo airlines (CARs) are easily classifiable for transporting cargo only. It is important to note that even today, some airlines with traditional business models are not profit maximizing companies. Pompl (2007, p. 99) noted that national prestige (especially flag carriers), provision of public services (mostly for regional airlines), and the stimulation of economic development are political objectives that often outweigh expected economic benefits.

After the de-regulation wave in the 1980s and 1990s, various new business models emerged. The most popular new business model are low-cost carriers (LCCs) that serve point-to-point networks with a very low cost structure (Shaw, 2016, pp. 100–101). At the other end of the service spectrum, super-differentiated airlines emerged to serve high-value business routes with a premium product as a cheaper alternative for private jets (Bieger & Wittmer, 2011, p. 98).

In recent years, certain authors have noted the convergence of business models into individual "hybrid" business models, which feature the characteristics of more than one business model (Lohmann & Koo, 2013, p. 7). The conceptual and empirical studies by Daft and Albers (2013, 2015) have supported this claim. Table 3.1 provides an overview of the differentiation schemes of airline business models in the literature.

Table 3.1 – Airline business model classifications in the literature[32]

Author	Full-service/legacy carrier (FSC)	Scheduled charter/leisure airline (SCA)	Regional carrier	Cargo airline (CAR)	Low-cost carrier (LCC)	Super-differentiated airlines	"Hybrid" business models
Bieger and Wittmer (2011)	x	x	x		x	x	
Daft and Albers (2015)							x
Doganis (2010)	x	x		x	x		
Gillen (2006)	x	x	x		x		x
Whyte and Lohmann (2017)	x	x	x		x	x	
Pompl (2007)	x	x	x		x	x	
Shaw (2016)	x	x			x	x	x
Sterzenbach et al. (2013)	x	x	x	x	x		
Wensveen (2015)	x		x		x		

[32] Source: Own illustration. based on literature mentioned in the table.

Full-service carriers (FSC)

Full-service carriers or legacy carriers mostly emerged from state-owned national flag carriers or private airline ventures immediately after the deregulation (Whyte & Lohmann, 2017, p. 110). On the basis of their previously protected home market, FSCs usually enjoy a strong market position due to excellent slot[33] portfolios and a huge customer base. At the same time, they suffer from a high-cost base, established during times of regulation when cost minimization was not a priority for many airlines (Gillen, 2006, p. 370). After the deregulation, most FSCs built efficient hub-and-spoke network structures with a combination of short-haul and long-haul routes. Their fleets are often heterogeneous and comprise multiple aircraft types from different manufacturers (Sterzenbach et al., 2013, p. 226). FSCs target a broad customer base and thus differentiate their product according to customer needs. This is expressed in different cabin classes, typically including First, Business, and Economy. In-flight frills, such as food, drinks, and entertainment, are usually free of charge. The bundling of services in combination with extensive frequent flyer programs requires sophisticated yield management systems, which often comprise more than 20 different booking classes (Shaw, 2016, pp. 212–214). The use of multiple distribution channels, including global distribution systems (GDS), direct online sales, and travel agencies, further increases the production cost of these carriers. Table 3.2 summarizes all the individual features by business model.

[33] Airports with high traffic volumes assign landing time windows (i.e., slots) to airlines to avoid congestion of the available infrastructure.

Table 3.2 – Key characteristics of airline business models[34]

	Full-service/ legacy carrier	**Scheduled charter/ leisure airline**	**Regional carrier**	**Cargo airline**	**Low-cost carrier**	**Super-differentiated airlines**	**"Hybrid" carriers**
Route types	Short-haul and long-haul	Short-haul and long-haul	Short-haul	Short-haul and long-haul	Previously only short-haul, recently also long-haul	Short-haul and long-haul	Short-haul and long-haul
Fleet	Large & diverse	Small & diverse	Small	All possible	Large homogeneous	Very small	All possible
Network type	Hub & Spoke	Point-to-point	Point-to-point	All types	Point-to-point	Point-to-point	All types
Focus airports	Major airports	Both major and secondary	Secondary airports	Cargo airports	Past: Secondary airports; recently all airports	No specific focus	Both major and secondary
Target customers	All travelers	Tourists	Mostly business travelers	Freight	Previously mostly tourists; Recently all travelers	Business travelers	All travelers
Product offering	Differentiated full-service	Standardized full-service	Standardized full-service	Cargo	Standardized no-frills product	High-end full-service product	A la carte product

34 Source: Own illustration. adopted from Sterzenbach et al. (2013, p. 225).

	Full-service/ legacy carrier	Scheduled charter/ leisure airline	Regional carrier	Cargo airline	Low-cost carrier	Super-differentiated airlines	"Hybrid" carriers
	product (First, Business, Economy)	product (single class)	product (single class)			(Business/ First)	combining full-service with no-frills
Pricing	Differentiated pricing with complex yield management systems	Block capacity sale to tour operators	Upmarket pricing with standard revenue management systems	Spot and block capacity sale	Cheap a-la-carte pricing with standard revenue management systems	Very upmarket pricing, no sophisticated revenue management systems	Differentiated a-la-carte pricing with complex yield management systems
Distribution channels	Multichannel distribution	Mostly via tour operators	Multichannel distribution	Direct sale to freight forwarders	Direct online sale to passengers	Mostly business travel agencies	Multichannel distribution

Scheduled charter airlines (SCA)

Prior to the deregulation, SCAs were not permitted to market single seats; rather, they could only sell seat allotments to tour operators (Bieger & Wittmer, 2011, p. 97). Post deregulation, many formerly independent airlines were integrated into larger tourism conglomerates[35] in order to reduce the transaction cost and adjust capacity more flexibly. SCAs are characteristically smaller than FSCs, although they can serve both short-haul and long-

[35] E.g., Hapag-Lloyd to Preussag (later TUI) in 1997, Condor to C&N Touristik (later Thomas Cook) in 1997.

haul flights. They serve the connections in their point-to-point networks with low weekly frequencies, especially for long-haul flights, reducing the complexity and allowing for a very high level of asset utilization (Doganis, 2010, p. 166). The typical product of a SCA consists of a single Economy Class, which offers in-flight frills similar to that of an FSC Economy Class. The distribution process is still dominated by tour operator allotments and also complemented with the direct sale of individual seats (Shaw, 2016, p. 154).

Regional carriers

Regional carriers focus on connecting secondary airports with small aircraft and mainly rely on the business travel demand between these airports. In addition, many regional airlines have contracts with FSCs to feed their hubs with traffic from smaller airports (Pompl, 2007, p. 102). They usually incur higher operating costs than other business models and often serve monopoly routes with limited but inelastic demand, which allows regional airlines to achieve higher yields compared to other business models (Whyte & Lohmann, 2017, p. 113). They typically offer a single class product with full-service features in order to satisfy the demand driven by business travelers. In some cases, they also receive government subsidies to connect remote locations as a public service (Pompl, 2007, p. 99).

Cargo airlines (CAR)

Cargo airlines exclusively carry freight, whereas airlines following other business models focus mainly on passengers[36]. Many cargo airlines are integrated either in an aviation conglomerate (e.g., Lufthansa Cargo or Emirates Sky Cargo) or in a global logistic forwarder (e.g., UPS, FedEx), allowing them to leverage the hub-and-spoke network of the parent companies. Independent pure players, such as Cargolux or Atlas Air, operate

---

[36] However, the revenue share of cargo in long-haul wide-body aircraft is up to 15% (Doganis, 2010, p. 306).

loose hub-and-spoke networks, which are much more flexible to accommodate short-term changes. Smaller fleets of cargo airlines (less than 30 airplanes) are typically homogeneous, whereas integrated express freight companies deploy large heterogeneous fleets. However, the business model of cargo airlines differs substantially from passenger airlines in three ways. First, the customers are companies and not individuals – in most cases freight forwarders. Second, the product differentiation is based on the cargo properties and timeliness rather than customer experience. Third, the sale of capacity in spot markets only occurs a few days before departure, so the network can be adjusted quickly to reflect changes in demand, especially if there are no blocked space allotments on a specific route (Doganis, 2010, p. 304).

Low-cost carriers (LCC)

The emergence of low-cost carriers was possibly the largest disruption in the airline business since the deregulation. LCCs maintain a very low cost base by combining a large, homogeneous fleet with a slim administration, a low degree of operational complexity, and decomposition of the traditional airline product (Shaw, 2016, pp. 103–111): aircraft manufacturers grant huge discounts for large orders, lowering unit capital cost dramatically. The standardization of both fleet and product reduces training and maintenance cost and increases flexibility, since aircrafts can be exchanged easily. Most low-cost airlines began as start-ups and thus avoided building an oversized administration as well as high wage contracts, a feature of better (regulated) times. Initially, LCCs purely served point-to-point networks between secondary (and uncongested) airports, which charged lower fees and guaranteed faster turnaround times to maximize asset utilization. The lack of transfer passengers reduced the complexity further, eliminating the need for schedule coordination (which is especially relevant for FSCs and regional carriers). Finally, LCCs decomposed the full-service product into a base product, which is the flight and a piece of hand luggage, and many ancillary services that can be assembled *a la carte* by the passenger to best suit his preferences. Ancillary revenues can generate up to 30% of the total revenues (Doganis, 2010, p. 152). This led to a focus on the load factor rather than average yield, since most ancillary revenues are generated after the actual booking. At the same time, sophisticated yield management systems, as used by FSCs, became obsolete.

Super-differentiated airlines

Super-differentiated airlines implement a focus strategy opposite to that of LCCs. Instead of focusing on the cost leadership, these airlines focus on providing the most luxurious travel experience to a price-insensitive customer base (Shaw, 2016, p. 151). The majority of this market is served by unscheduled business aviation providers that do not qualify as an airline according to the definition developed by Wensveen (2015). There were a small set of scheduled airlines offering scheduled Business Class-only services on high-yield business routes in the 2000s, many of which ceased operations during the financial crisis of 2008 (Shaw, 2016, p. 153). At the time of this study, only one of these airlines, namely the French airline La Compagnie still maintains scheduled Business Class-only flights as independent airline.

Hybrid carriers

With the market entry of the new LCCs, strategic reactions of the FSCs led to innovations in their own business model and service offering. Simultaneously, LCCs added premium services to their own product set, so that the lines between these business models became blurry (Daft & Albers, 2013, p. 47). The new breed of business models has often been called the "hybrid" business model, since they incorporate elements of both FSCs and LCCs in varying degrees (Lohmann & Koo, 2013, p. 7). Such business model convergence can occur in two different ways: first, airlines can alter their product portfolio. This entails either FSCs decomposing their bundled full-service product and offering *a la carte* ancillaries similar to LCCs; conversely, LCCs can start to bundle some of their *a la carte* products in something similar to full-service products (Daft & Albers, 2013, p. 50). Secondarily, airlines can establish their own LCCs to compete directly with the new market entrants and benefit from the low-cost structure of a newly founded airline. This results in large airline groups operating both FSCs and LCCs simultaneously but with clearly delimited scope and target markets (Pompl, 2007, p. 127). Airlines in North America have mostly chosen hybridization through product portfolio adjustments, whereas European airlines have deployed a mix of both hybridization approaches (Daft & Albers, 2015; Klophaus, Conrady, & Fichert, 2012).

3.2.4 Major business processes of airlines

The business processes of airlines can be roughly clustered in three groups: Commercial processes, operational processes, and administrative processes (Wensveen, 2015, p. 232). Administrative processes are usually staff functions reported directly to the Chief Executive Officer (CEO), whereas commercial processes are headed by a Chief Commercial Officer (CCO) and operational processes by a Chief Operations Officer (COO). Figure 3.4 provides an overview of the major processes in each category.

Operational processes are the responsibility of the classic cost centers and thus strive to provide a satisfactory level of service at minimal cost. Hence, efficiency is the most important innovation driver for operational processes (Wensveen, 2015, p. 248). Commercial processes are usually revenue centers, with the exception of NP, which can alternatively be a profit center that coordinates commercial and operational processes (Goedeking, 2010, p. 99). Strategic planning, including fleet planning, is usually considered an administrative function reported directly to the CEO (Wensveen, 2015, p. 241). Administrative processes are either cost or profit centers in the organization, depending on the responsibilities and decision-making rights assigned to them.

	Administrative processes	**Commercial processes**	**Operational processes**
Process types	Cost or profit centers	Revenue or profit centers	Cost centers
Major processes	▪ Strategic planning ▪ Finance ▪ Human resources ▪ Legal ▪ Communication & PR ▪ Information Technology	▪ Marketing & sales ▪ Revenue & yield management ▪ **Network planning**	▪ Flight Operations ▪ Ground Operation ▪ Engineering & maintenance ▪ Safety ▪ Training ▪ Crew planning

Figure 3.4 – Overview of standard airline processes[37]

3.3 Introduction to the network theory

Networks are omnipresent in almost all aspects of life and science. They can take different appearances, sizes, and strengths. Networks are clearly visible (e.g., a road network) or almost invisible (e.g., a social network). Even in airlines, there exist numerous network structures: route networks, airline alliance networks, computer intranet networks, and so on. In this sub-chapter, section 3.3.1 first defines the term "network" in general and discusses different network forms relevant for scientific research, with an aim to clearly delimit the airline route networks from other network types. Thereafter, section 3.3.2 presents the main scientific theories to describe and analyze networks. The most important theories are introduced in detail, namely the graph theory (section 3.3.3) and flow networks (sections 3.3.4 and 3.3.5).

3.3.1 Definition of networks

A network is a system constituting connected objects (Casti, 1995, p. 5). These objects can take several forms, based on the type and purpose of

[37] Source: Own illustration. following Wensveen (2015, pp. 233–263).

the network. In social networks, the objects are usually human actors or groups of actors and the connections are the relationship between these actors (Brass et al., 2004, p. 795). In technical networks, the objects can be computers, televisions, cities, or power plants as examples, and the connection is usually a physical connection, such as a wire, an electromagnetic signal, or a road.

The general purpose of a network is to enable the flow of “something,” using the connections between the objects. This “something” can be as diverse as information, passengers, or electricity. If the flow can be physically measured and expressed in a numerical demand figure or have a capacity constraint, the network is considered a “flow network.” Networks without specifiable flows and unlimited capacity are called “pure networks” (Bell & Iida, 1997, p. 19). The focus of the analysis in pure networks is usually on network structure and connectivity. In flow networks with additional path choices, the focus is on cost functions and demand and supply properties (Bell & Iida, 1997; Casti, 1995).

This study is concerned with *transportation networks,* which are classic flow networks. Network objects, which are usually called *nodes* in the context of transportation networks, can be points in space and time that have interaction potential. These points can include cities, industrial centers, or transportation facilities (Bell & Iida, 1997; Nakicenovic, 1995). In practice, transportation facilities, such as airports, ports, or train stations, are most frequently used as nodes in transportation networks. Network connections or *links* connect these nodes and materialize in the form of roads, railways, canals, or air and sea routes. Table 3.3 provides a summarized overview of network properties of different transportation networks.

Table 3.3 – Overview of transportation networks by transportation mode[38]

Transport mode	Network nodes	Network links	Individual transportation means	Community transportation means
Road	Spatial demand clusters (cities, industry centers, etc.)	Different road types such as highways, streets, etc.	Cars, trucks, bicycles	Buses, trucks
Railway	Train stations	Underground or above-ground rail tracks	Usually N/A	Trains
Water	Ports	Canals and sea routes	Variety of boats	Ferries, cruise ships, freight ships
Air	Airports	Air routes	General aviation planes & helicopters	Passenger aircraft and helicopters, cargo aircraft

For the analysis and optimization of a network, *network capacity* is of utmost importance (Casti, 1995). Capacity-constrained networks bear the risk of a flow shortage, which originates from capacity constraints in either network objects, connections, transmission modes, or a combination of these. Connections and transmission modes are usually only constrained if the network flow is quantifiable[39].

[38] Source: Own illustration. following Nakicenovic (1995), Bell and Iida (1997), and Frybourg and Nijkamp (1998).

[39] Let us consider social networks as an example. Network flows of affect are not quantifiable (Granovetter, 1973), and information and knowledge are at least difficult to quantify (Brass et al., 2004). The transmission of these flows in relationships is direct, i.e., there is no need for a transition mode. The only capacity supply constraint present in social networks are thus the network objects themselves – the amount of information, knowledge, and affect that social actors are willing or able to transmit in a social network.

Transportation networks possess not only capacity-constrained network objects but also constrained connections and transmission modes. Transportation facilities – the network objects of transportation networks – have a limited capacity to serve transportation modes; e.g., airports have a limited number of slots and limited terminal buildings. Moreover, most transportation networks have also capacity constraints in terms of network connections and transmission modes. There is only a certain amount of traffic that can be handled by a specific railway or road. At the same time, transportation modes, such as trains, buses, airplanes, and ships, have a limited capacity to accommodate passengers and freight.

The second property measure to distinguish network types is the *emergence* of networks. Social networks often have a hybrid emergence. While interpersonal networks often evolve unguided (at least in the non-professional context), interorganizational networks are generally strategically planned (Lavie, 2006; Provan, Fish, & Sydow, 2007). However, technical networks require dedicated infrastructure and transmission modes in order to fulfil their function. These networks rarely ever evolve spontaneously and need to be planned and created (Casti, 1995). Transportation networks is an exception here, since they may evolve without central planning, especially in emerging countries without sophisticated infrastructure and governmental planning. A couple of examples are need-based ride sharing and micro-logistic concepts in rural areas (Nakicenovic, 1995).

A final decisive criteria is *network reciprocity*, which describes the directional flow between two network objects (Garlaschelli & Loffredo, 2004, p. 795). In social networks, reciprocity is possible but not necessary. In contrast, transport networks require network reciprocity. It is logically impossible to move passengers only in one direction, without any passengers returning (including different return paths). After a while, there would be no passengers left to carry, and the demand center would disappear. For freight transportation, this phenomenon is slightly different since the carried goods may be consumed at the destination, but the transportation mode needs to return at some point to keep the network running. Counting deadheads as bi-directional network flow, reciprocity is a necessary condition for transportation networks.

This study focuses specifically on airline route networks. Therefore, the network objects – depending on the applied granularity level – are demand clusters or airports. The network connections are air routes served by airplanes as the transmission mode to enable the flow of passengers and cargo. All of these elements underlie the capacity constraints, which are further analyzed in section 3.3.4. Due to the asset and infrastructure specificity, airline networks are always the result of a deliberate planning process, called the airline network planning process. The reciprocity of network flows is a basic condition for all airline networks to function properly.

3.3.2 Distinction between the network theories

Network theory is an umbrella term for a multitude of individual theories and techniques related to network analysis (Provan et al., 2007, pp. 479–480). Network research in social sciences, including management science, has most often referred to social networks (Borgatti et al., 2009; Brass et al., 2004). A simple full-text keyword search on the Business Source Complete database supports this statement, with "social network" yielding over 6,000 scholarly articles, whereas "transport network" or "transportation network" result in less than 1,000 hits[40]. Despite this significant amount of network-specific literature, there exists no unanimous network theory across network types, not even for specific network types, such as social network or transportation networks (Borgatti & Halgin, 2011, p. 1168).

Since airline networks are technical networks, social network analyses cannot be applied to explain their characteristics. Thus, this study focuses

[40] Retrieved via EBSCOhost on October 30, 2017 with Boolean search phrase "social network" and "("transportation network") OR ("transport network")" and filter for peer-reviewed academic journals only.

on transportation networks and the associated network theories. Many scholars have intended to define a typology of transportation network theories, but there is no consensus in the broad range of research domains studying network-related phenomena. Bell and Iida (1997) propose to distinguish static and dynamic network analysis. Static network analysis is hereby concerned with network structure and properties, whereas dynamic network analysis studies the flows within networks. Figure 3.5 summarizes the concept pertaining to network theory discussed in this study. The research on transportation networks has usually been fueled by quantitative network theories (Bell & Iida, 1997, p. 17). From the static perspective, graph theory predominates the transportation network analysis (Casti, 1995), and it is introduced alongside basic network properties in the next section. However, transportation networks are flow networks and thus the dynamic view has traditionally been more prevalent in academic literature (Bell & Iida, 1997). Similar to the social network analysis, there is no single theory on the dynamic view of transportation networks. The representation and optimization of network flows can be summarized as the network optimization theory, comprising many individual optimization issues (Magnanti & Wong, 1984).

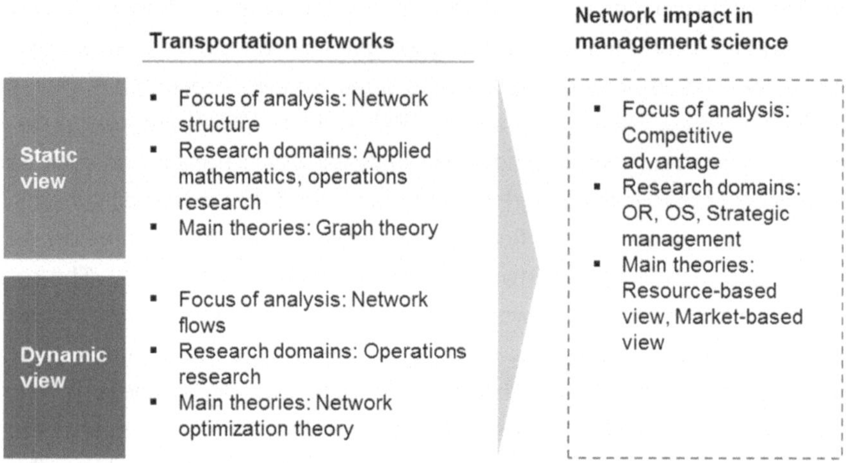

Figure 3.5 – Network theory in transportation networks[41]

Apart from theories describing the static and dynamic properties of networks, there also exist theories related to the impact of networks. From a strategic management perspective, the expectation towards a network – independent of its type – is to contribute towards building a competitive advantage (Gulati, Nohria, & Zaheer, 2000, p. 204). When considering the effect of networks in the management research domain, it is indispensable to relate networks to the common theories on competitive advantage in strategic management. For this purpose, section 3.7.5 discusses networks in the context of the resource-based view.

3.3.3 Fundamentals of the graph theory

The graph theory has mostly been developed by mathematicians and can be traced back to Leonhard Euler's Königsberg bridge theorem in 1736 (Casti, 1995; Newman, Barabasi, & Watts, 2011). Every graph consists of

[41] Source: Own illustration.

multiple nodes (Letters A to F in Figure 3.6), which are connected. Moving through the network via different connected links creates a path. If the origin node is also a destination node, the path is closed and thereby forms a cycle. The matter moving through the network is a flow, which is usually limited to the maximum *capacity* of the links. The terminology used in this study is collated in Table 3.4.

Table 3.4 – Graph theory terminology[42]

Term used in this study	Definition	Alternative terminol-ogy	Sources
Node	Junction of two or more links	Vertex	Bell & Iida, 1997; Casti, 1995; New-man, 2003
Link	Connection between two nodes	Edge, arc	Bell & Iida, 1997; Casti, 1995
Path	Sequence of nodes connected by links in one direction to enable a flow from the first to the last node		Bell & Iida, 1997; Casti, 1995
Cycle	Path where start and end point are the same node	Circuit	Bell & Iida, 1997; Casti, 1995
Flow	Movement between two nodes		Bell & Iida, 1997
Capacity	Maximum allowed flow in a time unit on a link between two nodes		Casti, 1995
Degree	The number of links connected to a node	Connectiv-ity	Newman, 2003

Directed graphs allow one flow direction for each link. In contrast, *undirected graphs* allow bi-directional flows between nodes (Newman, 2003, p. 172). All graphs can also be represented in a matrix. Figure 3.6 presents an undirected graph with six nodes, A to F, and five links. The properties of graph connectivity can be best elucidated using the three matrices in

[42] Source: Own illustration. following the authors mentioned in the table.

Figure 3.6. The *adjacency matrix* summarizes whether two nodes are directly connected via a link in a binary system. The node pair AB is connected by a direct link; hence, the adjacency matrix value is 1. Similarly, node pair BC has no direct link, so the adjacency matrix value is 0.

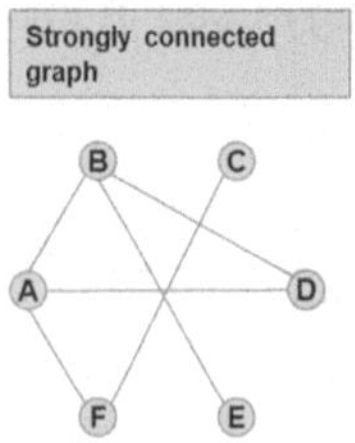

Adjacency matrix

	A	B	C	D	E	F
A	0	1	0	1	0	1
B	1	0	0	1	1	0
C	0	0	0	0	0	1
D	1	1	0	0	0	0
E	0	1	0	0	0	0
F	1	0	1	0	0	0

Reachability matrix

	A	B	C	D	E	F
A	1	1	1	1	1	1
B	1	1	1	1	1	1
C	1	1	1	1	1	1
D	1	1	1	1	1	1
E	1	1	1	1	1	1
F	1	1	1	1	1	1

Distance matrix

	A	B	C	D	E	F
A	0	1	2	1	2	1
B	1	0	3	1	1	2
C	2	3	0	3	4	1
D	1	1	3	0	2	2
E	2	1	4	2	0	3
F	1	2	1	2	3	0

Figure 3.6 – Connectivity matrices of an undirected, strongly connected graph[43]

The *reachability matrix* indicates whether a specific node pair is connected by a path, which could form a direct link or a combination of multiple links. The present graph is *strongly connected;* i.e., all the nodes are connected by at least one path. The reachability matrix indicates 1 for all node combinations. Since it is an undirected graph, even the origin node can be reached by moving back and forth. Finally, the *distance matrix* indicates by how many links it must move between the nodes. Nodes AB are directly connected; hence, the distance value is 1. Conversely, nodes AC are not directly linked but reachable via the path AFC, which constitutes the direct links AF and FC; thus, the distance is 2. If there is more than one possible path to link two nodes, the distance of the shortest path – the *geodesic path* – is shown. The longest geodesic path within a graph represents the *graph diameter*. (Casti, 1995; Newman, 2003)

Besides the strongly connected graph, there are other graph types that are depicted in Figure 3.7. A graph where every node is connected with direct links to all other nodes is called a hyper-connected graph (Casti, 1995). If

[43] Source: Own illustration.

graphs contain unconnected nodes or two sub-graphs that are not connected, these entities are called components (Newman, 2003, p. 173). The graph in the middle displays a two-component graph, consisting on the components DE and ABCF. Finally, there may be different types of links as depicted on right side of Figure 3.7. These links may differ according to the types of flows they transmit or in the flow capacity (Newman, 2003, p. 181). Examples of these networks are road-railway cargo networks or high- and low-voltage electricity networks.

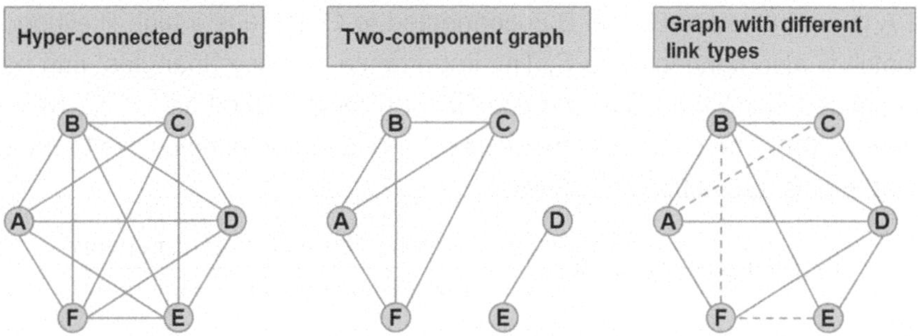

Figure 3.7 – Overview of graph types[44]

Besides graph connectivity, Albert and Barabási (2002, p. 71) have mentioned three key network attributes: average path length, clustering coefficient, and degree distribution. Newman (2003, p. 189) has added network resilience and betweenness to the attribute analysis.

The *average path length* describes the arithmetical average of all the geodesic paths of a network. This measure has received a large amount of public and scientific attention, triggered by Milgram's (1967) small-world problem, in which he found that the average path length of the social network of all humans on earth is between 6 and 7 links. In other words, most

[44] Source: Own illustration.

people are connected with at least half of the entire human population via 7 or fewer links. The implications of the small-world problem for graph theory are discussed at the end of this section. The *betweenness* or *centrality* measure indicates how many geodesic paths intersect at a specific node (Newman, 2003, p. 194). This also is the theoretical base for influencer modelling in social network analyses (Wasserman & Faust, 1994).

Transitivity or clustering in networks is a measure for the likelihood that friends of your friends are more likely to be friends with you. In other words, if A is connected to B, and B is connected to C, there is a high likelihood that A is also connected to C. The importance of these "triangles" can be quantified using the *clustering coefficient* (Albert & Barabási, 2002; Newman, 2003). The coefficient measures the relation of triangle links to "normal" triples, quantified as follows:

$$Clustering\ coefficient = \frac{3 \cdot \text{number of triangles in the network}}{\text{number of connected triples of nodes}}$$

If we take the graph in Figure 3.6 as an example, we can identify one triangle ABD, and ten triple relationships[45]. Therefore, the clustering coefficient is $\frac{3*1}{10} = 0.3$. As presented in Table 3.4, the degree of a node is the number of links connecting to the node. The *degree distribution* indicates the probability of a node *i* to have *k* degrees (Albert & Barabási, 2002, p. 73). Figure 3.8 exemplifies a degree distribution for the graph introduced earlier in this section.

[45] Triple relationships in undirected networks are counted bi-directionally. For example, the path ABE has its counterpart as EBA. The 10 triples in Figure 3.6 are ABE, AFC, BAF, CFA, DBE, DAF, EBA, EBD, FAB, and FAD.

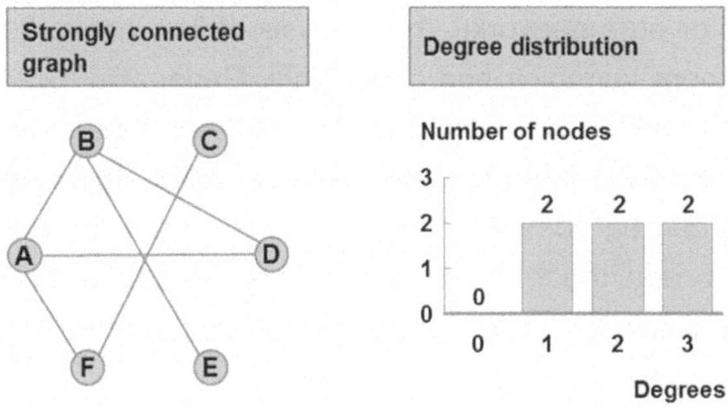

Figure 3.8 – Degree distribution example[46]

Network resilience measures the robustness of a network if individual nodes are removed. Usually, the average path length increases with the removal of nodes. The elasticity of the average path length in case of random or targeted node removal is the most common indicator for network resilience (Newman, 2003, p. 189). All of these network properties are highly relevant for airline networks and are discussed in that context in subchapter 3.4.

3.3.4 Network flows and network optimization

The network properties described in the previous sections focus primarily on network structure and evolution. For transportation networks, however, network flows are equally important. Hence, the optimization of network flows through the design of network structure, flow means, and schedule are key components of network theory. This section presents the basic concepts of network flow and network optimization that directly impact NP for airline route networks.

[46] Source: Own illustration.

In comparison with static or pure networks, the analysis of flow networks is performed with many more variables and constraints. Geospatial location of the network nodes and the type of links are shared features of both static and flow networks. However, flow networks always incorporate a flow demand component that can be completely satisfied if the links are not capacity constraint. In this case, the main concern of network optimization is simply to find the "best" route, be it the shortest or cheapest path to get a flow from one node to another (Bell & Iida, 1997, p. 19).

The physical properties of links in most real-world network types impose a certain capacity constraint. This capacity constraint becomes critical as soon as the demand exceeds the supply capacity. Now, certain flows cannot take the shortest or cheapest path but need to be re-routed to the next best path or cannot be transported at all (Casti, 1995). Especially in the case of transportation networks, there are multidimensional capacity constraints. Consider a railroad network; each railroad has a maximum number of trains that can operate safely in a specific time window. Additionally, for each train station, there is a maximum number of trains it can handle at one time, which is usually constrained by the number of platforms and outgoing rail tracks. Moreover, each train also has a maximum capacity for people or freight. In total, we find at least three network items with individual capacity constraints, namely links (railroad tracks), nodes (train stations), and transportation means (trains).

Flow networks have some more properties than static networks. The starting point of a specific flow is called the *origin* or source. The last node of a specific flow is the *destination* or sink. Nodes with a negative net flow are called *demand nodes,* since more flows originate than those that arrive. In turn, supply nodes have more arriving flows than originating flows, creating a positive net flow. If the net flow is zero, the node is called a *transshipment node* (Bazargan, 2016). If a network is separated into multiple independent networks by deleting one or more links, the combination of eliminated links is called the *cut (Casti, 1995)*.

In the following paragraphs, the most important network flow issues and their practical implications for transportation networks are introduced.

Shortest path problem

The shortest path problem is the most fundamental network flow problem and a basis for almost all network optimization theories. First formulated by Czech mathematician Otakar Borůvka in the 1920s (Nešetřil, Milková, & Nešetřilová, 2001), it aims to find the optimal paths for specific source destinations in higher-order networks. In static network theory, using a link comes with no cost, so the optimal path is always the geodesic path[47]. In a flow network, links get assigned a distance or a cost (Ahuja, Magnanti, & Orlin, 1993, p. 94). Hence, the problem is also known as the *minimum cost problem*. Consider a network such as the one depicted by the directional graph in Figure 3.9.

.

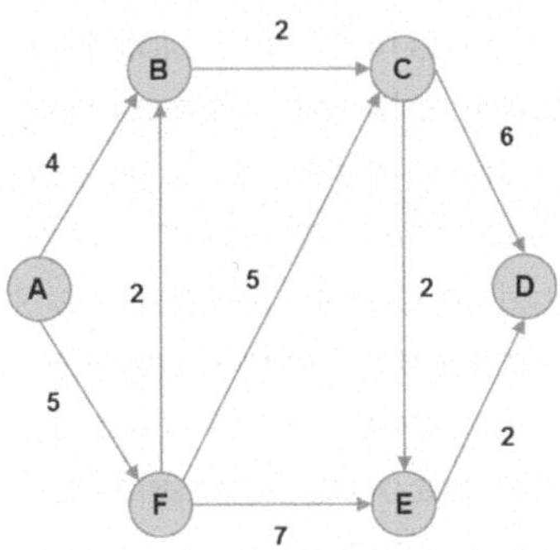

Figure 3.9 – Simple network with assigned link cost[48]

[47] The geodesic path is the path connecting two nodes with the smallest number of links.

[48] Own illustration following Bazargan (2016).

Each link has an associated flow cost that can also be viewed as the travel distance between two nodes. The geodesic paths connecting nodes A and D are ABCD and AFED. However, if we consider the link distances (cost), the shortest (cheapest) path from A to D is ABCED with a distance (cost) of 10, whereas the geodesic paths have lengths of 12 (ABCD) and 14 (AFED).

Since the shortest path problem does not consider any capacity constraints, it is not wholly transferable to most transportation networks. However, it is very useful to understand the basic mechanism of geographic routing that applies to all physical transportation networks (Goldman & Nemhauser, 1967). The most common application in real transportation networks is traffic planning on road networks, as it is applied by traditional navigation systems without real-time traffic information for example (Zhan & Noon, 1998, p. 66).

Consider that you want to drive from Frankfurt to Berlin at night with little traffic, so the capacity constraint of the road system is negligible. Most navigation systems provide you with two route options, the shortest and the most economic route. When considering the shortest route, the navigation system assigns distances to the links to calculate the shortest path. When choosing the most economic option, the navigation system assigns travel times (which equal cost) to the links to calculate the path with the shortest travel time. This example demonstrates that one network – in this case the German road network – can have varying allocations of distance and cost. Nevertheless, the algorithm required to determine this remains the same.

Over the last 90 years, the classical shortest path problem has produced a significant body of literature. Kruskal (1956) and Dijkstra (1959) proposed the first solution algorithms with exact but computational heavy solution algorithms that examined every network link. Subsequent research focused on reducing the computing time and not overly deteriorating the following empirical results obtained. Dreyfus (1969) and Ahuja, Magnanti, and Orlin (1991) presented a comprehensive overview over the development of solution algorithms. Deo and Pang (1984) provided a good summary on generalizations and specifications of the problem.

Maximum flow problem

The maximum flow problem is in many respects the counterpart of the shortest path problem and the second nucleus of the flow optimization theory. While the shortest path problem minimizes path lengths and costs without capacity constraint, the maximum flow problem isolates capacity constraint without assigning path length or cost (Ahuja et al., 1993, p. 167).

According to Ahuja et al. (1993, p. 184), the most important theorem of the maximum flow problem in the entire network optimization is the *max-flow min-cut theorem* introduced by Ford and Fulkerson in 1956. Based on empirical observations in the Soviet railway system, they developed a simple rule to determine the maximum flow capacity of a network. The maximum capacity of the network is the capacity of an individual cut with the smallest capacity of all cuts. Consider the same network as in the minimum path problem, depicted in Figure 3.10.

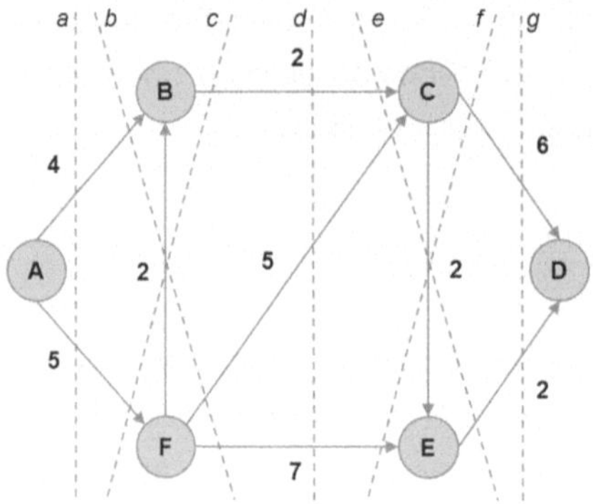

Cut	Left part	Right part	Capacity
a	A	BCDEF	9
b	AF	BCDE	13
c	**AB**	**CDEF**	**7**
d	ABF	CDE	14
e	ABFE	CD	9
f	ABFC	DE	15
g	ABCFE	D	8

Figure 3.10 – Maximum capacity determined by the max-flow min-cut theorem[49]

The number value now indicates the maximum capacity for each link. The dotted lines show all possible cuts of the network, which are summarized in the table on the right. The maximum capacity of each cut is the aggregated flows that can flow from the left part of the cut to the right part of the cut under the consideration of flow directions. For instance, cut *b* separates the left part AF from the right part BCDE. The links connecting the two parts are AB, FB, FC, and FE with an aggregated capacity of 13 flow units. Cut *c* relies only on the links BC and AF to connect the left part AB and the right part CDEF of the network. Here, the maximum capacity is only 7 flow units, which is also the maximum capacity of the entire network.

The generic problem with "bottlenecks" limiting the capacity of large transportation networks are most commonly observed in road and rail transport, but it is also present in airline networks and shipping networks. However, most capacity restrictions for the latter are determined by node capacity restrictions (airports and sea ports), although waterways, such as the Suez canal or the Panama canal, have capacity restrictions for shipping routes.

[49] Source: Own illustration. following Ahuja et al. (1993, p. 184).

Minimum cost flow problem

The minimum cost flow problem is the combination of the maximum flow and shortest path problems. In a directed network with one or more origins and one or more destinations, each link has both capacity restriction and associated flow cost. This is much closer to the reality of many transportation networks than the simpler problems presented earlier[50] (Ahuja et al., 1993, p. 295).

The objective of the problem is to determine how much of a single flow commodity is routed on every possible path from the source to the destination in order to minimize the total flow cost. Consider a two-origin and three-destination network with two transshipment nodes as depicted in Figure 3.11. The solid links have a capacity of 75 flow units and the dotted lines of 50 flow units. The numbers without an arrow frame describe the flow cost per link. Without capacity restriction, all commodities from B would have routed via D, since the total transport costs are lower than or equal to routing via C. However, the capacity restriction requires that 25 units flow via C. The resulting cost-minimizing flows are shown in the block arrows next to the links.

[50] The minimum cost flow problem has undergone multiple specifications and generalizations that lead to a variety of special cases and sub-problems. Ahuja et al. (1993, pp. 317–337) provided a comprehensive collection of these modifications as well as developed solution algorithms.

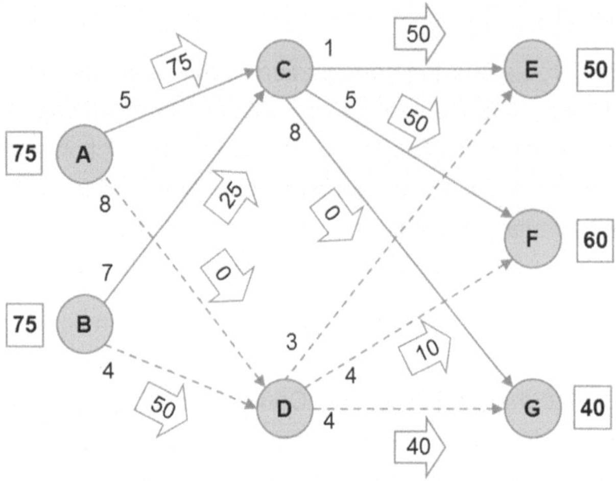

Figure 3.11 – Exemplary network and solution for the minimum cost flow problem[51]

The minimum cost flow problem and its derivatives are of central importance for transportation networks. First, it provides a sound set of solution algorithms for general routing problems. The network in Figure 3.11 could for example be understood as a simple network of a cargo airline transporting a single commodity. The intermediate stop D has a short runway and thus can only be served by small aircrafts, carrying up to 50 tons of cargo. The minimum cost flow problem here offers a simple routing algorithm to optimize this network.

3.3.5 *Design of flow networks*

While graph theory evaluates the properties and attributes of networks, network optimization determines optimal flows through the network; yet, a third component is missing for a complete understanding of NP. Neither graph theory nor network optimization recommend an optimal design of the

---

[51] Source: Own illustration. following Bazargan (2016).

network. Graph theory assumes that it either evolves randomly or probabilistically. In network optimization, the network and the corresponding properties are usually predefined; therefore, only the flows are optimized. However, network optimization is closely connected to network design, since efficient networks can only be designed by understanding the optimality conditions for network flows.

However, network design is in fact much more complex than network optimization. Network optimization problems are characterized by solving one well-specified problem, and more importantly, it is usually towards one single optimization parameter. However, network design requires encompassing and weighing all individual optimization problems and usually has multiple optimization parameters (Magnanti & Wong, 1984, p. 2). Consider airline network design as an example. Besides defining the most profitable network, you also want to design a feasible network, i.e., a network that can be flown with reasonable schedules and that exhibits some level of robustness towards external shocks[52].

Bell and Iida (1997, p. 20) have distinguished two archetypical network design problems: the *continuous* and the *discrete network design* problems. The continuous network design problem takes the network structure as given and aims to change the network characteristics, such as capacities and flow cost. Real-life examples of these design problems are the addition of a lane to an existing road or the installation of a traffic light. In airline networks, the determination of flight frequencies and the offered capacity (fleet assignment) are continuous network design choices (Bell & Iida, 1997, p. 20). Discrete network design problems are concerned with the determination of the network structure. In transportation networks, this can include infrastructure investments, such as the construction of a new road or railway, and the carrier route selection (Bell & Iida, 1997, p. 20). In an

[52] Changes in the network structure usually entail adding and deleting destinations; shocks such as political unrest or expired traffic rights can complement economic considerations for network changes.

airline network, the most common discrete network design problems are network type and route selection.

Discrete and continuous network design models can be viewed as a natural sequence[53]. Discrete network design choices usually have a longer planning horizon and require larger investments than for continuous choices (Guihaire & Hao, 2008, p. 1252). It is typically cheaper to repave or widen a road than to build a completely new road. However, real-life investment decisions require a holistic evaluation of the investment opportunities. An airline has to determine whether the newly acquired aircraft should be used to add frequencies on an existing route (continuous design choice) or to open a new route to passengers (discrete design choice). Therefore, mixed models have evolved to jointly analyze discrete and continuous network design problems (Yang & Bell, 1998, p. 258).

Most continuous network design models focus on infrastructure projects, more specifically on ground transportation, such as roads and railways (Bell & Iida, 1997, p. 20). This might result from the greater asset intensity of infrastructure projects than the network design of a transportation carrier (Farahani et al., 2013, pp. 281–282). While adding a new route for airlines or trucking companies comes with little to no asset investment, building a new road implies substantial financing. Hence, changing the characteristics of the network may often be more beneficial than changing the network structure.

3.4 Airline networks

Airline networks represent a special form of transportation networks and have many industry-specific properties. Section 3.4.1 presents the specificities of airline networks, following which section 3.4.2 outlines the most

[53] For an extensive overview of the existing network design models, see Farahani et al. (2013).

common types of airline networks. The underlying economics of airline networks are analyzed in section 3.4.3, before concluding the sub-chapter with an overview of airline network-specific measures of efficiency, effectiveness, and spatial distribution (section 3.4.4).

3.4.1 General properties of airline networks

The structure of airline networks is comparable to most other transportation networks. As a starting point, Table 3.5 collates the airline-specific network terminology. The nodes in an airline network are *airports* that are characterized by providing the necessary infrastructure for *airplanes*, the transportation means in airline networks (Burghouwt, 2007, p. 22). Essential infrastructural parts include runways, passenger terminals, cargo handling facilities, connections to other ground or sea transportation systems, and the offer of the required aviation services to enable flight operations (Burghouwt, 2007, p. 22).

Table 3.5 – Airline network terminology[54]

Graph theory terminology	Airline network terminology
Node	Airport
Central transfer node	Hub
Non-central transfer node	Station
Link	Route
Two unconnected nodes	Unserved route
Path	Itinerary
Demand source	Origin
Demand sink	Destination
Demand between specific sink and source	O&D demand
Flow event	Flight
Flow	Traffic
Transportation means	Airplane

[54] Source: Own illustration.

The flows in an airline network are usually referred to as *traffic*. Similarly, the demand for flow is the traffic demand. A single flow event between two airports is called a *flight*, and the link between two airports is the *route* (Goedeking, 2010, pp. 7–11)[55]. In fact, there exists almost an indefinite number of *unserved routes* in every airline network, since an airline can theoretically decide to fly to any suitable airport in the world. The routes with regular scheduled flights are called *served routes* and are the links of an airline network. In some cases, airplanes fly to more than one airport as part of the same flow. Goedeking (2010, p. 5) calls these multi-flight routes *itineraries*, which are especially relevant to cargo airlines.

If we look at the demand for airline network flows, the source of the demand is called the *origin*, and the sink of the demand is called the *destination*. The demand between a specific origin and destination is abbreviated as *O&D* demand (Bazargan, 2016, p. 32). The demand for air travel is usually not created at the airport itself but in the catchment area of an airport. Since airports are connected to other ground or sea transportation systems, passengers and cargo start their individual itinerary not at the airport but at individual homes, offices, or at manufacturing sites. Similarly, their journey does usually not end at the destination airport but at some location in the catchment area of those airports. These individual origins and destinations are called the *real O&D*.

Depending on the centrality of the node in the network, Burghouwt (2007, p. 24) differentiates between three types of nodes: decentral airports are simple *destinations*, where no flight connections are usually offered. Central airports can either be *hubs* if schedules are optimized for connection traffic or *stations* if connections are possible but the airline's schedule is

[55] The terminology for links is inconsistent in literature. While some authors refer to links as routes (Goedeking, 2010, p. 7), others use city pairs (Bazargan, 2016, p. 31) or flights (Burghouwt, 2007, p. 22).

not optimized for it. A typical example of stations are airports that are crew bases for low-cost airlines.

The geographic setup of airports connected via routes is the *spatial dimension* of an airline network (Burghouwt, 2007, p. 7). The analysis of the spatial dimension is rooted in graph theory and has become increasingly popular since the 1980s (Chou, 1990; Teodorović & Guberinić, 1984). The deregulation of air transport in the United States in the 1970s and in Europe in the 1990s has also attracted extensive research on the impact of deregulation on spatial structures of airline networks (Gillen, 2005; Gillen & Morrison, 2005). The most important spatial trend has been the increased centralization of airline networks around the so-called *hubs*. Rooted in the general network design theory (presented in the previous sub-chapter), scholars have identified the hub location problem as a central design problem for airline networks (O'Kelly & Miller, 1994).

The increasing importance of hubs and thereby of connecting flights has significantly impacted the planning and the analysis of airline networks. The *temporal dimension* of the network has become a crucial aspect: it is not only important *where* an airline is flying to but also *when* and more importantly *with what connection times* (Burghouwt, 2007, p. 8). Increasing airport congestion and new airline alliances that emerged with code sharing agreements further pronounced the importance of temporally optimized network (Burghouwt, 2007; Goedeking, 2010). Hence, scheduling has complemented network design as a vital activity in the NP process.

3.4.2 Types of airline networks

The structure of airline networks differs widely across business models, history, and market conditions. From an analytic perspective, network archetypes can be defined by considering the spatial and temporal concentration of the network. If a network is spatially concentrated, most traffic flows are directed through one central airport, the hub. Conversely, if a network is spatially dispersed, airports are connected directly and display little difference in the number of connections (Burghouwt, 2007, p. 12). The temporal concentration is expressed in the degree of flight coordination. Temporally concentrated networks enable shorter connection times for the customers and are called coordinated networks. In contrast, temporally un-coordinated networks have random connection times (Goedeking, 2010, p. 23). The following paragraphs highlight the four network archetypes and conclude with a reality check pertaining to the actual network structure of airlines.

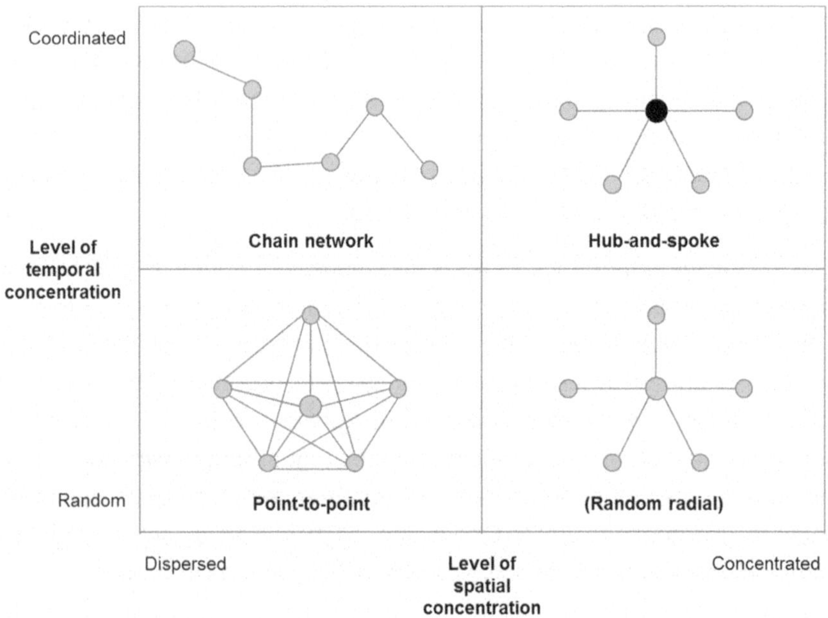

Figure 3.12 – Airline network archetypes[56]

[56] Source: Own illustration. following Burghouwt (2007).

Chain networks

Chain networks, also referred to as *tour networks*, *milk-runs*, or *linear networks* (Burghouwt, 2007, p. 14), are the oldest form of airline networks. The extreme case, as depicted on the upper left corner of Figure 3.12 , is characterized by two start/end points and several transshipment nodes. The chain network may comprise a long itinerary performed by a single aircraft or by a connection of multiple itineraries. In case of aircraft changes, the schedules need to be coordinated in order to avoid long connection times (Lederer & Nambimadom, 1998, p. 789).

In the early days of aviation, aircraft ranges were small and refueling stops common in connecting distant airports. Typical examples for chain networks were the intercontinental networks of European and North American airlines before the suitable long-haul aircraft was introduced in the 1970s[57].

Figure 3.13 exemplifies Lufthansa's South America network, spanning from Berlin to Buenos Aires in 1934, which featured no less than 14 intermediate stops and four aircraft changes (Airportzentrale, 2014). With the advent of economic long-haul airplanes, such as the Boeing 747, refueling stops became obsolete on most routes.

Since chain networks are less efficient than other network types (see section 3.4.3), most passenger airlines have developed different network structures. Today, chain networks are still common in cargo airlines and with some regional airlines connecting remote airports (Gillen, 2005, p. 61).

[57] Exemplary aircraft ranges: 1930s: below 2,500 km (Junkers Ju 52 or Douglas DC-3); 1950/60s: 6,000-8,000 km (Douglas DC-6, Lockheed Constellation, Boeing 707, Douglas DC-8); 1970s: above 10,000 km (Boeing 747, Douglas DC-10).

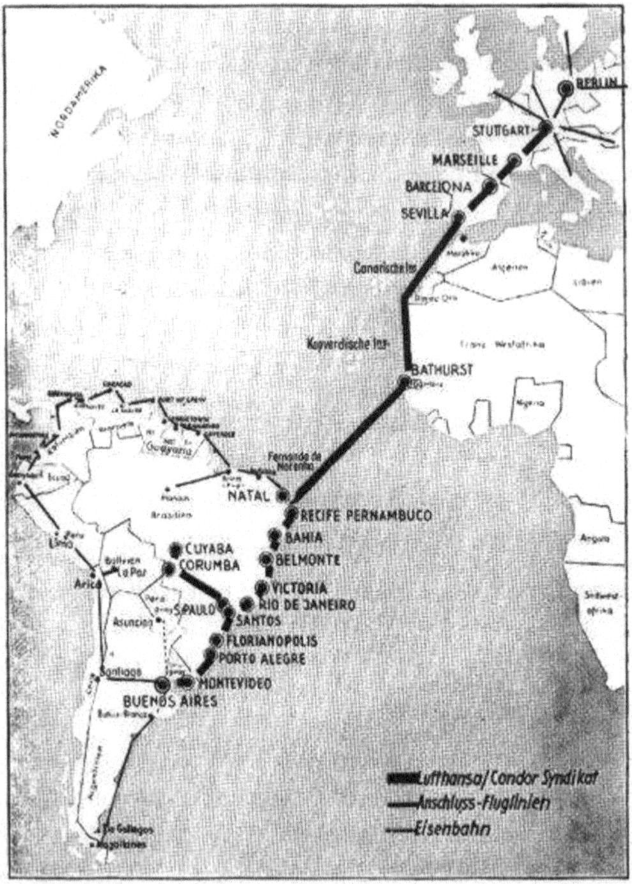

Figure 3.13 – Lufthansa's South America network in 1934[58]

[58] Source: Airportzentrale (2014).

Point-to-point networks

PP networks are dispersed and un-coordinated networks. The O&D connections are served by direct flights rather than connecting flights passing through a hub (Burghouwt, 2007, pp. 13–14). This has strong implications on the number of routes necessary to connect several airports. If we consider the six-airport graph in Figure 3.12, it requires 30 flights to connect all the airports in both directions. In a centralized HS network, only ten flights are necessary. However, as the schedules of the flights are not coordinated, airlines serving PP networks do usually not offer connecting flights at all (Goedeking, 2010, p. 32).

The standard structure in regulated markets is the PP network. Airlines apply for route rights at the regulator and get assigned a set of routes. The regulators usually favor direct connections, even between secondary airports, and thus, most domestic airline networks in regulated markets are PP networks to some extent. In exchange for a suboptimal network design, regulators often limit the competition on specific routes, so that the airlines can outweigh the cost disadvantage with higher fares (Lederer & Nambimadom, 1998). However, in the past 20 years, many low-cost airlines have chosen PP networks without any regulatory intervention. The driving forces behind this recent development are elaborated in section 3.4.3.

Hub-and-spoke networks

In the most extreme form of a HS network, all traffic flows are routed via a single hub. The upper right graph in Figure 3.12 schematically pictures such a "pure" HS network. The five spokes are only connected to one hub, and any O&D demand between the spokes must change flights at the hub.

Compared to PP networks, the HS model has obvious advantages. As mentioned in the last paragraph, much fewer flights are necessary to connect all the possible O&Ds. The freed capacity can be deployed to routes with the most demand, thus allowing for more flexibility in the schedule design (Goedeking, 2010, p. 33). Further advantages are economies of scale and scope, higher service levels, and an increased competitive position at the hub airports (Lederer & Nambimadom, 1998, p. 787).

Burghouwt (2007, p. 17) distinguished three types of hubs: global hubs, specialized hubs, and regional hubs. Global hubs not only connect short-haul with long-haul flights but also long-haul with other long-haul flights. Frankfurt, for example, is the global Lufthansa hub, which enables travelers from the United States to connect to India with reasonable connection times. Regional hubs optimize connections from short-haul to long-haul flights or simply from short-haul to other short-haul flights. Specialized hubs leverage their geographic location to bundle long-haul flights to a specific region and feed them with an associated short-haul network. Lisbon is a good example of a specialized hub for flights to Brazil that connect to a dense European short-haul feeder network.

Random radial networks

The spatial design of the random radial (RR) network is similar to the HS network but lacks the temporal coordination of the hub. This network type was the typical network for the European legacy carriers prior to the liberalization of traffic rights. Before the spread of the so-called *sixth-freedom rights*[59] or *beyond rights*, airlines were restricted to carry passengers only between two countries, one of them being the home country of the airline. Lufthansa, for example, could only carry passengers from Buenos Aires to Frankfurt (or vice versa) but not from Buenos Aires via Frankfurt to Mumbai. Connecting traffic flows thus had little relevance, and the schedule had little need for temporal coordination. With the increase of bilateral beyond-rights traffic agreements, European home base airports, such as Frankfurt,

---

[59] The sixth freedom right is the right to carry passengers or cargo from a second country to a third country by stopping in one's own country. Please refer to Annex 2 of Burghouwt (2007, p. 258) for a complete overview of the traffic right freedoms.

developed from central points of random radial networks to hubs in a HS network (Burghouwt, 2007, pp. 12–18).

Real-life airline networks

Very few airlines actually serve a pure network archetype; rather, there are varying shades of grey between these network types (Button & Stough, 2000, p. 26). The current networks are the result of a continuous network development, which has been influenced by changes in regulation, competition, aircraft technologies, and consumer preferences (Burghouwt, 2007, p. 2).

In the United States, for instance, networks first evolved from chain to PP networks due to the availability of long-haul aircraft, and then after the deregulation of the 1970s, they developed into HS networks. All the large United States (US) airlines have a multi-hub network, resulting from mergers in a consolidating industry. In general, there has been a clear tendency towards more spatial and temporal concentrations in the US airline networks (Burghouwt, 2007; Button & Stough, 2000; Gillen, 2005).

In Europe, the situation has evolved differently. The legacy carriers moved from chain to RR networks and then to HS networks. The spatial setup of the legacy carrier networks has not changed substantially (Bel & Fageda, 2010), but the temporal coordination has increased significantly (Burghouwt, 2007, pp. 3–4). The industry's consolidation in Europe has progressed slower than in the United States, but mergers in the past 20 years have produced more airlines with multiple hubs, such as Lufthansa, Air France-KLM, and the International Airlines Group (IAG)[60] (Lordan,

[60] Lufthansa Group currently operates with five hubs (Frankfurt, Munich, Zurich, Vienna and Brussels), IAG with two hubs (London Heathrow and Madrid) and Air France-KLM with two hubs (Paris Charles-de-Gaulle and Amsterdam).

2014, p. 1191). The Open Skies agreement between the US and the European Union (EU) has not led to further concentration but to an increased importance of alliances and joint ventures (Pels, 2009, p. 88).

The emergence of large low-cost airlines in Europe deserves additional remarks. Initially, LCCs had extremely dispersed networks, although they were far from being "pure" PP networks (Alderighi et al., 2007, p. 545). With the opening of more bases across Europe, LCCs such as Ryanair and Easyjet first decreased the spatial concentration of their networks; however, this trend reversed as they stationed more and more aircraft at each base (Burghouwt, 2007, pp. 57–59). In fact, networks of large LCCs are a combination of multiple RR networks around the operating bases.

3.4.3 Airline network economics

The size and the structure of networks have fundamental economic implications for airlines. Networks affect the cost structures, (de-)stimulate demand, and influence the competitive situation of an airline (Burghouwt, 2007, pp. 2–4). The literature on airline network economics has long assumed that in a deregulated market, the HS network type prevails, since airlines can harvest economies of scale and scope, provide a broader service offering, and increase the entry barriers to the airline industry (Goedeking, 2010, p. 108). However, the expansion of low-cost-carriers focusing on PP networks has led to a reconsideration of the traditional network economics in competitive markets (Takebayashi, 2013, p. 93).

A natural efficiency driver of network development are *economies of scale*. In the airline industry, economies of scale are defined as decreasing the average cost per passenger by increasing the network size (Burghouwt, 2007, p. 26). Although economies of scale on the firm level are disputed[61],

[61] While Caves, Christensen, and Tretheway (1984) found a constant unit cost at the firm level, Baltagi, Griffin, and Rich (1995) discovered economies of scale among North American airlines.

the existence of such economies of scale at a route level is widely acknowledged (Wojahn, 2001b). These cost advantages are often labelled as *economies of density*, which describe the decreasing average cost per passenger on a specific route when the number of transported passengers increases. Economies of density may be reached by using larger aircraft or increasing the frequency of flights on a specific route (Burghouwt, 2007, p. 28).

While economies of density can explain the focus on few high-density routes, it does not explain the spatial concentration of networks around a specific hub. This is where *economies of scope* come to play. In the airlines business, economies of scope are associated with "the joint production of heterogeneous products" (Burghouwt, 2007, p. 26). The core product of an airline is the transportation between an origin and a destination, i.e., an O&D connection. Passengers booking transportation on different O&Ds are considered to purchase different products. In a PP network, all passengers on a specific flight have purchased the same product, since the network does not permit connecting flights to a different destination. However, in an HS network, flights usually ferry passengers who have purchased completely different products. Imagine a Lufthansa flight from Zurich to Munich. Besides passengers flying only from Zurich to Munich, you may also find passengers with a different origin, for example, Nairobi; you may also find passengers whose origin is Zurich, but with a different end destination, for example, Delhi. The economic advantage of HS networks over PP networks is that they allow the bundling of different products and hence reduce the asset cost in offering these services (Wojahn, 2001b). Therefore, economies of scope can explain the formation of HS networks for airlines with a traditional cost structure.

The bundling effects of HS networks also have a positive impact on the demand side – the so-called *network effect*. Customers are more likely to choose an airline that offers a greater variety of products (all possible O&Ds); thus, customer retention becomes easier (Pels, Nijkamp, &

Rietveld, 2000, pp. 431–432). This positive demand network effect is also the primary driver for alliance formation, whereby airlines can virtually grow their network by offering code-sharing agreements with their alliance partners (Pels, 2008, p. 73). The temporal coordination of flights in an HS network also enables shorter connection times, thereby increases the attractiveness of the offered product (Goedeking, 2010, pp. 28–29). Several airlines use the *quality of service index (QSI)* to quantify these network effects. The QSI measures customer preferences for O&Ds, flight time, service quality, and price as well as the disutility of delays or connections. Based on these estimates, airlines can not only optimize the network structure but also the temporal coordination and used equipment for specific routes (Goedeking, 2010, p. 29). Serving a HS network provides more flexibility for network and schedule adjustments, since all the services are routed through the same hub.

Other than cost advantages and demand stimulation, there is a third factor explaining the historic development of HS networks. Concentrating traffic on one or more hubs increases the competitive position of an airline at these hubs. Since they provide a large share of the total traffic at these airports, they enjoy huge market power over the airports and the associated service providers (e.g., ground operations, catering, etc.). Besides the potential financial benefits, they often have a say on traffic right decisions and gate allocations. This market power increases the barriers on entry in the home markets of the HS airlines, whereby they can achieve a monopoly-like market position (Brueckner & Spiller, 1991; Oum, Zhang, & Zhang, 1995).

Establishing and developing a HS network also generates negative effects. Since great traffic is routed through the hubs, these airports are prone to congestion as they operate close to their capacity limit (Wojahn, 2001b). Congested airports bear a higher risk of operational delays, endangering the robustness of the network schedule. With the growing number of connections, the operational complexity also increases. Passengers and their baggage have to be transferred between the connecting flights. With such increasing complexity, the *minimum connection time (MCT)* increases and thereby the required turnaround time of the aircraft at the hub. If airplanes spend longer durations waiting for connecting passengers at the ground, the asset utilization decreases, and the marginal cost increase. These *diseconomies of complexity* have two concrete implications. First, there seems to exist a maximum network size with which airlines can operate efficiently. Merkert and Morrell (2012) found that the optimal network flow size is between 34 and 52 billion available seat kilometers (ASKs)[62]. Above 200 billion ASK, significant diseconomies of complexity seem to arise. Second, the cost structures become inflexible and enable the market entry of competitors with a simpler and lower cost structure (Pels, 2008, p. 74).

The entry of low-cost carriers (LCCs) in the market over the last 25 years has led to a revival of PP networks in aviation. In the HS model, there is little scientific evidence for the presence of network-wide economies of scale, since complexity (and hence cost) increases with network size. LCCs have radically reduced the network complexity by standardizing the offered product (single class, no frills) and operations (single aircraft type, no congested airports served). This has led to a much lower fixed cost base, enabling much better asset utilization than HS network airlines (Goedeking, 2010, pp. 31–35). These cost advantages of reduced complexity outweigh the lacking network effects and economies of density. Early scholars studying LCC development, such as Pels et al. (2000), concluded that a PP network was economically suitable only if the fixed cost base was very low. Airlines with a high fixed-cost base require economies of density and scope to remain competitive. However, recent research has empirically shown that even differences in the variable cost can make a HS network preferable to a PP network or vice versa (Takebayashi, 2013). In

[62] ASK is the unit measure of the total offered capacity controlled for route length. Take a flight with an Airbus A320 from Berlin to London as example: 180 seats are flown 950 kilometers, which results in 180 * 950 = 171,000 ASK for this specific flight.

conclusion, there is no clear answer to which among the HS or PP networks is more efficient. The efficiency depends largely on the cost structure and chosen business model of the airlines deploying these networks.

3.4.4 Airline network indicators

Measuring the properties and efficiency of airline networks is not a trivial task. Both graph-theoretical concepts, which are explained in section 3.3.3, as well as airline-specific network indicators can be used.

Airline network indicators from a graph theory perspective

Airline networks can be analyzed as unweighted and undirected graphs (Lordan, 2014, p. 1116). Guimerà et al. (2005) analyzed the entire global passenger air transportation network[63] and revealed that this network has evident small-world properties. The average shortest path length varied between 3.5 and 4.4, depending on the region. More than half of all airports could be reached using 4 flights. The clustering coefficient of the global air transport network is $C = 0.64$, which is significantly larger than the expected clustering coefficient for a random graph of similar size ($C = 0.049$). This is a clear indication of the small-world properties of the network.

Airline-specific network indicators

Airline-specific network indicators can roughly be classified under three categories. *Concentration measures* describe the distribution of traffic flows across the airline network. *Topological measures* evaluate the network structure, more precisely the airports and routes served (Wojahn, 2001b, p. 35). *Connectivity measures* describe the accessibility and centrality of airline networks (Burghouwt & Redondi, 2013, p. 37).

---

[63] They used the OAG database containing all the scheduled passenger flights between November 2000 and October 2001. The dataset contains over 530,000 unique flights between 3,883 distinct cities. 27,051 distinct routes have been identified.

Describing airline networks with geographical concentration measures has received most attention from the scientific community lately[64] (Alderighi et al., 2007, p. 530). The most commonly known indicator for spatial traffic concentration is a specific form of the *Gini index*[65], which compares the absolute available seat capacity per airport for all airports in an airline network (Wojahn, 2001b). In a completely decentralized network, such as the archetypical balanced PP network, we expect all airports to have the same available seat capacity. Since every airport is directly connected to every other airport with the same available capacity, absolute traffic flow numbers should be equal among airports. Accordingly, the Gini coefficient is 0, and the Lorenz curve should be a straight line with a 45° slope (see Figure 3.14).

In contrast, a perfect HS network with a single hub and three spokes has a huge traffic concentration at the hub and results in a Gini coefficient of 0.5 (Alderighi et al., 2007, p. 538). The Lorenz curve initially has a much steeper slope. The area between the diagonal and the actual curve is proportional to the Gini index of the network (Wojahn, 2001b, p. 34). Burghouwt (2007, p. 42) proposed the *Network Concentration* indicator, a derivate from the Gini index corrected for network size.

---

[64] Wojahn (2001b, pp. 26–37) and Burghouwt (2007, pp. 41–42) provided a comprehensive overview of the available spatial concentration measures.

[65] Wojahn (2001b) calculated the Gini index G as $G = \frac{1}{2n}\sum_{i=1}^{n}\sum_{j=1}^{n}|s_i - s_j|$, where n is the number of airports, s_i and s_j the traffic share of airports i and j.

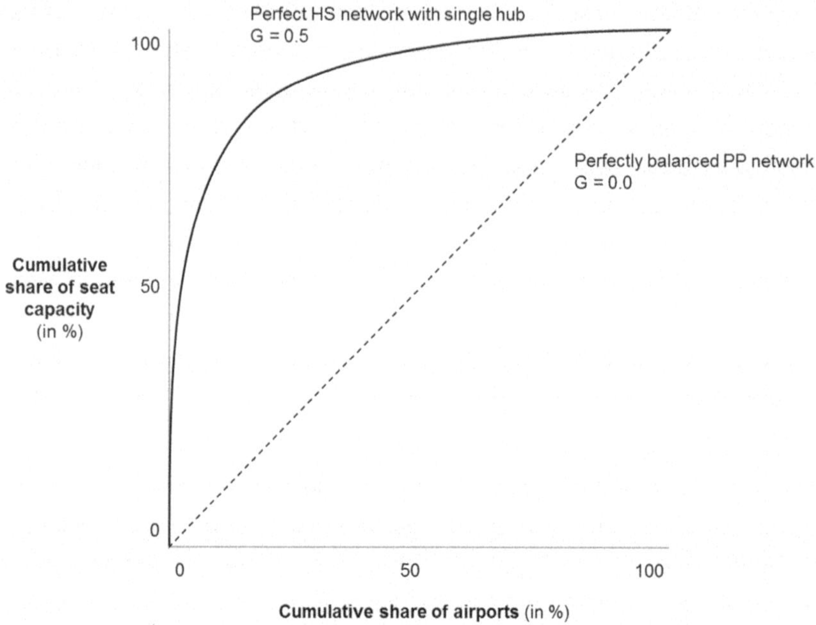

Figure 3.14 – Lorenz curves for the perfect PP and HS networks[66]

The Gini index does not provide information on the network centrality or the shape of the network. Alderighi et al. (2007, p. 538) recommended complementing the Gini index with the *Freeman index* of betweenness centrality[67]. Similarly, Wojahn (2001b, p. 44) developed the *topological hubbing index* to assess the network structure, which is derived from the Gamma index that measures the number of links compared to the number

[66] Source: Own illustration. following Alderighi et al. (2007, p. 538).

[67] Alderighi et al. (2007, p. 538) provided a highly accurate comparison between the Freeman Index and the Gini Index for a variety of networks.

of possible links in a network. In a normalized form[68], the topological hubbing index characterizes archetypical PP networks with a value 0 and an archetypical HS network with the value 1. The Freeman index works similarly but considers the perfect star network (HS network with 1 hub and 6 spokes) as graph theoretical reference.

Connectivity measures build on the finding that airline networks have small-world characteristics and aim to identify the best-connected nodes in a network, similar to the key influencer identification in social networks. Burghouwt and Redondi (2013) have identified 12 airline-specific measures of connectivity, which they distinguished in terms of accessibility and centrality measures. Accessibility measures consider airport connectedness independently of their hub function (e.g., Malighetti, Paleari, & Redondi, 2008). Centrality measures focus on defining the hub connectivity, focusing majorly on passenger transfer flows (Burghouwt & Wit, 2005). Recently, Boonekamp and Burghouwt (2017) developed a connectivity measurement model for cargo airline networks (called NetCargo), which presented different cargo categories to differentiate between networks.

Network profitability indicators

In addition to the graph-theoretical network indicators, the profitability analysis adds a strategic management indicator to the airline network analysis (Goedeking, 2010, p. 65). There are two alternative concepts for measuring network profitability: *route profitability* and *global network profitability*. While route profitability allocates all revenues and direct operating cost to specific routes, global network profitability also considers upline and downline revenues[69] (Sterzenbach et al., 2013, p. 383). Individual route profita-

---

[68] Wojahn (2001b) defined the topological hubbing index as $S(n,k) = \frac{n^2-n-2k}{n^2-3n+2}$, where n is the number of airports and k the number of routes.

[69] Upline and downline revenues emerge when a ticket is sold for an itinerary involving two or more flights. The total revenue is typically allocated to the individual flights of the itinerary by

bility analyses are only appropriate if airlines have no significant connecting traffic (Goedeking, 2010, pp. 102–104). This is true for most airlines operating within a PP network, such as low-cost carriers and regional carriers.

Individual route profitability analysis utilizes three contribution margins as profitability indicators, as displayed in Figure 3.15 (Goedeking, 2010; Niehaus, Ruehle, & Knigge, 2009; Sterzenbach et al., 2013).

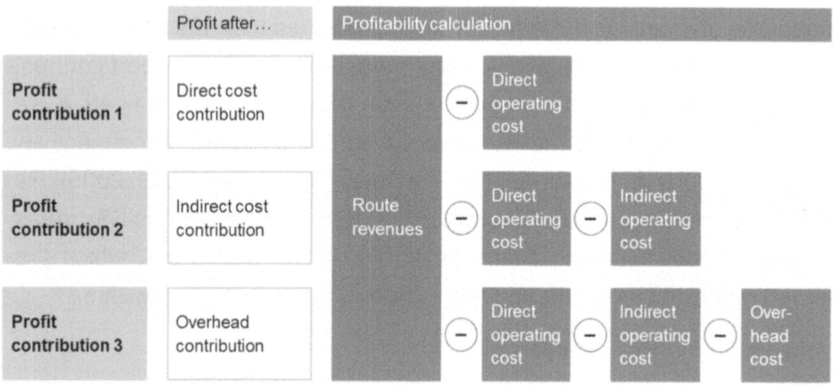

Figure 3.15 – Profit contribution margins in route profitability calculation[70]

The direct cost contribution margin indicates whether a flight covers its immediate variable cost. This should serve as an absolute bottom-line to decide whether a flight should be undertaken or not (Niehaus et al., 2009, p. 177). If a flight has a positive indirect operating margin, it also covers the

a distribution key, such as flight distance. The part of the ticket revenue that is not allocated to a specific flight is the upward revenue (for later flights of the itinerary) or downward revenue (for earlier flights of an itinerary).

[70] Source: Own illustration. following Niehaus et al. (2009, p. 177).

operational fixed cost, such as aircraft financing and maintenance expenditures. Ideally, a flight should cover its share of overhead cost in addition to the direct and indirect costs. This results in a positive overhead contribution margin as defined by Niehaus et al. (2009, p. 177).

If an airline network has a significant share of connecting traffic, the inclusion of upline and downline revenues is crucial in estimating the true value of a route for the entire network (Goedeking, 2010, p. 102). The importance of this can be best demonstrated with a real-life example. An economy class ticket for the itinerary Stuttgart–Frankfurt–New York generates a revenue of €1000. If the revenues are allocated according to distance, the flight from Stuttgart to Frankfurt gets allocated €24 (97 miles out of the total distance of 3953 miles equals 2.4%), whereas the flight from Frankfurt to New York gets allocated €976. Since Stuttgart–Frankfurt is a typical feeder route, with a high share of connecting passengers, the route profitability from Stuttgart to Frankfurt is probably on the alert screen of every network controller. However, the existence of the route enables the downline revenues of €976, which also needs to be considered when deciding on the network profitability impact of the Stuttgart–Frankfurt route. This obviously results in the double counting of revenues, but it provides a more reliable base for decisions on network and capacity adjustments (Sterzenbach et al., 2013, p. 389).

Niehaus et al. (2009, p. 177) presented a vertical and a horizontal method for calculating the global network profitability. With the vertical method, the contribution margins are calculated on a route level. Upline and downline elements are then added or subtracted from the respective route-specific margin. In contrast, the horizontal method includes the upline and downline revenues in the input revenue, from which the contribution margins are then calculated. While the vertical method reduces the need for two separate accounting systems, the horizontal method provides a more dynamic decision support, since changes in the network can be calculated on any margin level.

3.5 Network planning in airlines

Profit maximizing airlines aim to establish the most profitable network, realizing economies of scale, scope, and density. At the same time, the network schedule must be robust to allow for smooth operations and minimize the risk of total breakdown in case of external shocks. Furthermore, political and competitive considerations may shape a particular network and schedule (Burghouwt, 2007). Given the multifactorial environment, there is no “standard” NP process, neither defined in literature nor followed in practice. This sub-chapter deconstructs NP into distinct steps (section 3.5.1) and reviews the associated literature in passenger airlines (sections 3.5.2 to 3.5.5) and cargo airlines (section 3.5.6). Section 3.5.7 analyzes the literature on data needs for NP, before assembling a generalized NP process. The notion of “strategic” NP is finally discussed in section 3.5.8.

3.5.1 Components of network planning

From an analytical perspective, the NP process is the most complex transportation planning process (Bell & Iida, 1997, p. 3). Given the multitude of input factors and potential scenarios, one exact solution for all network planning problems is not feasible, even with today’s computing capabilities (Kölker & Lütjens, 2015, p. 901). There are two strategies than can be employed to overcome the complexity of NP.

First, the network planning problem can be broken into a sequence of smaller planning issues. This stepwise approach decomposes the NP process into different quantitative optimization and assignment problems. Grosche, Heinzl, and Rothlauf (2001, p. 258) have identified 14 sub-problems that can be solved independently in order to reach an optimal solution. The result of one optimization problem serves as an input for the next problem. However, the lack of feedback loops between the individual sub-problems creates a rather static NP tool, which is only recommendable for airlines in non-competitive or heavily regulated markets (Etschmaier & Mathaisel, 1985, p. 129).

A second option that can be adopted to overcome the complexity is heuristics that solve for a sufficiently good solution instead of calculating an exact solution. Those non-exact methods[71] have the advantage of being applicable to holistic NP models incorporating a multitude of sub-problems. Holistic models are dynamic and can be recalculated easily when critical input parameters change (e.g., the demand forecast for a certain route). This is especially relevant for airlines that operate in highly competitive market environments (Etschmaier & Mathaisel, 1985, p. 129).

Table 3.6 presents an overview of the fundamental literature pertaining to the process steps of NP and the relevant components or subproblems studied by the authors. It is evident that most authors focus on specific process steps rather than defining a holistic airline NP process. This also underpins the enormous complexity underlying airline NP.

In principle, four phases of airline NP can be discerned. *Long-term planning* refers to corporate strategy, long-term fleet planning, and long-to-mid-term demand forecast (Goedeking, 2010, pp. 93–94). The actual optimization of the airline network can be distinguished as *spatial optimization* and *temporal optimization* (Jacquemin, 2007, p. 61). The spatial optimization of the network aims to determine the optimal network structure (HS, PP, or any other network type) and select the most profitable routes of the network. The temporal optimization builds on the selected network structure and routes and determines the optimal flight frequency to satisfy the demand (given the available aircraft types). Further, it allocates concrete departure and arrival times to planned flights (Grosche, 2009, pp. 17–18).

[71] Leibold (2001) provides a superb overview of the relevant meta-heuristics, including simulated annealing, taboo search and genetic algorithms.

Table 3.6 – Overview of literature in airline NP processes[72]

		Wojahn, 2001b	Leibold, 2001	Grosche et al., 2001	Jacquemin, 2007	Grosche, 2009	Abdelghany & Abdelghany, 2009	Goedeking, 2010	Carmona Benitez, 2012	Bazargan, 2016
Long-term planning	Corporate strategy							M		
	Demand model	I		M	M		D		D	
	Fleet planning						M	M		
Spatial optimization	Network structure	D			D	D	M	M	D	M
	Route selection		M	M		M	M	M	D	M
Temporal optimization	Flight frequency		M	M		D	M	M		M
	Scheduling		M	M		D	M	M		M
Operational optimization	Fleet assignment			M		D	D			D
	Aircraft routing			M		D	D	M		D
	Crew assignment			M		D	D	M		D
Flight operations							D			D
Legend: D – Detailed ; M – Mentioned ; I - Input										

Operational optimization finally includes the assignment problems associated with operationalizing the network schedule. Fleet assignment entails the allocation of the optimal aircraft types to the planned flights. Aircraft

[72] Source: Own illustration. following authors mentioned in the table.

routing is the allocation of the individual aircraft to the planned flights[73], creating rotation plans for individual aircrafts. Crew assignment finally matches the available flight crews to individual flights (Bazargan, 2016, pp. 41–102). The NP process usually ends with the handover of the operational flight schedule to the flight operations department, which oversees the execution of the schedule, makes short-term adjustments, and reacts to operational irregularities (Bazargan, 2016, 133).

3.5.2 Long-term planning

Corporate and network strategy

The exact definition of corporate strategy for airlines varies across different research domains. While marketing scholars (e.g., Shaw, 2016) position product definition in the center of corporate strategy planning, finance researchers (e.g., Clark, 2017) consider a sound financial plan the key to strategy in a low-margin business, such as commercial aviation. Interestingly, network strategy plays a key role in most definitions of airline corporate strategy. Defining the network is a prerequisite for a compelling product definition as well as a key input for any financial planning.

Bieger and Wittmer (2011, pp. 78–81) proceed to put NP in the very center of corporate strategy definition. They view airline business models as a strategic reaction to the airline networks, enabling the creation of valuable resources to achieve a sustainable competitive advantage[74]. Sterzenbach et al. (2013, pp. 301–317) affirmed this perspective and noted that network strategy departments in many airlines directly report to the CEO. In this way, network planners contribute directly to the corporate strategy formulation. However, they assume that NP has an input role comparable to

---

[73] Aircraft routing is also called a tail assignment. This stems from the assignment of the individual aircraft registration, which is marked on the aircraft tail (at least the two last letters).

[74] Compare section 3.7.5 for a more detailed discussion on how airline network constitutes resources for competitive advantage.

other corporate functions, such as marketing and finance. The resulting corporate strategy, which has a larger time horizon, then serves as the starting point for the actual network strategy development. Similarly, Goedeking (2010, p. 94) cited corporate strategy (containing strategic objectives, fleet policies, and demand forecast) as an input for the NP process.

Contrary to Abdelghany and Abdelghany (2009), who consider corporate strategy a direct input for NP, Sterzenbach et al. (2013, p. 302) distinguished a planning phase between corporate strategy and network planning (compare Figure 3.16).

	Capacity planning (or network development)	**Network planning** (or flight scheduling)	**Network steering** (or revenue management)
Time horizon	5 – 2 years	2 – 0.5 years	0.5 years - departure
Planning content	▪ Capacity definition ▪ Fleet planning ▪ Fleet sourcing	▪ Itinerary definition ▪ Capacity optimization ▪ Fundamental pricing	▪ Detailed pricing ▪ Booking class steering ▪ Short-termed schedule and fleet adjustments
Process type	▪ Strategic planning process	▪ Network optimization and realization	▪ Market- and production optimization

Figure 3.16 – Airline network planning phases[75]

While corporate strategy has a long-term horizon of more than five years, the authors define *capacity planning* as an intermediate step covering the planning horizon between two and five years before departure. In this phase, an airline defines the capacity it wishes to offer based on the long-

[75] Source: Own illustration. following Sterzenbach et al. (2013, p. 302).

term demand forecasts and procures the necessary capacity in the form of airplanes.

Demand modeling

Forecasting airline demand plays a vital role not only in airline NP but also in other long-range planning activities, such as fleet planning and corporate strategy development (Goedeking, 2010, pp. 93–94). Air travel demand has a passenger and a ticket fare component, which need to be estimated in order to predict the expected revenues for specific markets or O&Ds (Carmona Benitez, 2012, p. 81). Here, we need to discern the estimation of the *unconstrained demand,* total *market size,* and the *market share* that an airline can expect to gain in the respective market. Estimation of the unconstrained demand is difficult and often not effective, so most researchers rely only on the market size and market share estimates (Holloway, 2008, pp. 99–102). Jacobs et al. (2012, pp. 39–42) proposed a two-step approach for market share evaluations, starting with an estimate of the total market size and then "splitting" this market among the competing airlines.

It is important to distinguish between constrained and unconstrained demand (see Figure 3.17). Unconstrained demand is the demand for transportation that is independent from price or the means. Constrained demand is the actual demand for a specific transportation service offered with defined transportation mean, times, and fares (Jacobs et al., 2012, 69ff).

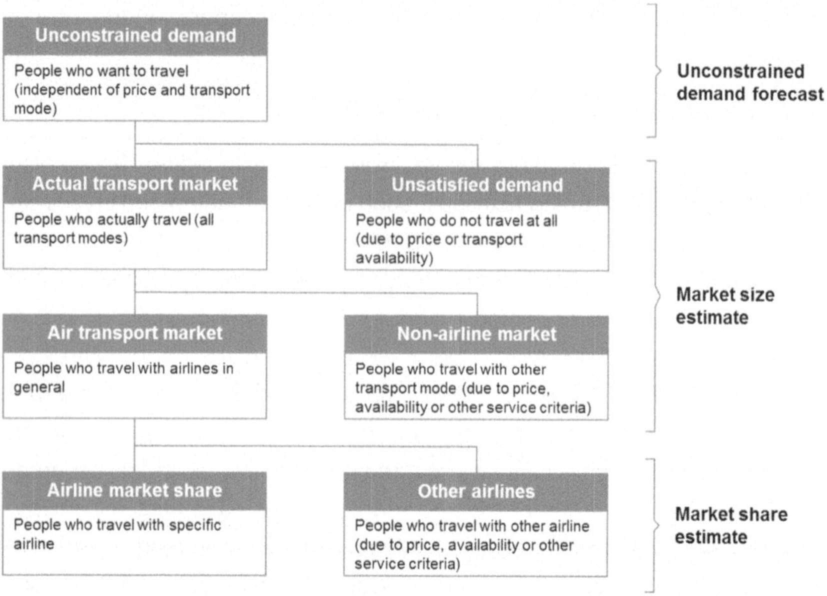

Figure 3.17 – Airline demand forecasting logic[76]

From the perspective of an airline, the two most important constraint factors that cause a demand spill are time and ticket price (Akartunalı et al., 2013, p. 794). Demand spill in terms of time applies when customers choose a different transportation means because the door-to-door travel time is faster or if customers do not travel at all because there are no satisfying travel options. The availability of alternative transportation modes is relevant only for a short-haul travel. From a modeling perspective, the time constraint is fairly stable, as air travel time is proportional to the distance (Jorge-Calderón, 1997, p. 27).

[76] Source: Own illustration. following Holloway (2008, p. 100).

Ticket prices are adjusted in real time in many airlines and are thus a very difficult input parameter in terms of long-term demand forecasts (Bazargan, 2016, pp. 113–137). Therefore, assumptions pertaining to the expected ticket fare need to be included in the demand model. There are two possible ways to include ticket price estimates in the model. They can be integrated in the market size model. These models are then *dynamic* or *demand-sensitive,* since the constraint is introduced during the actual market sizing. The sensitivity of the entire market to changes in ticket prices can thus be projected. Alternatively, market size estimates can be made on the basis of unconstrained demand, where the constraints in the market share models and other means of transportation and no-travel passengers are included. These are static or demand insensitive models.

Carson, Cenesizoglu, and Parker (2011, p. 925) distinguished between the macroscopic and microscopic *market sizing models*: in macroscopic models, the "dependent variable is an aggregate indicator of air travel demand in a certain country or region." Whereas, microscopic models "estimate the air travel demand between two airports, cities or regions." Microscopic models are thus more granular and require more accurate data than macroscopic models. Airlines typically use macroscopic models for general long-term market forecasts (up to 10 years) in informing their corporate strategy and fleet planning decisions. However, particular route selection decisions require demand forecasts on O&D levels to make various potential routes comparable.

Furthermore, there is an extensive body of literature on evaluating various mathematical methodologies for market size estimates. Grosche (2009, pp. 68–70) elucidated the most effective qualitative and quantitative methods (displayed in Figure 3.18). Almost all scholarly literature focuses on quantitative market forecasts, which can be categorized as time-series projections and causal models[77].

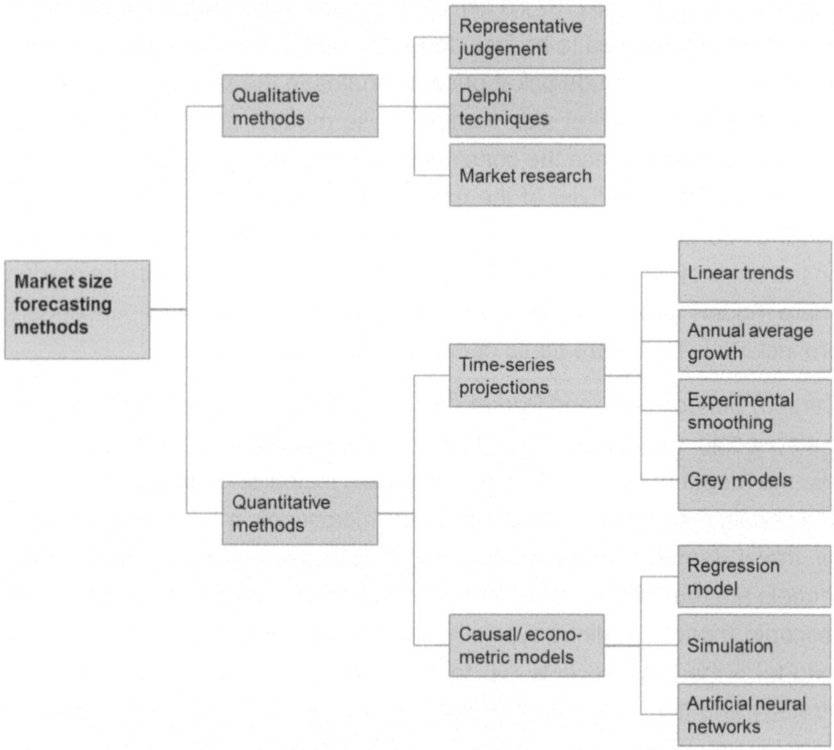

Figure 3.18 – Methods for market size forecasting[78]

Time-series projections usually extrapolate historic traffic data to the future. Unfortunately, there are few consistent data sets which cover a large

[77] Appendix 14 includes a comprehensive overview of the individual scholarly contributions on the different methods.

[78] Source: Own illustration. following Grosche (2009, p. 69).

number of O&Ds over a long period. Therefore, Grey models[79] have become increasingly popular among scholars, since they allow forecasting with a limited number of data points or with incomplete data sets (Carmona Benítez et al., 2013; Hsu & Wen, 1998). The time horizon for forecasts in literature varies from a few weeks (Saab & Zouein, 2001) to an astonishing 40 years owing to damp trend models (Carmona Benítez et al., 2013). Moreover, the mixed models combining time-series and causal approaches have evolved. Those models usually rely on geo-economic factors with readily available forecasts, such as population growth, and combine that with time-series data on air transport demand (Chen, 2012; Grubb & Mason, 2001; Profillidis, 2000).

Causal or econometric models try to identify variables that explain the past changes in air travel demand. The detected correlations then facilitate a demand forecast using assumptions regarding the future values of the explanatory variables (e.g., income per capita). There are two main groups of explanatory variables: geo-economic and service-related variables (Jorge-Calderón, 1997, p. 24). Geo-economic variables have geographic aspects (e.g., distance, geographic isolation), demographic aspects (e.g., population density, population growth), and economic variables (e.g., income per capita, gross domestic product growth). Service-related variables evaluate the factors for passenger utility. Those factors can be time related (total travel time), convenience related (number of stops, aircraft size, service level) and/or price related. There is a rich body of literature on causal methods using both types of explanatory variables, which is detailed in Appendix 14.

Based on market size estimates, *market share models* calculate the expected market share of a product offering. There are significantly fewer

[79] The Grey models complete partial theoretical constructs with real data; the used datasets can hereby be small.

studies than on market size models, which can be explained by the difficulty to model passenger preferences (Hsiao & Hansen, 2011). Furthermore, a gap between the academic and practical market share models is evident (Jacobs et al., 2012, p. 43). While researchers have mainly been focusing on discrete choice models, such as multinomial logit models (Coldren et al., 2003; Hsiao & Hansen, 2011), airlines often rely on the Quality of Service Index (QSI). The QSI was developed by the US Civil Aeronautics Board in the 1950s to calculate rate tables in the regulated airline environment. The latest version calculates the expected utility of each possible connection and splits the aggregated O&D demand between competitors utilizing a probabilistic model (Goedeking, 2010, pp. 29–30). Logically, all market share models include service-related factors similar to those described for market size models.

Fleet planning

The relationship between fleet planning and network planning is a classic chicken-and-egg problem. Most network planning tools and algorithms depend on a fleet plan as an input, and vice versa, fleet planning tools require a network to be served in order to calculate the most accurate results (Bieger & Wittmer, 2011, p. 79). Fortunately, in most airlines, there is both an existing fleet and an existing network, on the basis of which the other element can be estimated using long-term demand forecasts. Sterzenbach et al. (2013, p. 302) combined fleet size and network structure decisions in the *capacity planning* step, thus connecting corporate strategy with network planning (see Figure 3.16).

Traditionally, fleet planning was a long-term process, since aircrafts have to be financed and aircraft manufacturers have had a constant production backlog, resulting in waiting times of several years for newly built aircrafts (Clark, 2017, p. 25). More recently, fleet and capacity planning have become more flexible due to the leasing models for aircraft, a vivid second-hand market and an increasing number of the so-called ACMI[80] providers (Clark, 2017, p. 25). This enables airlines to adjust capacities to short- and mid-term changes in demand. Consequently, planning horizons for both fleet planning and NP can be shortened significantly.

For traditional airlines, Dožić and Kalić (2015) suggested a three-step fleet planning process. In the first step, an appropriate mix of short-haul, long-haul, and regional aircrafts is defined based on the draft network. The individual fleets are then sized based on the long-term demand forecast, before the most economic aircraft type within each fleet is finally selected.

However, not all airlines optimize their fleets to serve the predicted demand for air travel. In many cases, fleet planning decisions are influenced by political, emotional, or financial factors (Clark, 2017, p. 33). Political factors are especially common among state-owned airlines that want to promote local aircraft manufacturers (e.g., COMAC in China) or if economic sanctions limit the import of certain airplanes. Emotional factors are mostly prestige-based fleet decisions, e.g., the acquisition of Boeing 747s in the 1970s or the Concorde for Air France and British Airways. Financial factors often arise from the great discounts on new airplanes. LCCs, for example, place large aircraft orders[81] and realize volume discounts of up to 40% on the list price. This minimizes capital costs as these airlines can sell the airplanes even after 10 years for an amount not substantially less than the purchase price (Clark, 2017). The mentioned chicken–egg problem is thus solved at least for the large LCCs; here, the fleet planning comes first and lays the foundation for any NP.

---

[80] ACMI stands for Aircraft, Crew, Maintenance, and Insurance, which is provided by the leasing company (sometimes called wet-lease). Those contracts are similar to long-term charter contracts, where an ACMI company operates the flight for the lessor.

[81] Examples: Air Asia ordered 305 Airbus A320neo, Indian LCC IndiGo ordered 405 A320neo (Airbus, 2017).

3.5.3 Spatial optimization

Spatial optimization entails the geographic design of an airline network. It includes the definition of the network structure (i.e., network type and specific layout) and the selection of the optimal routes. The sequence of route selection and network structure definition in academic research is not well-defined. Certain authors have considered a set of airports as the input for network structure design (e.g., Barla & Constantatos, 2000; Lederer & Nambimadom, 1998). Others have selected cities and routes based on a network type hypothesis (e.g., Carmona Benitez, 2012). In practice, the network type for most airlines is presented by the existing network, so that route selection is merely a step after the decision on the network structure has been made.

Network structure

Based on the transport network designs described in section 3.3.5, the definition of airline network structure can be divided into a general and a specific network design. In the general design, the best-suited network type is determined (e.g., hub-and-spoke or point-to-point network). In the specific design, the best structure of a given network type must be found. The most prominent research field here is the hub location problem in hub-and-spoke networks (Alderighi et al., 2007).

There are few scholarly works on airline network design from scratch, since most airlines have a pre-existing network (Wojahn, 2001a, p. 267). The most fundamental study was conducted by Lederer and Nambimadom (1998), who examined the optimal network type from an economic cost perspective. Hence, an optimal network type is a network that minimizes both airline cost and passenger cost. They found that for short distances between airports, PP networks are more efficient, whereas HS networks are more efficient for long-haul networks and networks with mixed short- and long-haul routes. Moreover, HS networks are becoming superior to PP networks with an increasing number of destinations. Naturally, networks with equally high demand on its routes favor PP networks, whereas networks with huge differences in route demand can be better optimized following HS networks (Lederer & Nambimadom, 1998, p. 785). When designing an airline network from scratch, the demand for individual routes is often uncertain. Barla and Constantatos (2000) demonstrated that HS networks minimize cost risks in case of high demand uncertainty. Under the assumption of demand gravity[82], Wojahn (2001a) discovered a mix of HS and PP networks to be the optimal option, whereas multi-hub network structures are not cost-optimal.

Once the network type is defined, the optimal network structure becomes the center of attention. Whereas in a pure PP network the network structure is determined entirely through route selection (see next section), the structure of HS networks can vary greatly. An airline can operate in a single hub or multiple hubs. In single hub networks, the main design question is which airport to choose as the hub, whereas multi-hub networks offer a much wider range of design options. Besides the selection of spokes (which is essentially the route selection), the location of hubs and what spoke will be served from a particular hub need to be determined[83]. O'Kelly (1987) and Campbell (1992) pioneered the hub location research, formulating it however as a general problem without a specific context of airline network design. Alumur and Kara (2008) and Farahani et al. (2013) provide excellent

---

[82] Wojahn's (2001a, p. 268) gravity model of demand assumes that demand is not independent from geographical distance, i.e., the demand between close airports tends to be higher than the demand between distant airports.

[83] Jaillet, Song, and Yu (1996) first applied the hub location problem specifically to the airline industry and tested their algorithms on a sample of 39 US cities. They found that airports are more destined to be a hub due to their geographic location than for their local demand. Furthermore, optimal airline networks in the US are most probably not pure HS networks but mixed HS and PP networks (Jaillet et al., 1996, pp. 210–211). Adler and Berechman (2001) developed a dual-hub optimization model and applied it to the European aviation market. According to their findings, a network with the hubs London Heathrow and Stockholm Arlanda would be the most profitable dual-hub network combination in Europe.

and comprehensive overviews of the scientific body of literature, discussing general hub location problems[84].

Route selection

While the network design determines the network type and structure, route selection entails choosing the right nodes. These can be the spokes in an HS network or the most profitable airport connections in a PP network. In early research works, route selection was often integrated in the network design process. Chan (1974), for instance, views route selection as a step before the actual network design. He proposed a three-step approach to integrated route and network design: first, the most profitable O&Ds are determined. Second, a network structure is built to serve the demand at the lowest cost. Third, the network is constantly re-evaluated to identify more profitable routes to replace the least profitable routes. Although this approach is logical and resembles the real-life route selection processes, Chan (1974) assumes that airline networks are always PP networks and did not consider economies of scale and density.

Teodorović, Kalić, and Pavković (1994) and subsequently Hsu and Wen (2000, 2002) proposed a more theoretical approach. Under the assumption that the final schedule and thus the potential intermediate stops are unknown at the time of route selection, they created a set of the spatially shortest routes. However, serving this network would be highly inefficient, since the demand on some of the shortest routes would not justify a PP flight. In the second step, they aggregate the demand of spatially shortest routes on a feasible network. Wei, Chen, and Sun (2014) added a schedule robustness component to the route selection algorithm, which earlier was

[84] Alumur and Kara (2008) distinguished four sub-types of the hub-allocation problem: The *single allocation p-hub median problem* aims to minimize the total transportation cost incurred while serving a network with p hubs, n nodes, and a given flow demand, whereby every spoke can be connected only to one hub. In the *multiple allocation p-hub median problem,* spokes can be connected to more than one hub. If the fixed cost produced by the hub are introduced, we get *p-median problems with fixed cost.* Finally, the *p-hub center problem* minimizes the maximum cost to serve the given demand.

focused on profit maximization only. While all previously mentioned route selection models work with historic demand data as the input, Carmona Benitez (2012, pp. 140–145) integrates a dynamic demand and revenue forecast in the route selection algorithm.

3.5.4 Temporal optimization

Temporal optimization transforms a spatial network into a bi-dimensional airline network. It features two degrees of granularity: flight frequency definition and flight scheduling. Flight frequencies determine how often a specific route is served per period (usually per week). Flight scheduling defines the exact departure times and usually results in a draft rotation plan for an exemplary schedule week (Grosche, 2009, pp. 8–12).

Flight frequency

Flight frequency assignment is a combination of two decisions: How much capacity should be offered? What airplanes are required to provide this capacity? The offered capacity generally is a result of the demand forecast for a specific route in the airline network, including network-driven connection demand. If an airline has a homogeneous fleet, the decision pertaining to the offered capacity can be translated directly into required flight frequencies. In case of a heterogeneous fleet, there is an additional decision on whether less frequencies with larger aircraft or more frequencies with smaller aircraft are preferable to offer the intended capacity (Grosche et al., 2001, p. 258). Increased flight frequencies provide a more convenient service for customers and thus influence demand directly (Teodorović & Krčmar-Nožić, 1989, p. 14). On the other hand, operating smaller aircrafts to increase the frequency usually increases the cost of transportation and organizational complexity. Thus, cost-minimizing airlines aim to offer the capacity with the smallest number of flights possible (Teodorović et al., 1994, p. 103).

Teodorović and Krčmar-Nožić (1994; 1989) formulated a multicriteria model to balance passenger preferences and airline cost. Their model maximizes profits and the number of passengers flown by choosing the optimal number of flight frequencies on a given set of routes with a given aircraft fleet. Hsu and Wen (2000) incorporated planning constraints, such as maintenance requirements and spare aircraft reserves, into the flight frequency model.

Since flight frequency assignment has a direct impact on the service quality and thereby on demand, it is often incorporated in network design models (Grosche, 2009, p. 34). Most of the scholars mentioned so far have integrated flight frequency assignment either as independent sub-model (Hsu & Wen, 2000; Teodorović et al., 1994; Teodorović & Krčmar-Nožić, 1989) or as an optimization factor for the network design model (Lederer & Nambimadom, 1998; Wojahn, 2001a). However, it is treated as a separate NP process to reflect the realities in practice (see sub-chapter 4).

Flight scheduling

Grosche et al. (2001, p. 259) define *flight scheduling* as the "deliberate decision on departure times for each planned flight." The duration of a flight does not only include the time when the aircraft is airborne but also the time required to taxi and line-up. The time frame from the first movement (usually the push-back at the gate) to the last movement is called block time (BT), measured in block hours[85] (Goedeking, 2010, p. 19). The standing time at the gate is called the turnaround time (TAT). For flight scheduling, both BT and required TAT must be considered. In practice, the choice of the departure time automatically implies an estimated arrival time, which is the departure time plus the usual BT for the flight. The TAT needs to be added as well, which defines the earliest possible next departure time for the aircraft.

---

[85] Compare Goedeking (2010, p. 19): The term "block-time" originates from the chock blocks used to avoid aircraft movements when an aircraft is at the gate. If the chock blocks are removed ("off-block"), the block-time of the flight starts and ends with the setting of the chuck blocks after landing ("on-block").

Etschmaier and Mathaisel (1985, p. 128) delineated four critical input factors for flight scheduling: an O&D-based demand forecast that is ideally available for each day of the week or even on an hourly basis; a set of routes to be served, including intended flight frequencies, route distance, and operating restrictions, such as airport curfews, slots, and aircraft size restrictions; aircraft characteristics of the available fleet, including operating cost by route length; finally, any operational and managerial constraints, such as maintenance plans and crew rosters.

With the emergence of HS networks and thus an increasing number of connecting flights, the importance of scheduling has increased significantly. The connection time influences the total travel time for passengers, which is a key component of service quality (Goedeking, 2010, p. 30). Thus, flight scheduling has a direct demand effect, since passengers usually prefer short connection times. Airlines with HS networks have developed wave patterns to bundle the connecting passengers at their hub airports. Consider a hub for long-haul flights with short-haul feeder flights as example. First, a fixed time window called "inbound bank" is established where the short-haul feeder flights arrive (e.g., 10–11am). After a minimum connection time to allow passengers, baggage, and cargo to change planes (e.g., 60 minutes), an outbound bank is established (e.g., 12–1pm). During this window, the long-haul flights depart to minimize the total travel time for passengers. Those bank waves are naturally restricted by the airport's handling capacity (Goedeking, 2010, p. 45). In contrast, airlines with PP networks are not concerned with minimizing the total travel time for passengers, since they rarely offer connecting flights.

Schedules with banked hub operations have two major disadvantages. First, ground resources are often underutilized during off-peak times, thus creating higher operating cost. Second, TATs are longer than the operational minimum, since airplanes need to wait for connecting passengers. This leads to a decreased aircraft utilization and lower asset productivity (Jiang & Barnhart, 2013, pp. 831–832). Thus, many airlines have started to "de-bank" their hub operation, since additional operating cost are higher than the revenue increase that results from offering a better service through shorter connection times (Jiang & Barnhart, 2009, p. 338). However, some airlines seem to experience different economies and maintain a waved hub structure. Delta Airlines even re-established the waved hub structure at Atlanta after piloting the de-banked hub model (Goedeking, 2010, p. 72).

In the early literature on flight scheduling, the optimization goal was either to minimize required the fleet size (and hence cost) or to maximize the network-wide profits (Yan & Young, 1996, p. 380). More recently, additional optimization variables centered on schedule flexibility and robustness have been introduced. Flexibility indicates the "number of recovery options available to mitigate the effects of a disruption" (Burke et al., 2010, p. 823), but it can also be interpreted as flexibility in reacting to short-term changes in demand, e.g., by re-fleeting and re-scheduling (Warburg et al., 2008). Schedule robustness "is a measure for the probability of a delay to propagate through the schedule and the availability of local recovery strategies with a limited impact on the rest of the schedule" (Burke et al., 2010, p. 823). Since an increasing number of airlines are planning to introduce dynamic scheduling[86] to optimally serve their demand, the importance of

[86] Dynamic scheduling also influences the sub-processes of schedule development. Traditionally, the initial schedule was created and then iteratively evaluated and adapted (Etschmaier and Mathaisel, 1985, pp. 129–130). These sub-processes had two different solution models – a creation model and an evaluation model (Papadakos, 2009, p. 177). In dynamic scheduling, those sub-processes have to be merged to create optimal schedule solutions. Based on the work of Yan and Young (1996), Stojković et al. (2002) developed a dynamic day-of-operation scheduling model that combines both sub-processes to mitigate schedule disruptions. Yan, Tang, and Fu (2008) and Warburg et al. (2008) further adopted the integrated scheduling model to react not only to unpredictable schedule disruptions, but also to short-term changes in passenger demand on specific O&Ds. Jiang and Barnhart (2009) proposed a demand-weighting model to prioritize high-revenue connections in the process of dynamic scheduling. It is important to notice that a de-banked hub structure is preferable if an airline choses to adopt dynamic scheduling Jiang and Barnhart (2013, p. 832).

schedule flexibility and robustness has increased significantly (Warburg et al., 2008).

3.5.5 Operational optimization

The steps to operationalize the spatially and temporally defined flight schedules entail operational optimization. The three distinguishable steps are *fleet assignment* (allocation of aircraft type to each flight), aircraft routing (daily rotation plans for aircraft), and crew assignment (matching of crews and aircraft). Goedeking (2010) also considered maintenance planning a part of operational optimization. In line with a majority of scholars (Abdelghany & Abdelghany, 2009; Bazargan, 2016; Grosche, 2009), maintenance planning is considered as information input rather than a deliberate optimization step.

Fleet assignment

An aircraft type can be assigned to a specific flight at different points of time. The initial allocation is made simultaneously or shortly after setting the flight schedule. The so-called re-fleeting or demand-driven dispatch (Berge & Hopperstad, 1993) is a continuous adaptation of the fleet assignment according to changes in the demand pattern, which can occur at any time between the initial fleet assignment and the hand over to flight operations (Jarrah, Goodstein, & Narasimhan, 2000, p. 350).

The purpose of fleet assignment is to allocate the optimal aircraft type to each flight. Dispatching an aircraft type on a specific flight incurs a certain operating cost, which should be known as input. Furthermore, a specific aircraft type may be too small to serve the forecasted demand. This creates a passenger spill, since some passengers cannot be transported. A part of the spill may be recovered by offering alternative itineraries, but the difference between the total spill and recovered spill is foregone revenue, which is known as spill cost. Hence, the optimal fleet assignment needs to minimize both operating and spill cost for the airline network (Bazargan, 2016, pp. 46–49).

Fleet assignment is subject to a set of planning restrictions. First, all flights of the input schedule need to be undertaken. The sizes of individual aircraft fleets are usually pre-determined, and the utilization of the aircraft fleets should be balanced (Bazargan, 2016, pp. 50–54). Furthermore, the range of the aircraft type must exceed the route length, and both departure and arrival airports must be able to accommodate the aircraft type. Finally, the departing flight has to be operated through the same aircraft type, especially on multi-stop flights (Abdelghany & Abdelghany, 2009, pp. 65–68).

Fleet assignment has a strong interdependency with flight scheduling, since a change to a larger aircraft type may lead to the combination of two flights, or conversely, the use of a smaller aircraft type may lead to an additional flight (Abdelghany & Abdelghany, 2009, p. 75). Therefore, various scholars have published research on integrated fleet assignment and scheduling models (Bélanger et al., 2006; Ioachim et al., 1999; Papadakos, 2009; Sandhu & Klabjan, 2007; Yan & Tseng, 2002), which are examined further in section 3.5.7.

Aircraft routing

Aircraft routing, also known as tail assignment or aircraft rotation planning, is the "process of assigning each individual aircraft ('tail') within each fleet to flight legs" (Bazargan, 2016, p. 61). The most common objective of aircraft routing is the minimization of operating cost, since capacity and revenue-relevant decisions usually occur in the fleet assignment stage.

In practice, the schedule with fleet assignment is transformed into individual rotation plans for each aircraft. The planner needs to ensure that every planned flight is assigned an individual airplane and that the airplane utilization within each fleet is balanced (Bazargan, 2016, p. 61). Furthermore, the minimum TATs between flights need to be incorporated in the rotation plan (Abdelghany & Abdelghany, 2009, p. 79). The most prominent constraint here is the aircraft maintenance routing problem. Aviation authorities require regular maintenance activities, which are classified according to their scope, from regular nightly A-Checks (3–6 manhours, required every 60–200 flight hours) to D-Checks, which imply almost complete aircraft overhauls (several thousand manhours, required every 6–10 years). These maintenance checks need to be performed by an authorized provider, who holds a certification for the respective aircraft type. This implies that for aircraft routing, an aircraft scheduled for an A-Check must have a night overlay at an airport with a qualified maintenance facility (Gopalan & Talluri, 1998, p. 261).

Crew assignment

The crew assignment process matches individual crew members to specific flights and is considered to be one of the most computationally intensive combinatoric problems (Klabjan et al., 2002, p. 337). Therefore, this process is usually split into two sequential subproblems, *crew pairing* and *crew rostering* (Abdelghany & Abdelghany, 2009, p. 89). Since flight crews represent the second largest operating cost for airlines after fuel (Bazargan, 2016, p. 84), it is the most important objective of the optimization process to minimize cost through the effective management and planning of crews.

Aircraft crews comprise cabin and cockpit crew. Both job categories feature different ranks[87] and have certifications based on specific aircraft types (Abdelghany & Abdelghany, 2009, p. 89). The exact crew composition of a specific flight is regulated by the aviation authorities and depends on the aircraft size and flight duration. Additionally, airlines often have binding union agreements that specify the working conditions of the crew, such as a maximum number of days away from the crew base or crew rest times,

[87] See Abdelghany and Abdelghany (2009, p. 89): For cabin crew usually the purser and flight attendants, for pilots captain, senior first officers, and first officers.

which exceed the regulatory required minimum (Bazargan, 2016, pp. 94–95). Crews staying in hotels or requiring deadhead flight transfers generate additional cost; thus, airlines intend (at least in the short-haul network) to start and end crew duties at the home base.

The first part of the process – *crew pairing* – creates anonymous crew rotations (or trip-pair) for a sequence of flights over a period of two to seven days. These rotations are usually repeated on a weekly base over the scheduled period and comply with all the regulatory and contractual obligations. In the second part of the process – *crew rostering* – individual duty rosters are created out of draft trip-pairs for every cabin and cockpit crew member. These duty rosters are usually built on a monthly basis and also include vacation and standby duties (Abdelghany & Abdelghany, 2009, pp. 89–102).

3.5.6 Network planning in cargo airlines

The general process of NP in cargo airlines is quite similar to those of passenger airlines (Derigs, Friederichs, & Schäfer, 2009, p. 371). However, the air cargo business model presents some specific differences to passenger airlines (Feng, Li, & Shen, 2015, pp. 265–266):

- While passengers are a standardized single commodity from an airline's perspective, air cargo contains multiple commodities of different sizes, densities, and characteristics.
- Cargo demand tends to be much more volatile, complicating long-term demand and capacity planning.
- While passengers are always transported with passenger aircrafts, air cargo can be transported either in wholly freighter aircrafts (bulk cargo) or in the freight compartments of passenger aircrafts (belly cargo). This adds an additional layer of complexity to market share modelling.

- The planning cycles in air cargo are much shorter. Bookings for cargo flights open usually only 6–12 weeks before the flight, so the final schedule can be published much closer to the departure date.
- Non-express freight can usually be routed in various ways, as long as it arrives at the destination within a specific time window (only the O&D is booked, not the specific flight). This allows for much more active demand steering than in passenger airliners, where all the passengers are booked on a specific flight.
- Similar to passenger airlines, capacity is sold as fixed capacity commitments (hard block spaces) or as flexible capacity commitments (soft block spaces). In contrast to passenger airlines, there is usually no cancellation fee and price differences between fixed, and flexible capacity is much lower. This leads to significantly higher no-show rates and may thus influence aircraft routing.
- Most cargo airlines operate primarily from uncongested airports without fixed slot allocations, so they have more flexibility for short-term changes in planned aircraft routings.

Given the greater uncertainty and flexibility, NP and revenue management is more strongly interlinked in cargo airlines than in passenger airlines. The possibility to re-adjust the schedule and routings a couple of hours before departure also requires a closer collaboration with flight operations. The possibility to send cargo on different routes to the same destination renders cargo routing a specific planning step in the actual aircraft routing (Friederichs, 2010, pp. 20–22).

The immense complexity of air cargo NP in addition to the small scale of the industry compared to passenger airlines[88] is probably the reason for diverted attention towards passenger airlines in research. There are only

---

[88] IATA (2017a) estimates the global passenger airline market at ~800 billion USD, whereas the global air cargo market only accumulates around ~50 billion USD.

two scholars who aimed to develop integrated NP models for cargo airlines, namely Stefan Friederichs (Derigs et al., 2009; Derigs & Friederichs, 2013; Friederichs, 2010) and Shangyao Yan (Yan & Chen, 2008; Yan, Chen, & Chen, 2006).

Long-term planning

Literature on the corporate strategy of cargo airlines is scarce and mostly concerned with cargo alliances and revenue management (Feng et al., 2015, p. 267). Marsten and Muller (1980) proposed a fleet planning model for cargo airlines, based on a multi-hub network simulation. Naturally, the demand forecasting for air cargo is concerned with rather short-term demands and fluctuation predictions than long-term demand models. Long-term demand models usually rely on the gross domestic product (GDP) or a combination of GDP and foreign direct investment (FDI) as estimators in the econometric demand models (Chang & Chang, 2009). Suryani, Chou, and Chen (2012), for example, have applied fuzzy logic to a combined GDP/FDI simulation model to proxy the demand for air cargo. Totamane, Dasgupta, and Rao (2012) analyzed a series of general and economic influence factors[89] to predict the mid-term demand and booking ramp-up for a rolling three months period. Popescu et al. (2006) estimated the no-show rates for blocked cargo capacity on a 30-day horizon. Further revenue management–oriented demand forecasts are discussed by Feng et al. (2015, pp. 268–269).

Spatial optimization

Most cargo airlines, including express cargo airlines such as FedEx or UPS, operate multi-hub networks (Bowen, 2012). This is economically beneficial due to the close integration with ground transportation providers

---

[89] Day of week, proxy for holidays, GDP, inflation, industrial output growth, average cargo supply in first week of quarter, exports, imports.

and enables these airlines to route cargo flexibly through the network. Alumur and Kara (2009) and Lin, Lin, and Chen (2012) logically apply the hub location theory from passenger airlines to cargo airlines. Due to the short planning cycles, route selection and adaptation is usually demand driven and determined on an ad-hoc basis if a business opportunity arises. Antes, Derigs, and Zils (1997) addressed the route selection problem and employed the multi-commodity-flow network to determine an optimal set of routes. Derigs and Friederichs (2013) then extended that model to distinguish the two route categories, namely mandatory routes that are needed to maintain network flexibility and optional routes than can be served if the appropriate demand is anticipated. Yan et al. (2006) adopted a different approach and combined route selection with scheduling in a mid-term demand-based model. Azadian, Murat, and Chinnam (2012) went a step further and proposed a dynamic routing model, relying on real-time demand information, postponing routing decisions by up to six hours before departure.

Temporal optimization

Scheduling is less relevant for cargo airlines than for passenger airlines, since cargo is indifferent towards connection quality. However, if cargo airlines operate from capacity-restricted airports, scheduling becomes a necessary step for slot allocation. In the existing literature, scheduling is usually integrated with route selection and fleet assignment (Derigs & Friederichs, 2013; Friederichs, 2010; Yan et al., 2006).

Friederichs (2010, pp. 32–40) defined the "Air Cargo Scheduling Problem" as entailing flight selection, fleet assignment, rotation planning, and cargo routing, thus integrating all the temporal and operational optimization problems with the exception of crew scheduling. Tang, Yan, and Chen (2008) suggested a combined passenger and cargo scheduling model, since many large carriers, such as Lufthansa, Emirates, and China Airlines, deploy both cargo and passenger aircraft and transport a significant amount of belly cargo on their passenger flights.

Operational optimization

The integrated model of Friederichs (2010) covers all the relevant operational optimization problems, including the cargo routing problem. Li et al. (2006) combined fleet assignment and aircraft routing into an integrated model, leveraged from previous work on passenger airlines by Cordeau et al. (2001) and Mercier and Soumis (2007). Feng et al. (2015, pp. 269–273) also summarized additional operational problems, such as air cargo terminal operations, container loading, and aircraft loading. Since these activities are usually not performed by the NP department, they are excluded from analysis in this study.

3.5.7 Data needs of network planning

The analyzed literature on NP presents either empirical, theoretical, or mixed data models. A total of 72 publications have been examined in detail; the full overview is available in Appendix 15. There were 11 completely empirical contributions, i.e., the existing algorithms have been tested or verified with empirical data. In contrast, 25 models developed new algorithms, which were either untested or only tested with an artificially created set of test data. These publications are considered theoretical publications. Exactly half of the analyzed literature, 36 studies, follow a mixed approach to develop a new algorithm theoretically, which was subsequently tested with real empirical data.

Among the 72 contributions, 23 data types could be identified[90]. Table 3.7 summarizes the data types and most common data sources. Mostly, airlines have a specific set of internal data reflecting their planned or historic data. Additionally, there are private data providers (e.g., the Official Airline Guide, consultancies) who aggregate data from marketing information data tapes (MIDT) or published data from other sources. There are several

[90] The initial 25 categories were adopted from Grosche (2009, p. 9) and adjusted during the literature review.

types of organizations that publish relevant data either for free or for research purposes. These organizations include international organizations (e.g., IATA, ICAO and OECD), national statistic bureaus, public authorities (e.g., Federal Aviation Administration, EASA or other governmental agencies), and aircraft manufacturers such as Boeing and Airbus. Naturally, most research has been conducted either with an airline's internal data or with free public data (see Appendix 16 for a detailed overview of the used data sources according to contribution). Among the publications, 24 utilized internal data from the airlines and 16 processed data from public authorities or international organizations, while only 11 authors relied on private data providers.

Table 3.7 – Identified data types in network planning literature[91]

Data type	Example data	Most common sources
Actually flown flights	Actual departure time, arrival time, aircraft registration, passengers, load factor	Statistical bureaus, private data providers
Published schedules	Planned flights incl. departure and arrival airport, departure and arrival time, planned aircraft type, flight number, airline	Private data providers
Economic data	GDP growth, income per capita, imports, exports, foreign direct investments	Statistical bureaus, international organizations, public authorities
Demographic data	Population (absolute and growth), ethnic background	Statistical bureaus, international organizations, public authorities
Fare data	Average fare per flight, route or O&D	Airline internal data, private data providers
Set of airports/destinations	Airport name, geographic location, runway length, maximum take-off weight	Airline internal data, international organizations, private data provider
Competitor information	Fare data, schedules, planned routes, financial information	Statistical bureaus, international organizations, private data provider
Operating cost	Fuel, crew cost, maintenance cost, depreciation, airport fees, overflight fees	Airline internal data, public authorities, private data providers

[91] Source: Own illustration. based on literature listed in Appendix 16.

Data type	Example data	Most common sources
Aircraft specifications	Seats per booking class, crew requirements, range, fuel burn, runway and facility requirements, gross weight	Airline internal data, aircraft manufacturers, public authorities
Slots	Available time windows for departures, overflight and landings	Public authorities, international organizations
Maintenance requirements	Maintenance cycles by aircraft type, next planned maintenance by tail, maintenance station capabilities	Airline internal data, aircraft manufacturers, public authorities
Work rules	Legal restrictions (max. work hours, days away from home base, holidays), expense regulations	Airline internal data, public authorities
Crew resources	Job type, aircraft type certification, planned holidays, base salaries	Airline internal data
O&D demand	Number of passengers expected to travel between O&D (restricted or unrestricted)	Private data providers, aircraft manufacturers, international organizations
Market share	Expected market share given specified service level	Airline internal data, private data providers
Network structure	O&D offering, classification of airports in hubs and spokes	Airline internal data, private data providers
Routes	List of directly connected airports	Airline internal data, private data providers
Fleet information	Number of available aircraft per aircraft type	Airline internal data, private data providers
Flight frequencies	Number of flights per day/week for a specific route	Airline internal data, private data providers
Schedule	Exact time of departure for every planned flight	Airline internal data, private data providers
Fleet assignment	aircraft type for each planned flight	Airline internal data, private data providers
Aircraft routing	aircraft tail for each planned flight	Airline internal data, private data providers
Crew roster	Crew names for each planned flight	Airline internal data

Figure 3.19 illustrates the number of contributions using the 23 identified data types. The data types can be differentiated as input data and output data of the NP process. Input data is collected from beyond the NP process. The data source can be from within the airline organization, e.g., the finance department for operating cost. Alternatively, it can be an external data provider, such as an international organization that provides economic forecasts.

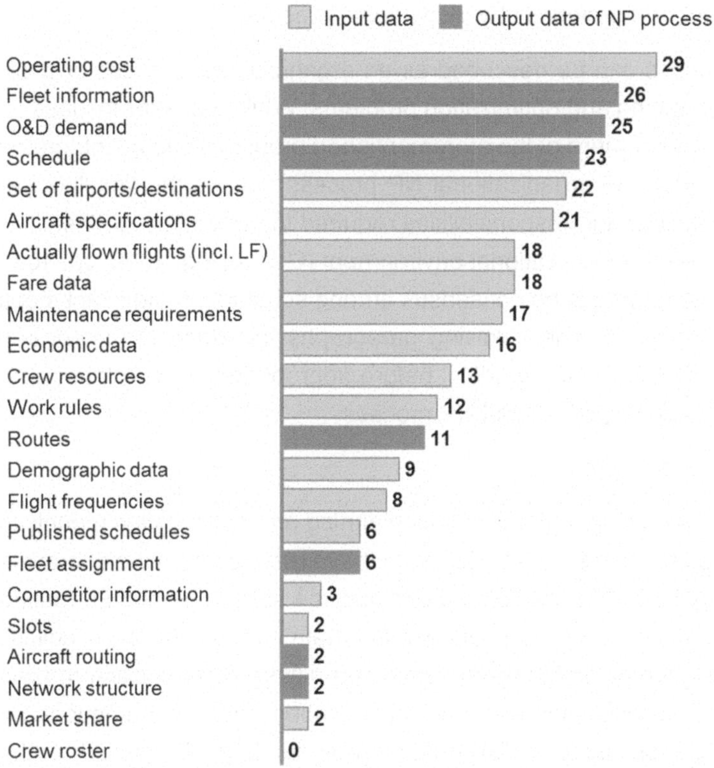

Figure 3.19 – Number of network planning publications, using specific data types[92]

Academic publications in the NP domain rely most frequently on operating cost and the output data produced early in the NP process. This is very logical as schedules, demand, and fleet information are essential data types for later NP process steps, such as fleet assignment or aircraft routing. The list of data types utilized in academic literature (see Table 3.7 and Figure 3.19) is the baseline for the status quo assessment of the used data types in practice, which is discussed in sub-chapter 4.2.

---

[92] Source: Own illustration.

Development of a generic network planning process

The NP process can be described as an organizational process or a sequence of planning and optimization problems. While the latter focuses on integrating one or more of the aforementioned problems into an integrated planning model, the organizational NP process defines the timeline, sequence, and roles and responsibilities required to operationalize the planning model in the organizational environment (Goedeking, 2010, pp. 108–109). However, there is no consensus among scholars on the exact steps and their sequence. The following paragraphs introduce the integrated planning and optimization models, before appropriately linking those with proposals for an organizational NP process.

Integrated planning models

Many authors have combined various planning and optimization models in an integrated planning model. This might have resulted from the non-availability of input data for the desired optimization step (e.g., aircraft routing data). Nevertheless, most authors aim to create a model that is as holistic as possible. Due to limitations in computing power, most existing models recommend solving planning and optimization problems sequentially (Kölker & Lütjens, 2015, p. 901). Some authors (e.g., Fitzgerald, 1993; Grosche, 2009; Kölker & Lütjens, 2015) have designed simultaneous models applying non-exact heuristics in order to achieve sufficiently good results.

Table 3.8 summarizes the contributions discussed in sections 3.5.2–3.5.5 that integrate two or more network planning and optimization problems. Additionally, it illustrates the integrated models discussed by Grosche (2009, pp. 34–42), who has also provided a detailed description of the mathematical properties of the models.

Table 3.8 – Integrated network planning and optimization models[93]

	Long-term planning			*Spatial optimization*		*Temporal optimization*		*Operational optimization*			
Author	Corporate strategy	Demand model	Fleet planning	Network structure	Route selection	Flight frequency	Scheduling	Fleet assignment	Aircraft routing	Crew assignment	Flight ops
Levin, 1971							x		x		
Chan, 1974			x	x	x	x		x			
Balakrishnan, Chien, & Wong, 1990				x	x						
Ghobrial, Balakrishnan, & Kanafani, 1992					x	x			x		
Teodorović et al., 1994					x	x					
Yan & Young, 1996							x	x			
Jaillet et al., 1996					x	x		x			
Clarke et al., 1996								x	x	x	
Desaulniers et al., 1997							x	x	x		
Rushmeier & Kontogiorgis, 1997								x	x	x	
Lederer & Nambimadom, 1998				x	x	x					
Barnhart et al., 1998								x	x		
Ioachim et al., 1999								x	x		
Hsu & Wen, 2000		x		x	x	x					
Erdmann et al., 2001				x		x	x		x		
Cordeau et al., 2001									x	x	
Mashford & Marksjö, 2001				x		x	x		x		
Wojahn, 2001b		x		x							
Klabjan et al., 2002							x		x	x	
Yan & Tseng, 2002				x		x	x	x	x		
Hsu & Wen, 2003		x				x					
Cohn & Barnhart, 2003									x	x	
Brueckner, 2004				x		x		x			

93 Source: Own illustration. based on literature mentioned in the table.

	Long-term planning			*Spatial optimization*		*Temporal optimization*		*Operational optimization*			
Author	Corporate strategy	Demand model	Fleet planning	Network structure	Route selection	Flight frequency	Scheduling	Fleet assignment	Aircraft routing	Crew assignment	Flight ops
Lohatepanont & Barnhart, 2004				x		x	x	x			
Sandhu & Klabjan, 2007								x		x	
Mercier & Soumis, 2007									x	x	x
Warburg et al., 2008							x	x			
Yan et al., 2008		x					x	x			
Grosche, 2009				x	x	x	x	x	x		
Haouari, Aissaoui, & Mansour, 2009								x	x		
Papadakos, 2009								x	x	x	
Weide, Ryan, & Ehrgott, 2010									x	x	
Carmona Benitez, 2012		x		x	x						
Pita, Barnhart, & Antunes, 2013							x	x			
Salazar-González, 2014								x	x	x	
Kölker & Lütjens, 2015					x	x	x				
Cacchiani & Salazar-González, 2016								x	x	x	

Of the 37 analyzed studies, only seven integrate three or more problems (see Figure 3.20). The model developed by Grosche (2009) integrates six problems, namely network structure, route selection, flight frequencies, scheduling, fleet assignment, and aircraft routing, and that is the most holistic model in literature. Interestingly, one of the earliest models developed by Chan (1974) does not only integrate five problems but is also the only one to integrate fleet planning in the analytical NP process.

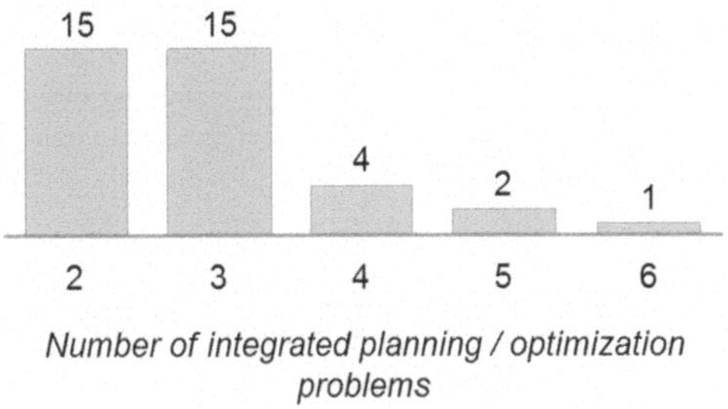

Figure 3.20 – Number of analyzed contributions by problem integration[94]

Figure 3.21 expresses the frequency and combination of NP and optimization problems. Every individual problem is represented by a grey circle, whose size indicates the number of models that have incorporated the problem. The lines indicate the combinations of problems, and the thickness of the line determines the frequency of combinations. Fleet planning, for example, is included in only one integrated model (Chan, 1974), which also contains network structure, route selection, flight frequencies, and fleet assignment. By analyzing the frequency of integration of individual network planning and optimization issues, it is evident that the problems from network structure and crew scheduling receive the greatest attention in literature. Long-term planning problems, such as corporate strategy, fleet planning, and demand models, are rarely integrated with other optimization problems. This is especially interesting since corporate strategy and fleet planning create the frame conditions for NP to operate in, and demand forecasting is one of the most important input data herein (see section 1).

[94] Source: Own illustration.

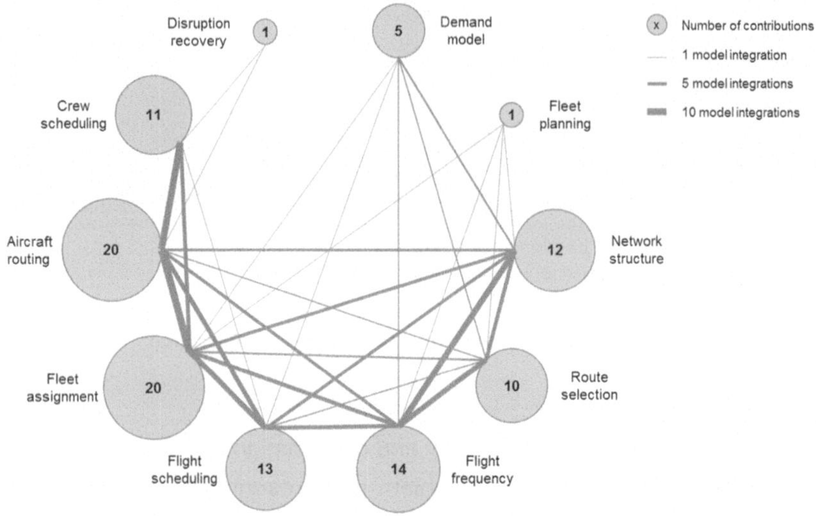

Figure 3.21 – Frequency and combinations of network planning and optimization problems[95]

The sequence of network planning and optimization problems derived in section 3.5.1 can be confirmed by graphical analysis of Figure 3.21. As expected, the problems are mostly integrated with their immediate "neighbor" problems (i.e., aircraft routing is mostly integrated with fleet assignment and crew scheduling and so on). With regard to the optimization problems, network structure and route selection are the only pair of neighboring problems in which this phenomenon is not observed. This can be justified by the fact that many authors treat the set of routes as an exogeneous input data variable (e.g., Brueckner, 2004; Wojahn, 2001b; Yan & Tseng, 2002) and network structure as an endogenous decision variable. For the

[95] Source: Own illustration. The total number of papers differs from the analysis in section 1, since only the contributions with integrated models containing 2 or more output data categories are considered. For the O&D demand forecast, for example, only 5 of the 19 contributions are considered from the total combined O&D demand forecast with another output variable.

sequence of spatial optimization steps, this poses a valid question of whether network structure defines route selection or vice versa. In practice, airlines usually have an existing network structure and add or delete routes without changing this structure (Ghobrial et al., 1992). Therefore, it is assumed that the network structure decision is an input information for route selection.

NP as organizational process

Mathematical network planning and optimization problems have attracted considerable attention over the past 40 years, and that has led to publications in the most renowned academic journals[96]. However, the organizational NP process has received little notice. The processes are mostly presented as a frame to the actual mathematical problems (Abdelghany & Abdelghany, 2009; Bazargan, 2016) and are rarely ever the core of the research. A noteworthy exemption is the work of Döring (1999), who analyzed the organizational NP processes from a cybernetic perspective.

Most researchers divide the NP process into three stages that can be roughly described as long-term planning, mid-term planning, and short-term planning (Abdelghany & Abdelghany, 2009; Döring, 1999; Goedeking, 2010; Grosche, 2009). Bazargan (2016) further sub-divided long-term planning into long-range planning and the market evaluation phase. Figure 3.22 summarizes the organizational planning phases and its components in the existing literature.

[96] 31 out of 37 analyzed contributions were published in journals with a VHB-Rating of A+, A, or B.

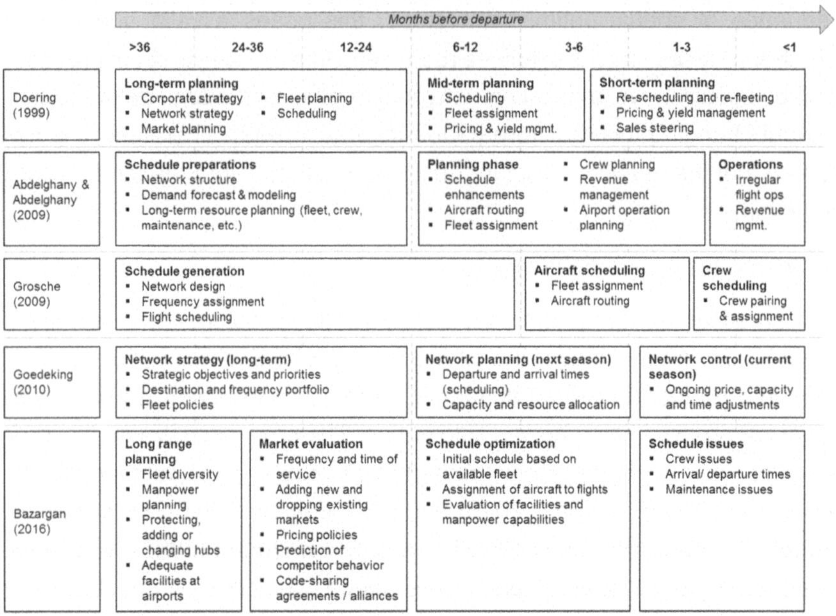

Figure 3.22 – Comparison of the network planning process models[97]

Long-term planning usually entails planning activities that take place at least 12 months before departure. It includes the three long-term planning items from the previous section, namely corporate strategy, fleet planning, and demand modeling. Spatial optimization is usually also added to long-term planning. Four authors have mentioned network structure/design, while Goedeking (2010) and Bazargan (2016) have explicitly also named route selection. Three authors also assigned temporal optimization, comprising frequency assignment and flight scheduling, to long-term planning. The terms “network strategy” and “market planning” used by Döring (1999)

[97] Source: Own illustration. based on the mentioned authors in the Figure.

include the planning steps of demand modeling, network design, and route selection.

In addition to the long-term planning and spatial optimization problems detailed in the previous sections, Abdelghany and Abdelghany (2009) and Bazargan (2016) have discussed long-term resource planning for crew, maintenance, and airport facilities to be part of long-term NP. Bazargan (2016) even added alliance and code-sharing coordination, pricing policies, and prediction of competitive behavior to this list.

Mid-term planning involves planning and optimization activities that are undertaken 12 to 3 months before departure. Almost all authors consider flight scheduling as part of this planning phase, although it may also be associated with long-term planning. All five authors considered fleet assignment in mid-term planning as well as aircraft routing. Grosche (2009) describes crew assignment as a short-term activity, whereas other authors categorize it as mid-term planning. In addition, Döring (1999) and Abdelghany and Abdelghany (2009) counted revenue management in mid-term NP. Bazargan (2016) and Abdelghany and Abdelghany (2009) added airport operations planning to the list of mid-term NP activities.

Short-term planning is the planning phase covering the three months before departure. It mainly deals with re-fleeting and re-routing and recovery of irregular operations. Döring (1999) and Abdelghany and Abdelghany (2009) also included revenue management in short-term NP activities.

Only Döring (1999) and Goedeking (2010) have mentioned organizational structures of NP departments. Döring (1999) proposed an integrated NP and revenue management function called "network steering." This department should have six main tasks: pricing, yield management and sales steering from the revenue management context, scheduling, fleet management, and operations control from a broader network management context (Döring, 1999, pp. 176–179). Goedeking (2010, pp. 99–100) views network management as an individual commercial revenue center or as a profit center in between a sales and revenue profit center and an operations cost center. The network management department can be structured functionally (network strategy, planning, controlling) or geographically (e.g., according to hub).

Towards a generic network management process

In practice, network management functions are usually dissociated from revenue management and operations (see sub-chapter 4). In order to develop a NP process that is practically applicable, revenue management and flight operations are excluded from the process. Figure 3.23 displays the generic network management process derived from the literature discussion in the previous sections. It constitutes 11 planning steps, 8 of which form the core of the NP process.

Corporate strategy and fleet planning are placed before NP chronologically, as they entail a very long-term perspective of more than five years (Bazargan, 2016, pp. 33–34). Furthermore, strategy and fleet planning departments are mostly staff departments that report directly to the CEO (Clark, 2017, p. 23), whereas NP departments are often part of a larger commercial function (Goedeking, 2010, p. 99). Demand forecasting is a difficult task to assign. The very long-term demand forecasts are used in strategy and fleet planning, while the more accurate mid-term forecasts are highly relevant for commercial NP decisions. Since demand forecasting is quite well integrated in NP models (see the first part of this section) while corporate strategy and fleet planning are fundamentally not integrated at all, the demand forecasting is treated as a specific NP process step.

Planning horizon	Process step	Central question to solve	Potential answers	Key literature
	Corporate strategy formulation	How do we differentiate from our competitors? What business model to follow?	▪ Full-service carrier ▪ Low-cost carrier ▪ Charter carrier	▪ Bieger & Wittmer (2011) ▪ Sterzenbach et al. (2013)
	Fleet planning	What is the best fleet mix to satisfy the demand?	▪ Diverse fleet of 30 A320 and 10 A350 ▪ Single A/C fleet of 50 A320	▪ Dozic & Kalic (2015) ▪ Clark (2017)
Long-term network planning	Demand forecasting	What will be the demand in the next 5-10 years?	▪ 1 million pax per year in 2025 from FRA to LAX	▪ Coldren et al. (2003) ▪ Carson et al. (2011) ▪ Jacobs et al. (2012)
Long-term network planning	Network structure determination	What is the best network layout given our business model?	▪ Hub-and-spoke ▪ Point-to-point ▪ Tour network	▪ Jaillet at al. (1996) ▪ Lederer & Nambimadom (1998) ▪ Barla & Constantatos (2000)
Long-term network planning	Route selection	Which routes (O&Ds) should be part of our network?	▪ FRA – JFK (pax) ▪ FRA – SIN – LAX – FRA (cargo)	▪ Teodorovic et al. (1994) ▪ Hsu & Wen (2000, 2002) ▪ Carmona-Benitez (2012)
Long-term network planning	Flight frequency determination	How many flights per week/day do we want to offer?	▪ FRA – JFK 2x daily ▪ FRA – LAX on days 2467	▪ Teodorovic et al. (1989, 1994) ▪ Hsu & Wen (2000, 2002, 2003)
Long-term network planning	Flight scheduling	What are the exact flight times for these flights?	▪ LH400: FRA 8:50 UTC – JFK 16:00 UTC	▪ Etschmaier & Mathaisel (1985) ▪ Yan et al. (1996, 2002, 2007, 2008) ▪ Jiang & Barnhart (2009, 2013)
Mid-term network planning	Fleet assignment	What aircraft type should serve a specific flight?	▪ Boeing 747-8 ▪ Airbus A380	▪ Abara (1989) ▪ Berge & Hopperstad (1993) ▪ Sherali et al. (2006, 2008)
Mid-term network planning	Aircraft routing	Which flights will be conducted by which individual airplane?	▪ D-ABYA on LH400 on January 1, 2018	▪ Feo & Bard (1989) ▪ Clarke et al. (1997) ▪ Gopalan & Talluri (1998)
Mid-term network planning	Crew assignment	Which crew can be assigned to which flights?	▪ CPT xyz, FO abc	▪ Rubin (1973) ▪ Klabjan et al. (2002) ▪ Guo et al. (2006)
	Disruption management	How can regular flight operations be restored?	▪ Cancelling LH568, rerouting of D-ABYC to LH400	▪ Mercier & Soumis (2007) ▪ Bazargan (2016)

Figure 3.23 – Generic NP process[98]

As discussed earlier, long-term NP includes spatial and temporal network design, including network structure definition, route selection, frequency assignment, and the initial scheduling. This phase ends with a draft schedule, which in practice is a model week for the schedule period. Re-scheduling is an ongoing optimization process, which corresponds better with

98 Source: Own illustration.

mid-term NP. Mid-term NP basically entails the operational optimization of the network, comprising fleet assignment, aircraft routing, and crew assignment. Any kind of disruption management, including short-term re-routings, is usually performed by the flight operations department, which is an operational unit and does not belong to the commercial revenue center (Goedeking, 2010, p. 104).

3.5.8 Definition of strategic network planning

To highlight the development of the term "strategic network planning" in literature, it is worthwhile to decompose the term into "strategic planning" and "strategic networks." Strategic planning describes a formal planning process that originated from strategic management (Mintzberg, 1994) and has swept to other research domains, such as IS, where an entire research stream on strategic information system planning has been established (Fitzgerald, 1993; Lederer & Hannu, 1996; Lederer & Sethi, 1988).

Similarly, logistics researchers selected the concept and developed a strategic logistic planning process (Korpela & Tuominen, 1996; Schmidt & Wilhelm, 2000). Crainic and Laporte (1997, p. 411) defined three planning horizons for the logistic planning process: *short term operational planning* is performed at a local level, where planners must react to a dynamic market environment (e.g., for vehicle routing and dispatch). *Mid-term tactical planning* entails an "efficient and rational allocation of existing resources in order to improve the performance of the whole system" (p. 411), including network design and route selection. Finally, *long-term strategic planning* involves the top-management level and entails making "decisions to determine general development policies and broadly shape the operating strategies of the system" (p. 411).

The term "strategic networks" is derived from organizational science. Jarillo (1988) coined the term "strategic network" in the context of organizational networks for firms, which are of strategic importance to a firm's success. Gulati et al. (2000) examined strategic organizational networks from a RBV perspective, defining strategic networks as a resource for competitive advantage[99]. However, strategic networks have rarely been used as a reference to transportation networks.

Literature from the logistics domain mostly defines strategic networks as supply-chain networks (Stadtler, 2005, p. 580), i.e., as production and distribution networks. In the field of supply-chain management (SCM), there is a reasonable body of literature[100] on "strategic network planning," which is used synonymously with "strategic supply chain planning" (Kauder & Meyr, 2009, pp. 508–509). Goetschalckx and Fleischmann (2005) have defined a strategic NP problem for supply chains of manufacturing companies, including structural decisions pertaining to facility locations, capacities, new products, and product/facility allocation, and operational decisions on the transportation flow of goods. Their strategic planning horizon spans 3–10 years and aims to maximize the net present value (NPV) from a specific SCM network (Goetschalckx & Fleischmann, 2005, p. 117).

"Strategic network planning" in airline-specific network planning literature

From the organizational process models presented in the last section (Figure 3.22), only Goedeking (2010) and Bazargan (2016) explicitly delineated "strategic" NP. Bazargan (2016) differentiated between tactical and strategic planning as follows: "Strategic development focuses on future schedules which may range from a few months to ten years depending on the air carrier's policies. Strategic developments respond to major changes in both business and operational environments. Tactical strategies [...] focus on short-term changes to the schedule and routes, sometimes on a daily basis. This is done by constantly monitoring markets, competitors and operations. The tactical strategy includes adding, dropping flights, and making changes to city pair markets and their frequencies" (p.32–33).

[99] See section 3.7.5 for a detailed discussion.

[100] Meixell and Gargeya (2005) provide an excellent literature review on strategic network planning in SCM.

Goedeking (2010) chose a three-step differentiation between strategic, tactical, and operational NP, much in line with Crainic and Laporte (1997).

Based on general as well as airline-specific concepts of strategic NP, a classification approach similar to that of Goedeking (2010) and Crainic and Laporte (1997) was adopted for this study, which distinguishes between strategic, tactical, and operational NP. Besides the time horizon of the planning steps, the interconnectedness and existence of natural break points (or hand-over points) in the NP process should determine the scope for each NP phase.

The natural candidates to be included in the *strategic NP* phase are the long-term planning items from section 3.5.2 (demand forecast, fleet planning, corporate strategy). If we assume that corporate strategy is usually beyond the network planner's control, we can classify this as a step situated temporally before the actual NP process. Fleet planning is a difficult process to allocate, but the high relevance of fleet information for other NP steps (see section 1) indicates including fleet planning in strategic NP. Finally, demand forecasting – the process step behind the O&D demand data type – proves to be a crucial, if not the most crucial, part of strategic NP. Moreover, the spatial optimization process steps of the network structure definition and route selection should be allocated to strategic NP, since they require a significant lead time to implement, especially for routes outside the European open sky agreement.

When analyzing temporal optimization, two aspects must be considered. First, scheduling and re-scheduling (or dynamic scheduling) must be separated. Scheduling is a process that can be clearly located in between spatial and operational optimization. On the contrary, re-scheduling is a recurring activity that adjusts the schedule as soon as new demand information is available. It ideally runs in parallel to the other NP steps and can thus not really be allocated to a NP phase. The second aspect to be considered is the existence of natural break points. The definition of a spatial network can be considered a natural break point, but in most organization, it is integrally connected with the temporal optimization step. Goedeking (2010, p. 99) differentiates between NP and network steering, where the initial draft schedule is the hand-over point. The natural break point is thus the first completed draft schedule, indicating that flight frequencies and scheduling should be allocated to strategic NP.

The operational optimization steps build on the draft schedule and allocate the available resources. This is consistent with Crainic and Laporte's (1997) definition of *tactical planning* as well as with the responsibilities of the "network steering" department described by Goedeking (2010). In this planning phase, the network planners (or network steerers) have to work closely with other departments, such as maintenance planning, crew planning, and revenue management. Therefore, fleet assignment, aircraft routing, and crew assignment are considered tactical NP steps. The amount of freedom is less than in strategic NP, but the complexity is comparable. However, the nature of the data changes. Data requirements for strategic NP entail a combination of internal and external elements. Whereas, tactical planning process steps rely heavily on internal data pertaining to available resources and booking ramp ups. In this study, the tactical NP steps are kept within the field of vision, but the focus is on the steps of the strategic NP process.

The last missing phase is the operations phase defined by Crainic and Laporte (1997). In airlines, this is mostly the so-called flight operations (Flight Ops) phase. The handover from network steering to flight operations usually occurs 72–24 hours prior to the flight. Changes in the schedule or resource assignment in the Flight Ops phase is only done due to operational requirements and not because of commercial considerations. That is also the reason Flight Ops is usually considered a cost center and is organizationally located in the operations department, whereas NP is either a revenue or profit center located in the commercial department

(Goedeking, 2010, pp. 99–101). Since flight operations have no real planning involved but a disruption management function, those steps are not considered in this study. Figure 3.24 displays the generic NP process with steps allocated to strategic, tactical, and operational NP.

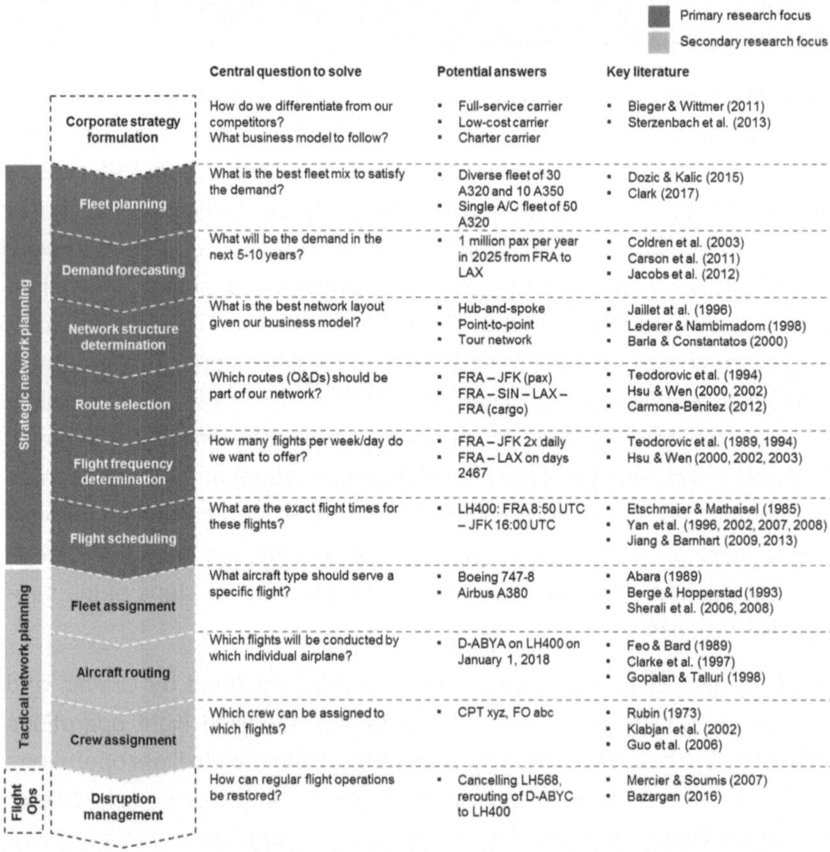

Figure 3.24 – Strategic network planning within the generic airline NP process[101]

[101] Source: Own illustration.

3.6 Big data

This sub-chapter begins with a general definition of data (section 3.6.1) and the specific properties of "big" data (section 3.6.2). Section 3.6.3 illustrates the use of big data in the context of the value chain concept. It is followed by a deep dive into the different categories of big data types for data collection in general (section 3.6.4) and within the airline and tourism literature (section 3.6.5). Section 3.6.6 closes this sub-chapter with a discussion on the risks of big data.

3.6.1 Definition of data

Data is omnipresent as it is the foundation of all information systems. When dealing with information systems research, it is vital to delimit the terms *data* and *information. Information* represents "data as processed, stored, or transmitted by a computer" (Oxford University Press, 2017). Therefore, information is a higher order construct that relies on processed data in order for it to be usable (Ackoff, 1989, p. 4). Rodriguez and King (1977, p. 45) added a value perspective and defined information as "evaluated data" that is usable for further processing. However, *data* and *information* are often used interchangeably in practice, which poses challenges to research on data and information (Wang & Strong, 1996, p. 7). In this study, the term *data* refers to the most atomic particle of information.

Data exists in innumerable formats and representations. The most widely accepted framework utilized to describe the nature of data is data structure. Traditionally, data was differentiated as structured and unstructured data. Structured data is what resides in fixed fields and is restricted to a predefined format (e.g., a date format). Unstructured data does not conform to fixed fields and can be presented in a variety of formats, e.g., text, video, or audio (Manyika et al., 2011, p. 33). In the 1990s, the possibility of tagging unstructured data with attributes (sometimes also called metadata) came to the focus of database research (Buneman, 1997, p. 117). The result of this attribution is known as semi-structured data. A research article in a scientific journal is a good example of semi-structured data. While the text body itself is unstructured, the file can be attributed with structured metadata, such as author, year, publication, or volume.

3.6.2 Characteristics of big data

With increasing computational capacity, improving data storage technologies, and the dispersion of computers, the amount of produced and stored data has been increasing exponentially[102]. Philip Russom (2011, pp. 6–7) developed earlier observations on e-commerce data by Laney (2001) and defined big data by *volume*, *velocity*, and *variety*. These three dimensions are now widely acknowledged in IS research (Abbasi, Sarker, & Chiang, 2016; Addo-Tenkorang & Helo, 2016; Mauro et al., 2015). Schroeck et al. (2012, pp. 2–3) introduced *veracity* as additional dimension; Chen, Mao, and Liu (2014, pp. 173–174) proposed *value* as a defining characteristic, building on research from Manyika et al. (2011, p. 2) who described the potential value generation from big data.

Table 3.9 – Definition criteria for big data in literature[103]

Author	Volume	Velocity	Variety	Veracity	Value
Laney, 2001	x	x	x		
Manyika et al., 2011	x				(x)
Russom, 2011	x	x	x		
McAfee & Brynjolfsson, 2012	x	x	x		
Schroeck et al., 2012	x	x	x	x	
Chen et al., 2014	x	x	x		x
Gandomi & Haider, 2015	x	x	x	x	x
Wamba et al., 2015	x	x	x	x	x

[102] Marr (2018) estimates that every day in 2018, 2.5 million terabytes of data is produced, which is 50 times more than in 2007 (estimate by Manyika et al., 2011).

[103] Please refer to Appendix 11 for a detailed overview of existing definitions.

Volume refers to the sheer amount of data available for storage, processing, and analysis. McAfee and Brynjolfsson (2012, p. 4) mentioned that in 2012, 2.5 exabytes of data were generated per day, and this amount was likely to double every two years (Akoka et al., 2017, p. 105). Waal-Montgomery (2015) expects the data volume generated in 2020 to be 50 times the data volume generated in 2015. This massive increase in the available data is mainly due to data produced by the Internet of Things (IoT) and the soaring use of social media, which generates large amounts of data-rich content, such as videos and images among others. Consequently, Manyika et al. (2011) defined big data as "datasets whose size is beyond the ability of typical database software tools to capture, store, manage, and analyze" (p. 1). Since the capabilities of information systems are advancing as well, there is no point in defining an explicit volume threshold for big data (Gandomi & Haider, 2015, p. 138).

Velocity describes the frequency of data generation and/or the frequency of data delivery (Wamba et al., p. 235). While data collection traditionally required an extract-load-transform process, it is collected and processed in real-time nowadays.

Variety refers to the structural heterogeneity in a dataset (Wamba et al., 2015, p. 235). Due to the increasing number of data sources, information systems must be able to cope with various formats of structured, semi-structured, and unstructured data. Big data analytics need to be able to integrate a great variety of heterogeneous data to generate useful information for businesses (Chen, Chiang, & Storey, 2012, p. 1166).

Veracity describes the inherent unpredictability of data quality. A major research focus of big data scholars is thus on developing techniques to manage and mine data with uncertain quality features (Gandomi & Haider, 2015, p. 168; Wamba et al., 2015, p. 235).

Value is probably the most controversial characteristic of big data, and it has not been defined unanimously. Manyika et al. (2011, p. 2) recognize the opportunity for additional value generation through big data and have estimated the potential value globally at above one trillion dollars per year. Various other scholars have supported the value generation principle (e.g., Chen et al., 2014, p. 174). Accordingly, Wamba et al. (2015) define value as "the extent to which big data generates economically worthy insights and or benefits through extraction and transformation" (p. 236).

For the remainder of this study, all data types that fulfil two or more of the five "V" characteristics are considered big data[104]. A detailed discussion on real examples is postponed to the discussion part of this study in order to avoid duplications (see sub-chapter 7).

Before proceeding to the practical research phases, the terminology pertaining to big data needs to be clarified. Big data *sources* are individual providers of data. Big data *types* are datasets that contain comparable information but may rely on different data *sources.* Social media data, for example, is a data *type* provided by multiple data *sources,* such as Facebook or LinkedIn.

A big data *opportunity or application* may include more components of the big data value chain than just data source. A big data *opportunity* can also contain processing, storage, and analytics services, which are all part of the offered solution. A concept for a system landscape covering the entire big data value chain is called big data *architecture.* The entirety of the big data *architecture* and all involved solution providers is called a big data *ecosystem.* A big data *project* is a transformation project whose goal is to exploit a specific big data opportunity or on a larger scale a big data ecosystem.

3.6.3 The big data value chain

Big data can be explained by the value chain concept that features four distinct steps: BD collection, BD processing, BD storage, and BD analytics

---

[104] Addressing RQ 1 – How can "big data" be defined for network planning in airlines?

(Gandomi & Haider, 2015, p. 141). Figure 3.25 describes the four-step value chain and includes the key properties of each step. An objective of this study is to identify suitable big data opportunities to improve airline NP. Since all big data opportunities include specific data sources, big data collection is the primary research focus. However, several big data opportunities also include other value chain steps as part of the offering, so the entire big data value chain is relevant for further discussion.

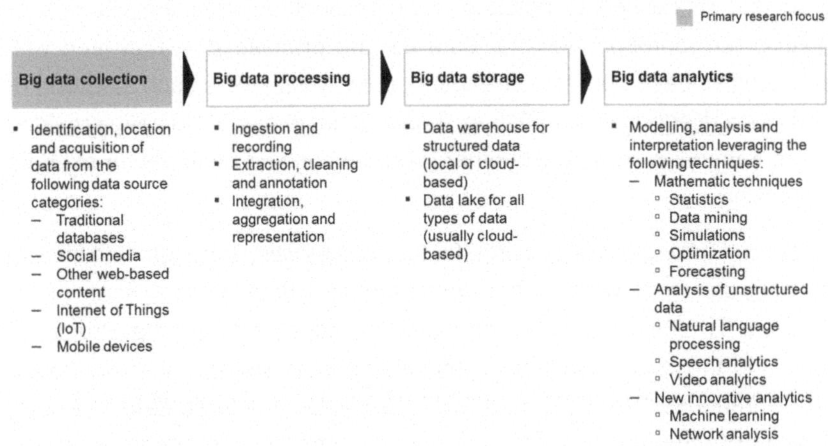

Figure 3.25 – Big data value chain[105]

First, big data needs to be collected from the available traditional and novel data sources. If direct access to a data source exists, the data can be ingested directly. Otherwise, companies must acquire access to data from a data collector, such as social networks or web search engines. Potential categories of data sources for airline big data are discussed in more detail in section 3.6.5.

---

[105] Source: Own illustration following Gandomi and Haider (2015, p. 141).

Once data is obtained, it needs to be processed in order to be usable for big data analytics. These processing steps include extraction from the original storage, data cleaning, and annotation with metadata, if required. Finally, data from different sources needs to be integrated and aggregated to an analyzable set of data (Gandomi & Haider, 2015, p. 141). There are currently two basic processing technologies, each of which exhibits a sophisticated environment of tools and applications. First, data can be captured and processed in batches using technology from the Hadoop or Skytree environment. Second, data can be processed in real time with technologies based on data streaming, notably with tools such as Storm or SAP Hana (Yaqoob et al., 2016, p. 1235). Chen et al. (2014) have provided a comprehensive overview of other technologies and methods for big data processing.

Processed data is typically stored for further analysis, although data stream analytics can work with the short-term storage of data (Yaqoob et al., 2016, p. 1235). Traditional data warehouses are capable of storing structured data, and these are available optionally as local storage or cloud-based data warehouses (Heilig & Voß, 2017, p. 33). Unstructured data or a combination of different data types is normally stored as raw data in cloud-based data lakes in order to minimize the pre-storage data processing effort. Processing layers, such as Hadoop or Storm, draw data directly from their dispersed storage in order to process it for analytics applications (Gandomi & Haider, 2015, p. 141).

Big data is not valuable without suitable methods to analyze the information. Analytic techniques thus play a key role in creating value from big data and receive the most attention from scientists and practitioners. Big data analytics can be clustered in at least three major categories: *mathematical models* use big data to improve or extend existing mathematical techniques, such as simulations or optimizations. New analytic techniques are required to *analyze unstructured data*, such as text, audio, images, or video formats. Furthermore, big data facilitates the development of completely *new innovative analytical techniques*, namely machine learning or advanced network analysis. Major techniques are described in Appendix 12)

3.6.4 Major types of big data

Since there is no uniform categorization of big data types in the literature, the most frequently mentioned categories are described herein.

Traditional databases mostly contain structured data and serve as a data pool for most big data analytics. With regard to the airline industry, some typical examples are flight plan data, fleet information, or crew schedules. Accordingly, database management systems are required to handle and maintain traditional databases.

The *Internet of Things (IoT)* is the totality of devices and sensors embedded in the physical world and connected by networks to computing resources (Manyika et al., 2011, p. 21). This also includes radio-frequency identification (RFID) chips, barcodes, and radio tags attached to any good (Chen et al., 2012, p. 1168). Concrete examples of "data-generating things" are Global Positioning System (GPS) devices, intelligent/smart cars, intelligent clothing, alarms, window blinds, window sensors, lighting and heating fixtures, and household electronics (Yaqoob et al., 2016, p. 1234). Cargo airlines are increasingly relying on sensors to control cargo parameters, such as temperature, pressure, and location (IATA, 2018b, pp. 27–29).

Mobile devices are technically a subset of the IoT, but these are often treated as a separate type due to the magnitude of their impact. They provide diverse data types, including location data, application usage, or health data. With the increasing penetration of smart phones and an ever increasing number of applications, mobile devices are the cornerstone of big data generation (Manyika et al., 2011, p. 68).

Social media is an umbrella term for many different, mostly web-based services. A narrower sense includes social networks such as Facebook and LinkedIn, media sharing services such as YouTube and Flickr, and hybrids of these two kinds such as Instagram (Yaqoob et al., 2016, p. 1235). Gundecha and Liu (2012, p. 3) also classified a variety of other services such as blogs, wikis, and rating pages as social media (see Table 3.10).

Table 3.10 – Social media services by Gundecha and Liu (2012, p. 3)

Social media services	Exemplary data sources
Online social networks	Google+, Facebook, LinkedIn, Xing, QQ Space, Renren, Myspace
Media Sharing	YouTube, Youku, Flickr, Instagram
Blogging	Huffington Post, Business Insider, TechCrunch
Microblogging	Twitter, Blogger, Tumblr, Sina Weibo
Wikis	Wikipedia, Internet movie database, Baidu Baike
Social news	Reddit, Digg, Newsvine
Social bookmarking	Pinterest, StumbleUpon, CiteULike
Opinion, reviews & rating	Yelp, TripAdvisor, Foursquare
Answers	Yahoo! Answers, WikiAnswers, Ask.fm

Other web-based content also contributes greatly towards big data. Almost every website collects information, much of which can be monetized. Good examples of web-based big data sources are search engines such as Google, Baidu, or Bing and many e-commerce websites. From an airline perspective, origin–destination search and booking data from online travel agencies especially need to be mentioned as potential valuable data sources.

3.6.5 Big data types in airline and tourism research

Airlines have been at the forefront of data management and data value creation even before the term big data was coined (Wixom et al., 2008), leading to the publication of several scholarly and practical studies on the use of big data in airlines. However, not a single contribution on big data in airlines focuses explicitly on NP or demand forecasting. In this section, the mentioned data types in literature are compiled and their applicability in NP is evaluated. This section also analyzes the big data types for tourism demand forecasting, which has received greater attention in the scientific community. Table 3.11 provides an overview of the big data types mentioned in literature[106].

Most scholarly literature on big data in airlines focuses on the value-generating big data use cases. The most commonly mentioned use case is predictive maintenance, which aims to reduce cost and minimize maintenance-related delays. Modern airplanes are capable of producing multiple terabytes (TB) of data per flight hour (Badea et al., 2018, p. 19), which can be transmitted to the ground stations for predictive maintenance and flight operations optimization (Chen et al., 2017, p. 27). Parts of the aircraft-transmitted data can also be used by air traffic controllers to improve the short-term traffic forecasting models (Ayhan et al., 2013, p. 2). The same data is also mined in certain airlines to improve fuel efficiency, thereby reducing fuel cost (Bradbury, 2018).

[106] The applicability of the data sources in Table 3.11 in airline NP is evaluated in sub-chapter 5.2.

Table 3.11 – Big data types mentioned in airline and tourism literature[107]

			Big data types										
Literature source	**Type of literature**	**Field of research / practice**	Flight tracking data	Airport data	Meteorological data	Airline info data	Market data	Passenger data	Aircraft data	Air Safety Reports	Social media data	Mobile location data	Search engine data
Larsen (2013)	Scholarly	Airline flight operations	x	x	x	x	x	x	x	x			
Badea et al. (2018)	Scholarly	Airline flight operations							x				
Ayhan et al. (2013)	Scholarly	Air traffic management							x				
Chen et al. (2017)	Scholarly	Airline marketing & flight operations			x			x	x		x		
Li et al. (2018)	Scholarly	Tourism demand forecasting									x	x	x
Miah et al. (2017)	Scholarly	Tourism demand forecasting									x	x	
Park and Pan (2018)	Scholarly	Tourism demand forecasting						x				x	x
Ross-Smith (2016)	Practical	Airline marketing					x	x			x		x
Bradbury (2018)	Practical	Airline big data						x	x	x			

[107] Source: Own illustration based on literature mentioned in the table.

The second airline-specific use case is improving customer interaction and revenue management with a 360-degree view of the passenger. Lufthansa combines internal passenger data with data from its frequent flyer program and social media to create a better journey for their customers (Chen et al., 2017, p. 25). Other airlines rely on a similar mix of internal, external, as well as search engine data to improve revenue management and demand forecasting (Ross-Smith, 2016).

Short-term forecasting and handling of irregular operations is the third use case discussed in airline literature. Larsen (2013) presents an extensive list of potential data sources that can be used to improve delay forecasting accuracy. Lufthansa also uses social media analysis to detect relevant external events for this purpose (Chen et al., 2017, p. 26).

The tourism industry frequently uses big data to enhance its mid- and long-term demand forecasts (Li et al., 2018, p. 318). They rely mostly on novel data sources, such as social media data (Li et al., 2018, pp. 305–307), mobile location data (Miah et al., 2017, p. 773), and search engine data (Park & Pan, 2018, p. 412).

3.6.6 Issues and risks of big data

Like many innovations, big data comes with not only benefits but also specific risk factors. These risks can be grouped into data quality risks, analytical risks, and managerial or organizational risks (Fan, Han, & Liu, 2014; Grover et al., 2018; Raguseo, 2018).

Big data has a considerable variety of data sources and formats. The resulting data heterogeneity poses a huge risk for *data quality*. The data cleaning and integration processes must be designed according to the increasing volume and variety (Grover et al., 2018, p. 413). Especially external data sources, such as social media data, must be verified since the content may be false. Furthermore, data may be skewed, since the sampling mechanisms have to be calibrated for each new data source (Fan et al., 2014, p. 294).

The volume of big datasets has also severe implications for statistical analysis techniques. Massive sample sizes and the multidimensionality of data leads to noise accumulation and spurious relationships in the datasets (Fan et al., 2014, p. 298). Traditional statistical methods need to be refined in order to detect and reduce these drawbacks. Fan et al. (2014) have provided an immaculate mathematical insight into the potential approaches to overcome these issues and to use statistical analytics on big data.

Furthermore, big data creates significant managerial and organizational challenges. Raguseo (2018, p. 194) found that managers are most concerned with data privacy and security, the required infrastructure and data investments, and the organizational reluctance towards big data. The growing importance of data in the economy comes with the increased threat of data breaches and hacking attacks (Grover et al., 2018, p. 415). At the same time, data privacy legislation has tightened, and companies need to significantly invest in order to comply with the new regulations (Raguseo, 2018, p. 194). The ever increasing volume of data also requires investments in appropriate computing infrastructure and data library technology, such as Hadoop or MapReduce (Fan et al., 2014, pp. 306–307). Similarly, data needs to be collected or purchased, which also binds firm capital (Raguseo, 2018, p. 194). The implementation of big data technologies requires a change in management processes to minimize the associated organizational risks. Many scholars have already studied organizational big data risks and determined the lack of required skills (Barton & Court, 2012; Grover et al., 2018), reluctance towards technology (Asay, 2014; Günther et al., 2017) and innovation, and appropriate organizational structures (Günther et al., 2017; LaValle et al., 2011) to be the main factors.

3.7 The RBV pertaining to data and network planning

The resource-based view is a general management theory, which has already been specified in many research domains. This sub-chapter presents the general theory of the RBV and the specifications relevant for this study. The RBV has been widely used in both information systems and logistics. (Big) Data and logistic networks have been conceptualized utilizing the RBV within their research domains. The last section 3.7.6 combines both perspectives and derives an RBV-based research concept appropriate for this study. Figure 3.26 displays the structure of this sub-chapter graphically.

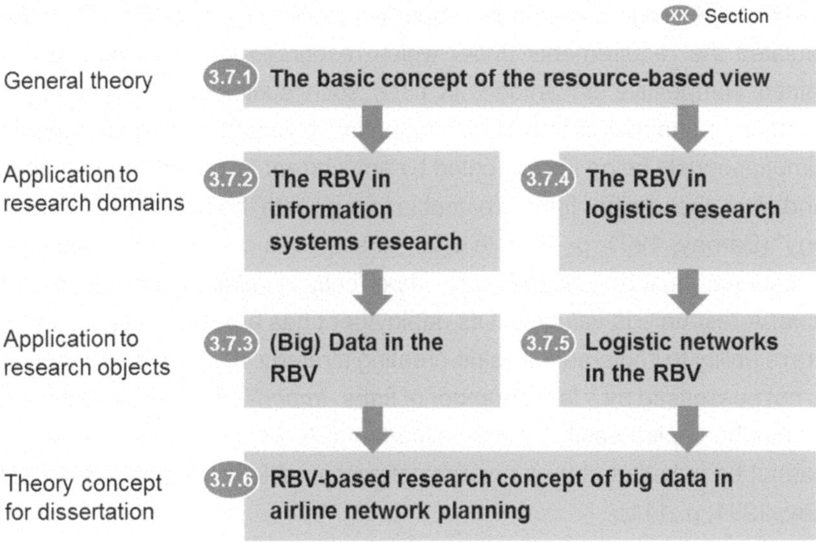

Figure 3.26 – Structure of sub-chapter 3.7[108]

3.7.1 The basic concept of the resource-based view

Over the past three decades, the resource-based view has become one of the most influential theories in strategic management, with hundreds of top journal publications and adaptations in almost all fields of management research (Barney, Ketchen, & Wright, 2011, p. 1300). The RBV is undisput-

---

108 Source: Own illustration.

edly a cornerstone of modern strategic management theories, which intends to answer the basic question of how firms can achieve a sustainable competitive advantage (Teece, Pisano, & Shuen, 1997, p. 509).

Jay Barney (1991) derived what is currently known as the first holistic theory of the resource-based view[109]. Based on the fundamental conditions of resource heterogeneity and the imperfect mobility of resources[110], he formulated the requirements under which resources can constitute a sustained competitive advantage. In case such sustained competitive advantage is attained, a firm is "implementing a value creating strategy not simultaneously being implemented by any current or potential competitors and when these other firms are unable to duplicate the benefits of the strategy" (Barney, 1991, p. 102). In order to sustain a competitive advantage, a resource must be *valuable, rare, imperfectly imitable*, and *non-substitutable*. A resource is *valuable* if its deployment has a positive impact on the firm's ability to implement a value-creating strategy. It is *rare* if the resource is not possessed by a large number of firms. *Imperfectly imitable* resources cannot be copied easily by competing firms. A *non-substitutable* resource cannot be substituted by a resource of comparable strategical value (Barney, 1991, p. 111).

In the 1990s, the RBV was further developed and refined. Margaret Peteraf (1993) specified the conditions for the existence of competitive advantage. In addition to the fundamental conditions of resource heterogeneity and imperfect resource mobility, she introduced ex-ante and ex-post limits to

---

[109] Barney developed the RBV based on a long history of scholars who studied the impact of firm resources on rent realizations. Early contributions of Penrose (1959), Stinchcombe (1965), and Andrews (1971) to the subject of superior rent realization by firms are noteworthy. In the 1980s, scholar such as Wernerfelt (1984) and Lippman and Rumelt (1982) defined important theoretical concepts, such as resource homogeneity.

[110] Barney (1991) defined resources as "all assets, capabilities, organizational processes, firm attributes, information, knowledge, etc. controlled by a firm that enable the firm to conceive and implement strategies that improve its efficiency and effectiveness" (p. 101).

competition. Ex-post limits to competition ensure that the resource's heterogeneity is durable after it has been acquired or developed by a firm. The ex-ante limit to competition draws on the ex-ante uncertainty on the expected return from a resource. This restricts excessive competition in the resource acquisition process.

Amit and Schoemaker (1993) split the construct of resources into two separate constructs: resources and capabilities. They defined resources as "stocks of available factors that are owned or controlled by the firm" (p. 35), whereas capabilities "refer to a firm's capacity to deploy resources, usually in combination, using organizational processes, to effect a desired end" (p. 35). Both resources and capabilities are considered strategic assets with similar properties to the resources described by Barney (1991). Teece et al. (1997) extend the capability concept into "dynamic capabilities." Dynamic capabilities enable a firm "to integrate, build, and reconfigure internal and external competences to address rapidly changing environments" (p. 516). Hence, agility becomes a significant driver of firm performance. The concept of dynamic resources was refined by Day (2011), who distinguished between dynamic and adaptive capabilities. As per his perspective, dynamic capabilities follow an inside-out perspective to make a company fit for a changing environment. Adaptive capabilities aim to foresee external development and shape such developments through a proactive outside-in-based adaptation of company capabilities (Day, 2011, pp. 187–189).

Grant (1996) introduces knowledge as a type of resource, essentially formulating the "knowledge-based view." He distinguished between tacit knowledge (knowing how) and explicit knowledge (knowing about). Explicit knowledge is transferrable in most cases, while tacit knowledge requires a high level of appropriateness to be useful. Barney, Wright, and Ketchen, Jr. (2001) have provided a much more detailed view on the individual streams of the RBV-related research in the 1990s.

In the 2000s, the focus of RBV research was on measuring the impact of resources and capabilities on firm performance empirically as well as on more theoretical extensions, which were summarized by Barney et al. (2011). In addition to the theoretical expansions of the RBV, many scholars have focused on applying the RBV on different industries and areas of management science. The subsequent sections focus on the application of the RBV to information systems research (section 3.7.2), data management (section 3.7.3), and logistics (section 3.7.4).

3.7.2 The RBV in information systems research

Mata, Fuerst, and Barney (1995) pioneered the application of the resource-based view in the field of information systems research. They reviewed the potential sources of competitive advantage that are influenced by information systems and contrasted them with the requirements defined by Barney (1991) and Peteraf (1993). Mata et al. (1995) found that managerial IT skills fulfill all criteria to create a sustained competitive advantage. Other factors such as technical IT skills, access to capital, or proprietary technology do not meet all the requirements but can still present a temporary competitive advantage. Subsequent research utilized the RBV to create more refined theories on how information systems can contribute towards superior firm performance. Two major research streams emerged in the years following Mata's publication: the refinement of the RBV in information systems, including IT assets, resources, and capabilities; and the IT business value research examining how information systems contribute to superior firm performance. Although both research streams build on each other, the critical milestones are highlighted individually for a better understanding of the concepts.

Ross, Beath, and Goodhue (1996) distinguished three IT-related assets that form the IT capability. First, *human assets* comprise the skills and talents of IT staff "who consistently solves business problems and addresses business opportunities through information technology" (p.33). Second, *technology assets* include databases and IT platforms, which are proprietary to the company. Third, *relationship assets* describe the alignment between IT and business departments. The parallel to Barney's (1991) trilogy of resources is obvious, with physical resources referred to as technology assets, human resources as human assets, and organizational resources as relationship assets. Bharadwaj (2000) first explicitly derived an IT capability based on Amit and Shoemaker's (1993) capability concept. The IT capability is hereby the "ability to mobilize and deploy IT-based resources in combination or co-present with other resources and capabilities" (p. 171). IT-based resources are defined as IT infrastructure, human IT resources and IT-enabled intangibles (compare Table 3.12).

Table 3.12 – Concepts of IT resources

Publication	Physical IT resources	Human IT resources	Organizational IT resources	Other factors
Ross et al. (1996)	▪ Well-defined IT architecture ▪ Data and platform standards	▪ Technical skills ▪ Business understanding ▪ Business problem solving	▪ Shared responsibility between business and IT departments	▪ None
Bharadwaj (2000)	▪ Computer and communication technologies ▪ Shareable technical platforms and databases	▪ Technical IT skills ▪ Managerial IT skills	▪ Know-how ▪ Corporate culture ▪ Corporate reputation ▪ Environmental orientation	▪ None
Melville, Kraemer, and Gurbaxani (2004)	▪ Infrastructure ▪ Business applications	▪ Technical skills ▪ Managerial skills	▪ Organizational structure ▪ Policies and rules	▪ Business processes (e.g., sales, logistics, manufacturing)

Publication	Physical IT resources	Human IT resources	Organizational IT resources	Other factors
			▪ Workplace practices ▪ Culture	
Wade and Hulland (2004)	▪ IS infrastructure	▪ IS planning and change management ▪ IS technical skills	▪ IS-business partnerships (manage internal relationships) ▪ Manage external relationships	▪ Market responsiveness ▪ IS development ▪ Cost effective IS operations
Bhatt and Grover (2005)	▪ IT infrastructure quality	▪ IT business expertise	▪ Relationship infrastructure	▪ None

Wade and Hulland (2004) built on the RBV to distinguish between information technology and information systems. IT is a purely asset-based resource, whereas IS include non-tangible resources and capabilities. Although this distinction is concise and clear, the two terms are still used interchangeably by many scholars. According to Wade and Hulland (2004, pp. 111–117), IS capability comprises nine resources. In addition to the abovementioned IT resource concepts, they include cost effectiveness, market responsiveness, and IS development as innovation parameters. Bhatt and Grover (2005) have defined three different IS capabilities, namely IT infrastructure quality, IT business expertise, and relationship infrastructure[111]. In an empirical study, they found that all of these capabilities are positively influenced by organizational learning. IT business expertise and relationship quality have a significant positive influence on firm performance, whereas IT infrastructure quality has no significant influence.

[111] IT business expertise is defined as the knowledge of IT staff regarding business strategy and processes; relationship infrastructure describes the degree of alignment and trust between IT and business departments.

Stoel and Muhanna (2009) studied IT capabilities as complex bundles of resources, which are focused either internally or externally. They discovered that the influence of IT capabilities on firm performance is highly influenced by the environment, i.e., the industry a company operates in. This implies that different resource bundles (i.e., IT capabilities) have different "fits" to a specific environment, and this explains the differences in firm performance. Kim et al. (2011) recommended sub-dividing IT capability into three distinct capabilities: IT infrastructure flexibility, IT management capability, and IT personnel expertise, where IT management capability and IT personnel expertise influence IT infrastructure flexibility. Studies in recent years (e.g., Chen et al., 2015) have proposed refined models for IT capabilities, but the topic has cooled down since. A remarkable contribution was made by Liu et al. (2013) who introduced the construct of IT assimilation, which is "the ability to diffuse and routinize IT applications in business processes within and across organizational boundaries" (p. 1455). This construct connects IT capabilities to dynamic capabilities and resonates with the findings of Stoel and Muhanna (2009) that IT capabilities should be adaptive to the developments in the environment.

3.7.3 (Big) Data in the RBV

Since the early days of information systems research, scientists have asked for the value of information and the data it is composed of. Rodriguez and King (1977, p. 45) stated that information based on "evaluated data" is an essential requirement of any strategic decision making and thus an indisputable source of value. Information systems help extract information from data and make it usable for strategic management. King (1983) attested that information is a "primary source of comparative business advantage in the marketplace" (p. iii). King, Grover, and Hufnagel (1989, p. 88) have defined information and information systems as two distinct resources for information management. Goodhue, Quillard, and Rockart (1988) then extended the definition of resource from information resources on data resources, which has also been acknowledged by Sabherwal and King (1991) who have described the information resource as "data that have been evaluated in such a way that it alters our expectations or our views of the alternatives that are available" (p. 193).

Although the focus of the early IT-related RBV literature has been on information systems as a holistic concept, the value of data has consistently been subject of research. Storey, Firth, and Wang (1995, pp. 623–624) consider data as a manufacturing output similar to product manufacturing, which undergoes the steps of raw data input, data processing, and finally, data products as the output. Similar to manufactured products, data products need to meet specific quality requirements in order to be of value (Redman, 1995, p. 100). Wang and Strong (1996) have developed a systematic definition of data quality attributes in order to create value for the data user.

Influenced by the data quality discussion, Levitin and Redman (1998) were the first to define the attributes of the data resource independent from the information resource. They differentiated between latent data and data records, which are "physical manifestation of latent data" (p. 91) that can be stored in databases or in paper files. They defined 13 dimensions of resource characteristics that are contrasted with human, financial, and physical resources. Table 3.13 summarizes the resource characteristics presented by Levitin and Redman and cross-references the relation to Barney's dimensions, which are discussed in the following paragraph.

Levitin and Redman (1998, pp. 92–95) noted that data records are *intangible* resources that are similar to financial, human, or organizational resources. Data records, in contrast to raw materials or financial resources, are *not consumable*, i.e., they can be used multiple times without disappearing. They are also *shareable* via physical or electronic transmission, so more than one user can benefit the data record. The shareability also implies the *copyability*, as data records can be recreated with or without transmission. Electronic transmission is very fast, so the *transportability* of electronic data records is also very high.

Table 3.13 – Data resource characteristics by Levitin and Redman (1998)

Resource characteristic	Latent data	Data records	Relation to resource characteristics by Barney (1991)
Intangible	No	Yes	No obvious relation
Consumable	No	No	Rarity
Shareable	Yes	Yes	Mobility
Copiable	Not applicable	Yes	Inimitability
Transportable	Not applicable	Fast	Mobility
Non-fungible	No	Depends	Non-substitutability
Fragile	Not applicable	Yes	No obvious relation
Versatile	Medium	Medium	Heterogeneity
Valuable	Maybe	Maybe	Value
Depreciable	Yes	Yes	Value
Sourced	External and internal	External and internal	Heterogeneity
Renewable	Yes	Yes	No obvious relation
Computer stored	No	Yes	No obvious relation

The term "*non-fungible*" was used by Levitin and Redman (1998, pp. 92–95) to describe the non-substitutability of resources. Some data records may be substituted by proxy data if, for example, the original data record is not accessible. However, in most cases, data records are not substitutable as they represent a given correct value. Data records are *fragile*, i.e., they can be destroyed and become unusable. This holds also true for physical resources but not for human or organizational resources.

Data records have a medium degree of *versatility*, meaning they can theoretically be used for many purposes but not universally for every possible application. They may also be *valuable* if they contribute useful information for management and operational steering. Most data records are *depreciable* since they lose value over time. Outdated data is clearly less valuable than updated data, especially if the timeliness of information is a driver of value creation.

Finally, Levitin and Redman (1998) defined three lifecycle characteristics. Data records can be either internal or external sources, the latter including data record purchases. Data records can also be renewed (updated) and replaced by a more current version. They can be stored electronically, which is a commonality with other resources.

Levitin and Redman (1998, p. 91) employed these resource characteristics to define and describe the data resource, but not to evaluate whether data alone can provide a competitive advantage according to Barney (1991).

In the 2000s, data as a specific resource has not drawn the attention of RBV scholars, who instead focused on the IT business value discussion and the refinement of IT capabilities (see section 3.7.2). With the arrival of big data analytics, the data resource discussion has gained momentum again as part of the definition process for a big data analytics (BDA) capability. Chen et al. (2012) introduced BDA as the latest wave in Business Intelligence & Analytics (BI&A), being a set of tools and methods to process large, varying, and real-time data sets.

Akter et al. (2016) developed a concept for a big data analytics capability, which was formerly included in a broader IT capability in literature. They define three sub-areas of BDA capabilities: BDA management capability, BDA technology capability, and BDA talent capability. Data records are not explicitly considered a resource in this BDA capability concept. Gupta and George (2016) proposed a different approach to define a BDA capability, differentiating human, tangible, and intangible resources. Human resources constitute the managerial and technical skills. Intangible resources build the counterpart to organizational resources, comprising organizational learning and a data-driven culture. Tangible resources – most similar to physical resources in the original RBV – are data, technology, and basic resources. Gupta and George (2016) have defined data as a physical, tangible resource that contrasts the definition by Levitin and Redman (1998), who consider data to be an intangible resource.

In the research model of Akter et al. (2016), all three sub-capabilities were found to have a significant positive effect on the BDA capability, with BDA talent capability having the strongest effect. The construct of BDA capability also had a significant positive effect on firm performance. Gupta and George (2016) also found a significant positive relation between BDA capability and firm performance; however, human resources have the strongest impact on BDA capability.

The business value of IT has been discussed controversially without consistent empirical results. However, the research on the value of data and data analytics has been less contentious. Originating from the data quality discussion in the 1990s, the value of information for attaining competitive advantage and thus the value of the underlying data has been widely acknowledged by scholars (Redman, 1995; Sabherwal & King, 1991). The discussion on the value of data then focused on the value of data quality with its various dimensions (Storey et al., 1995; Wang & Strong, 1996). Case studies on the business value of data warehouses have supported the hypothesis that (good quality) data can significantly improve management decisions, thus leading to a competitive advantage (Cooper et al., 2000).

Subsequent research on the business value of BI&A focused on defining value measurement metrics and processes (Lönnqvist & Pirttimäki, 2006) and creating an integrated BI&A framework featuring data as the input variable and BI systems as the production system to transform data into valuable information for management (Watson & Wixom, 2007; Wixom, Yen, & Relich, 2013). Similarly, Bharadwaj et al. (2013, p. 472) described the value of information and, in turn, the value of data as a crucial enabler for business value creation through digital business strategies. Seddon, Constantinidis, and Dod (2012) introduced possibly the most complete concept of measuring the value of BI&A. They derived a process and variance model comprising resources, capabilities, and mediators[112]. They found that technological and organizational capabilities contribute to most success cases, with readily-available high-quality data being a major contributor to the perceived business value.

Besides defining a concept for measuring the value for BI&A, various scholars have investigated the relationship between BI&A and firm performance. Trkman et al. (2010) observed a significant positive relationship between the deployment of business analytics and supply chain performance. Elbashir et al. (2013) demonstrated the importance of mediators such as shared knowledge and BI assimilation (i.e., a IT/Business alignment of BI systems) in this relationship. Both data accuracy and advanced analytics also have a significant positive influence on SCM initiatives and manufacturing planning, which results in a superior operational performance (Chae et al., 2014).

Building on the groundwork of BDA capabilities and the BI&A value discussion, recent contributions to literature have focused on the business value of big data analytics. Erevelles et al. (2016) consider big data to be a distinct resource, consisting of the combination of different data sources. This big data resource is mediated by the “traditional” three resources (human, organizational, and physical) to create dynamic and adaptive capabilities for marketing. The authors describe concrete value mechanisms within the marketing field, such as dynamic pricing and shortening product development cycles. Wamba et al. (2016) noted a strong significant positive effect of big data analytics capability on firm performance, moderated by process-oriented dynamic capabilities[113]. Most recently, Grover et al. (2018, p. 391) defined big data as a physical asset that needs to be complemented with

---

[112] The authors include technological, human, and organizational capabilities in the process model. The variance model tests for the direct resource influence of BA tools, data, and analytical skillset.

[113] Defined as a “firm’s ability to change (e.g., improve, adapt, adjust, reconfigure, refresh, renew, etc.) a business process better than the competition)” by Kim et al. (2011, p. 488).

the analytics technology to create a big data analytics resource. This is also the perspective for further discussion in this paper.

3.7.4 The RBV in logistics research

Being the pioneers in combining RBV and logistic concepts, Morash, Droge, and Vickery (1996) proposed an initial concept for a distinct logistic capability, composed of eight sub-capabilities, which entail a mix between activities (e.g., customer service) and performance measures (e.g., delivery speed). The five demand-side logistic sub-capabilities include pre-sale and post-sale customer service, delivery speed, and reliability and responsiveness towards target markets. On the supply-side, distribution coverage, availability, and low total cost are proposed as potential sub-dimensions for a logistic capability. However, the authors have not defined input resources for these capabilities. Logistical networks are indirectly present in all supply-side sub-capabilities, which include delivery speed, reliability, and target market responsiveness. Cho, Ozment, and Sink (2008) expanded the capability concept by three sub-capabilities: delivery information communication, web-based order handling, and global distribution coverage.

In a similar study, Closs, Goldsby, and Clinton (1997) developed 17 capabilities grouped under four competencies: positioning, integration, agility, and measurement. Despite opposing the RBV, the properties of a capability are not explicitly defined, and hence, there is a mix of resources and activities within the 17 capabilities. Interestingly, "network" is considered a distinct capability within the positioning competence.

In contrast to Morash et al. (1996) and Closs et al. (1997), Fawcett, Stanley, and Smith (1997) followed the capability concept of Amit and Schoemaker (1993), which views capabilities as bundles of resources. Strategic planning and information support systems here are the key resources to build five logistic-specific capabilities: delivery, quality, flexibility, cost, and innovation.

Olavarrieta and Ellinger (1997) proposed a generalized logistic capability as a solution to overcome the gridlocked discussion on the strategic value of logistics, but without specifying any resource and component. Zhao, Dröge, and Stank (2001) have defined two logistic-specific sets of capabilities, namely customer-focused and information-focused capabilities[114]. The authors found a strong significant correlation between customer-focused capabilities and firm performance but none between information-focused capabilities and firm performance. Lai (2004) formulated a service capability constituting 14 activities and then proved empirically that different types of logistical service providers require different service capabilities.

Yew, Wong, and Karia (2010) have defined a holistic logistic capability on the basis of five specific strategic resources: physical, human, information, knowledge, and relational resources. Physical resources comprise hubs, bases, and vehicles (e.g. aircraft) and human resources skills and qualifications. Information resources are slightly misleading, as they are measured exclusively with the IS system quality. Knowledge resources describe the organizational knowledge management processes and finally relate resources to the social network management capabilities of logistical firms. Similar to Lai (2004), these authors found that the combination of resources to gain a competitive advantage differs as per the logistical business model.

Cui and Hertz (2011) distinguished two types of logistical networks from a RBV perspective: networks of actors and networks of logistic service systems. Networks of actors are a type of social network that combine various logistical companies, either vertically (in a typical supply chain) or horizontally within the same supply chain level (e.g., cooperating trucking companies). The network of logistic service systems describes the actual physical

[114] Customer-focused capabilities include segmental focus, relevancy, responsiveness, and flexibility. Information-focused capabilities include information sharing, information technology, and connectivity.

network and the corresponding resource deployment. Based on this distinction, Cui and Hertz (2011, p. 1005) defined two different network management capabilities, one physical and one service based. They hypothesized that the success of logistical intermediaries, such as freight forwarders, relies more on the service-based network management capability, whereas carriers, such as airlines and shipping companies, rely primarily on the physical network management capability.

The most recent and holistic review of the RBV to the field of logistics has been provided by Gligor and Holcomb (2012). They define capabilities as “complex bundles of skills and accumulated knowledge” that “reflect the major role of strategic management in adapting, integrating and reconfiguring resources, organizational skills and functional competencies to respond to the challenges of the external environment” (p.445). In their extensive literature review, they examined over 20 scholarly articles on logistics and SCM capabilities, including most of the aforementioned authors. Gligor and Holcomb (2012) derived five meta-capabilities that provide a competitive advantage for activities of a logistic service system (see Table 3.14).

In summary, the application of RBV to logistics has produced a large body of literature, without a clear consensus on the role of resources and capabilities, partly caused by the definition problems with other theories. Some authors define logistic capabilities in close alignment with the original definition of capabilities as bundles of resources (Cui & Hertz, 2011; Fawcett et al., 1997; Yew Wong & Karia, 2010). Others cite greater degrees of freedom to align it with the activity-based capability definition of the logistic research domain (Cho et al., 2008; Lai, 2004; Morash et al., 1996). Logistical networks are seen both as a resource (Cui & Hertz, 2011; Xu, 2011), an explicit logistic capability (Closs et al., 1997; Yew Wong & Karia, 2010), and as a boundary condition for the functioning of a logistic service system (Fawcett et al., 1997).

Table 3.14 – Logistic capabilities defined by Gligor and Holcomb (2012)

Capability	Description	Authors (exemplary)
Demand-management capability	▪ Product or service differentiation ▪ Service enhancement for continuous distinctiveness by targeting a given customer base ▪ Unique, value-added activities	Cho et al., 2008; Morash et al., 1996; Zhao et al., 2001
Supply-management capability	▪ Total system cost minimization, with explicit consideration of cross-functional trade-offs ▪ Effective time management to eliminate capital and inventory wastage ▪ Response to demand fluctuations with less distortion of the order cycle process ▪ Use of resources to enable postponement speculation, modularization, and standardization	Cho et al., 2008; Fawcett et al., 1997; Morash et al., 1996; Zhao et al., 2001
Integration capability	▪ A state existing among internal organizational elements that are necessary to achieve unity of effort to meet organizational goals ▪ Includes internal and external components	Closs et al., 1997; Cui & Hertz, 2011; Lai, 2004
Measurement capability	▪ The degree to which a firm monitors internal and external operations ▪ Aligned with strategy to make accurate, detailed, relevant, and timely information accessible for strategic planning and daily decision making ▪ Enables the translation of business objectives into measurement specific operational and financial targets	Closs et al., 1997; Fawcett et al., 1997; Lai, 2004; Zhao et al., 2001
Information exchange capability	▪ Acquires, analyzes, stores, and distributes tactical and strategic information both inside and outside the firm ▪ Involves the application of hardware, software and networks	Closs et al.; Cui and Hertz; Fawcett et al.; Lai; Zhao et al. (1997; 2011; 1997; 2004; 2001)

3.7.5 *Logistic networks in the RBV*

After examining the RBV in IS, (big) data, and logistic research domains, the role of networks needs to be clarified. While inter-organizational networks have been widely discussed from a resource-based perspective[115], the literature on physical distribution networks remains underexplored. Cui and Hertz (2011, p. 1007) have defined a network management capability for logistic distribution networks, which assumes the existence of a physical network resource. Xu (2011, p. 47) adapted this view for airline networks. Bieger and Wittmer (2011, p. 79) have defined networks as assets that are the foundation for resource creation in the airline industry. Resources in this contribution include the airline brand, customer base, and position on a hub. Daft and Albers (2013, p. 50) view airline networks as a production factor but not a resource per se.

None of the mentioned authors provide a coherent discussion on whether airline networks qualify as resources based on Barney's (1991) definition of firm resources[116]. The two necessary conditions for the emergence of resources are resource heterogeneity and the imperfect mobility of resources (Barney, 1991, pp. 103–105). Airline networks are naturally heterogeneous, as airlines serve different routes with different fleets. Although two airlines could theoretically serve exactly the same spatial network in a deregulated environment, it is impossible to serve the same temporal network due to air traffic safety regulations[117]. In practice, even the spatial networks of airlines differ widely for historic reasons and competitive considerations (Gillen, 2005, pp. 50–51).

---

[115] Gulati et al. (2000) pioneered the application of the RBV to inter-organizational networks. Lavie (2008) refined this initial perspective, and Casanueva et al. (2014) applied it specifically to airline alliances.

[116] Please refer to section 3.7.1 for a detailed definition.

[117] Airports and airways are usually slot-restricted, so simultaneous departures and arrivals are highly unlikely.

The establishment of an airline network is a complex process requiring a number of specific assets to be accomplished, including suitable aircraft, traffic rights, and airport slots (Goedeking, 2010, p. 105). Since airline networks are a product of these assets, it is not easily moveable. Even if an entire airline that is in control of all of these assets is acquired, anti-trust legislations often impede the transfer of these assets[118]. Thus, airline networks can be viewed as imperfectly mobile, thus fulfilling both basic resource conditions stated by Barney (1991).

However, can a resource airline network contribute towards a sustainable competitive advantage? Airline networks are clearly *valuable*, since they have a positive influence on the associated firm's ability to implement a value-creating strategy. As outlined in section 3.5.8, NP and management are key elements of the airline strategy formulation and execution. The question of *rarity* cannot be answered that easily. The limiting factors of airline networks are the availability of slots and traffic rights. Since these assets are rare, the entire resource "airline network" is rare, even though every scheduled airline owns an airline network. As mentioned earlier, anti-trust legislation and slot and traffic right limitations also impede the resource airline network from easily being *copied* by competitors. When discussing *substitutability*, we need to differentiate between short- and long-term perspective and short-haul and long-haul airline network.

Potential substitutes for short-haul routes are mostly high-speed trains and similar transport facilities. The planning and construction of such infrastructure requires a large time horizon. Consequently, short-haul air routes can be substituted in the long term but not in the short term. At the time of writing this study, there is no substitute for long-haul air routes. New emerging technologies such as the Hyperloop may provide such a substi-

---

[118] A very recent example is the barred acquisition of Niki by the Lufthansa Group, in which Lufthansa intended to acquire all assets, including aircraft, slots, and traffic rights. The European anti-trust regulation imposed heavy concessions, so the transaction was not feasible.

tute in the far future. Since the planning cycles for major infrastructure projects are usually longer than for new air routes, airline networks are non-substitutable. In summary, airline networks can be defined as resources, since they are valuable, rare, non-copyable and not substitutable in the short term.

3.7.6 RBV-based research concept of big data in airline NP

The aim of this section is to bring together the separate concepts of airline networks and big data analytics to derive an RBV-based framework for this study. Based on the discussion in section 3.7.3, this study adopts the concept by Grover et al. (2018), whereby they define a BDA capability with data sources, processing technology, and analytic tools as foundation assets. This BDA capability is expressed in big data opportunities, which are the main focus of this study. This includes the identification of suitable data sources and the deployment of adequate data processing and analytics technology.

Airline networks are a distinct resource (see section 3.7.5) that consist of specific assets, namely the aircraft fleet, airport slots, traffic rights, the NP organization, and the supporting infrastructure. The supporting infrastructure includes IT systems and formal processes for NP. The NP organization includes the human and managerial assets that are responsible for planning and managing the airline network. The supporting infrastructure has an enabling effect for big data opportunities and is therefore taken as a secondary research focus. Similarly, the NP organization should be ready to adopt big data opportunities and is another secondary research focus.

In an ever-changing environment, fast reaction times become increasingly important to maintain a competitive advantage in the airline business (Takebayashi, 2013, p. 86). The ability to detect and forecast these changes becomes a key capability for network airlines. This is similar to Day's (2011) perception of adaptive capabilities, as described in section

3.7.1. Big data opportunities contribute towards making the NP capability more adaptive, since these can provide a real-time perspective leveraging appropriate data sources and analytic tools. Figure 3.27 displays the construct model and highlights the primary and secondary research focus of this study.

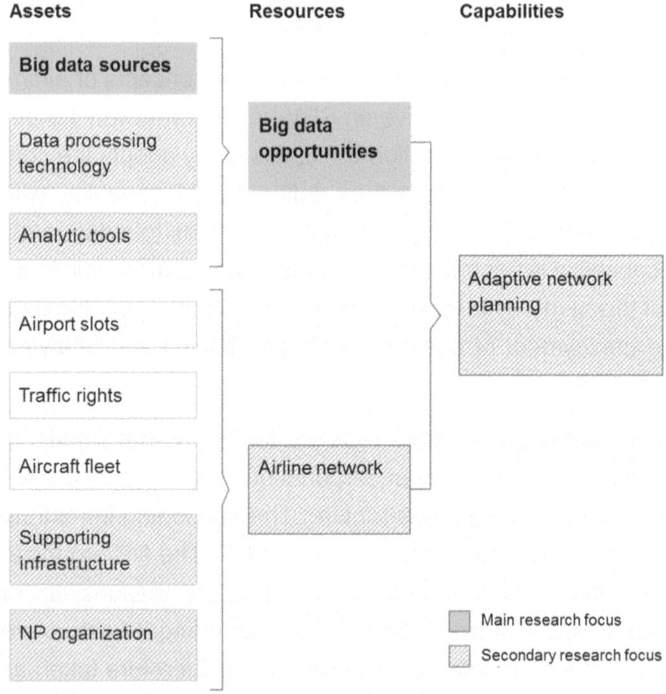

Figure 3.27 – Research focus in theoretical context[119]

[119] Source: Own illustration.

4 Status quo of strategic network planning in airlines

This chapter describes the status-quo of NP across airlines in the case study group. After a brief introduction to the organizational set-up and observed process structures (sub-chapter 4.1), sub-chapter 4.2 explores the data sources currently used for NP. Subsequently, the currently used IT systems for NP (sub-chapter 4.3) and the performance measurement within NP departments are detailed (sub-chapter 4.4).

4.1 The network planning process in reality

NP departments can assume a range of roles and responsibilities in the airline business process structure. While NP is usually integrated in commercial departments or placed as a mediator between the commercial and operation departments (Goedeking, 2010, p. 99), the actual set-up of the NP department and the related NP process differ widely across airlines.

4.1.1 Roles and responsibilities of NP departments

In line with the NP process, the responsibilities of NP departments can be defined temporally as well as spatially. While some of the carriers have NP departments that assume spatial responsibility in one central team, others divide NP functions based on hubs or sets of routes. The temporal responsibilities can be distinguished as long-term (strategic) and short-term (tactical) planning. The combination of temporal and spatial responsibilities results in four archetypes of NP departments, displayed in Figure 4.1.

M. Schosser, *Big Data to Improve Strategic Network Planning in Airlines*,
Schriftenreihe der HHL Leipzig Graduate School of Management,
https://doi.org/10.1007/978-3-658-27582-2_4

Spatial specialization	Responsibility split by process step	Responsibility for entire planning process
Global network responsibility	**Process-specialists for global network** ▪ All routes planned centrally ▪ Different teams cover long-term planning and short-term planning *Case examples: FSC 2, SCA 2, CAR 1, CAR 2, CAR 3*	**Global centralized network planning department** ▪ All routes planned centrally ▪ Same department for all relevant planning steps *Case examples: LCC 2*
Sub-network responsibility	**Highly specialized planning teams** ▪ Teams split between short-haul and long-haul routes ▪ Different teams cover long-term planning and short-term planning *Case examples: FSC 1*	**Geographically specialized teams for entire planning process** ▪ Teams responsible for short-haul or long-haul routes (FSC/SCA) or split by operation base (LCC) ▪ Teams cover all planning steps for their routes *Case examples: LCC 1 & SCA 1*
	Temporal specialization	

Figure 4.1 – Organizational responsibility model for airline network planning[120]

Global centralized NP department

The global centralized NP department is responsible for all the steps in the NP process on all route types. LCC 2, one of the airlines in the case study, uses this archetype to manage the entire network with a team of NP generalists. The advantage of this NP department structure is clarity in end-to-end process responsibilities, which makes the process itself more flexible due to the more lenient freeze and hand-over procedures. However, the generalist approach reaches its limits as complexity grows with increasing network size and connection traffic. In reality, this archetype may be suita-

120 Source: Own illustration.

ble only for LCCs and SCAs due to their drastically reduced network complexity by abstaining from indulging in connection traffic and complex aircraft routing schemes (Bley & Büermann, 2016, pp. 52–54).

Process specialists for a global network

In this NP archetype, different NP teams are specialized for specific process steps through the entire airline network. Most commonly, one team accounts for the strategic NP steps, which include long-term planning, route and frequency selection, and the preparation of a draft schedule. A second team operationalizes the schedule by assigning or updating fleet types and creating crew and aircraft rotation plans. The two teams usually form the NP department with a department head being responsible for the entire process. Five out of the nine case study airlines follow this model, including all cargo airlines, FSC 2 and SCA 2.

Geographical or route type specialist teams

In large carriers with both short- and long-haul operations, the NP teams can be structured around these route types. While one team manages the entire NP process for the long-haul route portfolio, a different team is in charge of the short-haul route portfolio. SCA 1 applies this logic because it benefits from a very limited number of transfer passengers, which reduces the need for coordination between long-haul and short-haul flights. Some low-cost airlines follow a different and much simpler model of geographical specialization. They assign aircrafts to specific operating bases, which are then responsible for selecting the appropriate routes and schedules. This decentralization of NP drastically reduces the planning complexity, as the same crew and aircraft rosters can be used for each station. Layover cost are reduced as well, since all the crew and aircrafts return to their home base every evening. LCC 1 follows this low-cost-specific version of NP specialization.

Highly specialized NP teams

For large and complex networks, it becomes necessary to combine spatial and temporal specialization. FSC 1 employs specialist teams for tactical and strategic NP, which too have both long-haul and short-haul sub-teams. This complex structure requires a very strict NP process with pre-defined freezes and hand-overs, significantly reducing NP flexibility. However, the complexity of a network of several hundred routes and aircraft and the integration with a major airline alliance increase the planning cycle duration in any case. The highly specialized teams in FSC 1 are supported by a dedicated data and IT team, which facilitates the use of highly sophisticated planning solutions (see section 4.3.2).

4.1.2 Sequence and time horizon of NP process steps

The sequence of real-life NP processes highly resembles the NP process that was derived from literature in section 3.5.7. However, the steps of the process are in many cases not purely sequential but run iteratively or in parallel. Figure 4.2 displays both the sequence and time horizon of the individual NP steps across the case study group.

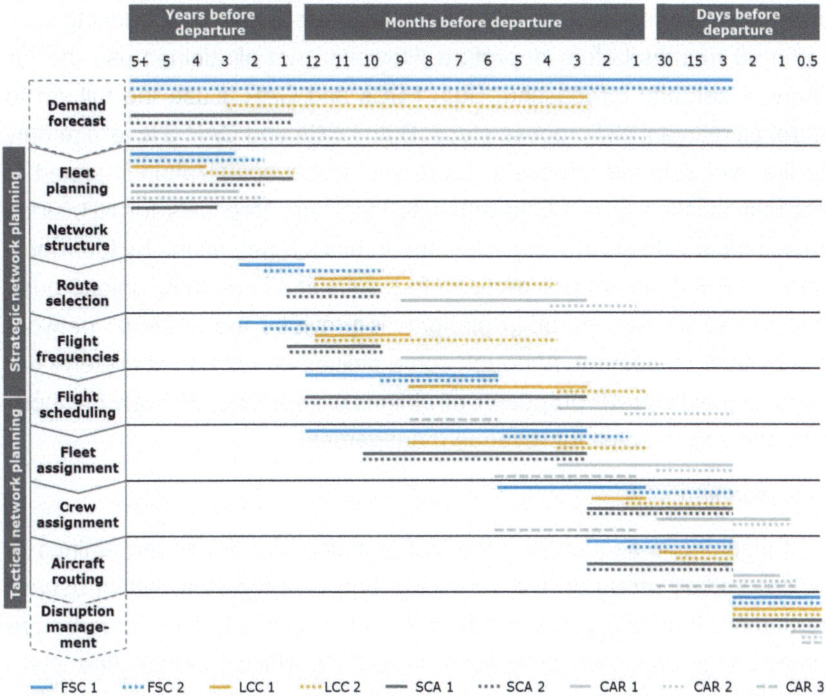

Figure 4.2 – Sequence and timing of NP process steps across case study participants[121]

Demand forecasting

Demand forecasts are a continuous process in all airlines, which is iteratively refined as forecasts become more accurate. It can be roughly distinguished as three individual demand forecasts: a long-term demand forecast that informs corporate strategy and fleet planning with a 3- to 10-year time horizon; a medium-term demand forecast informing strategic NP steps with a forecast horizon between 6 and 24 months; finally, a short-

[121] Source: Own illustration.

term forecast informing the tactical planning steps with real booking data starting 6 months before departure. However, not all airlines use the full trilogy of demand forecasting. Both FSCs and CAR 1 use the full set to inform all relevant NP process steps. Both LCCs and CAR 2 leverage only the first two demand forecasts, since the tactical optimization is aimed at cost minimization. The SCAs only use long-term forecasts for NP, since the schedule is finalized very early due to block reservations by tour operators. CAR 3 does not use demand forecasts at all due to its unique business model whose operation platform is provided the strategic network plan by their customers. Although some airlines do not use short-term demand forecasts for NP purposes, all airlines except for CAR 3 rely on short-term demand forecast for revenue management.

Fleet planning

Fleet planning is sequentially the first planning step for seven airlines of the case study group. It is a very long-term oriented step, which usually starts more than five years in advance and ends two to four years before a schedule period. Two exceptions are LCC 2, which conducts fleet planning within a shorter time span (one to three years), and SCA 1, which first plans the network structure and then procures the necessary fleet mix. The fleet of CAR 3 is provided by its shareholders, who are also responsible for the long-term fleet and capacity planning.

Network structure definition

SCA 1 is the only airline in the case study group that has an explicit network structure definition process step implemented as part of the long-term planning, three to five years before a schedule period, and this mainly includes the split between short-haul and long-haul routes. All other airlines take the current network structure as given and plan only incremental changes, such as addition and deletion of individual routes or the change of flight frequencies.

Route selection and selection of flight frequencies

Route selection is based on the fleet plan and the medium-term demand forecast. In all airlines, route selection and the determination of flight frequency occur simultaneously, since both are part of the same asset allocation problem. Opening a new route with an unchanged fleet size and composition always entails either reducing frequencies on an existing route or discontinuing a route. Therefore, both NP steps are conducted iteratively and in parallel, until the final route and frequency portfolio is defined. The airlines in the case study group exhibit large differences in the time horizon for these two process steps. FSC 1 starts as early as three years before a schedule period and defines the route portfolio 12 months in advance. All other passenger airlines begin the route and frequency selection 12–18 months in advance and conclude eight to ten months before a schedule period starts. LCC 2 is the only exception and ends the route and frequency planning phase only four months prior to departure. This is possible because LCC 2 serves many secondary airports without slot restrictions; therefore, the route and frequency portfolio does not have to be complete before the International Air Transport Association (IATA) slot conferences, which are hosted twice a year. Thus, airlines with heavy slot restrictions aim to finalize their route and frequency portfolio before each slot conference. Cargo airlines have a much shorter planning horizon and start route and frequency selection only nine to twelve months prior to departure. In case of CAR 2, the final route and frequency portfolio is finalized only a month prior to departure. This is possible as cargo airlines often fly to unrestricted airports and freight bookings open only six to twelve weeks before departure.

Flight scheduling

Of all network process steps, flight scheduling is the one handled most diversely within the case study group. FSC 2 and CAR 3 conduct flight scheduling as a sequential step between route/frequency selection and fleet assignment. Both SCAs and CAR 1 commence the scheduling process in parallel to route and frequency selection. The remaining airlines combine flight scheduling with fleet assignment in a parallel and iterative way. Most airlines undertake two iterations of flight scheduling, namely the preparation of a draft schedule for a standard week of operations and a detailed schedule for the entire schedule period. The draft schedule also serves as the formal hand-over product between the strategic and tactical NP teams in airlines that follow a temporal process specialization. Most passenger airlines begin the actual scheduling nine to twelve months before departure and freeze the schedule three to six months prior to departure. LCC 2 and two cargo airlines start scheduling only three months before departure and freeze their schedules one month ahead of it.

Fleet assignment

As mentioned in the previous paragraph, fleet assignment is often iteratively interconnected with flight scheduling. The two LCCs even combine it as a single step due to their homogeneous fleets. For the SCAs as well as for FSC 1 fleet assignment is most relevant for the second, detailed schedule iteration and can extend beyond the actual scheduling due to re-assignments. FSC 2 executes it explicitly after the scheduling process step. Fleet assignment may start as early as 12 months before departure (FSC 1) and as late as 30 days before departure (CAR 2). Most airlines freeze the fleet assignment between three and one month prior to departure. Only CAR 2 has a significantly late fleet assignment freeze, at 3 days prior to departure.

Crew assignment

Crew assignment always requires a detailed schedule and at least the assignment of an aircraft family (e.g., Airbus A319/320/321) in order to produce meaningful crew rosters[122]. Thus, crew assignment can only start af-

[122] Aircraft type ratings of crews usually comprise an aircraft family and not only the specific aircraft type.

ter the final schedule freeze, but it can run alongside aircraft re-assignments (within the same aircraft family) and aircraft rotation planning. In most airlines, crew rosters are not produced by the NP department but by a dedicated crew planning team. FSC 1 again has the longest planning cycle and starts rostering crews six months before departure. Most other airlines start crew assignments two to three months before departure and finish one month to three days before departure. The flexibility of crew rostering is greatly driven by labor agreements with crew unions, which often demand a final individual operation schedule for each crew member 30 days prior to departure. Therefore, airlines with a low degree of unionization and no common labor agreements enjoy more flexibility in their crew assignment process.

Aircraft routing

Aircraft routing depends heavily on individual aircraft maintenance plans and is either performed by the NP departments or directly by the maintenance department[123]. The final fleet assignment added with the frozen schedule is the main input for aircraft routing. Accordingly, aircraft routing always starts after scheduling and fleet assignment have been finished. It may be carried out alongside crew assignment, which is the case in seven out of the nine airlines. Passenger airlines start aircraft routing three to one month prior to departure. All of them finish with the rotation plan freeze three days before departure. The final rotation plan is the handover document from the NP department to the Flight Operations department, who then handle any short-term changes. Aircraft routing in cargo airlines starts one month to three days prior to departure, whereas the handover of the final rotation plan happens only 24 to six hours in advance.

[123] The NP department responsible in FSCs, LCCs, SCAs, and CAR 1; maintenance department in CAR 2 and CAR 3.

4.2 Data types used for network planning

After describing the procedural details of NP in the case study group, this sub-chapter focuses on the data employed to inform the NP process. The data types used in airline NP literature have been analyzed in section 1 and are summarized in Table 3.7 (p. 111). As practitioners are expected to use more and different data sources than researchers, an open question was asked in the first round of interview on the data sources currently used for NP. The results of the open-ended question were coded with the data sources derived from literature[124], as detailed in section 4.2.1. The additional data sources not mentioned in literature were coded separately and added to the list of data sources to be included in the subsequent survey that was used to evaluate the current use (detailed in section 4.2.2), reliability, and usefulness of the data sources (both presented in section 4.2.3).

4.2.1 Practical use of data types derived from literature

The open-ended question on the use of current data sources has been coded with the data types identified from the literature review in section 1. Data types that stem fully or partly from internal data sources were most frequently mentioned by the case study participants. All participating airlines use cost estimates, and all but one airline use internal booking information for NP. Other internal or mixed data types, such as traffic rights and slot information (5 mentions) and aircraft characteristics (2 mentions), are also utilized. However, maintenance requirements and work rules for crew planning were not cited at all. As pointed in the previous section, crew and maintenance planning are often not conducted by the NP department. Hence, these input data types seem less relevant to NP. Figure 4.3 summarizes the mentioned frequency of data types derived from literature.

[124] Please refer to section 4.2.2 for a detailed discussion on the used methodology.

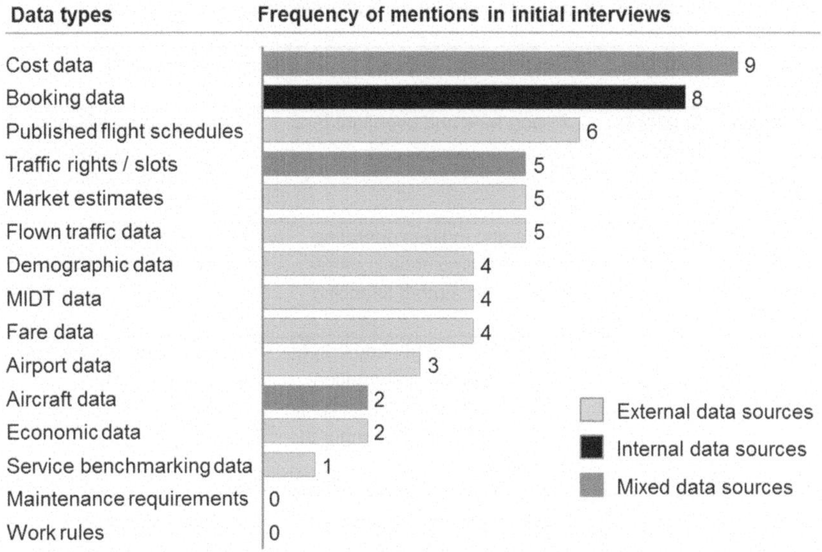

Figure 4.3 – Coding results based on open questions of first interview round[125]

The most frequently mentioned data type from external sources is published flight schedules, followed by economic market estimates and real traffic data on flown flights. Most airlines use a wide range of external data providers to satisfy their data needs. Public providers, such as industry associations, statistical bureaus, and international organizations, offer a broad selection of economic, demographic, and traffic data. Private data providers focus on aviation-specific data sets, such as published flight schedules, fare data, market analysis, and benchmarking data (e.g., Quality of Service Index). Table 4.1 provides a detailed overview of the coded data types, identified sub-types, and the corresponding data providers.

---

[125] Source: Own illustration.

Table 4.1 – Description of currently used data types derived from literature[126]

Data type	Subtype	Description	Data providers
Cost data	External fees	Airport fees and overflight fees	Either airport and flight control agency directly or third-party providers, such as Airpas
	Internal cost	Direct and indirect operating cost, including crew, maintenance, and aircraft financing cost	Internal controlling or finance department
Booking data	-	Complete list of booked tickets with all available information, such as fare, booking class, itinerary, additional passenger information, etc.	Internal controlling or revenue management
Published flight schedules	-	Complete list of planned flights, including airline, flight number, flight date, aircraft type, route, departure and arrival time	Private data providers, such as OAG, Flight Global and Innovata; IATA SRS provides schedule data from and for IATA members
Traffic rights / slots	Traffic rights	Database with contractual details of bi- or multilateral traffic right agreements	Usually internal database filled manually with information from government agencies; ICAO and WTO provide standardized databases.
	Slots	List of assigned slots per airport	Slot management or NP internal database
Market estimates	-	Ready-made market forecasts of air traffic volume development for next 5-10 years	Aircraft manufacturers, industry associations (e.g., IATA), consultancies (e.g., Seabury)
Real traffic data	Market-level data on actually flown flights	List of performed flights with departure and arrival times, operating airline, flight number, used aircraft	Official statistic authorities

[126] Source: Own illustration based on literature listed in Appendix 15

Data type	Subtype	Description	Data providers
	Airport traffic statistics	Number of passengers per route, potentially including ticket data	Airports
Demographic data	-	Demographic segmentation of airport catchment areas by age, ethnic descent, income, and social status	Airports, official statistical agencies
MIDT data	-	Anonymized booking data, including booking date, airline, booked flight, booking class, fare, number of passengers, itinerary; covers only the bookings processed by a specific global distribution system	Global distribution system operators, such as Amadeus, Sabre or TravelPort
Fare data	-	Includes average fares by date and route for specific booking classes	Private data providers (Infare, IATA PraxIS, CASS, WorldACD)
Airport data	Airport characteristics	Operation-relevant information, such as opening times, fees, allowed aircraft size, handling restrictions, meteorological specificities	From flight operation data providers (e.g., Jeppesen, Amadeus) or air traffic control entities (e.g., Eurocontrol)
Aircraft data	Service-relevant aircraft characteristics	Cabin layout, product quality level	Product management / maintenance
	Operation-relevant characteristics	Aircraft performance data, crew requirements	Aircraft manufacturers, maintenance, crew planning
	Maintenance data	Maintenance schedule for each aircraft	Maintenance
Economic data	Economic forecasts on country level	Forecasts on economic indicators, such as GDP growth, inflation, trade volumes	International organizations (IMF, World Bank), private research institutes (e.g., Oxford Economics)
Service benchmarking data	Quality of Service Index	Benchmarking of own offering with competitor offering based on connection time, price and product quality	Benchmarking data from large network planning system providers (e.g., Sabre, LH Systems)

4.2.2 *Currently used data types in airline network planning*

In order to classify and structure the used data types, it is important to recall the differences between data and information (compare section 3.6.1). Airline network planners are primarily concerned with information on the influencing factors for NP decisions. Three important factors can be derived from existing literature, namely demand information, cost information, and information on planning constraints (compare section 1). The data types used in the literature comprise these information objects, which are then used to perform and optimize the individual NP steps. The left side of Figure 4.4 displays the attribution of data types to information objects graphically.

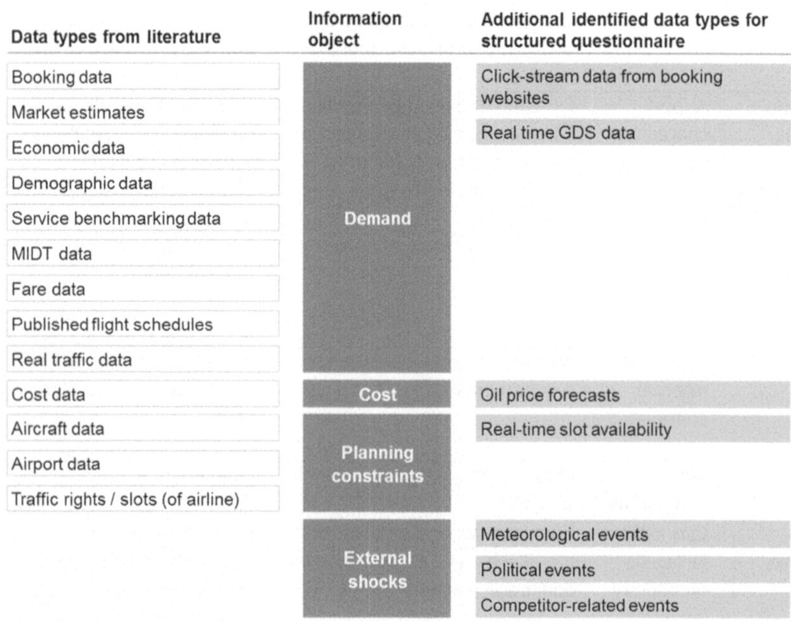

Figure 4.4 – Clustering of data types by information object[127]

[127] Source: Own illustration.

The previous section summarized the coding results mentioning the data types used in literature with primary codes. In the unstructured part of the first interview, practitioners mentioned additional data types that have not been cited in the literature. Building on the three identified information objects, four additional data types that were used in practice but not in the literature could be extracted from the initial interviews. In addition, airline network planners intend to forecast external shocks, namely meteorological, political, and competitor-related events. This introduces external shocks as the fourth information object of interest for airline NP, which contains data on the three mentioned shock types. Table 4.2 contains details on the seven additional data types.

Table 4.2 – Additionally coded data types not used in literature

Data type	Subtype	Description	Data providers
Booking website click-streams	-	Data feed with search request on flight booking portal, including set filters and subsequent behavior (e.g., purchase, drop-out, booked on different airline)	Skyscanner is actively commercializing data; Kayak or Expedia can potentially market similar data
Real-time external booking data	-	Real-time data feed on bookings per route but without additional MIDT data types	Global distribution system operators, such as Amadeus, Sabre or TravelPort
Oil price forecast	Five years aviation fuel price estimate	Estimate on oil price and kerosene price development and expected hedging strategies	External data from institutions, private companies, and financial markets[128] consolidated by internal

[128] Examples of institutions publishing oil price forecasts are the International Energy Agency (IEA), the U.S. Energy Information Administration (EIA), the Organization for Economic Cooperation and Development (OECD), and the Organization of Petroleum Exporting Countries (OPEC). Examples of private companies are almost all oil and gas-producing companies (e.g., BP, Royal Dutch Shell, ExxonMobile) as well as specialized oil price–forecasting companies (e.g., Deloitte, Kiplinger, etc.). Financial markets too provide oil price forecasts either through market institutions (e.g., the New York Mercantile Exchange (NYMEX)) or financial analysts (basically all the actors in the commodity exchange market, including banks and rating agencies).

Data type	Subtype	Description	Data providers
			fuel management or finance department
Real-time slot availability	-	Overview of available slots on slot-restricted airports	Two private data providers (ACL and e-airportslots), each covering different countries
Meteorological event forecasting	Mid-term forecast of extraordinary meteorological situations	15-day forecasts of hurricanes, floods, large bush fires that can influence air travel	Broad variety of local and international aeronautical meteorological forecasting companies
Political event forecasting	Systematic news screening	Identification of threats and opportunities evolving from political events (e.g., strikes, embargos, wars)	Specialized news screening companies
Competitor-related event forecasting	Competitor monitoring	Identification and forecasting of strikes, bankruptcies, and major strategic decisions	Specialized news screening companies and internal strategy department

The seven data types in practice complement the 17 data types and subtypes from the literature. Since maintenance plans and work rules are not primarily used by NP departments, only 22 data types were included in the structured online survey to evaluate their actual usage, reliability, and usefulness. All nine participating airlines filled out the online survey, resulting in a 100% participation rate. Figure 4.5 summarizes the survey results on the current usage of the 22 data types.

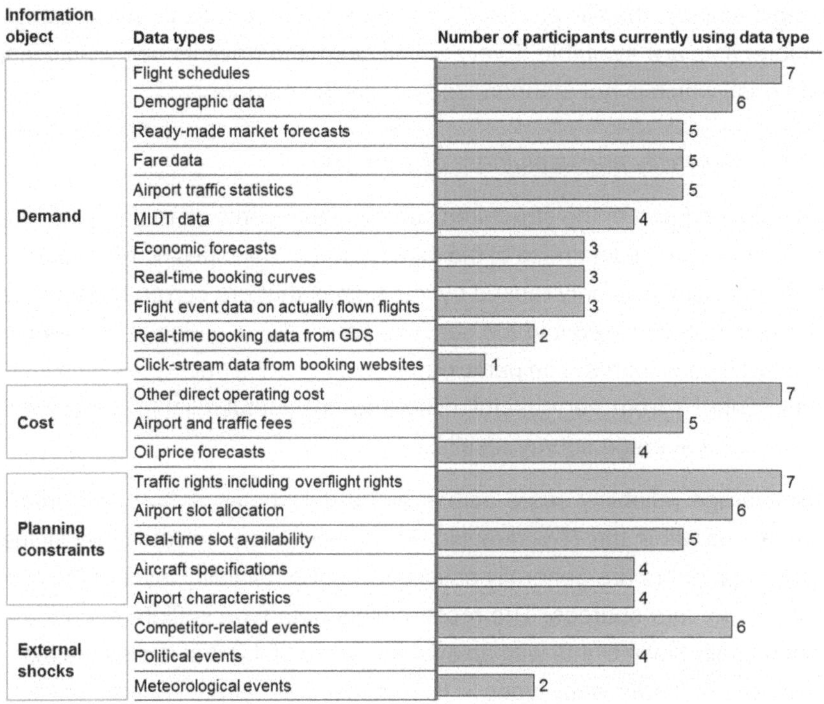

Figure 4.5 – Current usage of data types across case study group[129]

There is no common data type that is used across all airlines. Flight schedules, operating cost, and traffic rights are the most widely used data types (7 out of 9 airlines). Rather innovative data sources, such as clickstream data from booking websites and real-time data feeds from global distribution systems, are the least used data types, corresponding to the initial hypothesis that NP departments rely mostly on traditional sources for NP. Data on meteorological events is only used by two NP departments, since

---

[129] Source: Own illustration.

in most airlines, the NP process is concluded before reliable meteorological forecasts are available. Every airline seems to have its own traditional data pool, which is not standardized across the sample.

4.2.3 Reliability and usefulness of data types

In the second part of the structured survey, participants were asked to rate the reliability and usefulness of the data types for their specific NP process. While reliability was only ranked by the airlines that are currently using the data type or have used it in the past five years, the usefulness was evaluated by all participants. The participants could rate the data types on a four-point scale[130], from very useful/reliable to not useful/reliable. Figure 4.6 displays the average survey results.

The average reliability score across all 22 data types is 3.23, with most evaluations within the 75% quantile. This observation indicates that airline network planners are generally satisfied with the reliability level of the currently used data sources. The most reliable data type is flight event data from actually flown flights with an average score of 4.0 that is also the maximum score. Three data types – flight schedules, airport characteristics, and aircraft specifications – are also perceived as highly reliable with an average score of 3.7. Clickstream data from booking websites is perceived the least reliable with a score of 2.4, followed by ready-made market forecasts (2.6) and political event forecasting (2.7).

Average usefulness across all data types was evaluated at 3.30, which is slightly higher than the average reliability. This indicates that the currently used data sources provide satisfactory information. Operating cost are deemed most useful with an average score of 3.9, followed by real-time booking curves (3.8), airport slot allocation (3.7), and flight schedules (3.7).

---

[130] Compare section 2.3.3: scale following the very positive – slightly positive – slightly negative – very negative logic, as suggested by Berg (2004).

Meteorological event forecasting is perceived as the least useful with an average score of 2.4, followed by political event forecasting (2.8).

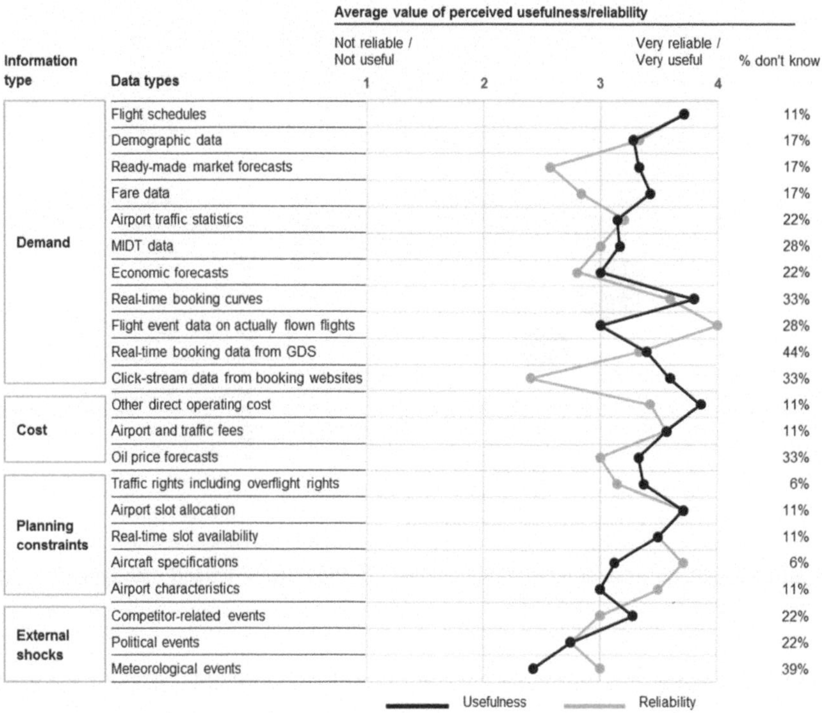

Figure 4.6 – Perceived usefulness and reliability of the 22 currently used data types[131]

The difference in scores for usefulness and reliability allow for a clustering of data types. When plotted on a matrix graph (Figure 4.7) with reliability along the X-axis and usefulness along the Y-axis, four generic clusters could be defined. If a data type is both useful and reliable (value over 3.0),

[131] Source: Own illustration.

it should be maintained for fully meeting its purpose. These are the *data essentials* for airline NP, comprising exactly half of all data types[132].

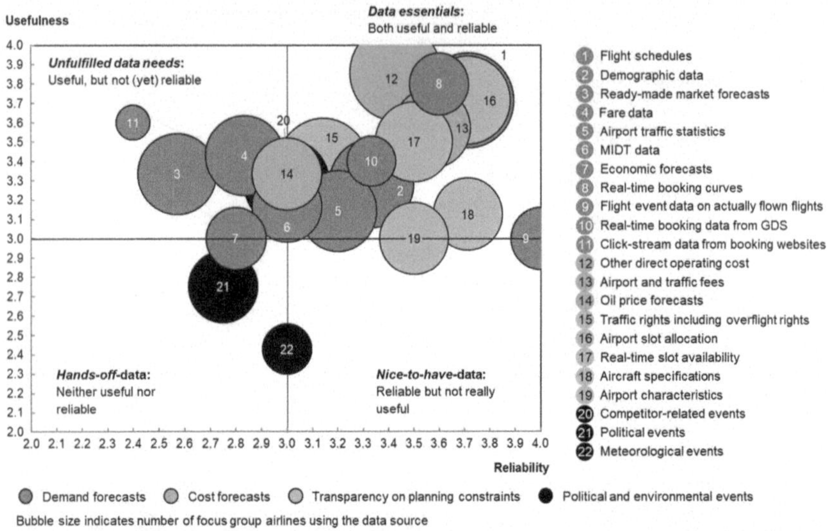

Figure 4.7 – Usefulness and reliability analysis of the currently used data types[133]

On the contrary, if a data type is neither useful nor reliable, it does not add any value to the NP process. It can even destroy value through bad decisions. Two data types fall in this cluster: political event forecasting and meteorological event forecasting. If airlines are not able to improve either the reliability or usefulness of these data sources, they should eliminate such *hands-off data*.

---

[132] Demographic data, real-time booking curves, real-time booking data from global distribution systems (GDS), oil price forecasts, MIDT data, fare data, airport traffic statistics, airport slot allocation, real-time slot availability, traffic rights, including overflight rights, aircraft specifications.

[133] Source: Own illustration.

Data types that are reliable but not useful can be retained if they do not incur additional cost; these are *nice-to-have* data. Operating cost and airport characteristics are the only ones in this category. Operating cost information is usually available from internal sources, and airport characteristics are procured for flight operations in any case.

The last cluster are data types that are very useful but not "yet" reliable. These "*unfulfilled data needs*" include seven data types, namely ready-made market forecasts, economic forecasts, clickstream data from booking websites, airport and traffic fees, flight schedules, flight event data on actually flown flights, and competitor-related event forecasting.

This clustering is the first step towards identifying BDOs for airline NP. In principle, big data can generate value in three different ways. First, it can improve the reliability of currently used data types by shedding light on "blind spots" or improving the validity of a data type. Second, it can improve the usefulness of a current data type by allowing for additional analyses that extract the right information for airline network planners. Finally, big data can create entirely new data types that complement the currently used set of data types. Clustering provides a starting point for the first two value generation mechanisms, as it highlights the improvement potential of the currently used data types. Sub-chapter 5.2 discusses the findings of this section to develop potential BDOs.

4.3 IT tools used for network planning

The data used for NP has to be processed and analyzed to generate useful information for NP staff. This sub-chapter analyzes the current market of IT tools for airline NP (section 4.3.1) and presents the practical use of these systems by the airlines of the case study group (section 4.3.2). The last section 4.3.3 draws on additional interviews with an IT system provider as well as on publicly available information in order to map out the data capabilities of existing NP IT solutions.

4.3.1 *Market of IT tools for airline network planning*

The easiest differentiation method from an outside-in perspective is the scope analysis. Taking the NP process developed in section 3.5.7 as the baseline, the coverage of available systems can be mapped.

	Vendor/developer	Solution name	Demand estimate	Network structure	Route selection	Flight frequency	Flight scheduling	Fleet assignment	Aircraft routing	Crew assignment		Input data/ Data sources used
Integrated NP solutions	Lufthansa Systems	NetLine	☑	☑	☑	☑	☑	☑	☑	☑	☑	OAG/Innovata, MIDT data, Fare data
	Sabre	AirVision & AirCentre	☑	☑	☑	☑	☑	☑	☑	☑	☑	Not disclosed
	Seabury	APGNet & APGFam	☑	☑	☑	☑	☑	☑	☑	☑	☑	Not disclosed
	Aviation Research Technologies	NetworkPlanner	☑	☑	☑	☑	☑	☑	☑			QSI data, "O&D market information", fleet data, cost & revenue assumptions
	Avio LINX	RAIDO			☑	☑	☑	☑	☑	☑	☑	forecast cost and revenue, expected passenger demand, fleet and crew capacity, flight time limitations, etc.
Strategic NP solutions	ICF	NetWorks	☑	☑	☑	☑	☑					QSI data, "O&D market information", existing airline schedules
	L.E.K.	CompetiShare	☑	☑	☑	☑						Industry databases, airline internal data, strategic assumptions
	Lift	LiftPlan, LiftHub, LiftSched, LiftFleet	☑		☑	☑	☑	☑				QSI, O&D demand data
Tactical NP solutions	AIMS	Commercial Planning - Flight Scheduling					☑	☑	☑	☑	☑	Not specified
	APM	SchedulePlanner, CrewLogic					☑	☑	☑	☑	☑	Not specified
	AVES	AVES Scheduler					☑	☑	☑	☑	☑	Not specified
	Hitit	Crane.SP, Crane.CREW					☑	☑	☑	☑		Not specified
	Optym	Amadeus SkyMax					☑	☑	☑			Flight frequency, Fleet info, Airport info, Revenue forecast per flight
	PDC	Flight planning tool					☑	☑	☑			Not specified

Figure 4.8 – Market overview over commercially available IT systems for airline network planning[134]

[134] List derived from Airline Software (2017); specific information derived from solution websites: AIMS (2017); APM Technologies (2017); AVES – Flight Operations Management Systems (2017); Aviation Research Technologies (2017); Aviolinx (2017); HITIT (2017); ICF

The Digital Solution Directory from Airline Software (2017) contains 66 IT solutions in the NP and scheduling field. Only 14 of these solutions cover more than two planning steps, all of which are included in Figure 4.8.

Three different types of IT solutions can be discerned. *Integrated network planning solutions* cover the entire NP process and may include various individual solutions bundled as a single suite. Currently, there are three all-in-one solutions provided by Sabre (AirVision Suite), Lufthansa Systems (NetLine Suite), and Seabury-Accenture (APG Suite). The Network Planner developed by Aviation Research Technologies encompasses almost the entire NP process and lacks only crew planning and flight operations functionality. Conversely, the RAIDO solution from Aviolinx omits network structure and demand estimates, otherwise covering the entire process from route selection to the flight operations phase.

Strategic network planning solutions focus on the strategic NP steps up to scheduling and fleet assignment. Typical examples for this are the solutions from L.E.K. Consulting and ICF, partly also the NP suite offered by Lift, a relatively new company in the market.

Tactical network planning solutions focus on technical schedule optimization and usually start with the flight scheduling process step. The IT tools from AVES, APM, and AIMS cover all process steps up to the flight operations phase, whereas the Crane Suite from HITIT has no flight operations functionality. The solutions developed by Optym and PDC only cover the core process steps of scheduling, fleet assignment, and aircraft routing.

System developer firms can also be distinguished in three groups. The first one includes large aviation system developers, covering a wide range of business processes. Sabre, Lufthansa Systems, and APM Technologies belong to this group. Boutique system developers that focus only on NP and flight operations are the second group, which includes Optym, Lift,

(2017); L.E.K. Consulting (2017); Lift – airline planning solutions (2017); Lufthansa Systems (2017); Optym (2017); PDC Aviation (2017); Sabre (2017); Seabury Consulting (2017)

PDC Aviation, Aviolinx, AVES, and AIMS. The third group are consultancies that have started to market their proprietary decision-support tools. L.E.K, Seabury (now part of Accenture), ICF, and Aviation Research Technologies are part of this last group.

It is remarkable that all the available solutions are provided by system developing companies with a specific focus on aviation. Large commercial software development companies such as Infosys, SAP, Oracle, or IBM do not offer any NP solutions for airlines. This further supports the hypothesis that airline NP is highly specialized and interlinked with other airline business processes.

4.3.2 Current use of IT tools in the case study airlines

Despite the diverse offer of IT solutions for NP, the participating case study airlines utilize solutions from only three providers. The NetLine suite developed by Lufthansa Systems is the most widely used NP system in the case study group. The NetLine/Sched application that covers the tactical planning process is used by five airlines, the strategic NetLine/Plan by one airline. AIMS and Sabre solutions are each used by two airlines. LCC 1 does not use any airline NP solution, relying solely on Microsoft Excel. Eight out of the nine case study airlines use Microsoft Excel as an important tool, making it the most important unspecific IT tool.

Furthermore, two airlines built their own market forecasting models, as they deemed existing ready-made market forecasts to be unreliable (compare previous section). One cargo airline employs a cargo-specific revenue management system (CHAMP) to inform NP decisions. Figure 4.9 summarizes the currently used IT systems.

System developer	Network planning system	FSC 1	FSC 2	LCC 1	LCC 2	SCA 1	SCA 2	CAR 1	CAR 2	CAR 3
Sabre	*AirVision™ Profit Manager*		☑							
	AirVision™ Fleet Manager	☑								
Lufthansa Systems	*NetLine/Plan*	☑								
	NetLine/Sched	☑			☑	☑		☑		☑
AIMS	*AIMS Scheduling*						☑		☑	
Others	*MS Office Excel*	☑	☑	☑	☑	☑	☑		☑	☑
	Self-developed market model	☑						☑		
	CHAMP								☑	

Figure 4.9 – IT systems currently used by the case study participants for network planning[135]

The reliance on Microsoft Excel and IT solutions for tactical NP has also been reflected in the current degree of process automation. While demand forecasting is partly automated in the NP process, strategic NP mostly remains a manual process with little IT support. Standardized business case calculations are[136] the only noteworthy automation, even in large airlines, before the flight scheduling process step. While FSC 1 and FSC 2 have started to automate the first steps beyond business plan creation, all other airlines rely on a fully manual strategic NP process.

With the exception of LCC 1 and LCC 2, the tactical NP process is more automated than the strategic planning process. In most airlines, the standard AIMS and NetLine functionality is used. FSC 1 and CAR 1 are currently working towards a complete automation of the tactical planning process. However, the extreme complexity of airline NP requires non-exact optimi-

[135] Source: Own illustration.

[136] With a fleet size of more than 100 aircraft.

zation heuristics that can cause significant re-planning in case of a parameter change (Kölker & Lütjens, 2015, p. 901). Figure 4.10 displays the current state of automation in airline NP graphically.

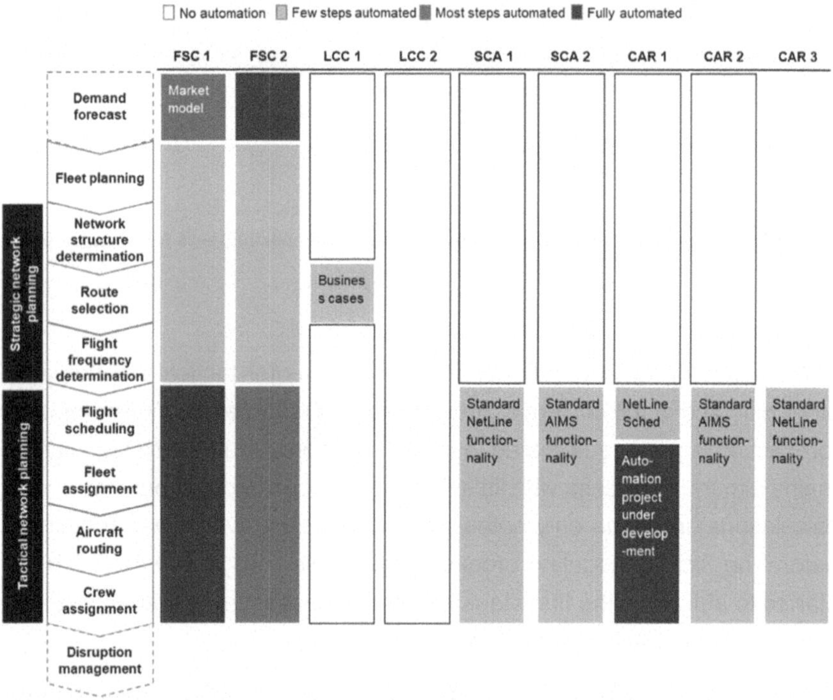

Figure 4.10 – Degree of automation in current NP process[137]

4.3.3 *Data capability of current IT tools*

Information on the data processing capability of current systems is difficult to obtain, since publicly available information exists for only 7 of the 14 IT solutions presented in section 4.3.1. When analyzing the publicly available

[137] Source: Own illustration.

information (right column of Figure 4.8), the commonalities among the different IT solutions are evident at the onset. Most IT systems rely on existing schedules, including revenue and QSI information and an O&D level forecast of expected demand. Airline internal data, such as operating cost and past booking data, as well as strategic assumptions on market and demand development can be handled by most systems. Not a single IT solution for NP claims to support real-time data, such as live bookings or search-engine data.

One system provider is included in the additional source tri-angulation and it provided information on the data capabilities of the NP solution. System developers distinguished primary from secondary data integration. The primary data integration occurs when databases are processed and analyzed directly by the system. In secondary data integration, assumptions based on primary data are entered without replicating the primary data structure. Only two data types from the analysis in section 4.2.2 are integrated by default, namely airport characteristics and publicly available statistical data on actually flown flights. Seven additional data types are mandatory to run the NP application. These need to be provided by the airlines and include flight schedules, MIDT data, fare data, operating cost, slots and aircraft characteristics. Furthermore, there are mandatory secondary data that need to be translated as assumptions. Market estimates, economic forecasts, and oil price forecasts are key assumptions to be entered for this.

Besides the mandatory data types, there are additional optional data types that can be processed by the NP IT system. Real-time internal booking data and external GDS data can be incorporated in addition to airport traffic statistics and traffic rights. Data from booking platforms (such as Skyscanner) is currently in a pilot testing phase.

Five data types cannot be integrated in the NP solution. Neither demographic data nor real-time slots and any data on external shocks are envisaged. Interestingly, these data types are widely used among the case study airlines[138]. Figure 4.11 summarizes the data integration in an exemplary NP IT solution.

Information type	Data types	Integration in network planning solution
Demand	Ready-made market forecasts	Secondary (assumptions)
	Economic forecasts	Secondary (assumptions)
	Demographic data	No
	Information on unconstrained demand	Pilot testing of primary integration
	Real-time booking curves	Primary integration possible
	Real-time booking data from GDS	Primary integration possible
	Flight schedules	Primary (airline provides data)
	MIDT data	Primary (airline provides data)
	Flight event data on actually flown flights	Primary (included)
	Fare data	Primary (airline provides data)
	Airport traffic statistics	Primary integration possible
Cost	Oil price forecasts	Secondary (assumptions)
	Airport and traffic fees	Primary (airline provides data)
	Other direct operating cost	Primary (airline provides data)
Planning constraints	Airport slot allocation	Primary (airline provides data)
	Real-time slot availability	No
	Traffic rights including overflight rights	Primary integration possible
	Aircraft specifications	Primary (airline provides data)
	Airport characteristics	Primary (included)
External shocks	Meteorological events	No
	Political events	No
	Competitor-related events	No

Figure 4.11 – Exemplary integration of the currently used data sources in airline network planning IT solution[139]

4.4 Performance measurement of airline network planning

The performance measurement in airline NP is closely connected to the role and responsibilities of the NP department in the organization (Goedeking, 2010, p. 99). Revenue, cost, or profit responsibility should define the primary KPIs in airline NP; however, secondary KPIs too can complement

[138] Among these, 66% use demographic data, 56% use real-time slot information, and 78% use at least one external shock data type.

[139] Source: Own illustration.

the performance measurement. Section 4.4.1 introduces the different NP responsibilities across the case study group and links it to the primary NP targets. Section 4.4.2 then presents the currently used primary and secondary KPIs across the case study group.

4.4.1 Planning and optimization goals for NP departments

Airline NP departments can be charged with revenue, cost, and profit responsibilities (see section 3.2.4). In our case study group, five airlines assigned profit responsibility to their NP department, while three airlines opted for cost responsibility and one chose revenue responsibility for this (see Figure 4.12).

One of the SCAs follows a shared-revenue responsibility model, in which revenue management and NP are jointly accountable for revenue generation. This makes the NP department a de-facto revenue center and requires their close collaboration with P&RM. Both the LCCs and CAR 3 charge their NP departments with a cost responsibility, which necessitates close engagement with flight operations and other operative departments. All other airlines place NP as a mediator between revenue centers – usually marketing and P&RM – and cost centers. Thus, NP holds a global profit responsibility that underlines its strategic importance for airlines' financial success.

The targets of an organizational unit should align with its role and responsibilities. If a NP department is considered a profit center, the primary target should ideally be profit maximization. Similarly, a cost center should strive to minimize cost and a revenue center should maximize revenue. Across our case study group, only seven airlines have aligned the stated primary target of NP with the assigned role for the department.

All profit centers are measured against aggregate route profitability (which excludes network effects) or network profitability. Here, the targets are aligned with NP departments' role as profit centers. In CAR 3, the sole purpose of the NP department is to minimize operating cost to an acceptable service level. Similarly, LCC 2's NP department is tasked with maximizing their asset utilization, hence minimizing unit cost. In all of these airlines, the targets are clearly aligned with the role of the NP departments.

Airline	NP responsibility	Primary NP target	Used KPIs (also for secondary NP targets)
FSC 1	Profit center	Network profitability	▪ Network profitability ▪ Forecast accuracy ▪ NP FTE efficiency
FSC 2	Profit center	Aggregated route profitability	▪ Route profitability ▪ Forecast accuracy ▪ Aircraft utilization
LCC 1	Cost center	Aggregated route profitability	▪ Route profitability (incl. new route performance) ▪ Aircraft utilization ▪ Operating cost minimization
LCC 2	Cost center	Aircraft utilization	▪ Aircraft utilization ▪ Schedule robustness ▪ NP FTE efficiency
SCA 1	Profit center	Aggregated route profitability	▪ Route profitability ▪ Aircraft utilization ▪ Operating cost minimization
SCA 2	Revenue center	Aircraft utilization	▪ Route profitability ▪ Aircraft utilization ▪ Forecast accuracy (only "negative surprises")
CAR 1	Profit center	Network profitability	▪ Network profitability ▪ Schedule robustness ▪ Load factor
CAR 2	Profit center	Aggregated route profitability	▪ Route profitability ▪ Aircraft utilization ▪ NP FTE efficiency
CAR 3	Cost center	Minimization of operating cost	▪ Operating cost minimization

Figure 4.12 – Performance management in NP departments[140]

LCC 1 assigns a cost center role to its NP department but ranks aggregated route profitability as most important target. Although secondary NP targets, such as aircraft utilization and operating cost minimization, are aligned with the departments' cost center role, the mismatch of role and primary target may result in difficulties in prioritizing big data investments for NP. SCA 2 exhibits an even greater mismatch in this regard. Despite assigning a joint revenue responsibility to its NP department, none of the

[140] Source: Own illustration.

primary or secondary targets focus on revenue generation. The primary target "asset utilization" is a cost target, and all secondary targets are cost or profit targets as well.

In summary, the targets in airlines, barring a few, are well aligned with its role and responsibilities. However, SCA 2 and LCC 1 present misalignments that can potentially complicate the benefit analysis pertaining to big data investments.

4.4.2 KPIs currently used for airline network planning

The primary cost, revenue, or profit objectives can be measured through a variety of direct and indirect KPIs. While direct KPIs express the immediate change in profit, revenues, and cost, indirect KPIs contribute towards the desirable improvements in direct KPIs. Since no pre-defined KPI framework for airline NP exists in the literature, a new framework has been designed on the basis of general airline KPIs summarized by Sterzenbach et al. (2013, pp. 389–416). This framework incorporates the KPIs used in the NP departments of the case study group (see Figure 4.13).

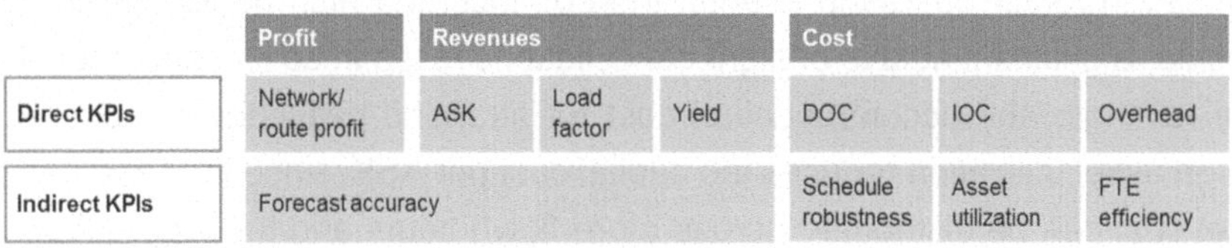

Figure 4.13 – KPI framework for airline network planning[141]

Direct KPIs squarely contribute to the profit and loss statement of an airline and are thus global performance measures within these organization. Airlines with a significant share of connecting traffic usually rely on network

[141] Source: Own illustration following Sterzenbach et al. (2013).

profit calculations, whereas other airlines use aggregate route profit figures[142]. Revenues depend on the available seat kilometers, which is considered the unit measure of the total offered capacity controlled for route length[143], the average load factor, and the yield per seat kilometer. In simple words, revenues can be raised if more capacity is offered, a larger share of capacity is sold, and the charged ticket price per kilometer increases. Airline cost are typically segmented as direct and indirect operating cost and non-operating overhead cost (see section 3.4.4).

Direct KPIs are influenced by many different organizational units of an airline. However, indirect KPIs can typically be associated with one specific department within the airline. NP departments across the case study group feature four major indirect KPIs, which are mostly under the complete control of the respective NP department. If demand forecasting is in the remit of NP, forecast accuracy is a crucial measure to assess planning quality, which enables network optimization, capacity planning, and pricing. Hence, it has an indirect effect on both profit and revenues. NP can also indirectly affect cost KPIs in three ways. First, a schedule's robustness reduces irregular operation events, thereby incurring high direct operating costs. Significant delays or flight cancellations result in costly repayments, re-routings, and accommodation cost for stranded passengers. Second, high asset utilization reduces the capital cost per ASK, since the fixed capital cost can be distributed across more flown hours and thus more ASK. Third, the NP department itself can become more efficient and reduce overhead cost. A typical efficiency measure is the number of routes

[142] See section 3.4.4 for a detailed discussion on the differences between network profit and route profit.

[143] Take a flight with an Airbus A320 from Berlin to London as example: 180 seats are flown 950 kilometers, which results in 180 * 950 = 171,000 ASK for this specific flight.

planned/managed per full-time equivalent (FTE)[144], which can be increased by using more useful information, IT system support, and automation.

The most frequently used NP KPI among the case study group is network/route profitability. It serves as the primary KPI for six NP departments and as secondary KPI for one other (see Figure 4.14).

Direct KPI | Indirect KPI | P Primary target | S Secondary target

Airline	NP responsibility	Profit	Revenues				Cost					
		Network/ route profit	Forecast accuracy	ASK	Load factor	Yield	DOC	IOC	Overhead	Schedule robustness	Asset utilization	FTE efficiency
FSC 1	Profit center	P	S									S
FSC 2	Profit center	P	S								S	
LCC 1	Cost center	P					S	S			S	
LCC 2	Cost center									S	P	S
SCA 1	Profit center	P					S	S			S	
SCA 2	Revenue center	S	S								P	
CAR 1	Profit center	P			S					S		
CAR 2	Profit center	P									S	S
CAR 3	Cost center						P	P				

Figure 4.14 – Primary and secondary NP performance targets in case study airlines[145]

Asset utilization ranks second, being the primary target for two NP departments and secondary target in four airlines. The minimization of direct and indirect operating cost is the primary KPI for CAR 3 and secondary target for two more airlines. Forecast accuracy, FTE efficiency, schedule robustness, and load factor are other subsidiary KPIs for NP in the airline case study sample. Three potential KPIs are not employed at all, two of those

---

[144] An FTE of 1.0 is equivalent to one full-time employee (40h per week).

[145] Source: Own illustration.

being the revenue KPIs “ASK” and “yield” and another being the direct overhead cost KPI. The fact that only one airline chooses a direct revenue KPI for its NP department also validates the finding that NP departments are considered profit or cost centers rather than revenue centers.

5 Big data opportunities for airline network planning

This chapter builds on existing research and practice to develop tangible BDOs for airline NP. First, the information needs of airline network planners are derived leveraging the currently used data sources and interview results from the case study group (sub-chapter 5). The BDOs that address the identified information requirements are described in detail in sub-chapter 5.2. In the last sub-chapter 5.3, the potential of BDOs to improve airline NP is qualitatively evaluated by network planners, and the feasibility of implementation is assessed. This chapter concludes with a classification of BDOs based on their potential and feasibility.

5.1 Information needs for airline network planning

Data needs to be translated into useful information to generate value for decision making (Ackoff, 1989, p. 4). In section 4.2.2, four major information objects, which airline network planners require information on, were identified. These can further be specified in information needs, which describe a cluster of logically similar information on a specific information object. Section 5.1.1 defines the relevant information needs for this study. In order to prepare the discussion on potential BDOs in sub-chapter 5.2, section 5.1.2 associates currently used data sources to specific information needs and indicates the gaps to be addressed with big data opportunities.

5.1.1 Definition of information needs for airline NP

Air transport demand is a broad concept involving all relevant actors in the market. Hence, airline network planners need information on various groups of actors as well as on the entire market system. Especially early in the NP process, long-term demand forecasts depend on a holistic perspective of the entire transportation market, including the air transport market as a specific sub-market. Furthermore, relevant trends in travel and transportation must be identified and evaluated. This results in two concrete information needs, the holistic *transportation demand forecast* and a

M. Schosser, *Big Data to Improve Strategic Network Planning in Airlines*,
Schriftenreihe der HHL Leipzig Graduate School of Management,
https://doi.org/10.1007/978-3-658-27582-2_5

more specific *trend identification.* Since both information needs focus on the entire market, the differences must be pointed out.

Transportation demand forecasts ultimately result in a concrete estimation of the people willing to travel over a specific time window between a certain O&D pair. The granularity of these estimates varies as do the forecast accuracy. High-level *transportation demand forecast* estimates the number of travelers across all transportation modes between large geographical entities, such as countries or continents on a yearly base. Whereas, granular *transportation demand forecasts* distinguish demand according to transportation mode and specify geographical areas down to individual catchment areas and hourly time windows. The value for airline network planners obviously increases with a higher degree of granularity and accuracy. *Transportation demand forecasts* tend to become more precise with a decreasing time horizon. Airline network planners use this information in all steps of strategic NP and even for tactical fleet assignment decisions (see Figure 5.1).

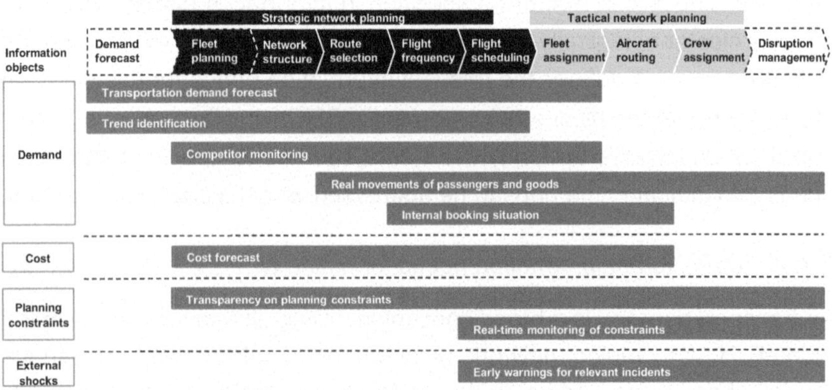

Figure 5.1 – Information needs throughout the airline NP process[146]

[146] Source: Own illustration.

Trend identification focuses on systematic changes in the transportation demand. On a higher level, this includes the identification of growth markets, mega-trends, and general travel preferences of customers. On a more granular level, *trend identification* aims to discover the recurring micro-seasonality for specific destinations (e.g., due to fairs or holidays) or the mismatches between accommodation and transportation supply for a specific region. While the end result of *transportation demand forecasts* is an estimated absolute demand figure, *trend identification* indicates the expected relative changes, thereby complementing the *transportation demand forecast.* Thus, airline network planners mostly rely on *trend identification* during the strategic NP phase up to the final scheduling.

Besides the information on the entire market, airline network planners require information on its main actors, mainly competitors, customers, and the airline itself. Information on competitors can be pooled as *competitor monitoring. Competitor monitoring* focuses either on regular or irregular operations. Information on regular competitor operations includes the backward-looking analysis of actually flown flights, delays, traffic volume, and reported yield. Forward-looking information consists mainly of published schedules, real-time fare data, and news analysis of planned routes or fleet decisions. The monitoring of regular operations is most relevant for strategic NP, as it informs an airline's route and schedule decisions. In contrast, irregular operations monitoring aims to exploit the short-term changes of a competitor's operation. This includes strikes, flight cancellations, and other unforeseen events that may justify the offering of additional flights or changes in fleet assignment. Consequently, information on irregular competitor operations are most relevant for tactical NP.

Information on airline customers has become possibly the most important need of P&RM departments (Chen et al., 2017, p. 25). While the focus of P&RM is mainly on understanding the customers' individual preferences, airline network planners try to understand the granular movement patterns of passengers and cargo. These so-called *real movements of passengers and goods* provide complete information on the real origin and the real destination of a passenger or a cargo item. Ideally, airline network planners should wish to know the exact address of both origin and destination for every passenger and every cargo item. Furthermore, even the travel patterns of non-airline customers are highly relevant for the identification of potential routes that can compete with railway and individual traffic. The *real movements of passengers and goods* are most relevant to the strategic planning steps, from route selection to flight scheduling. Cargo airlines especially benefit from the real-time location information of cargo items when a delayed delivery requires short-term re-planning.

The internal demand perspective of airlines is mostly shaped by the *internal booking situation.* Based on their experience and the current forecast, airlines define expected booking levels for specific flights during a defined period before departure. If the bookings are significantly above or below their expected level, schedule adjustments become necessary. The potential actions to adjust the schedule range from a permanent change in flight frequency to the addition or cancellation of individual flights up to a change in fleet assignment to reflect the specific internal demand. Accordingly, information on the *internal booking situation* is of utmost relevance in the mid- to short-term airline NP.

The information object "cost" is typically associated with the need for only one type of information: the *cost forecast. Cost forecasts* are typically structured in line with the airline cost classification scheme (Niehaus et al., 2009, p. 177). Because overhead costs are not in the remit of NP, the need for information is focused on direct and indirect operating cost. Most airlines utilize internal cost calculations to satisfy this need for information. *Cost forecasts* are relevant in all the strategic and tactical NP process steps, as they are required for any profitability analysis.

Information on planning constraints can be distinguished as two specific information needs. *Transparency on planning constraints* is concerned with the collection and organization of all relevant information for the NP process. This includes airport and aircraft characteristics, an updated list of available slots, and existing traffic right agreements. Airline network planners apply this information during the strategic NP phase to avoid technical planning mistakes[147]. The *real-time monitoring of planning constraints* checks for both the short-term changes in existing constraints (e.g., temporary runway closures) and the availability of slots and traffic rights for all tactical NP decisions. This need for information is relevant when airline network planners adjust the planned schedule by changing aircraft types or re-scheduling flights.

Finally, external shocks create the need for *early warnings for relevant incidents*. Airline network planners are primarily concerned with the political and meteorological events that may have a permanent impact on the travel demand or passengers' capability to fly to a specific destination. Political events include long strikes, travel restrictions, or conflicts that affect the stability of a destination. Meteorological events are usually less relevant for NP, since they usually cause only short-time interruptions. However, major catastrophes such as floods, tsunamis, or tropical storms may influence travel demand in the long term. Thus, *early warnings for relevant incidents* are relevant to both strategic and tactical NP, depending on the impact and severity of the shock.

5.1.2 Satisfaction of information needs with current data use

In this section, the currently used data sources are assigned to the information needs derived in the previous section. Figure 5.2 visualizes the allocation of currently used data sources to information needs. The usefulness and reliability classifications are included as the shaded areas of the data sources.

---

[147] Exemplary technical planning mistakes: aircraft too heavy for airport, night curfew not respected, aircraft range not sufficient for stage length, slot or traffic rights unavailable.

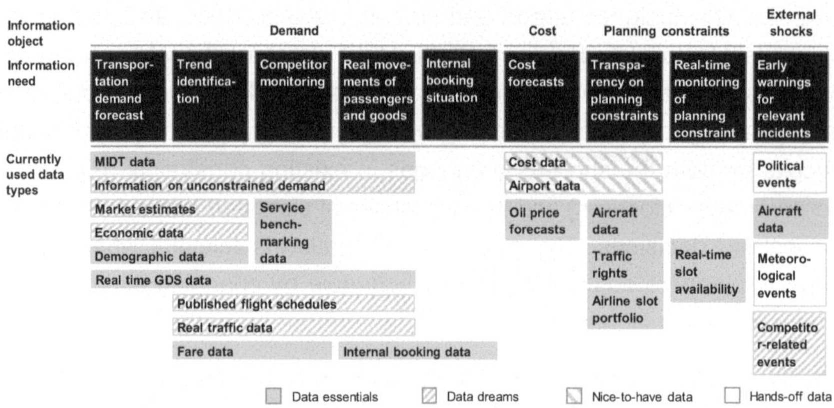

Figure 5.2 - Allocation of currently used data sources to airline NP information needs[148]

Transportation demand forecast

The current transportation demand forecasts are mostly developed around ready-made market forecasts and MIDT data, which are enriched by assumptions on economic development and demographic factors. One of the airlines uses clickstream data from booking websites to model their unconstrained demand, which is already considered a big data type. The usefulness of all five currently used data sources is rated as high; however, the reliability varies widely (see Figure 4.6, p. 180). Demographic data, MIDT data, and real-time GDS data are considered fairly reliable, whereas ready-made market forecasts, economic forecasts, and clickstream data from booking websites are considered rather unreliable. Furthermore, MIDT and GDS data cover only part of the market, namely the tickets sold via Global Distribution Systems. All of the data sources, excepting unconstrained demand, deliver data on actual bookings but not on the booking intentions.

---

148 Source: Own illustration.

Thus, there are multiple big data opportunities to improve the need for information on transportation demand forecast. First, BDOs may improve the reliability of economic forecasts, general market estimates, and unconstrained demand. Second, the data pool can be extended using data on booking intentions to predict actual bookings better. Third, a suitable proxy for real-time data on cargo demand is urgently required, as MIDT and GDS data cover passenger bookings only.

Trend identification

Trend identification relies on the same data sources as transportation demand forecast. In addition, airlines reference published flight schedules, real traffic data, and fare data to perform ex-post analyses and create time series in order to discover any relevant change. All currently used data sources exclusively contain airline-specific data. However, travel trends are often influenced by factors independent from the airlines, such as increasing tourism interest in a destination or specific events, such as fairs or concerts. Big data can add an outside-in perspective to complement the currently used data sources. In addition, big data needs to improve the reliability of the five data sources in the "data-dream" cluster (see Figure 5.2).

Competitor monitoring

Present day competitor monitoring occurs on multiple dimensions. Past traffic and fare data are evaluated through ex-post competition analyses. The current offering can be compared based on published schedules and service-benchmarking data. Bookings of competitors can be analyzed ex-post employing MIDT data or real-time GDS data. Flight schedules and traffic data appear to be the weak links, presenting great improvement potential in data reliability. Short-term schedule changes and aircraft type changes are usually not recorded in published flight schedules nor are charter flights. Big data can address these reliability issues by providing a complete picture on performed flights, complementing the currently used data sources.

Real movement of passengers and goods

Most data sources provide only the air travel–specific origin and destination, which includes the first and the last airport on the itinerary. MIDT data also contains the booking agent, but neither any personal address nor the internet protocol (IP) address used while making the booking. If a booking is made through the airline's website, most airline can locate the IP address, which indicated either the real origin or the real destination. However, no current data type can provide comprehensive real O&D information. Cargo airlines usually have the real shipping O&D for individual shipments, since it is a part of the air waybill. However, many freight forwarders consolidate individual shipments and issue new air waybills for such shipments. The shipping addresses are then the forwarder's airport facilities, which do not provide any further information on the real O&D of the consolidated cargo. Both passenger and cargo airlines can use big data opportunities to fill this gap and produce reliable information on the real O&D of their customers.

Internal booking situation

The internal booking situation is analyzed according to the airline's own booking data. In many airlines, P&RM has already established sophisticated analytics and forecasting tools, often linking their booking data to a 360-degree view of the customer. Furthermore, the airlines in the case study group consider real-time booking curves as both highly reliable and useful. There exist big data applications for hyper-granular customer prediction. However, improving the analysis of the internal booking situation does not appear to be a priority of airline NP departments.

Cost forecasts

Two of the three main data sources are highly reliable but of limited utility. Both operating cost and airport fees are considered must-have factors by airline network planners, since these need to be included in the route and network profitability calculations. However, they are not in the remit of the

NP departments. Flight operations departments across airlines are currently investing heavily in big data applications in order to reduce operating cost; however, little is invested to improve cost forecasts. From the airline NP perspective, there seems to be little need to invest in BDOs to improve cost forecasts.

Transparency on planning constraints

All of the currently used data sources are highly reliable for airline NP. However, many interview participants confessed that the data sources are not connected, and the actual useful information has to be compiled manually. Big data not only consists of new data sources but also a combination of existing data sources. Therefore, there is great big data harmonization and automation potential in planning constraint data. The harmonization aspect is considered part of the real-time planning constraint solutions, which are introduced subsequently.

Real-time monitoring of planning constraints

At present, the real-time monitoring of planning constraints is limited to the use of slot information systems, which mostly cover airports in free market economies[149]. These platforms are meant for information purposes only; a trading or swapping function does not exist. Furthermore, there is no means to track the use of traffic rights, e.g., for overflight contingents. These shortcomings of the current data sources are concrete opportunities to establish big data solutions and add a new real-time dimension in planning constraint monitoring. At the same time, a real-time platform should link all the available existing data sources to guarantee transparency in the status quo of planning constraints.

---

[149] ACL International covers UK, Canada, Ireland, Luxemburg, New Zealand, Poland, and the United Arab Emirates. e-Airportslots covers Australia, France, Belgium, Germany, Netherlands, Philippines, Spain, Tunisia, and Mexico.

Early warning systems for relevant incidents

The current early warning systems on meteorological and political events have been proved to be both unreliable and useless. While meteorological warning systems may benefit from a larger time horizon[150], political warning systems must deliver more airline-specific results. New big data technologies, such as natural language processing, may be able to increase relevance significantly. The same applies for competitor information, which is currently compiled via daily news briefings.

5.2 Development and evaluation of BDOs for airline NP

A two-step idea generation process identified potential BDOs for airline NP. First, the big data types in the literature were reviewed and contrasted to news articles and reports on the big data types used in other airline functions. In the second step, concrete ideas are developed to address specific information needs in preparation for the second interview round with airline network planners. Section 5.2.1 demonstrates the development of 23 specific BDOs. These are subsequently detailed in sections 5.2.2–5.2.7, which are structured as per the primarily addressed information needs.

5.2.1 Specific BDOs for airline NP information needs

Yaqoob et al. (2016, p. 1234) elaborated on social media, the Internet of Things (IoT), mobile device data, and other web-based content as primary big data types. These data types have emerged over the past 15 years. They produce large volumes of both structured and unstructured data, which can often be transmitted in real time. Traditional “small” data types

[150] The current systems warn for specific meteorological events, such as a thunderstorm or a hurricane. However, a generalized analysis, such as one on the occurrence of fog at a specific airport, can indicate specific times of day during certain months with a high fog risk, thus informing scheduling.

complement the big data types. The airline-specific big data types identified in section 3.6.5 can be classified under these categories (see Table 5.1).

Table 5.1 – Classification of airline big data types[151]

Airline big data type	Social media data	Internet of Things	Mobile device data	Other web-based content	Traditional small data
Flight tracking data		x			
Airport data					x
Meteorological data		x			
Airline info data	x			x	x
Market data	x			x	x
Passenger data	x		x	x	x
Aircraft data		x			x
Air Safety Reports					x
Social media data	x				
Mobile location data			x		
Search engine data				x	

Social media comprise services such as social networks, (micro-)blogs, and review platforms, which present valuable information on passengers, competitors, and the general market development. Social networks contain an abundance of *demographic data*, which can be accessed to improve granularity and reliability of demographic customer profiling beyond aggregated statistical bureau data. Social media data can also be used to improve economic forecasting. *Consumer confidence* can be measured in real time based on unstructured social network and social blogging data

151 Source: Own illustration.

(Tuckett et al., 2014). Social media data can then be used in combination with search engine data to determine the specific or aggregated *consumer price elasticity* (Ghose, Ipeirotis, & Li, 2018). Travel-specific social media, such as travel rating platforms or travel blogs, present valuable data on transportation streams. Reviews and visitor volumes can indicate *shifts in travel trends* (Bowen, 2015). Clickstream data[152] from travel rating platforms can also reveal *travel patterns of consumer groups*. The analysis of specific *events in social networks* may yield a better prediction of one-time travel flows, e.g., for large concerts or industry fairs.

The IoT provides multiple BDOs, especially for air cargo network planners. The *location transmitting sensors* attached to individual shipments can reveal the real O&D and further indicate short-term delivery delays. Alternatively, a cheaper RFID-chip can be attached to cargo carrying an *improved electronic air waybill. Flight tracking data* can complement competitor monitoring and fill gaps in MIDT data and published flight schedules. The increasing number of weather-tracking devices can improve the usefulness of long-term *meteorological forecasts*. Similarly, machine learning-based *image recognition tools* can use geo-spatial images to predict the impact of extreme meteorological events and even improve economic forecasting.

Aggregated and anonymized *mobile location data* can draw a seamless picture of all travel movements, independent from the chosen transportation mode. Airline network planners can discern a real-time view on travel behavior, market shares, and real O&Ds.

Furthermore, there are multiple BDOs using other web-based content. The most prominent opportunity is conducting an analysis of search engine data to predict future bookings. This can either be based on *general search engine data* (e.g., Google, Baidu) or on specific *clickstream data from meta-search websites* for flights (e.g., Kayak, Skyscanner). Another important data source is e-commerce platforms (e.g., Amazon, Alibaba).

---

[152] A clickstream is the sequence of hyperlinks followed by a unique website visitor. The clickstream is presented chronologically and allows retracing the search pattern of customers.

Data on cross-border orders can reveal trends in air *cargo demand from e-commerce*; this is predicted to become a major air cargo growth driver in the coming years (IATA, 2017b). Moreover, e-commerce pricing data can be used to *track inflation in real-time* in order to better inform economic forecasts (Cavallo & Rigobon, 2016).

Improved scraping[153] technology enables the collection of information from different web-based services. Airlines can *analyze daily hotel prices* to identify micro-seasonality in specific destinations or identify a supply mismatch between transportation and accommodation. Similarly, cargo airlines can collect *data on industry fairs and related exhibitors* in order to predict cargo flows. Online forwarders quote *public rates on the major shipping lines*, which can indicate the expected booking situations in a manner similar to passenger airline fare intelligence. The scraping of unstructured data in combination with natural language processing (NLP) analytics can vastly improve *news monitoring and political risk assessments*.

Two of the BDOs identified do not fit the classification scheme presented in Table 5.1. First, an *integrated real-time slot trading platform* can facilitate short-term schedule adjustments and decrease the need to freeze the schedule before the IATA slot conferences. A *real-time traffic right information platform* can bundle all the relevant information on global traffic rights and indicate potential violations, e.g., overusing an overfly contingent. In total, 23 BDOs have been identified. Figure 5.3 schematizes the BDOs by their primarily addressed information need[154].

---

[153] Scraping describes a technique in which a computer program extracts data from human-readable output, coming from another program or website.

[154] Please refer to Appendix 17 for a different view structured by the NP process steps.

Big data opportunities	A Transportation demand forecast	B Trend identification	C Competitor monitoring	D Real movements of passengers and goods	E Internal booking situation	F Cost forecasts	G Transparency on planning constraints	H Real-time monitoring of planning constraints	I Early warnings for relevant incidents
A1 Geo-spatial image analysis	■	□	□	□					□
A2 Real-time inflation forecasts	■	□							□
A3 Consumer confidence from social media	■	□							
A4 Detailed demographic profiling with social networks	■								
A5 General search engine data	■	□	□		□				
A6 Click-stream data of meta-search websites	■	□	□	□	□				
A7 Social media mining to determine price elasticity	■				□				
A8 Analysis of rates from online air cargo portals	■	□	□		□				
A9 Analysis of exhibitor data of industry fairs	■	□		□					
A10 Shipping data from e-commerce platforms	■	□	□	□	□				
B1 Analysis of reviews in travel rating communities		■							
B2 Click-stream data from travel platforms	□	■							
B3 Analysis of local hotel prices	□	■			□				
B4 Analysis of events in social networks		■							
C1 Real-time flight tracking with transponder data			■			□		□	□
C2 Network-relevant competitor news monitoring			■						□
D1 Mobile location data from smartphones	□	□	□	■					
D2 Extended electronic AWB with shipper address		□		■					
D3 Location-transmitting sensors for cargo shipments				■	□			□	
H1 Real-time slot trading platform							□	■	
H2 Real-time traffic right information platform						□	□	■	
I1 Global meteorological warning platform	□					□			■
I2 Global political risk assessments	□								■

■ Primary information need addressed □ Secondary information need addressed

Figure 5.3 – Addressed information needs of BDOs[155]

Since many of the BDOs address more than one specific need for information, the secondarily addressed information needs are also displayed in

[155] Source: Own illustration.

light grey. In line with the argumentation presented in the previous subchapter, no BDO is included for internal booking situation and cost forecasts. The transparency in planning constraints is addressed as a secondary need for information in real-time platforms.

The following sections, which are organized according to the addressed information needs, describe each BDO in detail.Appendix 18 summarizes the big data properties of each opportunity and indicates the potential data providers and applicable BDA methods to generate useful information from the data.

5.2.2 Transportation demand forecast

A1 – Geo-spatial image analysis

The current economic forecasts mostly consist of econometric extrapolation models, using indicators at the country or regional level. The most widely used economic growth indicator – GDP – is calculated on the basis of a variety of secondary indicators, such as industrial production and unemployment rate (Angelini et al., 2011, C30). This bears three shortcomings for its use in airline NP. First, ensuring a high data quality of the input indicators requires a thorough statistical recording of economic activity. Developing countries often do not have acceptable data quality standards in place to support meaningful economic growth forecasts (Klein, 2001, pp. 65–69). Second, current growth forecasts are rarely available on the local level. Especially in the route selection process, accurate local economic activity forecasts can inform the choice between several airport candidates within a shared catchment area. Third, global growth forecasts are usually updated only on a quarterly base[156]. Thus, these changes in economic activity are only incorporated after a significant time lag.

The analysis of geo-spatial images, which usually are captured using satellites but more recently also with drones, can help overcome all three shortcomings of traditional growth forecasting. In the scientific community, Henderson, Storeygard, and Weil (2012) pioneered the approach and showed that the nighttime light intensity analysis is a better predictor for economic growth in developing countries than traditional forecasts. Similarly, Jean et al. (2016) have predicted poverty levels with this approach. Keola, Andersson, and Hall (2015) have contributed land cover data as an additional image-based indicator for economic forecasts. Gennaioli et al. (2014) proved that geo-spatial image analysis generates robust economic forecasts on sub-regional level.

Several start-ups are now commercializing geo-spatial imaging data. The Japanese company Nowcast uses nighttime data to estimate sub-regional economic growth (Allan & Ito, 2016). The American start-ups Orbital Insight and SpaceKnow have developed industry-specific image analysis applications, including hyper-granular economic forecasts (Komissarov, 2017). All of these companies use supervised machine learning to inform the algorithms to recognize specific patterns within satellite or aerial images. The list of recognizable items is becoming longer every day. Orbital Insight analyzes mass retail revenue by counting cars in supermarket parking lots or construction activity by the deployment of construction cranes (Orbital Insight, 2018). SpaceKnow predicts trade flows by counting the shipping containers in port storages and truck movements on highways (SpaceKnow, 2018).

---

[156] The International Monetary Fund updated the World Economic Outlook quarterly, Word Bank, and OECD every six months.

The primary use case for airline NP is the precise analysis of local economic activity, which can improve both the reliability and usefulness of economic forecasts. Furthermore, a geo-spatial image analysis can reveal the travel and trade trends by counting vehicles in tourist destinations or ships and trucks on trade lanes. If the frequency of imaging is further increased[157], image analysis can be used to monitor competitors by revealing the position of spare aircraft, maintenance activities, or cargo shipment routing. Similarly, real O&D monitoring can become feasible, perhaps more so for cargo than for passengers. Outsized cargo can be tracked from the real origin to destination and reveal all the involved transportation providers. Several companies already use this technology for their early warning systems for political risks and natural disasters, which can also become relevant for airline NP (Komissarov, 2017).

Geo-spatial imaging data is of utmost relevance for the NP process steps of demand forecast and route selection. Demand forecast can be based on much more granular economic forecasting, allowing for more accurate O&D-specific forecasts. Route selection can benefit as granular growth data informs idea generation (e.g., what is the next best Chinese airport to serve) and airport decisions in large agglomerations with multiple airports.

A2 – Real-time inflation forecasts

High inflation rates directly influence the air transportation demand and indirectly endanger revenues if tickets are sold in local currencies (Wadud, 2014). Inflation measurement and forecasts are often unreliable, especially in countries with high inflation rates. In a sample of Latin American countries, Jalles (2017) found that inflation forecasts are highly volatile and not dependable. Extreme cases, such as that of Venezuela, show that prolonged high levels of inflation significantly affect the demand for air travel, as it lowers the purchasing power of the population (Echenique, 2018).

---

[157] The current maximum data frequency is daily (Orbital Insight, 2018).

Furthermore, the official inflation statistics are not reliable in some countries.

Driven by the manipulated official inflation statistics in Argentina, researchers at the Massachusetts Institute of Technology (MIT) began recording online retail prices to monitor inflation (Cavallo & Rigobon, 2016). The so-called "Billion Prices Project" has been expanded subsequently, and it is now providing daily inflation figures for 22 countries based entirely on online retail data (The Billion Prices Project, 2018). The data is commercialized by the spin-off PriceStats (PriceStats, 2018).

Real-time inflation measuring and forecasting can improve both the usefulness and reliability of economic forecasts. The data can also reveal short-term trends and thus serve as an early warning system for political risks, e.g., for protests due to high inflation or poor economic development. Airline network planners can anticipate routes with high demand risk better due to inflation and thus adjust flight frequencies or the route mix. It impacts the three NP process steps of demand forecasting, route selection, and flight frequency determination.

A3 – Consumer confidence measurement with social media

Consumer confidence indices are the central input factors for GDP growth forecasts (Angelini et al., 2011, C30). Currently, consumer confidence is measured through representative polls conducted on a monthly basis by statistical bureaus and research facilities (Dominitz & Manski, 2004, pp. 52–53). Since regular large-scale polls are expensive and fail to measure real-time results, scholars have proposed to employ the sentiment analysis of social media postings to measure consumer confidence in real time. Daas and Puts (2014) have shown that the sentiment analysis of Dutch Twitter and Facebook posts resembles the traditional consumer confidence index while delivering faster results. Similarly, Tuckett et al. (2014) utilize the sentiment analysis of broker and analyst reports to measure business confidence.

Despite scientific pioneering, there are no commercial providers of a real-time consumer confidence index. Nevertheless, airlines can use the published methodology to build their own consumer confidence index for countries, but that does not provide sufficient reliable data. This data can complement the assumptions regarding consumer confidence in economic forecasts on the country level to improve their reliability. Furthermore, trends in changing consumer confidence can be detected easily to adjust economic forecasts instantaneously. This would directly impact the demand forecasting process step, although there may be little impact on other steps.

A4 – Detailed demographic profiling with social networks

Airlines currently use a variety of demographic indicators to estimate travel demand from the O&D level (Itani, O'Connell, & Mason, 2014, p. 129). One SCA of the case study group utilizes the ancestry data provided by American airports to estimate source demand to Europe, since a large proportion of Americans travels to their ancestor's home country. One LCC uses official statistical data on migration background in order to identify routes for ethnic travel. Other airlines use trade data to estimate the extent of business connections between two different regions. However, the current sources of demographic data are fragmented and of varying quality. Data provided by airports may differ by methodology and definitions, which makes it difficult to compare across route candidates. Data from official statistical bureaus is usually reliable but restricted to larger geographic entities, and they sometimes miss important variables. In Germany, for example, a breakdown by country of origin is only available for foreigners living in Germany but not for naturalized Germans (Statistisches Bundesamt, 2017). A German of Kurdish origin, for example, may still travel frequently to Turkey or Iraq to visit his extended family. For business travel, trade volumes are only a rough proxy for the actual business travel.

Scientific research on innovative demographic data has concentrated mostly on extraction methodologies from social networks (Filippova, 2012) and micro-blogging services such as Twitter (Sloan et al., 2015). Despite the increasing importance of ethnic travel in the aviation industry (Itani, 2017), there exists no scientific study on the use of social media to improve the current data sources of demographic data.

Three categories of demographic data are most relevant for airline NP, namely ethnic background, business contacts, and economic status. Large social networks, such as Facebook, contain vast information on ethnicity and economic status. Professional social networks, such as LinkedIn, contain data on direct global business contacts. Facebook offers a free analytics tool called "Audience Insights" that allows the segmentation of the targeted audience through both demographic and socio-economic factors (Facebook, 2018a). The user can either segment a specific audience (e.g., the followers of his/her page) or the entire public audience. It offers segmentation criteria, such as language, gender, and educational background. Until August 2018, the data could be extracted through an open application programming interface (API)[158], but Facebook discontinued this API after a massive data scandal (Johnson, 2017). Now, companies have to use the integrated "Audience Insights" tool to process raw data.

LinkedIn currently does not commercialize the network connection raw data but only pre-filtered audience data for marketing and recruiting purposes (Cohen, 2016). However, LinkedIn provides researchers with network raw data if they join the LinkedIn research platform (Agarwal, 2017). Since data on global business contact is valuable to many business models, LinkedIn may start commercializing this data as well. Besides social networks, there is a group of aggregator companies that facilitate data management and analytics across platforms[159]. Most companies started

[158] An open API, also known as a public API, is an application programming interface that allows the owner of a network-accessible service to give universal access to other developers.

[159] The main competitors include SproutSocial, Spredfast, agora Pulse, Salesforce Social Studio, and Socialbakers.

as cross-platform marketing tools, which then developed analytical functionalities. However, almost all companies only offer analytics for a company's own social media audience and not on the entire user population. SproutSocial is currently developing a cross-platform analytics solution, but the launch date is yet to be announced (York, 2018).

Airline network planners can use demographic data from social networks in various ways to improve the usefulness and reliability of current demographic data. Data from global platforms and LinkedIn allow for seamless analyses across locations, thereby overcoming the issue of varying data quality from different data sources. Moreover, demographic data can be narrowed down to the city level (Facebook, 2018a), allowing for a greater data granularity. Filtering by language or interests may yield a much more accurate picture of people with a migration background than official statistics. If professional networks, such as LinkedIn, begin marketing direct business contact data, the demand for business travel may be forecasted more accurately. All of this affects the need for information pertaining to transportation demand forecast. Demographic data is mostly utilized in the strategic NP process steps from demand forecast up to route selection.

A5 – General search engine data for detailed O&D demand

All the booking data that airlines currently use for demand forecasting is based on actual bookings, even if it is updated in real time. Thus, it reflects booking decisions that have already been made. Many potential passengers search for flights in search engines before they actually process the booking. Analyzing search engine data could thus indicate future booking intentions, which makes it a truly future-oriented data source. In addition, search engine data can indicate real O&D demand, since people are likely to search for their real destination. IP analytics allow for the detection of the geographic origin of the search, so that airlines have indications for both the real origin and the real destination.

Search engine data has attracted significant attention in the scientific research community. Disease prediction was the first proven application

(Lazer et al., 2014), although the range of opportunities is infinite (Choi & Varian, 2012). Carrière-Swallow and Labbé (2013) employed Google Trends data to measure economic indicators in emerging markets in real time. In tourism research, Google Trends has been widely used to predict tourist flows (Önder & Gunter, 2016; Park, Lee, & Song, 2016; Yang et al., 2015) and hotel room demand (Pan, Chenguang Wu, & Song, 2012; Rivera, 2016). Indeed, there is no research on predicting air travel demand with search engine data, but a similar methodology as for hotel demand forecasts may be applicable.

All major research is conducted using Google data, which can be explained by its high market share of about 90% in the global search engine market (StatCounter, 2018). Google offers its proprietary "Google Trends" webtool to analyze search volumes. It allows the comparison of different search terms, which are displayed in a normalized scale. One can obtain absolute search volumes using the Google Adwords plug-in "Keywords." The search statistics can be filtered geographically down to the city level in North America or to the regional level in other continents (Google, 2018). Searches can then be displayed as a time series with daily search data for up to ten years. The data is also available through a Google Trends API (npm Inc., 2018).

Airlines can combine the search term "flight" with a list of potential destinations and filter these results by the intended origin geographies. The results should indicate changing preferences and seasonal patterns. The data needs to be controlled for different booking lead times and conversion rates for different O&Ds. On some routes, people may search and book several months ahead, whereas on other routes, the lead time is much shorter. In any case, search engine data indicates booking intentions and may thus be a highly valuable complement for actual external and internal booking data. The broadness of information comes at the cost of specificity and reliability. Google Trends data have to be adjusted to booking lead times, conversion rates, and search terms. This requires significant data processing before it becomes reliable.

Network planners can use general search engine data to fine-tune demand forecasts and identify unserved markets. Furthermore, this data can reveal trends in booking and travel behavior. Due to its general character, this data contributes to various information needs. Primarily, it can improve transportation demand forecasts and also inform trend identification and the internal booking situation. In combination with competitor search terms (e.g., Aeroflot + Moscow), it can enrich competitor monitoring and serve as an early warning indicator. The broad range of applications makes the data valuable for almost all NP process steps. Long-term demand forecasts can benefit from 10-year trend patterns, while mid- and short-term forecasts can be directly informed by concrete booking intentions. This not only affects the strategic process steps like route selection and flight frequency determination but also the tactical scheduling and fleet assignment decisions.

A6 – Clickstream data of meta-search websites for flights

Meta-search websites for flights can provide much more focused data than general search engines. However, the market is fragmented and features multiple players, such as Skyscanner, Kayak, and Expedia (Reals & Hadwick, 2015). Since every player can commercialize only their own clickstream data, these datasets have limited market coverage. In turn, the data contains complete search information, including set filters, clickstreams, and IP addresses (Skyscanner, 2018). The IP address can indicate the real origin of the passenger.

There is no recent literature on the use of clickstream data from meta-search engines, which may be due to the recency of data availability. Around mid-2018, only Skyscanner had commercialized its clickstream data to airlines. Skyscanner established its “Travel Insights” platform in 2016 and entered into a partnership with the air route portal Anna.aero to promote the “unserved route of the week”, a weekly feature identifying the next-best direct flights according to the Skyscanner clickstream data (Anna.aero, 2017). Their direct competitor Kayak, a brand of Booking Holdings, launched a “Travel trends” feature in 2018. This service does not provide actual clickstream data but only processed trending searches and destinations (KAYAK, 2018). Expedia offers “creative partnerships” for customized data solutions (Expedia Group, 2018) but no standard clickstream product that is comparable to the Skyscanner solution.

The clickstream dataset allows airline network planners to identify O&Ds by search volumes, thereby revealing unserved potential non-stop routes. In addition, airline network planners can retrace how many passengers have booked with competitors or have not booked at all[160]. All data is transmitted daily, so that booking intentions can be tracked in nearly real time. If a sample can be generalized based on the assumed market coverage and possible biases, such as a skew towards leisure travelers, airlines can model O&D demand much more granularly than with the existing market forecast models.

Clickstream data from meta search websites can improve the usefulness and reliability of transport demand forecasts by increasing the granularity and specificity of O&D demand estimates. If the data is compiled to a time series, airline network planners can also identify demand trends. The clickstream data supports competitor monitoring and market share modelling, since competitor bookings are visible in this data. At the same time, internal bookings can be traced. With the IP address included, the real origin of passengers may be approximated. This information primarily serves the demand forecast as well as route selection and scheduling. Scheduling, especially, can be improved through this, since clickstream can contain preferred departure and arrival time windows. Fleet assignment can also

---

[160] All the results can also be refined by the filters that users have set, e.g., to identify price-sensitive or time-sensitive customers.

be informed by improving the forecast accuracy of the internal booking situation.

A7 – Social media mining to determine price elasticity

Traditionally, price elasticity in airlines was calculated based on published ticket data (e.g., the US Department of Transportation DB1B database) or MIDT-data (Brons et al., 2002). Price elasticity was determined on a route level and based on the total fare, omitting ancillary revenues. With the increased unbundling of air fares, researchers strived to calculate the price elasticities for individual service items (Granados et al., 2012). The availability of booking data from online booking portals and airlines' internal booking systems allow for elasticity calculation at the flight level (Mumbower, Garrow, & Higgins, 2014). The next granularity step is calculating the price elasticity on an individual customer level, which was pioneered by Ghose et al. (2018) on a Google Product Search dataset. They enriched a structural econometric model with unstructured social media data in order to understand individual customer preference factors. These preference factors were then mapped to a set of hotel rooms reserved by the same customer group to determine the price elasticity. Airlines can use a similar approach to estimate the individual price elasticity of their own customer base.

In general, price elasticity in airlines is crucial for P&RM departments. However, the price elasticity informs revenue estimates for route forecasts and is thus also vital for airline NP. Network planners can prioritize destinations with relatively low price sensitivity and adjust flight frequencies and fleet assignment accordingly. Besides adding an additional layer of granularity, price elasticity at the customer level improves the interpretation of the internal booking situation, as abnormal booking levels may be correlated with changing price elasticities.

A8 – Analysis of air cargo rates from online freight portals

While passenger airlines can rely on the real-time price intelligence of established providers, such as Infare or DataCrops, cargo airlines only have access to their internal accounting data on freight rates and to the market rate levels published one month after being cleared by the IATA or WorldACD. Rates between forwarders and cargo airlines have long been negotiated bilaterally, so there was no data source to access real-time prices. With the digitization of the logistic transportation chains, cargo rate intelligence providers have entered the market in recent years and are trying to bring transparency similar to those of passenger airlines.

Digitization is changing the air cargo industry at lightning speed. Online freight forwarders, such as Freighthub or Instafreight, are challenging the established freight forwarding companies (Vaske, 2017). They offer not only tailored services but also price transparency to the shipper. Moreover, they offset volume disadvantages with slim service charges due to a lean digital business model. Many incumbents, such as DHL, have reacted and now offer online quotes as well; cargo airlines, such as Lufthansa Cargo (Lufthansa Cargo, 2018a) and Emirates Sky Cargo (Emirates Sky Cargo, 2018), have also started to circumvent the issues with traditional forwarders and enable direct quotes and bookings. The availability of online quotes is fueling the business model of freight rate comparison websites, such as Freightos (Carey, 2017) and Xeneta (Air Cargo News, 2017). With an increasing number of cargo rates being available, Cargoguide (2018) has developed a freight rate intelligence software, which is comparable to the Infare solution for passenger fares.

Real-time price intelligence is even more important to air cargo NP than to passenger airlines, since their planning cycles are much shorter. Cargo airlines can be required to start new routes with only a few weeks preparation; thus, sensing the rate development of potential cargo routes can be a significant leap forward. Network planners for cargo airlines can use real-time price information to improve the reliability of demand forecasts and identify trends rapidly. Furthermore, cargo rate intelligence can improve competitor monitoring and explain the internal booking situation. This has an impact on almost all NP process steps from demand forecasting until the final aircraft routing, which can be changed if short-term demand increases in the spot market are detected.

A9 – Analysis of exhibitor data of industry fairs

Fairs for industrial goods are the main driver of the micro-seasonality in cargo airlines. Especially those fairs that involve high value goods such as cars or specialized machinery, usually rely on air cargo services. Identifying cargo flows associated with industry fairs requires two components: an exhaustive list of industry fair events must be complemented with the analysis of the manufacturing facilities of the exhibitors to predict the micro-seasonality at the O&D-level. While the cargo airlines in our case study group maintain an exhaustive list of the most important industry fairs, they all lack transparency in terms of the entire industry fair landscape. In addition, trade flows are only recorded by experience, not predictively. Cargo airlines have currently no transparency in manufacturing sites from exhibitors that can help them predict the exact demand origins.

A machine learning-supported data mining tool can increase transparency in industry-related trade flows. Data on industry fairs, exhibitors, and their manufacturing sites, as well as the products per manufacturing site can be derived from publicly available web-sources, using professional scraping services, such as Data Crops (DataCrops, 2018b). Such data can be linked to historical internal booking information to identify industry fair-related shipments. Furthermore, the data can be linked to published cargo volumes and rates from the WorldACD or IATA Cargo Accounts Settlement System (CASS) databases. With sufficient data points, industry fair-specific trade lanes can be identified and incorporated in the NP process.

Air cargo network planners can use such data to plan for industry fair-specific extra stops that can be actively marketed to potential shippers. By offering a more direct flight connection, the trucking cost can be reduced and a value proposition for exhibitors can be created. Let us consider the

Tecnoshow Comigo as an example. It is the largest agricultural technology show in Brazil, featuring more than 500 exhibitors and over 100,000 annual visitors (Tecnoshow Comigo, 2018). It occurs in Rio Verde, a medium-sized town, southwest of Brasilia. As of 2018, only domestic cargo airlines serve the closest airports of Brasilia and Goiânia, since most international cargo arrives in the airports of the Sao Paulo agglomeration. Offering an industry fair-specific stopover in either Brasilia or Goiânia can attract cargo, which would otherwise have been flown to Sao Paulo and then be trucked to Rio Verde for one day. Big data analytics on the exhibitors and their manufacturing facilities can indicate the most likely origins of the cargo. Network planners can leverage this information to create a better product for potential shippers and incorporate the micro-seasonality with one or two additional stops on regular cargo flights to Brazil.

Predicting industry fair-related cargo streams contributes towards both transportation demand forecast and the identification of trends, including micro-seasonality. In addition, it may reveal the real movement of goods by detecting the true origin and destination. This information can be used both for long- and short-term demand forecasts. Network planners may choose to add a new route temporarily or add a frequency on an existing route to serve the demand. They can also schedule additional stops on an existing route and adjust the aircraft type, based on the expected cargo volume and characteristics.

A10 – Shipping data from e-commerce platforms

Cross-border e-commerce is one of the major growth factors of air cargo demand (IATA, 2017b). Large e-commerce platforms, such as Amazon, Alibaba, eBay, and JD.com, facilitate most e-commerce transactions (Minges et al., 2016). They own the transaction data, including the real O&D of the shipment, size of the goods, and chosen delivery mode. While Amazon is increasingly integrating logistic services, including air cargo in its own product portfolio (Chamlou, 2018), Chinese platforms Alibaba and JD.com have not yet entered such logistics fulfillment yet. Furthermore, the growing cross-border e-commerce market opens new route opportunities for air cargo network planners. Belgian ASL Airlines, for example, started a direct service from the West-Chinese city of Urumqi to Europe, supposedly driven by such e-commerce demand (Kauffman, 2018).

E-commerce platforms without integrated logistics service have a genuine interest in offering their customers the optimal shipping services. They may be willing to share their data with carriers for this purpose. If airlines can anticipate e-commerce cargo flows, they may be able to react quickly and adjust their own network dynamically to market needs. If Alibaba, JD.com, and similar e-commerce platforms share shipping data on a daily base, airline network planners can refine their demand forecasts and inform new route decisions, frequency changes, schedule adjustments, or changes in aircraft types. Thus, cross-border e-commerce shipping data influences the entire NP process up to actual aircraft routing.

Besides improving the demand forecasts, e-commerce shipping data can be used to identify trends and extract real movements of e-commerce shipments. Detailed shipping data can help classify airline internal bookings and monitor competitor actions pertaining to e-commerce demand.

5.2.3 Trend identification

B1 – Analysis of reviews in the travel rating communities

The popularity of travel destinations can change over time, as illustrated by Cuba. Many Cuban hotels and tourist facilities increased their prices, anticipating the relaxation of visa regulations in the United States, which would surge tourist numbers. However, they failed to invest in better services, so the perceived value for money in their tourism industry dropped sharply (Whitefield, 2017). European tourists opted for other destinations, and the overall air travel demand to Cuba dropped sharply in 2016. European charter airlines did not anticipate this trend and were faced with massive overcapacity during winter, which had to be adjusted on a short notice.

Data from large travel communities, such as TripAdvisor or Foursquare, can indicate such travel trends. Monitoring the average reviews for a destination and its tourist facilities (hotels, restaurants, etc.) can indicate whether the destination's image is improving or deteriorating (Kladou & Mavragani, 2015). Similarly, the number of reviews over a specific period reflects whether the popularity of the destination changes. In theory, this data can be obtained from a range of travel communities, but data commercialization has started only recently. TripAdvisor publishes curated travel trend analyses, without disclosing raw data (Tripadvisor, 2018b). However, TripAdvisor promotes its "Business Advantage" product as customizable analytics solution (Tripadvisor, 2018a). The rating communities Foursquare (2018) and Yelp (2018) already have both commercialized review data. Since the data is publicly available, it can also be retrieved using a data scraping service. In this case, the data processing and cleaning must be performed by the airline.

Airline network planners can use trends in travel reviews to inform the market growth expectations of their demand forecasts. Destinations with an increasingly positive review trajectory can be identified as potential new routes. Similarly, destinations with decreasing volume and quality of reviews may be candidates for frequent reviews. Thus, travel review data is most important for the strategic NP steps, as it indicates long-term trends rather than the transient short-term demand.

B2 – Clickstream data from travel platforms

Clickstream data from travel platforms, such as TripAdvisor, comprises information regarding travelers' choice preferences and individuals' travel patterns. While reviews reflect the image of a location, clickstream data displays its popularity. It includes absolute page view numbers und unique page view numbers (Tripadvisor, 2018a), which proxy the general interest in a destination. While reviews contain historical information[161], page views

[161] The reviewer has already been at the reviewed point of interest.

may indicate travel intention. It thus has a more forward-looking character and may be useful in predicting the next season's travel flows.

NP managers can use clickstream data for three purposes. First, they can forecast future travel flows as per travel intentions. Second, they can rank potential destinations by their popularity to identify route candidates. Third, they can monitor the trends in popularity using time-series clickstream data. While the first use case supports a mid-term demand forecast, the rest aim to primarily identify long-term trends. Therefore, demand forecasting is the most impacted NP process step. Network planners can further use clickstream data for route selection. Mid-term travel flow forecasts may enable schedule adjustments and fleet assignment decisions.

B3 – Analysis of local hotel prices

Transportation represents only one side of the coin in a travel system. The other is accommodation, which largely includes hotels, where leisure and business travelers are lodged (Bieger & Wittmer, 2006, p. 40). Hotels are bound to their location and usually know the local demand specificities much better than any transportation carrier. They may reflect events in their pricing, of which airline P&RM departments are completely unaware (Herrmann & Herrmann, 2014). It may be a good strategy for airline network planners and P&RM departments to leverage the local pricing knowledge for their own decision making.

Hotel prices present two important pieces of information for network planners. They indicate micro-seasons driven by specific events, which are expressed through temporary price spikes. It is likely that the demand for transportation also increases during these price spikes, which may justify an additional frequency or the deployment of a larger aircraft. If hotel prices are structurally lower than comparable hotels in other destinations, airlines should check their own booking ramp up. Low hotel prices may be a symptom of a transportation supply shortage, leading to a concrete business opportunity – adding transportation capacity to a destination. If a route is extraordinarily well booked while hotels remain cheap, network planners may add flights to benefit from the misalignments.

Many rate management software providers offer a hotel rate intelligence functionality. The most advanced rate intelligence product in the market is RateGain, which features a proprietary service quality index to compare hotels across destinations according to service standard (RateGain, 2018). Amadeus recently acquired the market leader, TravelClick, for more than Euro 1 billion (O'Neill, 2018). Octorate (2018) features a similar functionality and includes Airbnb and vacation rental apartments. All these hotel rate intelligence solutions are highly powerful analytics tools, with much more functionality than pure rate comparison. It may be sufficient for an airline to scrape hotel rates from one online travel agency, such as Booking.com, to understand local micro-seasonality. Specialized data scaping services, such as DataCrops (2018a), can provide a daily data batch with the desired prices.

Airline network planners can use hotel prices to fine-tune their demand forecasts at the O&D level and make the schedule more dynamic for local micro-seasons. This implies short-term route addition, flight frequency adjustment, and fleet assignment changes.

B4 – Analysis of events in social networks

A different approach to detect micro-seasonality is the analysis of events in social networks. It starts with the detection of events accommodating a critical audience size among the thousands of public events in social networks, such Facebook or MeetUp. These events then need to be assigned to (potential) destination airport catchment areas. Ideally, the event data includes demographic audience information, e.g., the stated location of participants. This would enable network planners to anticipate the actual travel demand and allow for the filtering of events with a large number of non-local attendants.

Scientific research has mostly focused on event analysis based on unstructured data, such as pictures and videos (Liu, Wang, & Huet, 2016). In this approach, a pre-existing event list is used to tag social media content, based on image recognition or a simple metadata analysis (Stieglitz et al., 2018). However, analytics related to events without a pre-defined event list have not widely been researched so far (Liu et al., 2016, p. 445). Until mid-2018, Facebook allowed access to public event data via the Export API (Facebook, 2018b). However, the data scandal of 2017 drove the depreciation of the API (Burgess, 2018). The only option remaining is to scrape event data randomly via the “Discover Events” function, which allows for filtering by time, location, and category. MeetUp provides free access to group metadata via API (MeetUp, 2018).

Airline network planners can use social network event data for similar purposes as hotel price patterns. The major applications entail the fine-tuning of demand forecasts and the dynamization of the schedule, which affects NP process steps from frequency selection to fleet assignment.

5.2.4 Competitor monitoring

C1 – Real-time flight tracking with transponder data

Airlines experience multiple blind spots in competitor monitoring. Traditional MIDT data do not convey information on direct airline website bookings, which account for the increasing amount of total bookings (Sheivachman, 2017). Published flight schedules do not include charter flights, e.g., for sport events or cruises. If airlines lose tenders for charter flights, they often do not know which airline gained the opportunity. Finally, airlines have limited visibility in terms of the operational issues of competitors, such as grounded aircrafts or heavy delays.

The emergence of the Automatic Dependent Surveillance Broadcast (ADS-B) technology enabled the real-time tracking of ADS-B-equipped aircraft. Most commercial aircrafts now have an ADS-B transponder installed, which permanently transmits data on position (longitude and latitude), speed, altitude, hex-code for aircraft identification, and the aircraft registration or flight number (Flightradar24, 2018). Companies such as Flightradar24 and FlightAware maintain their own receiver network to capture the ADS-B data in relevant regions. The data is already commercialized and can be purchased through a real-time data feed subscription or as batch data.

Research on ADS-B data has focused almost exclusively on air traffic control applications (Strohmeier et al., 2014) and air traffic flow research (Schäfer et al., 2014). Older research has focused on the security aspect of the transmission protocol and general technology adoption issues (McCallie, Butts, & Mills, 2011).

Batch data can be used to fill the gaps of MIDT and flight scheduling data. Since almost all the commercial airplanes are equipped with an ADS-B transponder, the dataset includes a seamless recording of flight movements in the covered geographies. By being aware of the outline data of charter tenders, airlines can retrace the winning competitors. Real-time data also enables the detection of the operational issues of competitors, which can be used to selectively increase frequencies or change aircraft types to the airline's benefit. The recorded flight paths can support cost calculation for new routes, since the likelihood of specific air routings can be estimated. In summary, transponder data primarily serves competitor monitoring and has secondary applications in cost forecasting and as an early warning system.

While airline network planners conduct cost forecasting and competitor monitoring throughout the entire NP process, the real-time monitoring component is most vital for short-term tactical NP. Airlines may re-fleet or reschedule if a competitor has severe operational issues, but this is not relevant to the strategic planning and scheduling process steps.

C2 – Network-relevant competitor media monitoring

The bankruptcy of Air Berlin in 2017 represented the impact of competitor events on airline NP. Competitors took over or opened more than 100 new routes from Berlin and Düsseldorf in the summer of 2018, which posed a huge NP challenge for all airlines (Recklies, 2018). As a consequence, on-time performance suffered dramatically, as airlines operated with non-robust schedules to secure the slots that they inherited from Air Berlin (Reichert, 2018). Early warnings concerning such significant competitor incidents, such as bankruptcies, strikes, or forced groundings thus become increasingly important. Airlines in the case study group mostly rely on traditional news briefings and scenario planning to monitor competitor events.

Research on new media monitoring technologies has mostly focused on social media (Batrinca & Treleaven, 2015). However, the advent of machine learning-based NLP technologies has also transformed established media monitoring companies. Machine-learning algorithms allow for a more holistic news coverage, including foreign language media and advanced sentiment analysis to predict the likelihood of certain events (Gersuni, 2016). The American media analytics company Meltwater (2018) offers an "Executive Analytics" product that supports strategic decision making, based on media monitoring that is aided by artificial intelligence. The large incumbent Universal Information (2018) offers cross-platform analytics that is capable of processing all types of unstructured data, including videos and podcasts.

Airline network planners can use these specialized media monitoring techniques to filter those competitor events that may have an impact on NP. Larger events such as bankruptcies mostly have a lasting impact and influence strategic NP. Temporary events such as strikes or groundings may call for tactical actions, such as the scheduling of additional flights or a change in fleet assignment. In any case, advanced media monitoring benefits the airlines in terms of competitor monitoring and serves as an early warning system for critical events.

5.2.5 Real movements of passengers and goods

D1 – Mobile location data from smartphones

Airline network planners have only extremely limited data on the real origin and the real destination of their passengers. Recorded IP numbers of direct bookings are often misleading, and location tracking with an airline's mobile app covers only a small portion of the passengers. The widespread prevalence of mobile phones has created a completely new opportunity for location tracking. Every time a cell phone receives a call or message or data package, mobile network operators can link the phone to the transmitter catchment area. In the early years of mobile phones, operators could locate users only when they placed or received a call or text message. However, the increasing popularity of data flat rates have caused constant flows of data package exchanges and allows mobile operators to track smartphones seamlessly in their networks (Bonnel et al., 2015, pp. 381–385).

Researchers started using mobile location data for urban travel flow analysis around ten years ago (Calabrese et al., 2011). Subsequently, more studies on urban travel flows based on mobile location data have been conducted (Çolak et al., 2015; Iqbal et al., 2014). Tolouei, Psarras, and Prince (2017) demonstrated that properly processed mobile location data is as reliable as traditional travel surveys, but it has the advantage of a much larger sample size. Mobile network operators cover a significant part of the population, resulting in highly representative samples.

Telecommunication providers are increasingly commercializing their mobile location data. In Europe, Deutsche Telekom founded the subsidiary Motionlogic only to process and market location data (Motionlogic, 2018). Similarly, Telefónica created Telefónica NEXT, which cooperates with the Swiss location analytics company Teralytics (Telefónica Next, 2018). All three companies agreed to share certain information for this study and were included in the data provider group. Current data analytics can record movements down to the radio cell level (in Germany) and identify the mode of transportation. Data protection laws require companies to anonymize users and display only aggregate movement flows, including at least five users. The current datasets are limited to national mobile networks. If a user crosses a country's border and connects to a new network, he is assigned a completely new anonymized random code, making cross-border tracking difficult. However, all providers are currently working to integrate their European mobile networks into one coverage zone.

The American start-up Streetlight Data, which also joined the data provider group, follows a different approach. As against using mobile phone signals, Streetlight Data purchases the GPS-tracked location data from over 400 application providers and now covers over 30% of the mobile phone users in the US (StreetLight Data, 2018). GPS-based location data has the advantage of being recorded independent from the mobile network and thus can be tracked across country borders.

Mobile location data provide a broad application range for airline network planners. They draw an accurate picture of the relevant travel streams across all transportation modes, which can be filtered by origin, location, time of travel, and mode of travel. No other data type currently provides a comparable information depth across transportation modes. Airline network planners can employ mobile location data to precisely define the catchment areas of airports. Moreover, in case of low flight frequency, they can track the real origins and destinations of their passengers[162]. If GPS data is used, passengers can be matched to flights, even at busier airports. The data allows also for competition monitoring, since location data is not limited to their own passengers. The time series of mobile location data reveal changing travel patterns, including the used transportation mix. The data can be combined with an event list (see *B4 – Analysis of events on social networks*) to identify the origin of event visitors. Micro-seasonality

[162] Data is currently available as 15-minute time stamps; if a limited number of flights arrive or depart during a 15 minutes time window, passengers may be allocated to the individual flights.

can also be identified by analyzing the absolute numbers of travelers per day.

This information can be used across the strategic NP process. Demand forecasts can be enriched with real O&D granularity, and the alternative transportation modes can be included. Transparency pertaining to the catchment areas of airports can influence hub decisions and route selection. Information regarding time-of-day travel patterns can inform scheduling and flight frequency decisions. The application for tactical planning is rather limited, since the data reflects actual travel and not intended travel.

D2 – Extended electronic air waybill with shipper address

Air cargo network planners lack transparency in terms of the real O&D of shipments when the shipments are consolidated by a freight forwarder. The current paper-based air waybills (AWBs) require the logistics facilities only before and after the air transport, so there is little information on the real origin and destination addresses. The digitization of air waybills is now a major initiative of the IATA, who defined the report and information standards for electronic AWBs (IATA, 2018a). However, the e-AWB resembles the data entry fields of the paper-based AWB, thus not solving the information transparency issue for air cargo network planners.

The digitization of logistical supply chains was mentioned by researchers as early as 2001, when Forster and Regan found that the e-AWB would aid significant operational performance improvement. However, the role of freight forwarders as intermediaries impeded their support in electronic data exchange with other supply chain members for another decade. Only in recent years has the electronic waybill (which also covers terrestrial and sea cargo) attracted the attention of scholars. Bakhtyar, Holmgren, and Persson (2013) have found positive synergies between electronic waybills and intelligent transportation systems. Bakhtyar and Henesey (2014) employed standard e-waybill data fields to train a machine learning algorithm to predict cargo volumes and products for land transport. However, there exists no air cargo-specific scientific literature on electronic waybills. The IATA started the e-AWB initiative in 2010, aiming to digitize all AWBs by 2025 (IATA, 2018a).

In order to improve the usefulness of e-AWB for air cargo NP, the standard template defined in the IATA Resolution 672 needs to be changed. A detailed composition list of the consolidated cargo must be added as a mandatory data field. This change has to be backed by an air cargo industry initiative, since all cargo airlines would benefit from the increased real O&D transparency. However, it is unlikely that freight forwarders will agree to this change, since they fear that direct sales from cargo airlines will endanger their business model.

If such changes are applied and all e-AWBs contain real O&Ds, the need for information related to real O&Ds would be fully satisfied. Real O&D data for cargo shipments is absolutely crucial for strategic NP decisions. It would enable a substantially more granular demand forecast based on the real O&D areas, thereby allowing the optimization of the route portfolio and flight frequencies. Since a large portion of air cargo is trucked over large distances, a reconfiguration of the network structure may be useful to create shared value for airlines and shippers.

D3 – Location-transmitting sensors for cargo shipments

Another solution for the lack of transparency of real O&Ds for cargo shipments is the attachment of location tracking sensors to cargo shipments. An increasing number of shippers request real-time tracking of location and environmental parameters (e.g., temperature, air pressure, gravity peaks), especially for expensive and highly sensible cargo (Boylan, 2016). Cargo airlines, such as Cathay Pacific and Lufthansa Cargo, cooperate with sensor producers to offer real-time cargo tracking as a service to their customers (Air Cargo News, 2018; Lufthansa Cargo, 2018b). However, the currently available tracking solutions are costly, since the devices need to be leased for about USD 1.50 per day (Lufthansa Cargo, 2018b). Multiple providers of cargo tracking devices offer sensors directly to shippers, without leasing them (Cargo Signal, 2018; Sendum, 2018; Sensitech, 2018).

The increasing importance of Internet of Things (IoT) solutions has boosted the demand for a low bandwidth communication network. The existing mobile networks provide increasing transmission bandwidth but are restricted in the number of devices that can be connected at the same time. Many IoT sensors do not require a high bandwidth to upload their data, but the sheer number of sensors requires networks with a much larger device capacity than current mobile networks. Thus, industry associations and mobile network operators have founded the LoRa Alliance (2018) to promote a new Low Range Wide Area Network (LoRaWAN) standard that can complement the planned 5G networks with a low-bandwidth alternative for IoT sensors. Poenicke et al. (2018) have already described the applicability of the LoRaWAN technology for air cargo tracking sensors, which are expected to be significantly cheaper than the current solutions.

The increasing popularity and decreasing cost of real-time tracking sensors for shipments present a great opportunity for air cargo network planners. Similar to mobile location data for passengers, they can get a complete picture of the real O&Ds of cargo shipments. However, data ownership remains a question. Since shippers would probably not share location data automatically, airlines can only access data sent to LoRaWAN receivers in their airplanes. Ideally, the mobile network operators should anonymize and aggregate location data as with mobile location data, which can then be commercialized for cargo airlines.

Cargo location data can have a substantial impact on the entire NP process. Air cargo network planners can employ this data to conduct hypergranular O&D analyses to retrace the end-to-end shipment streams. This data can be used to optimize network structure, route portfolio, and flight frequencies. If the data is available in real-time, prediction models for short-term spot bookings can inform scheduling and fleet assignment as a reaction to foreseeable demand shifts. Real-time location data can also inform aircraft routing and short-term dispatch, since it increases visibility in terms of whether booked shipments will arrive on time or not.

5.2.6 Real-time planning constraint monitoring

H1 – Real-time slot trading platform

Airports with high traffic volumes assign landing time windows (i.e., slots) to airlines to avoid congestion in the available infrastructure. Airport slots are allocated using the grandfathering principle, implying that the slot owner keeps the slot if he complies with a specified use quota (e.g., 80% of days used). If an airline fails to comply with the use quota or stops a service, the slot ownership is retracted by the airport or the regulator (depending on the country). The slot are then re-allocated based on the published allocation criteria (Madas & Zografos, 2006, p. 54).

Scholars have long argued that the grandfathering concept is economically inefficient and proposed alternative allocation strategies. Brueckner (2009) argued that congestion can be regulated most efficiently either through congestion-dependent landing fees or by auctioning slots. Some scholars go even further and demand a secondary market for slots, which would enable the transfer of the ownership right from airports to airlines once the slot has been allocated or auctioned (Madas & Zografos, 2006; Verhoef, 2010). While monetary slot trading is not permitted in most regulatory regimes (except for the US and the United Kingdom), airlines can swap slots through bilateral agreements (Madas & Zografos, 2006, p. 53).

Airline network planners are faced with two transparency issues with regard to airport slots. First, many countries do not support transparency in the slot register, i.e., the database containing all the allocated and available slots. Second, slot changes require in almost all countries (except for the

US and the United Kingdom[163]) regulatory approval and thus significant time investment. Therefore, slot swaps are often agreed during the semi-annual IATA slot conferences, which drastically reduces scheduling flexibility.

Currently, only two companies have transparency in the slot registers of mostly free-market economies. The UK-based Airport Cooperation Limited (ACL) covers slot-restricted airports in eight countries, including UK, Canada, and New Zealand (Airport Coordination Limited, 2018b). The German company e-Airportslots serves nine markets, including Germany, Spain, France, Mexico, and Australia (e-Airportslots.aero, 2018). ACL provides a slot-trading platform for the UK, which has facilitated 55 slot swaps or trades in 2017 (Airport Coordination Limited, 2018a).

A more flexible trading or exchange mechanism would reduce the required lead time for the scheduling process dramatically, since the required slots can be acquired simply. The slot acquisition cost must be integrated in the business plan for the new route or frequency. Any trading scheme comes with complete transparency on the slot database, thus solving both transparency issues. The European Commission has proposed the liberalization of secondary slot trading in the entire EU (Buyck, 2018), and the US Federal Aviation Authority proposed a similar deregulation three years ago (Federal Aviation Authority, 2015). To realize the full potential in this area, more countries need to liberalize slot allocation mechanisms, including growing markets such as China and India.

Real-time slot trading platforms can potentially be integrated in standard scheduling solutions to automatically indicate when a desired slot is available. Airline network planners will be able to use the information from the route selection process to test the financial and operational feasibility more

---

[163] UK enjoys a special exception from the current EU regulations; slot trading in the US is restricted to a limited number of congested airports (Fukui, 2010).

rapidly than today. Flight frequency changes and (re-)scheduling will also become more dynamic.

H2 – Real-time traffic right information platform

Traffic rights, including overflight rights and transport freedom rights[164], are usually negotiated between two countries and codified in a bilateral agreement. The exceptions are multilateral agreements, such as the European Single Sky Agreement, where one agreement includes multiple countries. Those agreements are legal documents and usually comprise a public and a classified part.

Both the International Civil Aviation Organization (ICAO, 2018a) and the World Trade Organization (WTO, 2013) maintain global traffic right databases, which suffer from similar shortcomings. The databases contain only the public information regarding the agreements, which sometimes lacks penalty and contingent information. Furthermore, the databases are updated infrequently (the last WTO update was in 2013), so they may not reflect the latest legal situation. In addition, the coverage of agreements between countries with poor reporting standards is low. Consequently, most airlines from the case study group maintain their own databases on traffic rights, which are evaluated as reliable and useful in section 4.2.3. Airlines usually contact the respective government authority to gather information on relevant existing traffic rights in case they plan to serve a new route. Moreover, the airlines sometimes experience denied overflights due to a non-public overflight contingent, which is not recorded in official databases and is not tracked real time.

This process is both time and labor intensive and can potentially be simplified by a global traffic right database, which is linked to a real-time tracking

[164] Transport freedom rights regulate how airlines can transport passengers and goods from and to a specific country. The ICAO (2018b) defines nine freedom rights, from simple overflight rights (First Freedom) to the right for a foreign airlines to serve domestic routes within the home country (Ninth Freedom).

tool, such as flight transponder data. Modern text mining algorithms can simplify the labor requirement to scan and analyze bilateral agreements and deliver instead just the relevant information. Such information, e.g., number of permitted overflights per day, can then be cross-checked against the published schedules and real-time flight tracking data.

Real-time transparency in traffic rights can save airline network planners their manpower in the strategic planning steps, as they can easily extract information. It would also flag risks, such as late flights, which may lead to denied overflight permits or additional fees. The risks of paying additional fees and the cost of diversions can then be considered in the cost forecast of a route. Tactical NP can benefit from real-time information on the use of traffic rights, e.g., if the overflight quota has already been fulfilled. In this case, the aircraft routing can be adjusted to avoid additional cost. All of these are of utmost relevance for charter and cargo airlines that frequently change routings and schedule additional flights at short notice.

5.2.7 Incident monitoring

I1 – Global meteorological warning platform

Two types of meteorological events may influence airline NP. Recurring meteorological phenomena, such as the occurrence of a morning fog in a specific location, can influence scheduling decisions. The forecasting and impact assessments of meteorological disasters, such as floods, hurricanes, and droughts, should indicate the shifts in short-to mid-term demand, which may cause re-routings or temporary route suspension.

Scholars and practitioners are applying big data analytics to both meteorological forecasts and disaster impact assessments. Larsen (2013) proposed to use historical meteorological data to inform flight planning systems, which is a central IT tool of the flight operations process. Artificial intelligence is being used to forecast turbulence development (Williams, 2014) and provide decision-making tools in case of significant weather phenomena (Choi et al., 2016; McGovern et al., 2017). A research project conducted by the University of Michigan has developed an algorithm to detect weather patterns, which can inform airline scheduling (Moore, 2014). In practice, The Weather Company (2018), a subsidiary of IBM, is already commercializing turbulence forecasts for aviation.

Disaster forecasting and assessment is a predestined application for BDA. High volume real-time data from a variety of sources must be examined to obtain useful information. Akter and Wamba (2017) found that data mining techniques using social media and geo-spatial information are most commonly used for disaster management applications. IBM is researching artificial intelligence forecasting algorithms with data from Australia and New Zealand (Mareels, 2018). However, there is no commercialized big data disaster forecasting solution yet.

A global meteorological warning platform addresses three types of information needs. It is primarily an early warning platform to mitigate the impact of meteorological events. It further informs short- and mid-term demand forecasts in case of natural disasters and cost forecasts by calculating the expected cost due to irregular weather situations. Disaster impact assessment is most useful for route selection and flight frequency determination to react to demand changes. Finally, airline network planners can use weather pattern forecasting for schedule optimization.

I2 – Global political risk assessments

Like natural disasters, unexpected political events, such as strikes, military coups, and civil wars can significantly influence travel demand. Airline network planners rely on risk reports evaluating risks based mostly on human judgement and media analysis. These are provided by professional risk consultancies. Airline network planners of the case study group rated these risk reports low both in usefulness and reliability.

Big data analytics may provide a means to improve in both dimensions. The American start-up Geoquant (2018) uses 250 risk indicators to calculate a real-time political risk index (Shieber, 2017). Other companies develop media monitoring algorithms that scan relevant sources every 30 seconds and flag potentially critical events (Muñoz, 2016). The Chinese company Grisk combines NLP and machine learning to produce sectorial risk indices, considering the different vulnerability levels of specific industries towards political events (Grisk, 2018).

Airline network planners can use political risk assessments to adjust their demand forecasts and subsequently route portfolio and flight frequencies. The applicability in tactical NP is rather limited. However, unexpected political events may be relevant to flight operations if they require short-term re-scheduling or re-routing of flights.

5.3 Evaluation of BDO potential

This sub-chapter presents the qualitative potential assessment of the 23 BDOs identified. All the BDOs have been introduced to the airline network planners in the case study group, including data properties, NP applications, and potential data providers. The airline network planners then scored the potential of the BDOs for their specific airline NP process on a scale of 0 to 5. A score of 0 means that the respective BDO has no potential use in the airline's NP process, and it will not be considered even if the data is available for free. Conversely, a score of 5 indicates that the airline would invest significantly in data acquisition and data analytics to leverage the specific BDO.

5.3.1 Qualitative assessment of BDO potential

All nine case study airlines participated in the qualitative potential assessment. The evaluation scale ranged from 0 for no potential to 5 for very high potential. The arithmetic mean across all the BDOs is 2.2, which is slightly less than the median of 2.5. This indicates that the overall potential of the BDOs is considered only low to medium. Only four BDOs were scored with an overall potential of more than 3 (A5, A6, H1 and H2). A9 was assessed by the airline network planners with the lowest potential across all BDOs, with a score of 0.5. Figure 5.4 visualizes the overall potential scores (black line) and the score range across all individual assessments (grey line).

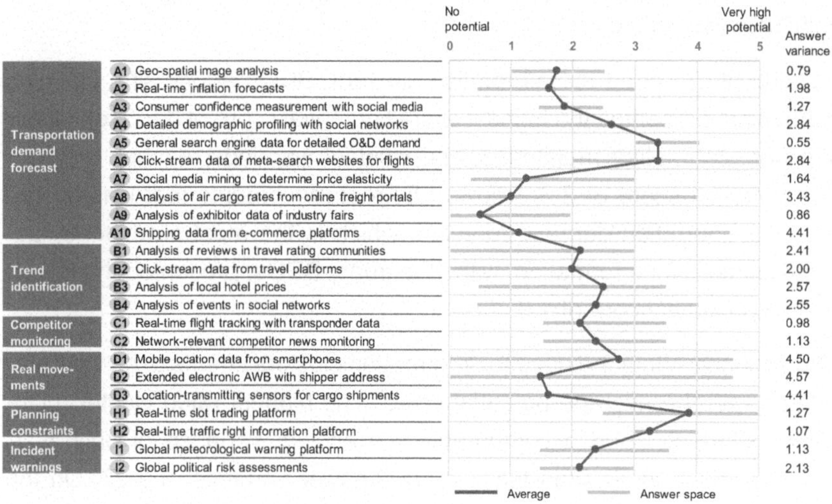

Figure 5.4 – Overall qualitative potential assessment of BDOs[165]

The variance in the assigned scores for potential across the case study group is 2.27 on an average, indicating significant differences in BDO potential for airlines. Location transmitting cargo sensors (D3) exhibited the largest differences. Two CARs estimated the potential to be very high (5.0), while five out of the six passenger airlines see absolutely no potential in this BDO. The differences seem to be business model specific and are examined further in the section 5.3.2.

[165] Source: Own illustration.

Furthermore, there are also BDOs with comparably uniform potential estimates. Some BDOs for economic forecasts (A1, A3) presented similar potential for all business models. Moreover, the potential for a real-time traffic right information platform and the incident warnings did not differ dramatically between airlines.

Looking at the need for information clusters, BDOs addressing planning constraints presented the highest overall potential score of 3.6. Trend identification, competitor monitoring, and incident warnings reached an average potential score of 2.3, followed by real movements that was scored 2.0. Transportation demand forecast, which is the most prominently addressed need for information, with 10 primary BDOs, presented the lowest overall potential score of 1.9.

The variance within the need for information clusters seems to be inversely related with the average potential score. The highest rated cluster "planning constraints" had a comparably low answer variance of only 1.17, which is much lower than the average answer variance of 2.27. On the contrary, real movements had an extraordinarily high variance of 4.41, and it was rated below average with a potential score of 2.0. However, a simple correlation analysis performed on BDO level does not support this assumption. The correlation[166] between the variance and average score is -0.23, which is a negligible value, at most indicating a mild association between variance and potential score.

5.3.2 Differences in BDO potential by business model

Due to the specificities of airline business models, airlines may evaluate the potential of BDOs differently according to their information needs. Figure 5.5 visualizes the assessment results by business model.

---

[166] The Pearson correlation coefficient has been calculated using the score variance as the independent variable and the average score as the dependent variable.

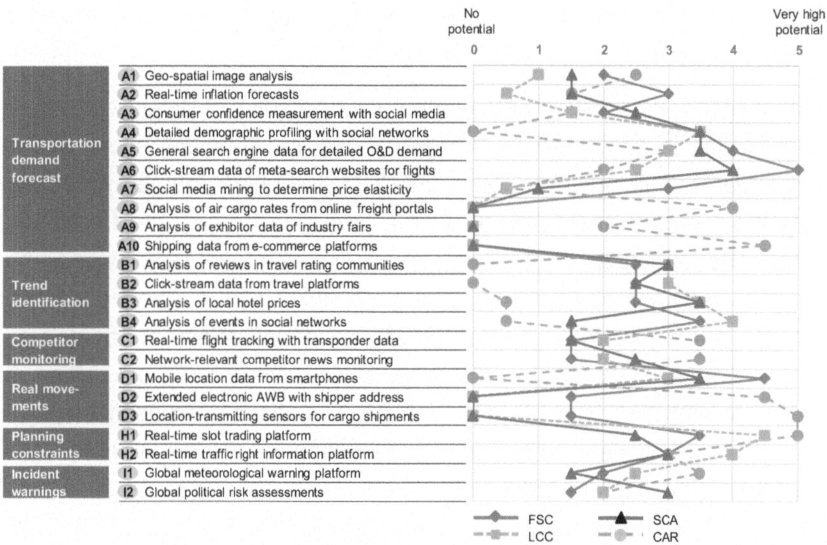

Figure 5.5 – BDO qualitative potential evaluation patterns by business model[167]

Full-service carriers find the highest potential in data from meta-search websites (5.0) and from general search engines (4.0). Mobile location data (4.5) was also highly ranked, whereas cargo-specific data sources A8-A10 were mostly not deemed to have any potential in FSC NP. The average potential assigned by the FSC network planners was 2.3 and thus slightly higher than the global average of 2.2. FSCs see more potential in the travel demand forecasting and trend identification BDOs than other airlines (see Appendix 19). This can be explained by the longer planning horizon of FSCs, which emphasizes on the need for accurate long- and mid-term demand forecasts and the early identification of trends. In contrast, competitor monitoring and incident warnings were rated with less potential than the global average. Due to their inflexible schedules, FSC may benefit less

[167] Source: Own illustration.

from real-time information, which would allow them to react to competitor problems or other events at a short notice.

In most cases, low-cost carriers evaluate the potential of BDOs lower than FSCs, which is confirmed by the below-average potential score of 2.0 across BDOs. Both planning constraint BDOs bear high potential for LCCs, since they would benefit from real-time data due to their short planning cycles. The identification of micro-seasonality with local hotel prices and events is also considered to have high potential by LCC network planners. Demographic profiling can further benefit the identification of underserved ethnic markets, which is a considerable traffic driver for LCCs. Looking at need for information clusters, LCCs rated BDOs above average in the planning constraint cluster and in the trend identification cluster. Whereas, the potential of BDOs for transportation demand forecast and real movements was scored lower than average. This aligns with the findings on the LCC NP process, which is highly dynamic due to short lead times. LCCs want to identify unserved revenue pockets, which is reflected in the serving of ethnic routes and schedules reflecting micro-seasonality.

The ranking profile of scheduled charter airlines combines aspects from the FSCs and LCCs. Search engine and mobile location data were evaluated with high potential in addition to demographic profiling and mobile location data. SCAs have longer planning cycles than LCCs, which increases the need for trend identification and transportation demand forecasting information. Moreover, SCAs also target ethnic travel and try to identify the underserved point-to-point connections. This makes demographic data and mobile location data valuable. SCAs can also leverage the current hotel prices to identify supply shortages in tourist destinations and benefit from adding capacity. Overall, SCAs evaluate BDOs similar to how LCCs do so, with an average score of 2.0, which is lower than the global mean. Trend identification is the only need for information cluster rated higher by SCAs than by the global average of all airlines.

Cargo airlines show a completely different evaluation pattern than the other business models. They see high potential in a real-time slot trading platform, which is in line with LCCs and caused by the short planning cycles of the cargo NP process. However, besides the real-time slot trading platform, cargo airlines highly rated those BDOs that have an explicit role in cargo demand forecasting and tracking. Overall, CARs rated the 23 BDOs with an average potential of 2.3, which is similar to the FSCs and higher than the LCCs and SCAs. They rated all the need for information clusters except for trend identification higher than the average of the case study group. Table 5.2 shows the BDOs ranked by business model.

Table 5.2 – BDOs ranked by business model[168]

Code	Big data opportunity	Overall rank	Rank by business model			
			FSC	CAR	LCC	SCA
H1	Real-time slot trading platform	1	4	1	1	9
A6	Clickstream data of meta-search websites for flights	2	1	12	11	1
A5	General search engine data for detailed O&D demand	3	3	9	6	4
H2	Real-time traffic right information platform	4	7	10	2	6
D1	Mobile location data from smartphones	5	2	20	7	5
A4	Detailed demographic profiling with social networks	6	5	21	5	3
B3	Analysis of local hotel prices	7	10	19	4	2
C2	Network-relevant competitor news monitoring	8	16	7	12	11
B4	Analysis of events in social networks	9	6	17	3	13
I1	Global meteorological warning platform	10	13	6	10	14
B1	Analysis of reviews in travel rating communities	11	11	22	8	7

168 Source: Own illustration.

Code	Big data opportunity	Overall rank	Rank by business model			
			FSC	CAR	LCC	SCA
I2	Global political risk assessments	12	18	13	14	8
C1	Real-time flight tracking with transponder data	13	17	8	13	15
B2	Click-stream data from travel platforms	14	12	23	9	10
A3	Consumer confidence measurement with social media	15	14	16	15	12
A1	Geo-spatial image analysis	16	15	11	16	16
A2	Real-time inflation forecasts	17	8	15	17	17
D3	Location-transmitting sensors for cargo shipments	18	19	2	19	19
D2	Extended electronic AWB with shipper address	19	20	3	20	20
A7	Social media mining to determine price elasticity	20	9	18	18	18
A10	Shipping data from e-commerce platforms	21	21	4	21	21
A8	Analysis of air cargo rates from online freight portals	22	22	5	22	22
A9	Analysis of exhibitor data of industry fairs	23	23	14	23	23

Real-time slot trading platforms were the highest ranked BDO for both LCCs and CARs, and the fourth highest for FSCs. It was also the only shared top 5 BDO of CARs with any other business model. Within the passenger airlines, demographic profiling appears in the top 5 of all three business models. Four BDOs appeared twice in the business model-specific top 5, namely clickstream data of meta-search websites, mobile location data from smartphones, general search engine data (all FSCs and SCAs), and analysis of local hotel prices (LCCs and SCAs). In total, 12 different BDOs appeared at least once in the top 5 of one business model, which are highlighted in grey in Table 5.2.

Comparing the business model-specific evaluation patterns, significant contrasts are detected. The sharpest contrast is between cargo airlines and passenger airlines. Cargo airlines assessed the potential of seven BDOs (A4, A7, B1, B2, B3, B4, and D1) with a score below 1, thereby denying any potential of these BDOs in their airline NP. In six out of seven cases (except for A7), there was not a single passenger airline that rated the potential of the BDO less than 2. Thus, these BDOs seem to create value for passenger airlines but not for cargo airlines. Conversely, five BDOs (A8, A9, A10, D2, and D3) seem to create significant potential for cargo airlines but little to no potential for passenger airlines. This indicates that there are three application classes of BDOs.

Data opportunities can be applicable to either cargo airlines or passenger airlines, or they can generate potential for all airline types. Figure 5.6 illustrates the allocation of BDOs. Only transportation demand forecast and real location clusters include both passenger and cargo-specific BDOs. The trend identification cluster is only relevant to passenger airlines, while competitor monitoring, planning constraints, and incident warnings exclusively make for general BDOs.

If the low assessments of potential for cargo and passenger-specific BDOs are excluded from the analysis[169], the global arithmetic mean increases from 2.2 to 3.0. From the 23 BDOs, 12 reached a recalculated mean of 3.0 or higher, indicating medium to high potential for the respective business models. These 12 BDOs coincide fully with the 12 BDOs identified in the analysis by business model earlier. Appendix 20 presents the BDOs sorted according to the recalculated mean, and it indicates the individual business model-specific evaluation scores.

[169] The assessments of passenger airlines for cargo-specific BDOs and the assessments of cargo airlines for passenger-specific BDOs have been excluded.

	Cargo airline specific BDOs	Passenger airline specific BDOs	General BDOs
Transportation demand forecast	A8 Analysis of air cargo rates from online freight portals A9 Analysis of exhibitor data of industry fairs A10 Shipping data from e-commerce platforms	A4 Detailed demographic profiling with social media mining	A1 Geo-spatial image analysis A2 Real-time inflation forecast A3 Consumer confidence measurement with social media A5 General search engine data for detailed O&D demand A6 Click-stream data of meta-search websites for flights A7 Social media mining to determine price elasticity
Trend identification		B1 Analysis of reviews in travel rating communities B2 Click-stream data from travel platforms B3 Analysis of local hotel prices B4 Analysis of events in social networks	
Competitor monitoring			C1 Real-time flight tracking with transponder data C2 Network-relevant competitor news monitoring
Real movements	D2 Extended electronic AWB with shipper address D3 Location-transmitting sensors for cargo shipments	D1 Mobile location data from smartphones	
Planning constraints			H1 Real-time slot trading platform H2 Real-time traffic right information platform
Incident warnings			I1 Global meteo warning platform I2 Global political risk assessments

Figure 5.6 – Cargo vs. passenger-specific BDOs[170]

5.3.3 Implementation of BDOs in current IT systems for NP

This list of 23 BDOs was presented to a major system developer for IT NP solutions in order to evaluate the ease of implementation. The evaluation was not based on the feasibility in gathering and analyzing the data from

[170] Source: Own illustration.

the BDO (which is discussed in the next section) but the possibility of the current NP software solution to integrate the analytics result. The scores were given on a 6-point scale from 0 (not possible to implement) to 5 (very easy to implement). Since the current system is focused on passenger airline NP, all cargo-specific BDOs were evaluated with the lowest score of 0.

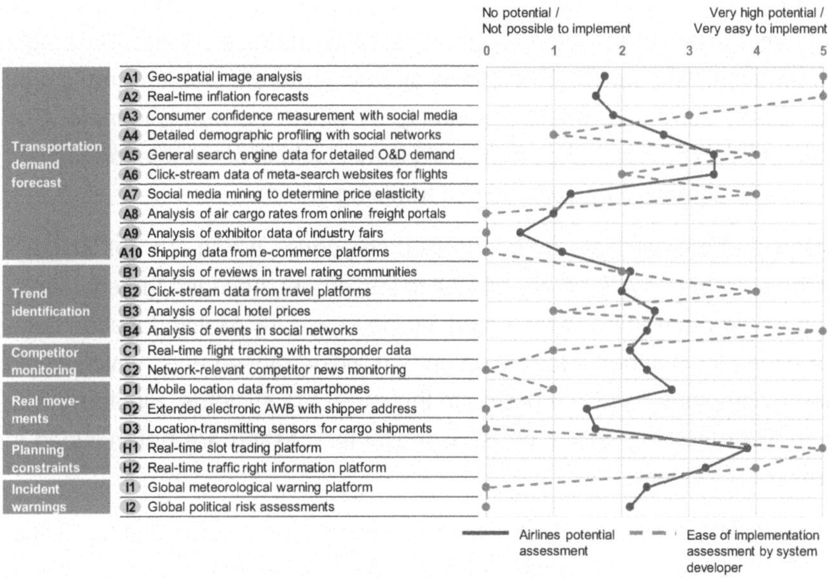

Figure 5.7 – Ease of implementation assessment for current NP IT system[171]

The answers displayed in Figure 5.7 show that the analytical results from BDOs are in most cases either very easy or very hard to implement, with a few exceptions that show a medium degree of ease of implementation. All BDOs that influence assumption values in the NP software solutions

---

[171] Source: Own illustration.

are easy to integrate. This group includes economic growth and inflation forecasts as well as assumptions concerning O&D demand and price elasticity. A second group of BDOs that are comparably simple to integrate are those providing structured demand data, which can be calibrated to inform O&D growth forecasts. This includes search data (both Google and flight websites), clickstream data from travel platforms, and event data from social media.

The third group of easy-to-implement BDOs includes slots and traffic right information. The current IT systems already feature a slot and traffic right database, currently updated manually by airline network planners. The data pull can be automated if the data is available in a suitable format, i.e., a table of current slots and codified traffic rights.

BDOs that provide data on information categories which are not included in the current IT systems are difficult to implement, because the entire system would need to be recalibrated for the new data. Mobile location data, for example, includes information on non-airline movements, which would add a completely new dimension to the current IT systems. Similarly, real-time flight tracking and micro-seasonality forecasting are not included in present IT systems.

Existing NP software are not able to process unstructured data. Thus, BDOs that are likely to produce unstructured output data, such as all incident warning platforms, cannot be integrated into the current IT systems.

5.3.4 *Feasibility assessment of BDOs*

This section evaluates the implementation feasibility of the 23 BDOs to complement the potential assessment of the last sections. In the first step, a feasibility evaluation framework must be constructed to meaningfully assess the BDOs. In the literature, there is no data-specific feasibility assessment framework available. Most existing frameworks have focused on IT project feasibility evaluations, resulting in a large body of literature being published in the early 2000s. However, the focus of most research lies on the financial feasibility evaluation (Milis & Mercken, 2004) instead of technological and legal feasibility aspects. Other literature follows a strategic perspective and classifies the feasibility assessment as an important process step in IT project planning (Willcocks, 2009, pp. 239–259). However, it does so without further specifying the feasibility criteria apart from financial feasibility. Similarly, Ehie and Madsen (2005) found that feasibility is the third most important step in an implementation process for enterprise resource planning through an empirical analysis.

Although there is no data-specific assessment framework, scholars have proposed various frameworks to assess the readiness of big data analytics. Chen et al. (2014, pp. 175–176) listed the challenges for big data implementation, including data availability, data representation, legal restrictions, and the availability of analytical methods. Comuzzi and Patel (2016) developed a maturity model for BDA, constituting a specific data dimension focusing on data acquisition, management, and analytics. Based on the scarce literature, a five-dimensional model is developed to cover data availability, legal restrictions, and analytics. The evaluation model comprises four feasibility levels, ranging from 2 to minus indefinite. A score of 2 always indicates the highest feasibility of a dimension, whereas a minus indefinite specifies that either data collection, processing, or analytics are impossible. If a BDO receives a score of minus indefinite on any dimension, it is excluded from further analysis immediately. The ease-of-implementation assessment provided by one system provider in the previous section was not considered, because it represents the isolated view on one NP system. Figure 5.8 summarizes the assessment model and presents the five dimensions and feasibility scores.

	Scoring: 2	1	0	-∞
A How **technologically feasible** is the data collection?	Feasibility proven	Feasible, but not yet proven	Potentially feasible	Not feasible
B What are **legal or political restrictions** to the use of data?	No restrictions	Minor restrictions	Severe restrictions	Use of data not permitted
C How is **data ownership** organized?	Internal data	Data commercially available	Data potentially available	Data not available
D How **aggregated (holistic) is the available data**?	Single provider of aggregated data exists	Various providers of partly aggregated data	Various providers of un-aggregated data	Data not available
E How **accessible are analytics tools** to process the data?	Analytic tools integrated with data	Analytic tools commercially available	Analytic tools need to be developed	Analysis not possible

Figure 5.8 – Feasibility assessment model for big data acquisition and analytics[172]

The data collection and acquisition related to a BDO needs to be technologically feasible. Ideally, the specific dataset should already have been recorded, which proves the technological feasibility (score 2). If data collection is technologically not feasible, the BDO needs to be dropped. This would hypothetically apply for real-time satellite images, since that would require an unrealistically high number of geostationary satellites. Furthermore, there can be legal or political restrictions on data collection. Data privacy laws may restrict the use of raw data or make it completely illegal. Individual, non-anonymized mobile location tracking is an example of legally restricted data collection. Even if there are no technological and legal barriers to data collection, the data may simply not be available because data ownership lies with a company that does not want to share it. Data on the real O&Ds of cargo shipments exists already, but freight forwarders are data owners and have no interest in commercializing the data for cargo airlines. The fourth feasibility criterion is the variety of data sources. Ideally,

[172] Source: Own illustration.

all data should be available at the same source, which is the case for transponder data or Google Trends. BDOs with multiple data sources, such as mobile location data or clickstream data from meta-search engines, require data aggregation, thus reducing the feasibility of the BDO. Finally, there should be analytic tools to process the data. In an ideal case, the analytic tool is integrated in the data set, which is true for the hotel rate intelligence software. In the worst-case scenario, analytic tools cannot handle the data meaningfully, e.g., when data quality is poor.

Table 5.3 summarizes the individual feasibility assessments for all 23 BDOs. Examining the individual dimensions, technological and legal feasibility are the least restrictive criteria, whereas data ownership and accessibility of analytic tools hinder the implementation feasibility most.

For 16 out of the 23 BDOs, it could be proven that data collection is technologically feasible. This proof stems from either a commercialized use or scientific research using the data source. Three BDOs gave no proof of technological feasibility. Extraction of exhibitor manufacturing sites (A9) may be feasible, but there is no real-life example for such a scraped data set. Similarly, there is no example for a real-time information platform for traffic rights that connects transponder data with text mining from bilateral agreements. The extended e-AWB suffers resistance from forwarders who have blocked a technological proof of concept. However, all three BDOs appear potentially feasible and are rated with a score of 0.

Table 5.3 – Feasibility assessment of BDOs[173]

Code	Big data opportunity	How technologically feasible is the data collection?	What are legal or political re-strictions to the use of data?	How is data ownership organized?	How aggregated (holistic) is the available data?	How accessible are analytic tools to process the data?	Total score
A1	Geo-spatial image analysis	2	2	1	1	1	**7**
A2	Real-time inflation forecasts	2	2	0	2	1	**7**
A3	Consumer confidence measure-ment with social media	2	2	0	0	0	**4**
A4	Detailed demographic profiling with social media mining	2	1	1	0	0	**4**
A5	General search engine data for detailed O&D demand	2	2	1	2	0	**7**
A6	Clickstream data of meta-search websites for flights	2	2	1	0	0	**5**
A7	Social media mining to determine price elasticity	1	1	0	0	0	**2**
A8	Analysis of air cargo rates from online freight portals	2	1	1	2	2	**8**
A9	Analysis of exhibitor data of in-dustry fairs	0	2	0	0	0	**2**
A10	Shipping data from e-commerce platforms	2	2	0	1	0	**5**
B1	Analysis of reviews in travel rating communities	2	2	0	1	0	**5**
B2	Clickstream data from travel plat-forms	2	2	0	2	0	**6**
B3	Analysis of local hotel prices	2	2	1	2	2	**9**

[173] Source: Own illustration.

Code	Big data opportunity	How technologically feasible is the data collection?	What are legal or political restrictions to the use of data?	How is data ownership organized?	How aggregated (holistic) is the available data?	How accessible are analytic tools to process the data?	Total score
B4	Analysis of events in social networks	1	1	0	1	0	**3**
C1	Real-time flight tracking with transponder data	2	2	1	2	0	**7**
C2	Network-relevant competitor news monitoring	2	2	1	0	1	**6**
D1	Mobile location data from smartphones	2	0	1	1	1	**5**
D2	Extended electronic AWB with shipper address	0	1	2	0	0	**3**
D3	Location-transmitting sensors for cargo shipments	2	1	0	0	0	**3**
H1	Real-time slot trading platform	2	0	0	0	0	**2**
H2	Real-time traffic right information platform	0	1	0	0	0	**1**
I1	Global meteorological warning platform	1	2	0	0	0	**3**
I2	Global political risk assessments	1	2	1	0	1	**5**
	Average score	1.57	1.52	0.52	0.74	0.39	**4.74**

Two BDOs suffer severe legal restrictions, and seven BDOs have minor legal or political restrictions. A real-time slot trading platform relies on the cooperation of national regulatory authorities, and so far, only free-market economies have provided the necessary access to slot data. Transparency in slots may not be desirable for countries that wish to protect their national aviation industries or use slots as a means of political pressure. Mobile location data suffers from severe legal restrictions, since all the data needs to be anonymized and aggregated, making it impossible to track individual customers. BDOs with minor legal restrictions are mostly constraint from data privacy legislation.

Only the extended e-AWB can be counted as internal data, since it needs to be transmitted for every shipment. If the real O&D were to be added as a mandatory field, the BDA can use the internal AWB database as a primary data source. Further, 12 BDOs are not yet commercialized, which requires bilateral negotiations with the current data owners to access these data. Six BDOs have a single source of data, which reduces the effort of data matching and processing. Another 12 BDOs work with dispersed and unstructured data, which, in turn, makes complicated data matching and processing even more complicated. Intelligence software for cargo rates and hotel prices include analytic tools to draw useful information from given data. Five other BDOs offer analytics as an add-on service that needs to be procured. Integrated platform analytic tools, such as Google Trends or Facebook Audience Insight, were not rated in this category, since they are not customizable. The output data from Google Trends or Audience Insight must be processed and analyzed subsequently for the specific BDO purpose of airline NP.

If we contrast the potential and feasibility of all 23 BDOs, four clusters can be derived (see Figure 5.9). *Top priorities* are the BDOs with high potential (3.0 or above) and high feasibility (score of 5 or above). Six BDOs are located in this cluster, including the two most feasible BDOs. Solutions for cargo rate and hotel price analytics are readily available and need to be only subscribed. Search engine and clickstream data is also already available, although not all meta-search websites have commercialized their data yet. Mobile location data is being commercialized, and first pilot applications for public transportation do exist. Finally, shipping data from e-commerce platforms exist, but airlines need to negotiate with platform operators, such as Alibaba or JD.com, to access the data.

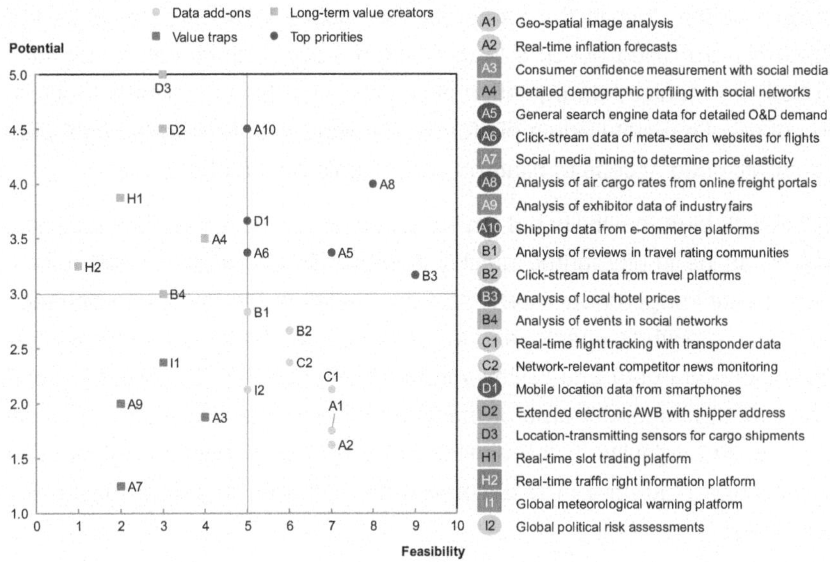

Figure 5.9 – Potential and feasibility evaluation matrix for BDOs[174]

Long-term value creators are BDOs with high potential that currently have limited implementation feasibility. Raw data on demographic profiling can be accessed from Facebook, but there is no automated data transmission and the queries need to be set manually. Furthermore, airlines can approach LinkedIn to drive the commercialization of business network data. Event extractions from Facebook are complicated due to the discontinued API, but third-party developers with full API access can potentially provide a customized solution for airline network planners. Airlines should actively lobby the IATA to include a mandatory real O&D field in the e-AWB. Similarly, airlines should approach mobile network providers to commercialize

[174] Source: Own illustration.

cargo location data in the same way as mobile location data, once LoRaWANs are rolled out at a large scale. Finally, airlines can lobby for a globally harmonized deregulation of slot trading rules to facilitate the creation of real-time slot trading platforms. Similarly, real-time traffic right platforms will need access to bilateral agreements on a global scale.

BDOs with high feasibility but limited potential can serve as *data add-ons*, which can be implemented quickly if a specific information need arises. Geo-spatial image analysis and real-time inflation forecasts can enhance economic growth forecasts, and travel trends can be identified by analyzing clickstream data and reviews from travel platforms. Competitor monitoring with transponder data or media monitoring may be valuable in case of increased volatility in the airlines industry. The services of global risk assessment platforms may become more important if political instability increases.

Four BDOs are potential *value traps*, since they are difficult to implement and have a low potential to satisfy information needs in airline NP. Consumer confidence measurement with social media is possible, but it is only a very minor input assumption in the economic growth models that are used by airlines. Furthermore, the data does not dramatically improve the traditional survey-based consumer confidence indices. Moreover, social media mining to determine price elasticity is a major technical challenge, since many input data need to be connected to specific customer profiles. Data privacy legislation further complicates this analysis. In reality, this BDO may be more valuable for the P&RM department of an airline, as it allows for individual pricing (if legally permitted). While data on industry fairs and exhibitors is easily available, it is problematic to identify the corresponding manufacturing sites and predict trade flows. Airline will need to match the data with their own bookings and invest heavily in data mining to extract relevant trade flows. Finally, meteorological warning platforms are the most relevant for flight operations but not for airline NP. Airlines should restrain from investing in *value traps*, unless their primary purpose is to serve a different function (e.g., flight operations).

The next chapter develops a cost and benefit evaluation scheme for the *top priorities* and *long-term value creator* clusters. The BDOs in the *data add-on* and *value trap* clusters are not included in the cost–benefit analysis, as those data sources are most likely not the primary investment candidates for airline NP. This gives us 12 BDOs for further analysis, including four cargo-specific BDOs (A8, A10, D2, D3), four passenger-specific BDOs (A4, B3, B4, D1), and four general BDOs (A5, A6, H1, H2).

6 Financial impact of big data for airline network planning

The selection of the appropriate BDOs to support the NP process is a key challenge for airline network planners. This chapter aims to develop a logical process that can help airline network planners to choose the most appropriate BDO and provide a framework to estimate the cost and benefits of a BDO investment. Figure 6.1 displays this logical process and links it to the relevant sections of this chapter.

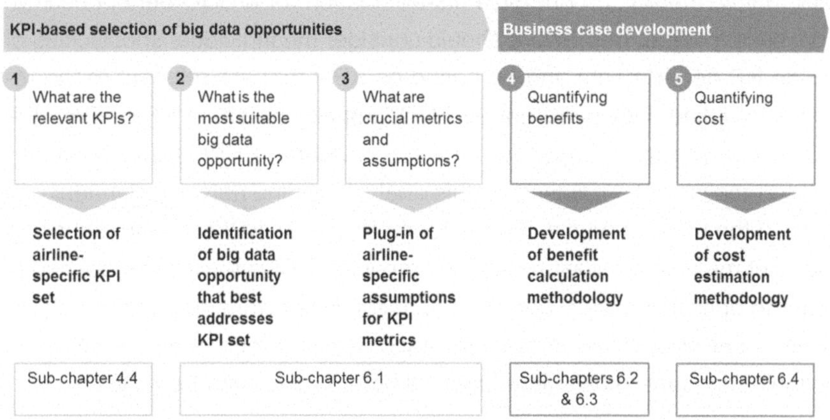

Figure 6.1 – Logical process to derive cost and benefit estimate for BDOs[175]

Since NP departments and processes differ significantly across airlines, the choice of the right BDO should always be based on specific KPIs of an airline NP department. Sub-chapter 6 presents a qualitative evaluation of the 12 selected BDOs based on the KPIs utilized in the NP departments of the case study group. Subsequently, the best metrics to measure the KPIs in the BDO context are chosen. Sub-chapter 6.2 develops a benefit calculation framework based on these metrics. Sub-chapter 6.3 operationalizes

---

[175] Source: Own illustration.

M. Schosser, *Big Data to Improve Strategic Network Planning in Airlines*,
Schriftenreihe der HHL Leipzig Graduate School of Management,
https://doi.org/10.1007/978-3-658-27582-2_6

the benefit calculation framework through a fictive airline example before sub-chapter 6.4 finally adds the cost perspective for the 12 selected BDOs.

6.1 Choice of appropriate BDOs based on KPIs

The status quo analysis of the current performance measurement practices reflected that airlines use a broad set of KPIs to measure their NP activities. Since the organizational setup and role of NP departments differs widely, there is no one-size-fits-all solution for a BDO benefit estimation. An expedient framework should consider the individual specificities of airline NP departments and be based on KPIs that are relevant to the respective airline. However, not all BDOs impact the same KPIs. First, the BDOs that are most impactful for each individual KPI need to be determined (section 6.1.1). Based on this analysis, airline network planners can choose the most promising BDOs for their specific KPI set. Subsequently, the right metrics to measure the KPI impact of BDOs have to be defined in order to operationalize a benefit calculation framework. Section 6.1.2 presents a set of possible metrics for each KPI and then chooses the most suitable measure to calculate financial benefits resulting from BDOs.

6.1.1 Impact of BDOs on airline NP KPIs

The case study group primarily uses indirect KPIs as well as aggregated route and network profitability to measure NP performance. The direct KPI load factor, direct operating cost (DOC), and indirect operating cost (IOC) are also used as secondary KPIs by some airlines. IOC and DOC are combined in a direct cost KPI, since all airlines use them in this form only. Similarly, network and route profitability are joined for the analysis. Figure 6.2 recapitulates the currently used KPIs from chapter 4.

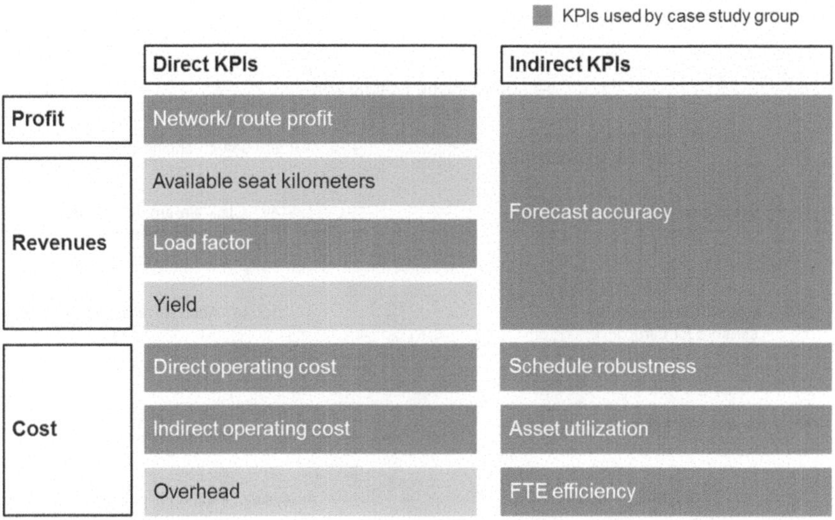

Figure 6.2 – Direct and indirect KPIs currently used by the case study group airlines[176]

In the last interview round, the participating airline network planners were asked to assess the impact of the 12 BDOs selected in chapter 5. The rating scale ranged from 0 (no impact) to 5 (very high impact), and each primary or secondary KPI that the respective airline used was assessed. The average scores across the case study group were calculated using an equally weighted arithmetic mean of the answers[177]. The average scores were used to produce spider graphs for each KPI, which visually indicate the estimated impact by BDO (Figure 6.3 to Figure 6.9). Cargo-specific BDOs were evaluated only by cargo airlines, while passenger-specific BDOs were evaluated only by the FSCs, LCCs, and SCAs. General BDOs were evaluated by all the applicable airlines.

---

[176] Source: Own illustration.

[177] Only answers from the airlines which use the respective KPI are included.

Route and network profitability

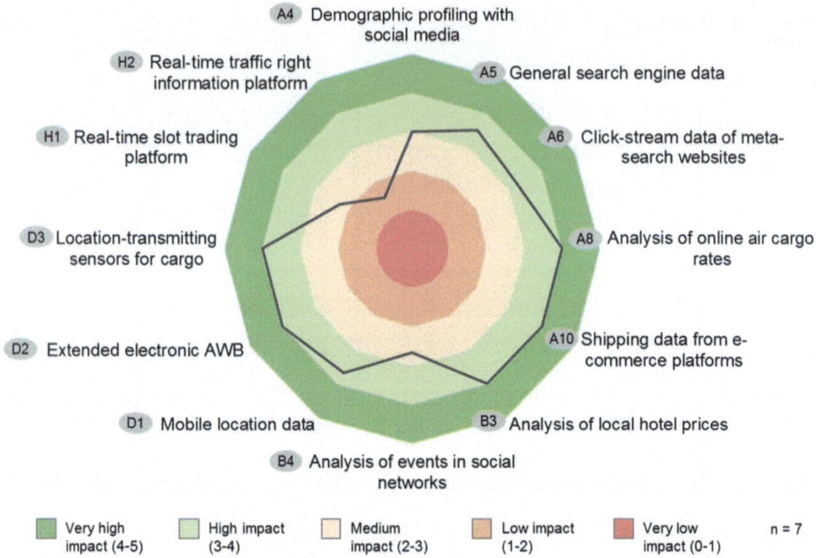

Figure 6.3 – Estimated impact of BDOs on route and network profitability[178]

Seven of the case study group airlines use route or network profitability as primary or secondary KPI[179]. All of the business models are represented. The four cargo-specific BDOs achieved the highest scores of 4.0, which indicates that cargo airlines expect a very high impact of all BDOs on profitability. Passenger airlines expect the highest profitability impact from hotel price analysis (4.0) and mobile location data (3.7). General search engine data received a high impact score on profitability across all airlines (3.5). The two "planning constraint" BDOs were rated the lowest, with low

---

[178] Source: Own illustration.

[179] LCC 2 and CAR 3 do not use route or network profitability.

and medium impact scores of 1.5 and 2.3 respectively. Besides the low ranking of the "planning constraint" BDOs, there was no clear pattern across the need for information clusters.

Load factor

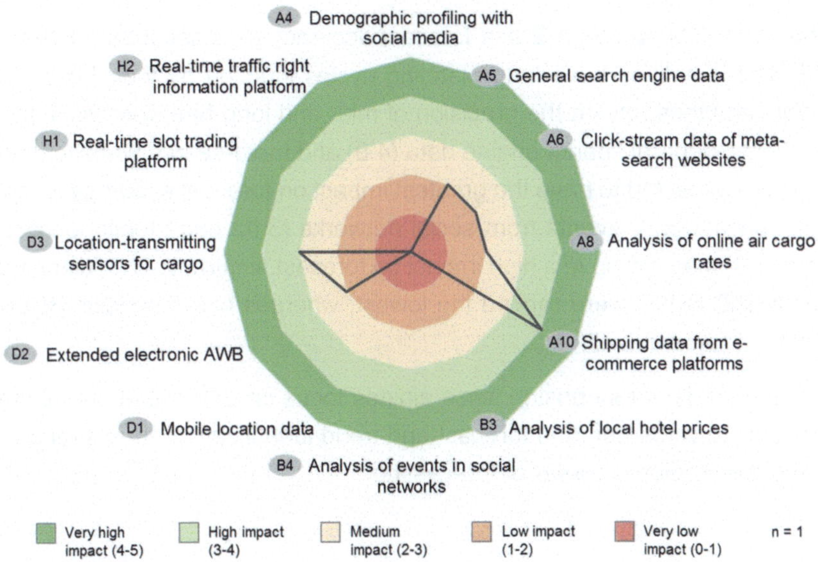

Figure 6.4 – Estimated impact of BDOs on load factor[180]

Only CAR 1 uses load factor as a secondary KPI for the NP departments. Thus, Figure 6.4 represents the answers of only this airline. Shipping data from e-commerce platforms is the only BDO with an expected very high impact on the load factor. E-commerce usually entails small merchandise in boxes, which can be assimilated on pallets. Thus, a detailed forecast of e-commerce shipments can improve load planning, thereby improving the

[180] Source: Own illustration.

load factor. Similarly, cargo airlines can use real-time location data for cargo (impact score of 3.0) to predict late arrivals and fill the load space with alternative cargo, if possible. None of the other BDOs are expected to have significant impact on the load factor.

Forecast accuracy

The two FSCs and SCA 2 use forecast accuracy as a secondary KPI for NP. These airlines have long planning cycles induced by their business model and thus rely on the precision of mid- and long-term forecasts. Accordingly, general search engine data (4.0) and meta-search website data (3.7) are expected to have the greatest impact on forecast accuracy. Local hotel prices (3.3), events from social networks (3.0), and mobile location data (3.0) may still have a high impact on forecast accuracy. The “planning constraint” BDOs were ranked the lowest, whereas cargo-specific BDOs were not ranked at all.

The pattern is not surprising since airlines focus on BDOs that contribute primarily towards demand forecast and trend identification, thus strengthening the predictive power of forecasting.

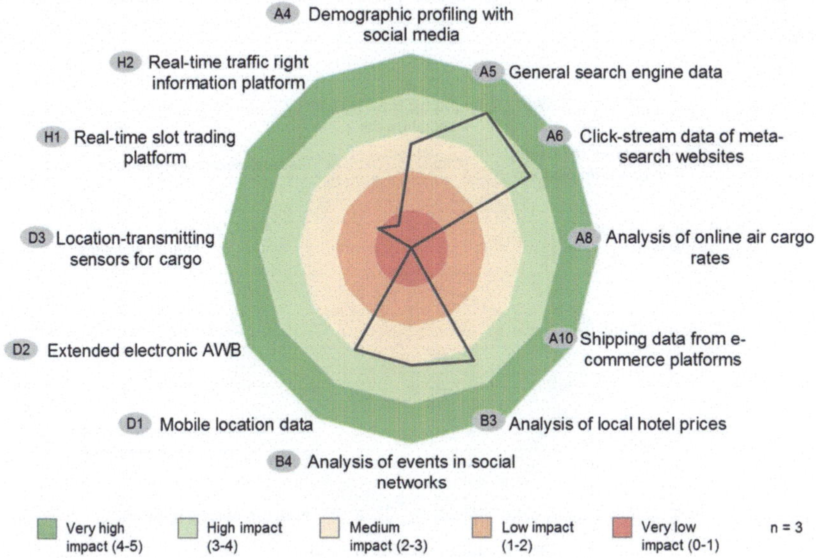

Figure 6.5 – Estimated impact of BDOs on forecast accuracy[181]

Schedule robustness

LCC 2 and CAR 1 measure schedule robustness as a secondary KPI for their NP departments. The late deliveries of cargo shipments are a major driver of delays in the air cargo business. These can be mitigated by obtaining data from real-time location transmitting cargo sensors, which are assigned a very high potential (4.0) by CAR 1. LCC 2 expects information on the age structure of passengers from demographic profiling. This information can help anticipate the likelihood of passengers requiring special assistance, which is a major driver of ground operations handling delays

[181] Source: Own illustration.

for LCC 2. All other BDOs bear no to medium impact for schedule robustness.

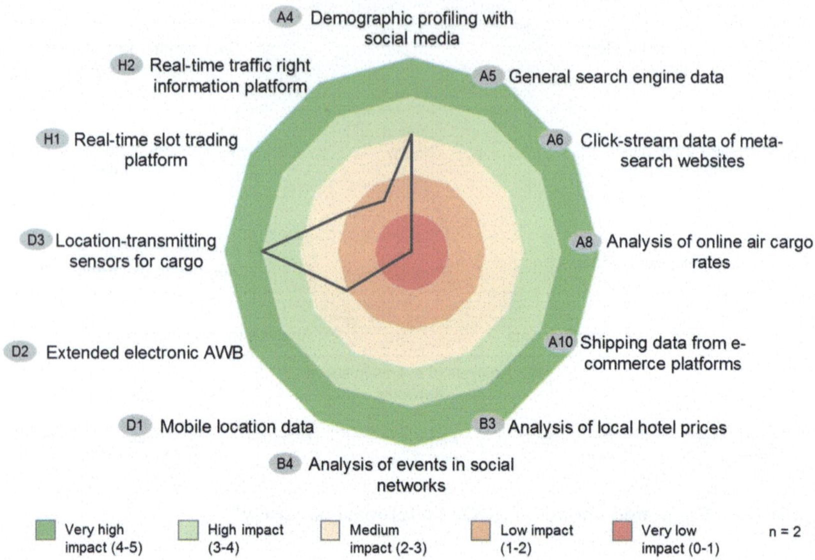

Figure 6.6 – Estimated impact of BDOs on schedule robustness[182]

It is surprising that none of the "planning constraint" BDOs are expected to have a high impact, since information on slots and traffic rights can help calculate the impact of delays at specific airports (e.g., due to unavailability of later slots). In contrast, the low expected potential of "demand forecast" and "trend identification" BDOs seems logical, since the influence of demand on schedule robustness is limited.

[182] Source: Own illustration.

Asset utilization

Six airlines across all business models consider asset utilization to be a KPI for NP[183]. Asset utilization can be improved by changing the route mix, i.e., closing schedule gaps by adding additional flights or re-scheduling existing flights. For cargo airlines, idea generation for the next best route is a crucial lever, which is supported by their high impact rating for air cargo rates (4.0) and e-commerce shipping data (4.0). Both the BDOs contribute towards identifying value pockets in the form of unserved or underserved routes, which air cargo network planners can use to optimize their route mix.

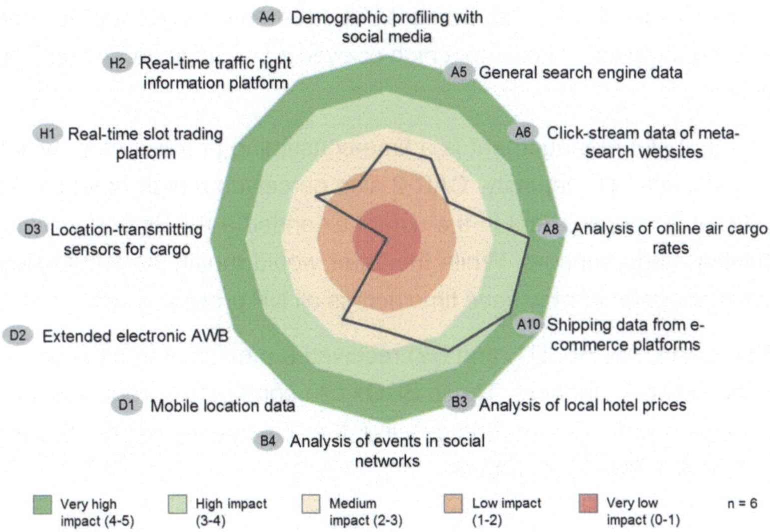

Figure 6.7 – Estimated impact of BDOs on asset utilization[184]

[183] LCC 2 and SCA 2 use it as a primary KPI; FSC 2, LCC 1, SCA 1, and CAR 2 use it as a secondary KPI.

[184] Source: Own illustration.

Passenger airlines rated local hotel price analysis the highest (3.5), as that may enable the discovery of untapped revenue pockets and adjustment for micro-seasonality. Real-time BDOs are not deemed relevant for asset utilization across passenger and cargo airlines. The airline network planners attested that several BDOs have a medium impact on asset utilization (A4, A5, A6, B4, and H1), but there is no clear recognizable pattern. However, cargo airlines expect more impact potential on asset utilization than passenger airlines.

FTE efficiency

Three airlines (FSC 1, LCC 2, and CAR 2) calculate FTE efficiency as a secondary KPI for the NP department. All three airlines attested to real-time slot trading platform having a high or even a very high impact on FTE efficiency.

It seems that slot management is a time-consuming process step, which binds significant FTE capacity. CAR 2 also perceives a high potential for FTE efficiency improvement in the use of extended e-AWBs and location transmitting cargo sensors. While the latter would mostly benefit tactical NP, slot management may save time across all NP process steps.

Five BDOs (A4, A5, A6, D1, and H2) received a medium impact score by the airline network planners. Those BDOs can contribute to reducing time for information gathering and processing, thereby making NP employees more efficient in their daily routine.

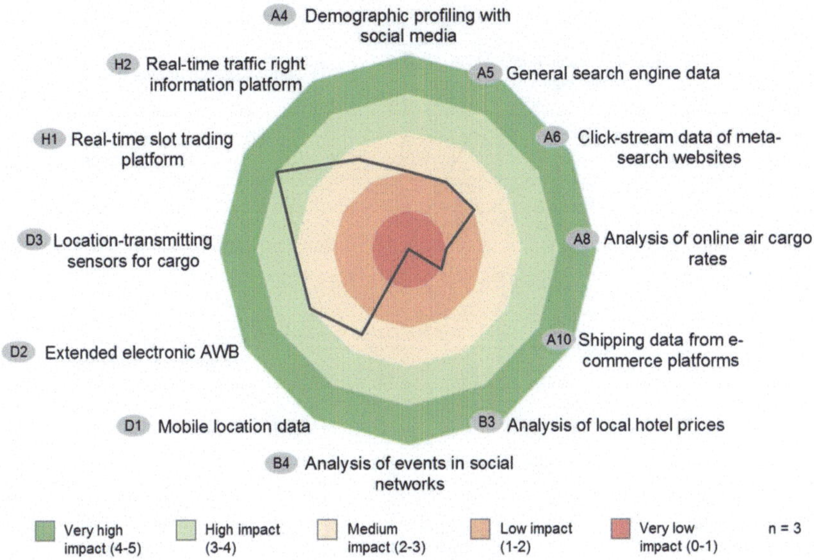

Figure 6.8 – Estimated impact of BDOs on FTE efficiency[185]

Direct and indirect operating cost

SCA 1, LCC 1, and CAR 3 use DOC and IOC as cost KPI for NP. In contrast to other KPIs, the "planning constraint" BDOs received high impact scores. A real-time slot trading platform has very high potential for cost reductions (4.0), and a real-time traffic right information platform has a high potential (3.5). Real-time slot management and traffic right information can help reduce delay-induced cost and fines for exceeding traffic rights or missing assigned slots. Mobile location data achieved a medium impact score of 2.0, whereas all the other BDOs were considered to have low or no impact.

185 Source: Own illustration.

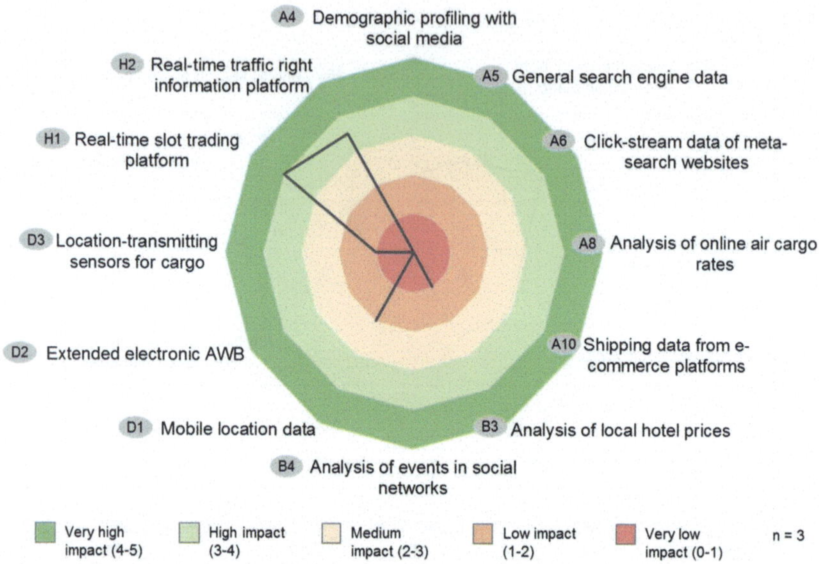

Figure 6.9 – Estimated impact of BDOs on DOC and IOC[186]

If the impact of BDOs is compared across the seven different KPIs, it is noteworthy that no BDO has a high impact on all the KPIs, but every BDO influences at least one KPI highly or very highly (see Table 6.1). Furthermore, every BDO has "blind spots," meaning that it has no significant impact on one or more KPIs. Therefore, there is no single BDO that suits all NP KPIs. Thus, airline network planners should select the suitable BDOs based on their specific KPI mix to maximize the impact.

---

[186] Source: Own illustration.

Table 6.1 – Impact of BDOs on airline network planning KPIs[187]

BDOs	Route & network profitability	Load factor	Forecast accuracy	Schedule robustness	Aircraft utilization	FTE efficiency	Direct cost
Detailed demographic profiling with social media mining	◕	○	◑	◕	◑	◑	○
General search engine data for detailed O&D demand	◕	◑	●	○	◑	◑	○
Clickstream data of meta-search websites for flights	◕	◑	◕	○	◑	◑	○
Scraping of published rates of cargo shipping portals	●	◑	○	○	●	◔	○
Shipping data from e-commerce platforms	●	●	○	○	●	◔	○
Scraping of regional hotel prices	●	○	◕	○	◕	○	◔
Analysis of events on social media platforms	◑	○	◕	○	◑	◑	◑
Mobile location data	◕	○	◕	○	◑	◑	○
Extended electronic AWB with shipper address	●	◑	○	◑	○	◕	○
Location-transmitting sensors for cargo shipments	●	◕	○	●	○	◕	◔
Real-time slot trading platform	◑	○	◔	◑	◑	●	●
Real-time traffic right information platform	◔	○	○	◔	◔	◑	◕

Legend: ● very high - ◕ high - ◑ medium - ◔ low - ○ very low/none (rating derived from Figures 6.3-6.9)

[187] Source: Own illustration.

It is worth noting that the results of the impact assessment are not statistically significant, since the number of individual assessments is low due to the limited size of the case study group. Including more airlines in a broader survey will increase the external validity of the analysis and bridge the assessment gaps, such as that of the load factor, which were assessed by one cargo airline only. However, the result patterns confirmed the earlier hypothesis that there is no one-size-fits-all solution for airlines when it comes to choosing the most suitable BDO for airline NP.

6.1.2 Suitable KPI metrics for BDOs in airline NP

Airlines must select the right KPI metrics to calculate the expected benefits from BDO deployment. For most KPIs, there are multiple potential measures, including static and dynamic metrics as well as metrics focusing only on a KPI aspect that is relevant for NP. Dynamic metrics measure the change in a specific KPI over time and are preferable to static measures, which measure a KPI at a specific point of time[188]. Furthermore, the metrics should fall in the domain of airline NP. External factors, such as fuel prices or economic downturns, should be excluded from the NP-specific benefit analysis to represent the actual impact of BDOs on NP.

Figure 6.10 collates a range of possible metrics for each of the seven KPIs used by the case study group. Route profit, for example, can be calculated using static metrics, such as the total or average route profitability for a given period. This global static metric is influenced by several internal and external factors (e.g., economic cycle, fuel prices) with limited influence by the NP department. Alternatively, only the routes with long-term negative performance can be used as an indicator for unsuccessful route decisions. This metric is static but focuses on a remit that is more controllable by a

[188] BDO impact should be assessed over an investment time period (e.g., 5 years) to inform a business case calculation.

NP department if the objective is to minimize loss-making routes. A dynamic metric can measure the performance of new routes, which are fully under the responsibility of the NP department. This metric is a concrete measure for decision-making quality, which should also be improved by the deployment of BDOs. Including dropped routes would tune the metric to become more holistic in terms of NP responsibility, as it also reflects the decisions on terminated services[189].

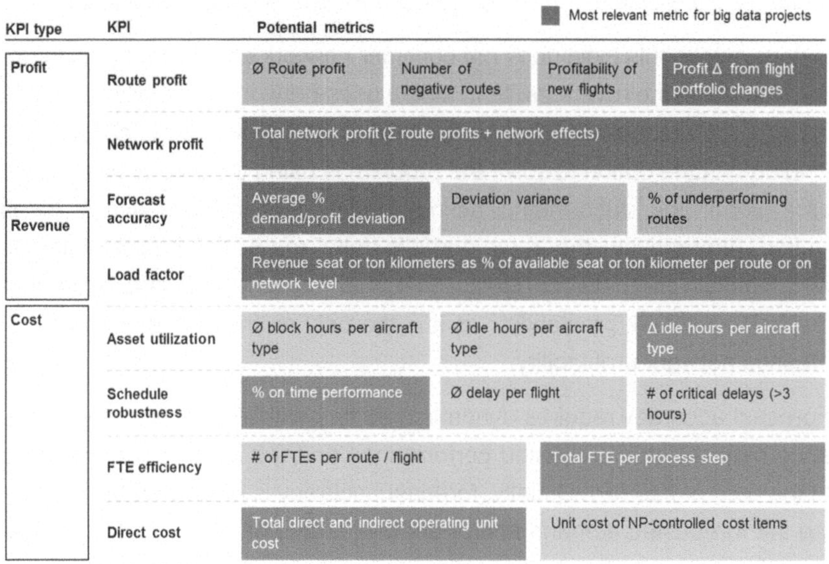

Figure 6.10 – Relevant metrics for KPI calculation in airline NP[190]

The metric "profit delta from flight portfolio changes" compares the financial performance of new flights with the financial performance of terminated services. Ideally, the new flights should show a significantly higher profitability than the ended flights, thus proving the value added by NP. Choosing

[189] Otherwise, highly profitable routes can be replaced with other profitable routes, which will not affect the total route profit for the airline.

[190] Source: Own illustration.

"profit delta from flight portfolio changes" or only the "new flight performance" depends on the capacity development of the airline. An airline with little capacity growth needs to replace its existing services if it wants to pursue new route opportunities, while an airline with strong capacity growth can simply add new flights without terminating the existing ones. For airlines with high capacity growth, the "new flight performance" metric is more suitable. For all other airlines, the "profit delta from flight portfolio changes" metric is preferable to measure the BDO impact on route profitability.

Unfortunately, this logic does not consider network effects, comprising upline and downline revenues. If an airline uses network profitability as a KPI instead of route profitability, the extraction of the NP-specific impact is challenging[191]. One option to solve the problem is using the total network profit as a global and static metric, acknowledging that the influence of NP is limited. Alternatively, the "route portfolio delta" metric can be calculated as well, omitting the network effects. The total network profit is chosen as a metric for network profitability, as it is the only metric that specifically addresses network profitability.

Forecast accuracy requires dynamic metrics by definition, since the difference between the forecasted performance and the actual performance is at the core of this KPI. Usually, forecast accuracy is measured by comparing the forecasted demand and/or profit with the actual figures for a single period at the route level. The average relative forecast deviation then expresses the accuracy of the forecast. If an airline wants to reduce extreme outliers, the deviation variance can be calculated as well. Some airlines accept deviations if they are "positive surprises" but want to control negative forecast deviations. However, considering only the negative deviations creates an incentive for the NP departments to forecast demand and profit very conservatively. This can lead to the refusal of new route opportunities,

[191] Upline and downline revenues tend to display significant variance on many routes, so the dynamic comparison is diffused (Sterzenbach et al., 2013, p. 393).

although they would be financially beneficial. The initially presented metric "average forecast deviation per route" is the most holistic measure of forecast accuracy and is thus recommended for a BDO benefit analysis.

The load factor calculation is standardized, since it expresses the percentage of available capacity that has been sold. In order to balance different route lengths and aircraft sizes, the load factor is calculated on a unit basis, which is seat kilometers for passenger airlines and ton kilometers for cargo airlines. Like network profitability, load factor is a global and static metric, influenced by many factors. Low-cost carriers tend to increase the load factor by aggressive pricing, which may lower yield and profit, despite high load factors. Load factors are only partially in the remit of NP and require extensive assumptions if used as a KPI for the evaluation of a BDO.

Asset utilization is typically measured with the average block hours that aircrafts fly per day. The objective is to minimize the unproductive time on the ground and distribute the aircraft financing cost along more flight hours, thereby reducing the indirect unit cost. The aircraft utilization can be differentiated by aircraft type, as long-haul and short-haul aircrafts have significantly different operation patterns. However, asset utilization cannot be increased indefinitely, because maintenance schedules and turnaround times are required in every rotation plan. For this reason, some airlines use an alternative metric, called "idle hours." "Idle hours" measure only the unproductive time during which an aircraft is parked idle on the ground. NP departments are responsible for the minimization of the unproductive ground time with schedule optimization and find suitable flights instead. Therefore, "idle time" is fully in the remit of NP, but it is still a static measure. The metric can be dynamized by measuring only the change in average idle time per aircraft over two different periods. These times are aggregated and converted to a reasonable number of flights that can be operated in this idle time to create a monetary benefit value. This metric is both dynamic and NP controlled. Hence, it is preferred to assess BDO value contribution.

Schedule robustness is often directly related to the delay statistics of a schedule period. The standard metric is used to measure the average delay of flights by comparing the block times of each flight with the scheduled block times. Schedule deviations of less than five minutes are not considered delays, and airlines can easily track only delayed flights using an on-time performance metric. This metric indicates the flights with a delay of more than five minutes as a percentage of all flights. Longer delays are usually more costly than short delays, since passengers can claim compensation and additional services. Thus, certain airlines may track only cost-significant delays that pass a pre-defined threshold (e.g., 3 hours). All schedule robustness metrics are partially in the remit of the NP department, since it can build in time buffers and maintain spare aircraft to react to operational and technical delays. Since minor delays of less than five minutes are not financially relevant, on-time performance is the most holistic measure for schedule robustness.

FTE efficiency in the NP department can be measured in relation to the route portfolio or in relation to the individual NP process steps. Several airlines from the case study group measure FTE efficiency by the number of routes that an individual FTE is managing, which in some cases is differentiated by long-haul and short-haul. However, this measure can be misleading, since some routes require greater planning and managing effort than others. A more meaningful measure is based on a process workload analysis that investigates the number of FTE working on individual process steps. As BDOs can support very specific process steps, this metric facilitates benefit calculation for any BDO deployment.

Several airlines from the case study group report that direct and indirect costs are used as KPIs for NP departments. If a NP department is a profit center, it may be useful to consider all DOCs and IOCs as the unit cost in performance analyses. However, most cost items are not under the direct control of NP departments. An alternative approach considers only the incurred costs that are directly controlled, namely airport and traffic fees and delay costs. Since these cost items are only a small fraction of the total cost, the use of this metric is not meaningful. Although the overall unit costs are not under the full responsibility of the NP department, it is the only meaningful holistic cost metric. In any case, it is difficult to relate NP-specific BDOs to company-wide cost. Thus, it should only be considered in special cases to justify BDO investments for NP, where a causal relation to specific cost categories can be created.

6.2 Financial benefit calculation for big data opportunities

Based on the recommended metrics for each KPI, this sub-chapter develops an estimation methodology to quantify a BDO's benefit. The input data required for the metrics are discussed along with the estimations on the impact of BDOs. The sub-chapter is structured according to the eight KPI metrics, which are discussed consecutively. The metrics are operationalized in sub-chapter 6.3. Table 6.2 summarizes the required input data and estimations for each KPI metric.

Table 6.2 – Required input data and estimations for KPI metrics[192]

KPI	Metric	Required input data	Estimations to be made	BDO financial benefit
Route profit	Profit delta from flight portfolio changes	▪ Aggregate profits from discontinued flights ▪ Aggregated profits from new flights	▪ Number of flights to be changed ▪ Average profit for big data–supported route/flight frequency decision ▪ Average profit of discontinued flights	Increase in average profits for new routes expected

[192] Source: Own illustration.

KPI	Metric	Required input data	Estimations to be made	BDO financial benefit
Network profit	Total network profit	▪ Aggregated route profits adjusted for network effects	▪ Percent increase in network profit due to NP BDO	Increase in network profitability
Forecast accuracy	Average forecast deviation per route	▪ Demand/profit forecast per route for a given period ▪ Actual booking figures for the same period (if demand forecast) ▪ Actual profit figures per route (if profit forecast)	▪ Reduction potential of average deviations due to NP BDO	No direct financial benefit
Load factor	Average load factor in %	▪ Available seat kilometers and revenue seat kilometers for the entire network for a specific time period	▪ Percentage point increase due to NP BDO	Increase in RSK/RTK multiplied with expected yield
Asset utilization	Average idle hours per A/C type	▪ Average number of idle hours (ground time minus turnarounds and maintenance) for last schedule period per aircraft type	▪ Number of potential additional flights per A/C type to reduce total idle time	Profit from additional flights
Schedule robustness	On-time performance	▪ Planned flight schedule ▪ Actual departure and arrival times (on/off block)	▪ Reduction potential of schedule-related delays due to NP BDO	Reduction of delay cost
FTE efficiency	FTE per process step	▪ Number of NP FTE ▪ Allocation of FTE to process steps	▪ Automation potential by process step due to NP BDO	Reduction of FTE cost
Direct cost	Operating cost (indirect and direct)	▪ Report on DOC and IOC for chosen time period	▪ Cost reduction potential through NP-specific BDO	Reduction of direct and indirect operating cost

Profit delta from flight portfolio changes

The profit delta from flight portfolio changes is a financial performance measure, calculated by subtracting the total profits of all discontinued flights from the total profits of all new flights. A discontinued flight may be the result of a discontinued route or reduction of flight frequencies on continued routes. Flights that are simply re-scheduled without change in flight number are not considered for this metric. Similarly, new flights can either be all the flights of a new route or individual new flights on an existing route, following an increase in flight frequency. Thus, the calculation is as follows:

$$(1)\ \Delta P_{(portfolio\ chan\quad)} = \sum_{i=1}^{m} P_{i\ (new\ flights)} - \sum_{j=1}^{n} P_{j\ (discontinued\ flights)}$$

where:

$\Delta P_{(portfolio\ change)}$	= profit change resulting from installation/discontinuation of flights [USD]
$P_{i\ (new\ flights)}$	= profit of the ith newly installed flight [USD], (i = 1 ...m)
m	= total number of newly installed flights
$P_{j\ (discontinued\ flights)}$	= profit of the jth discontinued flight [USD], (j = 1 ... n)
n	= total number of discontinued flights

The primary input data is the aggregated profits of new flights and the aggregated profits of discontinued flights. For the estimations, the average profits for both categories have to be calculated as well. The key estimations for BDO impact calculation are the expected number of flight changes and the expected average profit for BDO-supported new flight decisions.

The number of flight changes can be predicted by analyzing the same variable from previous schedules. However, the number of flight changes may increase as more attractive route opportunities are identified using big data.

The hypothesis is that BDO-supported new flights should yield higher profits than flights added without BDO support. Therefore, the $\Delta P_{(portfolio\ change)}$ should be higher after BDO implementation.

Total network profit

The total network profit is calculated by adding all the individual route profits and adjusting for network effects (see section 3.4.4 for a detailed discussion of network profitability). The general nature of this metric makes it difficult to connect the impact of a specific BDO causally to the measure. As the total network profit is influenced by all the airline departments and external factors, airline network planners have to make a high-level assumption on the BDO impact. This means that, in practice, a percentage value must be defined as an estimation for the financial BDO impact. Due to the superficiality of this metric, it cannot be recommended for justifying investment calculations for BDOs.

Average forecast deviation on route level

The average forecast deviation at the route level is the arithmetic mean of all absolute individual route forecast deviations. The forecasts may apply to either the demand or profit. In both cases, the required input data is the forecast at the route level for a specific time period – typically a calendar year – and the actual demand or profit figures at the route level for the same period. Logically, this metric is an ex-post analysis. Therefore, the calculation for *k* number of routes is as follows:

$$(2)\ \overline{FD} = \frac{\sum_{k=1}^{n}\left[\frac{\left|Q_{k\,(actual)} - Q_{k\,(forecast)}\right|}{Q_{k\,(forecast)}}\right]}{n} \cdot 100$$

Where

$\overline{\mathrm{FD}}$ = average forecast deviation in percent

$Q_{k\,(actual)}$ = actual demand of the kth route [number of passengers or USD], (k = 1 … n)

$Q_{k\,(forecast)}$ = forecasted demand of the kth route [number of passengers or USD], (k = 1 … n)

n = total number of forecasted routes

The investment in BDOs should decrease the actual forecast deviation, hence improving the forecast accuracy. Since the current forecast accuracy depends on the currently used forecasting methods and tools, there is no single range of reasonable accuracy improvements through the BDOs. An airline that is currently only extrapolating past data may see a dramatic improvement of forecast accuracy, while an airline with a sophisticated multi-factorial forecasting model may only improve by a few percentage points using the same BDO. This estimation needs to be conducted by airline network planners who have transparency in the accuracy performance of their own forecast models. In any case, improving forecast accuracy does not directly translate to financial benefit. This KPI is a moderator that enables better NP decisions, then resulting in higher route profitability or an increased load factor.

Average load factor

The average load factor is calculated by comparing the available capacity with the actual sold capacity (compare section 4.4.2). Passenger airlines use seat kilometers as a unit for load factor calculation; cargo airlines rely on ton kilometers. Therefore, the mathematic expression to calculate load factor for passenger airlines is as follows[193]:

$$(3)\ LF = \frac{\sum_{i=1}^{n}(r_i \cdot d_i)}{\sum_{i=1}^{n}(c_i \cdot d_i)} \cdot 100$$

Where

LF = load factor in percent

r_i = sold seats of the ith flight [number of seats], (i = 1 … n)

c_i = seat capacity of the ith flight [number of seats], (i = 1 … n)

d_i = stage length of the ith flight [kilometers], (i = 1 … n)

n = total number of flights

Similar to network profits, the load factor is a general metric influenced by all the commercial departments. The direct effect of a NP-specific BDO on the load factor is difficult to estimate, especially in airlines with very long-term NP processes. Airlines with a flexible NP process may influence load factor through re-scheduling and re-routings, but the NP effect is difficult to isolate. If airline network planners wish to justify a BDO project with increased load factors, they need to make a highly accurate estimation pertaining to the improvement potential driven by a specific BDO. This is likely to be very speculative, and therefore, this metric is not recommended as a single justification of BDO investments.

Average idle hours per A/C type

Idle hours refer to the unproductive ground-time of an aircraft, i.e., all the ground time that is not used for maintenance, turn-arounds, or spare

[193] For cargo airlines, the seat capacity is replaced by metric ton capacity and the sold seats by sold metric tons.

aircraft assignments. These must be calculated using the aircraft rotation plans, where it is necessary to subtract planned block hours and productive ground time from the total available time. Idle hours constitute the contingent that can be used to increase aircraft productivity by optimizing the schedule without further operational optimization such as shorter turn-arounds or shorter maintenance events. Therefore, the calculation of average yearly idle time T_{idle} for a number of aircrafts is the following:

$$(4)\ \bar{T}_{idle} = \frac{\sum_{i=1}^{n}\{(365 \cdot 24) - T_{i\,(BT)} - T_{i\,(TAT)} - T_{i\,(maintenance)} - T_{i\,(spare)}\}}{n}$$

where

$\bar{T}_{idle}$	= average yearly idle time per aircraft [hours]
$T_{i\,(BT)}$	= yearly block time for the ith aircraft [hours], (i = 1 … n)
$T_{i\,(TAT)}$	= yearly turnaround time for the ith aircraft [hours], (i = 1 … n)
$T_{i\,(maintenance)}$	= yearly maintenance time for the ith aircraft [hours], (i = 1 … n)
$T_{i\,(spare)}$	= yearly spare aircraft time for the ith aircraft [hours], (i = 1 … n)
n	= total number of aircraft

BDOs can enable these optimizations by creating transparency in planning constraints and identifying potential routes to use aircrafts in their idle time. Many short-haul aircrafts are parked overnight at their base airports without any scheduled maintenance. BDOs could help identify financially feasible overnight routes to reduce this idle time. The profit resulting from these additional flights can be directly attributed to the BDOs. Since short-haul and long-haul fleets have very different rotation plans[194], the fleet types should ideally be kept separate. This metric is not recommendable if existing night rotations are incurring losses. In such a case, the termination of these flights will increase profits and idle hours[195].

The main input data is derived from the analysis of past rotation plans, in order to calculate the average idle hours per aircraft for each fleet type. To estimate the impact potential of any BDO, it is crucial to analyze the composition of idle-time blocks. If idle time is dispersed in blocks of few minutes between scheduled flights, the schedule needs to be packed more tightly in order to enable an additional flight. This might not be feasible if the idle time is deliberately maintained as time buffer for increasing schedule robustness such that the overall BDO impact potential is low. In contrast, if idle-time blocks are large, such as overnight stays without maintenance, the potential for identifying route opportunities using BDOs is higher. Section 6.3.2 provides an example for actual BDO-benefit calculation.

On-time performance

On-time performance is typically calculated as the percentage of flights departing within 15 minutes of the scheduled departure time. Departure is regarded as the first movement of the aircraft, which can be the push-back on the ground or the start of taxiing. The off-block time is recorded and can be compared with the scheduled departure time in order to calculate the deviation for every flight. Small delays are usually not financially relevant and can be recuperated during the flight or absorbed by time buffers that are built into the schedule.

---

[194] Long-haul aircrafts typically have fewer overnight stays but longer turn-around times and maintenance blocks than short-haul aircrafts.

[195] In this case, the use of asset utilization as KPI for network planning should be reconsidered – profitability metrics might be more appropriate.

BDOs can improve on-time performance by revealing regular delay factors and real-time information pertaining to cargo and aircrafts. Large delays produce huge delay costs, which need to be mitigated by airline network planning. Delays are never planned, but a robust airline schedule contains sufficient time buffers and spare aircrafts to accommodate operational irregularities. Therefore, the impact of BDOs can rarely be linked with the mitigation of specific delay events and only with a general reduction of major delays. The calculation of the financial impact of delays proves to be difficult for many airlines, and there is no standard methodology available for this purpose (Cook et al., 2009). The most practical approach is to segment the delays into small, medium, and large categories and to assume a cost-per-hour value based on the aircraft type. Cook et al. (2009) provide a comprehensive overview of cost-per-hour delay costs for a broad range of aircraft types. The final estimation for BDO benefit calculation, therefore, requires the definition of a percentage of small, medium, and large delays that can be mitigated by BDOs. An example calculation is included in the business case framework presented in section 6.3.2.

FTE per process step

The FTE per process step metric is a simple allocation of workforce in the NP department to the individual NP process steps. Major input data is an airline-specific NP process map[196] and a workforce allocation analysis. Many companies rely on employee surveys to estimate the share of time spent on individual process steps if the staff is responsible for multiple process steps. The distribution can vary significantly between airlines, and as such, no standard allocation is available.

BDOs can help automate specific tasks (e.g., creating a long list of potential routes) or facilitate information gathering (e.g., by a real-time slot-trading platform). This improvement should result in spending less time on

[196] The generic NP process portrayed in section 3.5.7 can serve as a baseline but needs to be adapted to airline specificities and feedback loops.

a specific process step such that the time saved can be quantified in FTE. Naturally, the BDO-benefit potential is highest for large NP departments with little automation, and it is the lowest for small or highly automated NP departments. The financial benefit can then be easily calculated based on airline-specific FTE costs and the number of saved FTE.

Operating cost (indirect and direct)

Operating costs include all direct and indirect costs that are related to the operations of an airline. Direct operating costs are immediately related to flight operation and include fuel, airport and traffic fees, ground handling, and passenger-related expenses. Indirect operating costs occur independent of the performed flight. The most prominent costs are aircraft-financing cost, flight crew salaries, and maintenance cost. NP controls none of these cost factors exclusively[197]; it can, however, influence the overall cost by including reasonable estimates in route profitability forecasts.

BDOs can help sharpen cost forecasts and avoid unnecessary direct costs such as diversion cost due to missing a slot or penalties for disregarded traffic rights. Thus, the historic costs of these specific applications must be assessed as the main input factors for benefit calculation. In a second step, it is necessary for airline network planners to estimate the number of DOC and IOC relevant incidents that can be mitigated with BDO support, in order to calculate the financial benefit of the BDO.

6.3 Business case framework for big data in airline NP

This sup-chapter introduces Example Air, a fictive mid-sized full-service carrier, whose operational and financial specifics are derived from real-world airlines (section 6.3.1). Subsequently, the benefit calculation for a

[197] In one SCA of the case study group, the NP department negotiates airport and ground handling fees. However, in most airlines, this is performed by the airport relation or procurement department.

big data business case is shown as example for each of the relevant KPIs (section 6.3.2).

6.3.1 Introduction of Example Air

Example Air is a mid-sized full-service carrier with a dual-hub network structure and a healthy financial performance. Its total revenues amount to six billion USD, 500 million USD of which results as operating profit measured as earnings before interest and tax (EBIT). It operates a homogeneous two-type fleet of 100 aircrafts, with three-quarters of the total being short- and medium-haul aircrafts and the remaining long-haul aircrafts. There is no planned capacity increase over the next five years.

From its two hubs, Example Air connects 100 destinations on three continents. This results in 150 routes, as some destinations are accessible from the both hubs. The routes are operated 12 times a week on average, which results in a total of 1,750 return flights and 3,500 individual flights per week. The total offered capacity is 70 billion ASK, of which Example Air could sell 60 billion – a load factor of 86%. The overall on-time performance is 85%, but only 1% of flights are delayed by 1 hour or more.

The network is managed by a temporally specialized NP department that consists of 15 FTE. Ten of these manage the strategic network planning steps, while five are dedicated to tactical network planning. The NP department is responsible for demand forecasting and has produced an average forecast deviation of 11% in the previous year. Figure 6.11 summarizes the basic characteristics of Example Air.

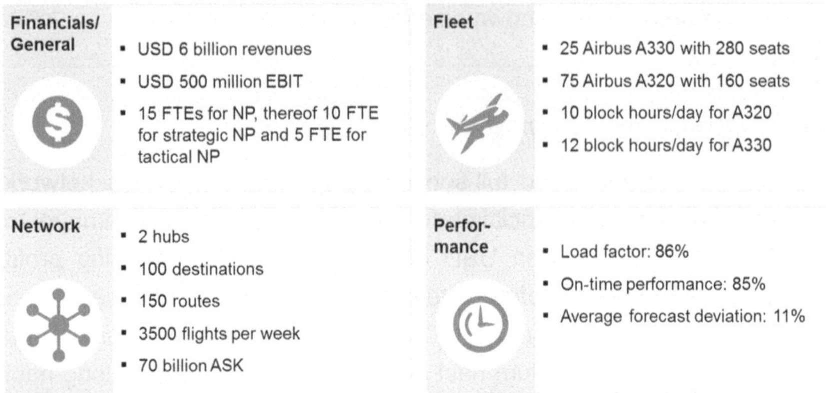

Figure 6.11 – Profile of Example Air[198]

In order to create reliable benefit estimates for motivating BDO investment business cases, Example Air must make realistic estimates for the BDO impact on relevant KPIs. Figure 6.12 contains all relevant input metrics and estimates for Example Air, which are based on the discussion in sub-chapter 6.2. The estimates of BDO impact in the right column are provided as an example, and they depend on the specificities of each airline. These values are only used to demonstrate the calculation methodology in the context of this study.

---

[198] Source: Own illustration.

Metric	BDO value creation	Input data needed	Example Air values	Example Air estimates
Profit Δ from flight portfolio changes	Increase in average route profit for new routes	▪ Ø profit of new routes: ▪ Ø profit of discontinued routes:	4000 USD/flight - 500 USD/flight	▪ BDO – supported new routes : 4500 USD/flight ▪ 150 permanent yearly flight number changes
Total network profit	Overall profit increase	▪ Overall network profit:	500 million USD/year	▪ 1% profit increase
Average forecast deviation per route	Reduction of forecast deviation	▪ Distribution of forecast errors by error margin	11% deviation on average: ▪ 55% less than 10% ▪ 25% between 10% and 20% ▪ 15% between 20% and 30% ▪ 5% more than 30%	 ▪ 1% improvement ▪ 2% improvement ▪ 3% improvement ▪ 5% improvement
Load factor	Overall load factor improvement	▪ ASK and RSK	▪ 70 bn ASK ▪ 60 bn RSK ▪ Load factor 85.7%	▪ 0.2% RSK improvement
Idle hours per A/C type	Additional flights in idle hours	▪ Idle hours composition for A/C type:	▪ A330: 4 hours, fragmented ▪ A320: 2 hours fragmented, 5 hours en bloc	▪ 10% of A320 5 hour blocks can be used productively
On-time performance	Decrease of delay cost	▪ Delay distribution ▪ Delay cost per hour	▪ 85% - on time ▪ 10% - 15-30 minutes ▪ 4% - 30-60 minutes ▪ 1% - > 60 minutes	▪ Reduction of 10% across all delay classes
FTE per process step	Automation of manual tasks	▪ FTE breakdown by process step	▪ 10 FTE for strategic NP ▪ 5 FTE for tactical NP	▪ 1 FTE automation potential in strategic NP steps
Operating cost	Reduction of NP-influenced operating cost	▪ Operating cost break-down	▪ 1 billion USD fees and charges	▪ 1% reduction on fees and changes

Figure 6.12 – Input data and estimates for the calculation of KPI metrics for BDO-benefit evaluation[199]

6.3.2 Calculation of BDO impact for relevant KPI groups

Profit delta from flight portfolio changes

If the operating profit of 500 million USD is broken down to the flight level, it is noted that the average flight contributes 2,750 USD. Naturally, not all flights are equally profitable. Figure 6.13 shows the entire flight portfolio sorted according to average flight profitability[200]. Some flight numbers are even loss-incurring and therefore make candidates for discontinuation. The aim of a NP department is to replace low-performing flight numbers with

[199] Source: Own illustration.

[200] A flight is a flight event on a specific date. A flight number is a series of flights with the same schedule characteristics. For example, flight number XX1231 departs every Monday at 8 am from Airport A to Airport B. The specific flight on Monday, October 8, could then be specified as XX1231-1008. It is important to compare flights, as seasonal flight numbers contain less flights than permanent flight numbers.

better-performing ones. For Example Air, the average flight event of a discontinued flight number generates losses worth 500 USD. In contrast, the average flight profit of new flight numbers is 4,000 USD without the support of any BDO.

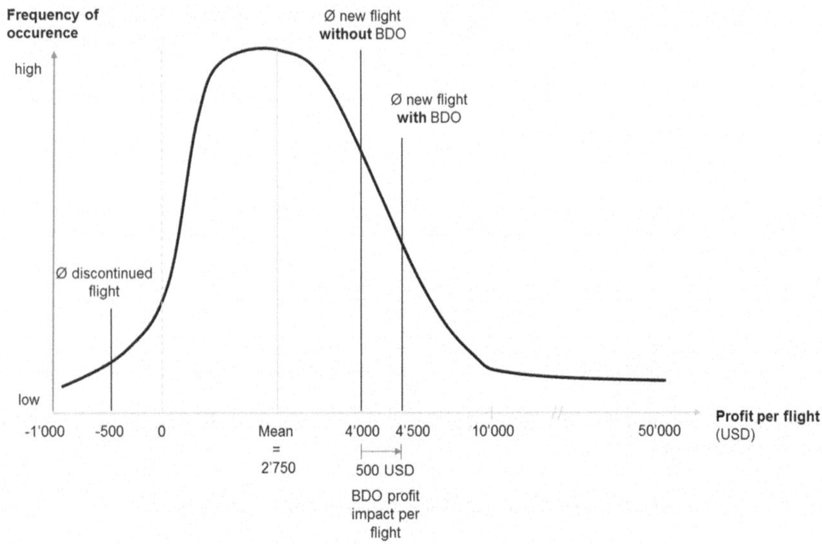

Figure 6.13 – Illustrative flight portfolio by average flight profit[201]

For Example Air, the deployment of a BDO increases the average profit of new flights by 12.5% to 4,500 USD. This results in 500 USD of benefit per flight, which is directly attributable to the BDO. Furthermore, Example Air expects to replace 150 flight numbers per year, which is about 4% of the entire flight portfolio of 3,500 flights per week. The average flight profit of discontinued flight numbers is expected to remain constant. If the BDO

[201] Source: Own illustration.

enables 500 USD additional profit for 150 flights per week, the yearly benefit amounts to 3.9 million USD in this Example (see Figure 6.14).

150	x	**500 USD**	=	**75'000 USD**	x	**52**	=	**3'900'000 USD**
New flights per week (flight portfolio changes)		*BDO benefit per flight*		*Weekly BDO profit impact*		*Weeks*		*BDO profit impact per year*

Figure 6.14 – Example benefit calculation for profit delta from flight portfolio changes[202]

Total network profit

The calculation of the total network profit is simple. However, the BDO-impact estimate remains on a high level as Example Air expects a specific BDO to increase total network profits by 1% from a combination of better route selection and more precise demand forecasting. The benefit resulting from BDO deployment would hence amount to 5 million USD per year (see Figure 6.15). In practice, it may be difficult to directly attribute the changes in total network profit to a specific BDO.

500 million USD	x	**0.01**	=	**5 million USD**
Yearly EBIT		*1% expected BDO profit impact*		*Yearly BDO profit impact*

Figure 6.15 – Example-benefit calculation for total network profit[203]

[202] Source: Own illustration.

[203] Source: Own illustration.

Average demand forecast deviation per route

Example Air's average demand forecast deviation per route is 11%; however, the distribution is skewed towards the lower end (see Figure 6.16). If the distribution is segmented by absolute forecast deviation, 55% of all the forecasts diverge 10% from reality at most. At the other end, 5% of the forecasts deviate more than 30% from the actual demand.

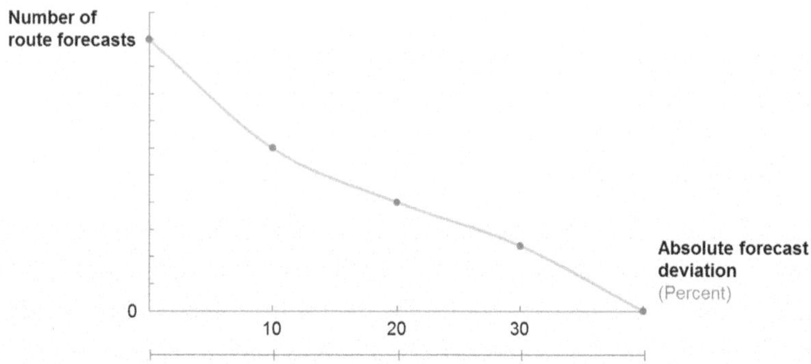

% of forecasts	55%	25%	15%	5%
Average deviation	4%	13%	23%	40%
BDO improvement target (in PP)	1PP	2PP	3PP	5PP
Average deviation with BDO deployment	3%	11%	20%	35%

Figure 6.16 – Illustrative distribution of forecast deviation for Example Air[204]

Example Air estimates that the improvement potential is highest for those forecasts that have the highest deviation. Accordingly, the potential improvement for the segment with more than 30% deviation is estimated

---

[204] Source: Own illustration.

to be at 5 percentage points, while the segment with the smallest deviations should improve only 1pp due to BDO deployment. If the new averages of the segments (bottom line of Figure 6.16) are consolidated, the new overall forecast deviation is 9% instead of 11%. The BDO impact therefore constitutes 2pp of the forecast deviation. However, forecast deviation only has indirect financial benefits, and therefore, this KPI metric is not suitable for motivating a business case creation.

Load factor

In a similar manner as total network profit, load factor is a holistic KPI. The direct influence of a specific BDO deployment is difficult to assess, thereby necessitating a global estimate. Example Air has a load factor of 86%, which results from a capacity of 70 billion ASK, of which 60 billion have been sold (revenue seat kilometer, RSK). Example air estimates that BDO deployment can increase the load factor by 0.2% at constant yield. Yield per RSK is 0.10 USD[205], and hence the positive revenue impact can be quantified at 13 million USD per year. Applying a constant operating profit margin of 8.3%[206], the profit impact of the RSK increase is 1.08 million USD per year. Figure 6.17 displays the calculation method.

[205] Revenue per RSK: 6 billion USD/60 billion RSK = 0.10 USD per RSK.

[206] Operating profit margin: EBIT / Revenues = 500 million USD / 6'000 million USD = 8.3%.

$\frac{\text{60 billion RSK}}{\text{70 billion ASK}}$	=	85.7%	+	0.2%	=	85.9%	x	70 billion ASK	=	60.13 billion RSK
Sold capacity over total capacity per year		*Load factor without BDO deployment*		*BDO impact on load factor*		*Load factor with BDO deployment*		*Constant capacity per year*		*RSK of new load factor*

130 million RSK	x	$\frac{\text{0.10 USD}}{\text{RSK}}$	=	13 million USD	x	8.3%	=	1.08 million USD
Additional RSK due to BDO deployment		*Constant yield*		*BDO revenue impact per year*		*Constant EBIT margin*		*BDO profit impact per year*

Figure 6.17 – Example-benefit calculation for load factor[207]

Average idle hours per aircraft type

Idle hours for aircrafts can be derived directly from the rotation plans. Figure 6.18 displays two schematized rotation plans for both aircraft families. The short- and medium-haul A320 aircrafts are used mainly during the day and remain parked at night. 33% of the fleet undergoes maintenance during the night layovers each day. There is fragmented idle time between some flights, which cannot be utilized for additional flights unless all rotation plans are rearranged. The nightly idle time could potentially be used for additional flights, and according to Example Air estimates, 10% of the idle-time blocks can be activated to add to the productive flight hours after BDO deployment.

The rotation plans of long-haul A330 aircrafts differ significantly from the A320. They take two or a maximum of three long-haul flights per day, and idle time is fragmented between these flights. The overall utilization of the A330 fleet of Example Air is also higher than the utilization of the A320 fleet.

---

[207] Source: Own illustration.

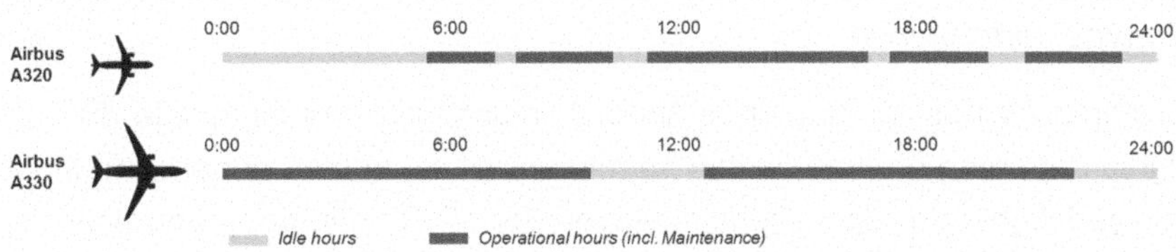

Figure 6.18 – Schematized rotation plans for Example Air aircraft types[208]

If the deployment of a BDO reduces idle-night blocks for A320 by 10%, Example Air can fly five additional round-trips per day, i.e., a total of 10 additional flights. Since shorter flights generate less profit than long-haul flights, an average flight profit of 1,500 USD is assumed (see Figure 6.19). The 3,650 additional flights per year hence result in an extra profit of 5.48 million USD, which can be completely arrtibuted to BDO deployment.

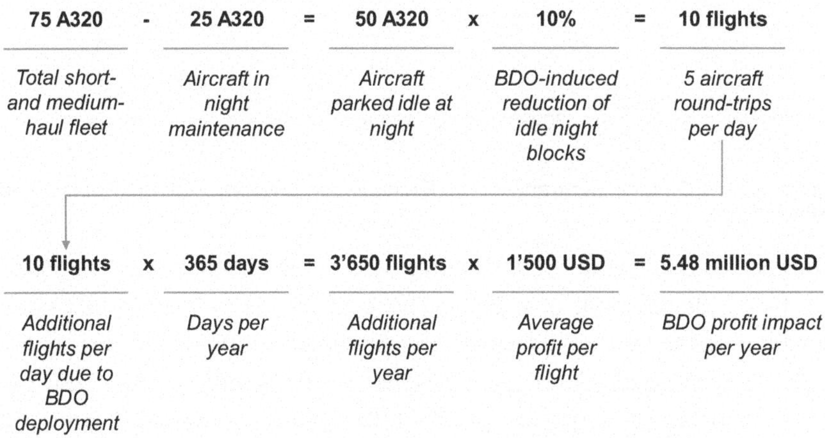

Figure 6.19 – Example-benefit calculation for idle hours per aircraft type[209]

[208] Source: Own illustration.

[209] Source: Own illustration.

On-time performance

Example Air has an industry-standard on-time performance, with 85% of flights departing on time (within 15 minutes of scheduled departure). Most delayed flights are only slightly delayed (by 15–30 minutes), and only 1% of the flights is delayed by more than one hour (see Figure 6.20).

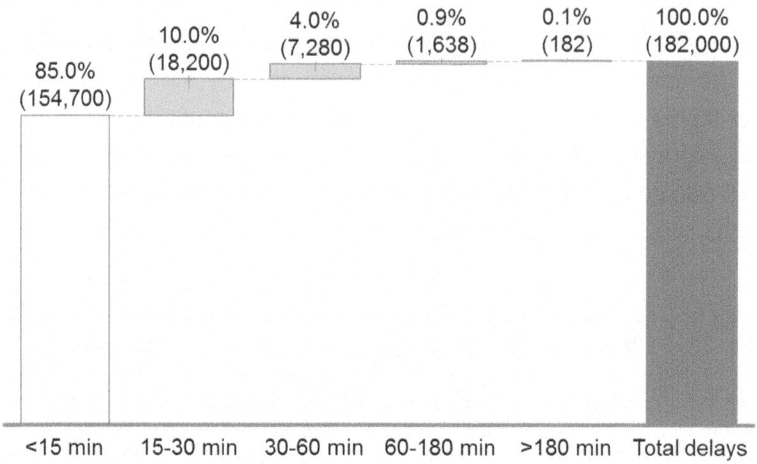

Figure 6.20 – On-time performance of Example Air (percent and total number of flights)[210]

Example Air expects to reduce delays by 10% across all delay categories due to the deployment of a BDO. The cost per delay minute has been studied in detail by Cook, Tanner, and Anderson (2004) for a Eurocontrol study. They discovered that delay cost below 15 minutes is only 1 USD per minute and hence negligible (p. 99–100). Delays between 15 and 180 minutes are calculated on an average with 72 USD per minute, and larger delays with 240 USD per minute. For the business case, it is assumed that all delays are in the lower bound of each category, in order to reach a conservative estimate. This calculation is purely presented as an example

[210] Source: Own illustration.

since every airline has specific cost structures and, therefore, individual delay cost. The total delay cost currently incurred is 50.32 million USD. If the use of a BDO reduces delays by 10%, this can generate annual savings of 5.03 million USD.

Delay range	Delay cost per minute depending on delay severity		Minimum minutes of delay in delay range		Number of delays in delay range		Minimum delay cost per delay range		Minimum total delay cost
15-30 min:	**72 USD**	x	**15**	x	**18'200**	=	**19.66 million USD**	Σ	**50.32 million USD**
30-60 min:	**72 USD**	x	**30**	x	**7'280**	=	**15.72 million USD**		
60-180 min:	**72 USD**	x	**60**	x	**1'638**	=	**7.08 million USD**		
>180 min:	**240 USD**	x	**180**	x	**182**	=	**7.86 million USD**		

Figure 6.21 – Example-benefit calculation for on-time performance[211]

FTE per process step

Example Air has a NP department with 15 FTE. The tactical network planning is already partly automated, and as such, the saving potential due to automation is limited. For strategic network planning, Example Air plans to implement a BDO-featured decision support tool that automatically proposes the next-best route and prepares a draft business case for the route decision. It expects to save 10% of the manhours that are currently required for strategic network planning. Given that 10 FTE are dedicated to strategic network planning, 1 FTE could potentially be saved. Assuming an FTE cost of 200,000 USD, including all incidental wage costs, the BDO-induced cost savings would amount to 200,000 USD on a yearly recurring basis.

211 Source: Own illustration.

Operational cost reduction

The Example Air NP department holds the responsibility of negotiating airport and traffic fees and meeting cost targets in these cost categories. The "fees and charges" cost category makes up 15% of the entire cost base of 5.5 billion USD. This translates into a cost block of 825 million USD, about 50% of which NP can influence directly. Example Air expects to reduce the 412.5 million USD NP-controlled fees and charges by 1%, with an improved slot and traffic right information system, which translates into BDO-induced cost savings of 4.13 million USD per year.

6.3.3 Scenario-based sensitivity analysis of KPI benefits

After demonstrating the calculation methodology employed in the Example Air case, the sensitivity of each KPI metric is now compared on the basis of four different big data project scenarios. The scenarios, which are summarized in Table 6.3, describe archetypical big data investment cases.

Table 6.3 – Big data project scenarios[212]

Scenario	Implementation cost (one-time)	Recurring yearly cost	Yearly benefit requirement for break-even[213]
Small big data project	20,000 USD	50,000	54,796
Medium big data project	200,000 USD	200,000	247,963
Large big data project	1,000,000 USD	500,000	739,816
Very large big data project	5,000,000 USD	1,000,000	2,199,079

A small BD project is based on already processed and filtered data, such as search engine data queries or hotel price intelligence reports. Thus,

[212] Own illustration following estimates of Rouda (2014) and Heilig and Voß (2017).

[213] NPV of 0 with 10% discount rate, no terminal value considered.

implementation costs are very low; however, a significant yearly data subscription fee must be considered. Costs for additional big data storage and processing are negligible in this scenario.

Medium big data projects require some implementation and configuration of the big data ecosystem[214], which includes storage options, processing services, and analytics (see sub-chapter 6.4). Many storage, processing, and analytic solutions incur subscription-based or use-based cost, and significant yearly recurring cost must be considered.

With increasing data volume and variety, the big data ecosystem becomes more complex, and thus implementation costs increase. Large big data projects may well generate implementation costs that are twice as high as the yearly recurring cost (Rouda, 2014). Analysis of events from different social networks could blong to this project category, as a large volume of raw data from different sources has to be extracted, processed, stored, and analyzed.

Very large projects differ from large projects due to their even larger complexity. Data processing and analytics usually involve advanced BDA technology such as machine learning, NLP, or a combination of various methods. It usually features unstructured data and requires the development of a tailored analytics solution, which increases the initial implementation cost drastically. The only short-listed BDO that may require a very large big data project is the real-time traffic right information platform, as it combines multiple complexity drivers[215]. For the scenario

[214] In the big data context, the term "ecosystem" refers to a very dynamic system architecture, which is usually platform-based and allows for the combination of different vendor services (Heilig and Voß, 2017, p. 33).

[215] Complexity drivers: unstructured data (law texts), real-time data feed (flight radar data), high volume of streamed data, NLP technology for the extraction of useful content from law texts required, large number of data sources.

analysis, the break-even NPV is calculated for a time period of five years without the consideration of a terminal value (see Appendix 23).

All implementation costs are allocated to the first year, and the recurring cost applies to all five years. The right column of Table 6.3 contains the required yearly benefit necessary to reach a NPV of zero, assuming a discount rate of 10% and an equal distribution of the benefits across the five-year period. For small big data projects, the required yearly benefit is 55,000 USD, while very large projects require a multi-million USD value of recurring benefits. Naturally, these numbers are not representative and serve only the purpose of comparing sensitivities of the various KPI metrics in the case of Example Air.

In a second step, the required value of BDO benefit to reach a NPV of 0 is calculated for each KPI metric and big data project scenario (see Table 6.4). For instance, the BDO profit impact for a newly added flight was estimated to be 500 USD per flight in the previous section, which resulted in yearly benefits of 3.9 million USD. This benefit would clearly justify each of the project scenarios, as it even exceeds the required 2.2 million USD annual benefit necessary for very large big data projects. For the sensitivity analysis, the inverse question is asked: How large does the BDO benefit need to be in order to break each of the project scenarios even?

The required BDO profit impact per flight varies between 7 USD and 282 USD. Compared to an average flight profitability of 2,750 USD for Example Air, these figures do not seem overly ambitious. Similarly, the number of required additional flights in idle time seems manageable. Four additional flights a day (two return flights) in a fleet of 75 A320s are sufficient to justify even a very large big data project. The feasibility of global KPI metrics, including load factor, total network profit, on-time performance, and operational cost reduction, are more difficult to judge, as they depend on the individual airline's performance, regardless of whether the BDO impact is realistic or not.

Table 6.4 – BDO benefit requirement for break-even of BD project scenarios[216]

KPI metric	BDO benefit requirement	Small project	Medium project	Large project	Very large project
Profit delta from flight portfolio changes	Required BDO profit impact per flight in USD	7.03	31.79	94.85	281.93
Total network profit	Required percent increase	0.01%	0.05%	0.15%	0.44%
Load factor	Required load factor increase in percentage points	0.01	0.04	0.13	0.38
Idle hours per aircraft type	Daily additional flights needed	0.10	0.45	1.35	4.02
On-time performance	Percent delay reduction needed	0.11%	0.48%	1.43%	4.24%
FTE per process step	FTE reduction needed	0.3	1.2	3.7	11.0
Operational cost reduction	Operational cost reduction required	0.01%	0.05%	0.15%	0.44%

The only KPI metric that seems not suited to justify large or even very large big data projects is FTE per process step. Assuming that one FTE costs 200,000 USD per year at most, it would require massive FTE reductions between 4 and 11 FTE to generate sufficient financial benefit. Since NP departments in most airlines are smaller than 30 FTE, this would require large-scale automation, which is less feasible than the operational improvements mentioned above.

6.4 Cost evaluation of big data opportunities

The huge expansion of project scope across big data projects calls for a unifying framework to estimate the cost of big data projects. Although this study cannot assign exact prices to individual BDOs, the potential cost

216 Source: Own illustration. based on Appendix 24 which contains the detailed calculation.

components of big data projects are outlined and connected to recent research (section 6.4.1). Section 6.4.2 then highlights the cost components that are relevant to specific BDOs in order to provide a guideline for BDO-specific project cost estimates.

6.4.1 Cost composition of big data projects

Cost for big data projects can be structured along the big data value chain that has been used in some variations both by scholars (Gandomi & Haider, 2015; Heilig & Voß, 2017) and practitioners (Keuning & Balkir, 2013). The basic big data analytics value chain introduced in section 3.6.3 can serve as a basic framework; however, it requires more detailing in order to capture relevant cost items. Specifically, big data storage and big data processing must be distinguished in order to account for the different underlying technological platforms.

The simplest useful big data value chain for cost estimates entails four major components, namely acquisition, storage, processing, and analytics of big data. Cost can be derived either directly from the usage of data and technology, which includes one-time cost or subscription fees for different technological platforms, or from the implementation and configuration effort. Google, Amazon, and Microsoft have established cloud-based big-data ecosystems that provide all the relevant services across the big data value chain (Heilig & Voß, 2017). Cloudera and Hortonworks offer a platform-as-a-service (PaaS) ecosystem, where users can select different providers for each value chain component, which are connected through the PaaS technology. Figure 6.22 summarizes potential cost components and structures them along the big data value chain.

BD value chain	Data & technology cost		
	Batch data	Streaming data	Implementation cost
Big data acquisition	o Batch purchase or subscription	o Data subscription	
	o Data scraping volume cost component		o Scraper development cost
	o Cost for data ingestion (e.g., Streamsets, Talend, Informatica)		o Initial setup cost
Big data storage	o Hardware for local storage o Cloud storage subscription o Data lake (e.g., AWS, MS Azure, Google)		o Initial architecture design cost o Initial storage configuration o Maintenance cost (for local hardware only)
Big data processing	o Batch processing technology (e.g., Hadoop, Skytree)	o Stream processing technology (e.g., Kafka, Storm)	o Initial processing configuration
	o Platform-as-a-Service (Cloudera, Hortonworks)		
Big data analytics	o Analytics layer (e.g., machine learning technology) o Serving layer (data aggregator such as Sybase) o Frontend layer (e.g., Tableau, QlikView) o Integration in network planning IT tools		o Initial analytics layer configuration o Development cost of analytic tool if no off-the-shelf solution available

Figure 6.22 – Cost components of BDA projects structured along the big data value chain[217]

In the *big data acquisition* phase, data is recorded or acquired by the airline. Data can be transferred in batches or as a data stream. While data batches are self-contained datasets that can be updated at a chosen frequency, data streams transfer data continuously and enable real-time data feeds. The technologies for ingesting these data types differ fundamentally, as do the pricing concepts of data providers (Heilig & Voß, 2017, p. 32). Batch-data can be purchased like a physical product in a singular transaction (e.g., mobile location data set for one month) or as a data subscription that includes the delivery of multiple data batches during the subscription period (e.g., monthly traffic statistics). Data streams are usually only available as a subscription model, especially in the case of real-time data (e.g., live flight radar data). The price of the data batches or

[217] Source: Own illustration. following Heilig and Voß (2017).

the data subscriptions differs widely between BDOs and cannot be assessed globally.

In addition to the pure data acquisition cost, airlines incur cost for ingestion technology and implementation services. Ingestion technology bridges data acquisition and data storage by cleaning and annotating data wherever necessary (Gandomi & Haider, 2015, p. 141). In other words, data ingestion technology makes data fit for storage, if it is intended as such in the big data ecosystem. Heilig and Voß (2017, p. 36) compared the pricing schemes for data stream processing of the Amazon, Google and Microsoft ecosystems and found that streaming volume and required computing capacity are the main cost drivers, even though the actual pricing differs widely between the ecosystem providers [218]. Most independent technologies for data ingestion require an initial configuration, which is typically offered as a service by the technology provider. If data is collected with a data scraper, the initial development of the scraper must also be included in the cost calculation.

Big data storage comprises various possibilities of local and cloud-based data storage architectures. Traditional local data warehouses are often still able to store structured batch data and even recorded and aggregated streaming data (Heilig & Voß, 2017, p. 33). Cloud-based storage solutions enable distributed file systems that form decentral data lakes that can be accessed directly by data processing technology such as Hadoop. Raghupathi and Raghupathi (2014, p. 5) call this the “middleware” solution, as it passes the task of structuring and integrating the data on to data processing technologies. The middleware solution is, therefore, best suited for unstructured data that can be stored without large transformation efforts. Cloud-based storage solutions can certainly also provide

[218] Monthly cost for a data stream with 100 data records per second with a size of 35KB per record varies between 50 USD (Amazon Kinesis) and 200 USD (Google Cloud Pub/Sub).

distributed data warehouse solutions for the management of structured databases (Heilig & Voß, 2017, p. 33).

Rouda (2014) compared the actual cost of local and cloud-based storage solutions, including implementation cost. He discovered that cloud-based storage solutions are 21% cheaper on an average than local hardware storage, if all related costs are considered. Heilig and Voß (2017, pp. 38–39) compared the storage pricing of the three ecosystem providers, Amazon, Microsoft, and Google. The pure storage price differs between 2.5 and 3 US cents per gigabyte (GB) and month for distributed data lakes. However, all three providers charge for database query requests, which can add another 1.5 cents per GB and month. The choice of storage provider hence depends upon the use pattern and data volume. The pricing for cloud-based data warehouses depends only on the stored volume and not on query requests (Heilig & Voß, 2017, p. 41).

Big data processing technology manages data integration and annotation, especially if raw data storages such as data lakes are used. The most common technology family is the Apache Hadoop cluster, which is an open-source technology that needs to be licensed for use. Hadoop can manage both batch and stream data; its strengths, however, lie in the processing of unstructured and structured batch data, while its relative Apache Kafka is a comparable technology for streamed data (Keuning & Balkir, 2013). Hadoop applications are organized in clusters, which are connected by so-called virtual machines (VM) (Heilig & Voß, 2017, p. 33). This decentralized architecture enables the matching of unstructured data in order to process it for further analytics use.

The number of VMs is also the main driver of the licensing cost for Hadoop applications, alongwith data volume and a time-sensitive pricing component. Heilig and Voß (2017, p. 40) compared the Hadoop solutions of the three integrated ecosystem providers (Amazon, Google, and Microsoft). They discovered that the hourly cost of use for a Hadoop cluster is between 60 and 70 US cents per VM, while the additional storage capacity required for processing is charged at 10 to 20 US cents per GB per month. A dataset of 25 TB, which requires 150 VM hours per day, generates a total cost of 4,000 to 8,000 USD per month. Thus, data processing is significantly more expensive than data ingestion or data storage of a similar dataset[219].

Big data analytics is an umbrella term that includes several technology layers contributing to the analysis of processed data. A BDA application with a complex analytics layer based on machine learning algorithms will obviously generate a much higher cost than a slim data visualization application that uses a standard solution such as Tableau. The monthly cost can vary between a low double-digit dollar figure for simple frontend layer solutions and several thousand dollars of recurring cost for "deep" BDA solutions that require multiple layers (Heilig & Voß, 2017, p. 43).

Similarly, implementation costs vary widely. Not every big data project requires the setup of an entire big data value chain environment. If the source data is structured, analytics tools may be applied directly on the raw data, which lowers the implementation cost dramatically. In contrast, the setup of an entire environment produces huge upfront development costs. A study of the IT consultancy Existek (2018) shows that a mid-sized development project requires 40-60 FTE months, producing additional cost of 250.000 to 600.000 USD[220].

6.4.2 Cost drivers for big data opportunities

Many BDOs do not require the setup of a new big data analytics environment along the entire value chain. This section analyzes which value chain components are relevant for each BDO and how this impacts the expected overall costs. The costs of each value chain component are influenced by several cost drivers, which may overlap. Table 6.5

---

[219] All calculations were performed with the same dataset of 25 TB data per month.

[220] Cost difference based on project location and degree of outsourcing.

summarizes the cost risks of different cost drivers for the entire big data value chain.

Table 6.5 – Cost risks of cost drivers for value chain components[221]

Value chain component	Cost driver	Cost risk		
		Low	Medium	High
Big data acquisition	Type of data	Query results	Processed data	Raw data
	Data velocity	Batch data	Stream data	Batch and stream data
	Pricing	Free access	Subscription	Volume dependent
	Scraping required	No	–	Yes
Big data storage	Data volume	Small: < 1 GB per day/batch	Medium: 1 GB–1 TB per day/batch	High: > 1TB per day/batch
	Data structure	Structured only	Unstructured only	Structured and unstructured
Big data processing	Data structure	Structured only	Unstructured only	Structured and unstructured
	Data sources	Single source	2–5 sources	> 5 sources
BD analytics	Analytical complexity	Simple: Statistics, visualizations	Medium: Econometrics, data mining	Advanced: Machine Learning, NLP
	Tool availability	Integrated	Available	Development need

The acquisition and ingestion costs mainly depend on the provider pricing and the data properties. Some data sources are free (e.g., Google Trends, Facebook Audience Insights), while other data needs to be purchased by subscription (e.g., cargo rates and hotel price intelligence) or by volume-dependent batch procurement (e.g., mobile location data). Cost risks are the highest with volume-dependent pricing, as large datasets can generate significant costs. Data volume is also driven by the type of data. Raw data

221 Source: Own illustration.

typically constitutes larger volumes than processed data. Data sources with integrated filtering options (such as Google Trends or hotel price intelligence) produce query results that are even more compressed than processed data (e.g., mobile location data or clickstream data). The use of data ingestion technology, such as data scraping or data stream recording, produces additional acquisition cost.

Costs for big data storage mostly depend on the data volume and the data structure. If the data is structured, it can be stored in a traditional data warehouse, be it local or cloud-based. Unstructured data and data from multiple sources require data lakes that minimize pre-storage processing cost but increase data storage cost. The data volume drives storage cost in any chosen storage model. Big data processing becomes increasingly complex and costly if multiple data sources are required to be connected and if unstructured data is present. However, the required processing scope has to be defined on a case-by-case base, in order to consider specific BDO requirements.

The costs of BD analytics are both driven by the analytical complexity and the availability of tailored analytic tools. If the analytical complexity is high, such as for machine-learning or NLP applications, the tools require various analytic layers that increase costs. In contrast, simple statistical analyses and visualizations can be performed directly by frontend tools such as Tableau and do not require further integration. The availability of tailored analytical tools varies widely between BDOs. Hotel price intelligence and cargo rate intelligence have the analytical functionality included in the solution, and therefore, no additional investment is necessary. BDOs that deliver structured and processed data (e.g., mobile location data) can typically be analyzed directly with analytical front-end tools. Only BDOs with more complex data properties (e.g., a real-time traffic information platform) require the development of tailored analytical solutions, which then increase BD costs.

6.4.3 *Cost estimation framework for BDOs*

The cost drivers of Table 6.5 can be assigned directly to BDOs (see Appendix 21). Subsequently, a scoring model (see Appendix 22) is developed in order to indicate the expected cost risks for the 12 shortlisted BDOs[222]. Table 6.6 summarizes the scoring results by value chain component.

Detailed demographic profiling with social media data (A4) and general search engine data (A5) produce the lowest acquisition cost, as the data is already a filtered query result, thereby delivering batches of structured data for free. Extended electronic AWBs with shipper address (D2) are also freely available after implementation since the e-AWB data must be recorded in any case in order to process the shipment. However, the large volume of the raw data may incur additional cost. All other BDOs will produce more data acquisition cost, as the data is only available for a charge. Furthermore, most other BDOs transmit either non-filtered or non-processed data or include a real-time data stream that is costlier to capture.

Big data storage costs are low for BDOs that deliver small and structured data sets. This is the case for all BDOs transmitting only query results (A4, A5, B3, and H1). All BDOs except the real-time traffic right information platform use structured data only[223] and can be stored both in a central data warehouse or a decentral data lake. Furthermore, only four BDOs are likely to produce high data volumes of more than 1TB per batch (or data stream per day).

---

[222] Cost drivers with low cost risks are assigned 2 score points, cost drivers with medium risks 1 score points, and cost drivers with high cost risks 0 score points. If a BDO achieves less than 50% of the potential score, it is assumed to bear a high cost risk; if a BDO achieves more than 75% of the potential score, it is assumed to bear a low-cost risk. The logic applies to each value chain step and to the overall cost risk.

[223] Further BDOs using unstructured data (A1, A3, A7, A9, B1, C2, I1 and I2) have all been de-prioritized in sub-chapter 5.3.

Table 6.6 – Estimated cost risks of BDOs[224]

		Estimated cost risk				
Code	**BDO**	***BD acquisition***	***BD storage***	***BD processing***	***BD analytics***	***Overall cost risks***
A4	Detailed demographic profiling with social media data	○	○	○	◗	○
A5	General search engine data for detailed O&D demand	○	○	○	◗	○
A6	Clickstream data of meta-search websites for flights	◗	◗	◗	◗	◗
A8	Analysis of air cargo rates from online freight portals	◗	○	○	○	○
A10	Shipping data from e-commerce platforms	◗	◗	◗	◗	◗
B3	Analysis of local hotel prices	◗	○	○	○	○
B4	Analysis of events in social networks	●	◗	◗	◗	●
D1	Mobile location data from smartphones	◗	◗	◗	◗	◗
D2	Extended electronic AWB with shipper address	◗	◗	◗	◗	◗
D3	Location-transmitting sensors for cargo shipments	◗	◗	◗	●	●
H1	Real-time slot trading platform	◗	○	○	◗	◗
H2	Real-time traffic right information platform	●	●	●	●	●

Legend:
Cost risk: ● High (<50 % of max. score) - ◗ Medium (50-75% of max. score) - ○ Low (>75% of max. score)

[224] Source: Own illustration. based on cost driver analysis.

Mobile location data and cargo location sensors produce high data volumes even after anonymization and aggregation if a high granularity level is chosen. Extended electronic AWBs with shipper address and real-time traffic right information platform rely on raw data, which can also cause to the generation of high data volumes and increased storage cost.

Big data processing costs are the lowest for BDOs that originate from a single data source and deliver structured data. In these cases, the actual data processing is already performed by the data provider (such as Facebook, Google, or the hotel price intelligence tool), which reduces the cost for airlines using the processed data. BDOs that rely on multiple data sources necessitate a matching of the different data sets, which increases the cost of processing. The real-time traffic right information platform (H2) requires the most elaborate data processing due to the fact that structured data (flight radar information) and unstructured data (law texts) must be matched as well as batch data and streamed data.

Similarly, the real-time traffic right information platform also requires the development of a complex analytic engine that is able to match text mining results with real-time streaming data. B4, D3, and H1 involve the development of new analytical tools, which may result in significant implementation costs. In contrast, the data providers of air cargo rates and hotel rates (A8 and B3) have integrated analytics tools such that little additional investment in big data analytics is required.

In summary, the real-time traffic right information platform is expected to produce the highest implementation cost by far, as it is the only BDO relying on unstructured data that drives storage, processing, and analytics cost. Detailed demographic profiling with social media data and general search engine data are likely to be very economic, as they provide filtered and structured data for free, which only need analysis. Likewise, analysis of air cargo rates (A8) and hotel rates (B3) require subscription fees to use the platforms but relieve airlines from additional investments in storage, processing, and analytics as the entire analytics tool is included in the platform offering.

6.5 Comparison of benefit and cost potential of BDOs

Sub-chapters 6.2 and 6.3 have evaluated the benefit potential of specific KPIs and the potential of the BDOs to influence these KPIs. It was argued that forecast accuracy has no direct financial impact and is hence not suited as a KPI to financially justify BDO investments. Overhead cost savings in the form of increased automation to reduce FTE are not sufficient to justify large big data investments in most cases.

In contrast, reduction of idle time and the improvement of route profitability through higher profits from new routes are well suited to justify BDO investments. These two KPI metrics are directly attributable to BDO deployment, and they are under the complete control of the NP department. The remaining KPI metrics are global performance indicators that can be used if the BDO impact is directly accountable and if the NP department is confident enough to be measured against a metric that is influenced by many departments.

This logic can be transferred into a scoring model to weigh the individual benefit potential scores, ranging from 0 to 5, that were assigned to the BDOs by the network planners of the case study group[225]. The BDO scores for route profitability and aircraft utilization are counted as double, as these KPIs seem to be particularly well suited for justifying BDO investments. BDO impact scores for FTE efficiency and forecast accuracy are excluded, as they are not suited. BDO scores for the remaining KPIs are included with their original score. Appendix 25 contains the associated calculations.

If the weighted individual benefit estimates are aggregated, the benefit impact score can be calculated. It needs to be noted that the impact score

---

[225] Compare sub-chapter 6.

has an indicative character due to the small sample size of the case study group. However, this figure contains two important pieces of information. First, it is based on the impact score that was assigned by case study participants and hence includes the practitioner perspective. Second, the weighing ensures that the scores of the KPIs that are easier to influence count more and provide significant potential to justify BDO investment.

The highest possible financial impact score is 35, resulting from two double-weighted KPIs and three single weighted KPIs[226]. However, none of the BDOs has been assessed by the airline network planners to be relevant for all KPIs. D3, H1, and H2 are relevant for four KPIs, while all the other BDOs are relevant only for three KPIs (excluding FTE efficiency and forecast accuracy). Furthermore, none of the BDOs has been evaluated with the highest impact score of 5 for any of the KPIs (see section 6.1.1). As a result, the highest financial impact score is 20 for shipping data from e-commerce platforms (A10) – a cargo-specific BDO. It scores high on both double-weighted KPIs and is furthermore relevant for load-factor improvements. The analysis of events in social networks (B4) scores lowest, as it primarily influences forecast accuracy, which is not financially quantifiable.

Table 6.7 summarizes and classifies the financial impact score. The range of the financial impact score is from 10.3 to 20, which allows for the relative assessment of the BDOs . A score of 16 or higher can be considered high, while scores below 12 indicate a comparably low financial benefit. The right column recapitulates the cost potential evaluation of Table 6.6 (p. 312). Both evaluations are indicative, as an exact calculation is only possible if the airline specificities are known. Hence, the following summary is a first assessment based on the present case study group.

---

[226] Two double-weighted KPIs: 2 * 10 = 20; Three single-weighted KPIs: 3 * 5 = 15.

Table 6.7 – First indicative comparison of financial benefit and cost risks[227]

Code	BDO	Financial impact score	Financial benefit evaluation	Cost risk evaluation
A4	Detailed demographic profiling with social media data	14.0	Medium	Low
A5	General search engine data for detailed O&D demand	14.0	Medium	Low
A6	Clickstream data of meta-search websites for flights	12.5	Medium	Medium
A8	Analysis of air cargo rates from online freight portals	18.0	High	Low
A10	Shipping data from e-commerce platforms	20.0	High	Medium
B3	Analysis of local hotel prices	16.0	High	Low
B4	Analysis of events in social networks	10.3	Low	High
D1	Mobile location data from smartphones	14.3	Medium	Medium
D2	Extended electronic AWB with shipper address	12.0	Medium	Medium
D3	Location-transmitting sensors for cargo shipments	16.0	High	High
H1	Real-time slot trading platform	15.2	Medium	Medium
H2	Real-time traffic right information platform	11.3	Low	High

Still, the comparison enables a rough evaluation of the cost–benefit ratio of individual BDOs. The analysis of air cargo rates (A8) and hotel prices (B3) both have a high financial benefit potential with very limited cost risks. They have in common the fact that the analytics tool is integrated in the data vendor product, which means that the subscription fee and minor storage and processing expenses are the only relevant cost factors. At the same time, both BDOs have a high impact on asset utilization and route profitability.

[227] Source: Own illustration.

On the other side of the spectrum, the analysis of events in social networks (B4) and the real-time traffic right information platform (H2) promise comparably low financial benefits and require significant development investments. Three further BDOs have a higher financial benefit evaluation than cost potential (A4, A4, A10), while five BDOs have a balanced evaluation (A6, D1, D2, D3, H1).

Although the assessment has an indicative character due to the small sample size, a preliminary conclusion can be drawn from a cross-airline perspective. In any case, every airline should conduct a thorough analysis of its specific network planning characteristics and KPIs in order to inform the choice of appropriate BDOs. This chapter has developed a framework for guiding these considerations and presents a decision-making logic that can be applied by airline practitioners in the same way.

7 Discussion and contrast with the scientific body of knowledge

This chapter aims to connect the literature analyzed in chapter 3 with the research findings of the previous three chapters. The structure of this chapter follows the order of the theory discussion.

Discussion sub-chapters	7.1 Status quo of NP in airlines	7.2 Big data in airline NP	7.3 Big data for airline NP in the RBV
Theory sub-chapters	▪ 3.2 Airline business models ▪ 3.3 Introduction to network theory ▪ 3.4 Airline networks ▪ 3.5 Network planning in airlines	▪ 3.6 Big data	▪ 3.7 The resource based view applied on data and network planning
Practical research sub-chapters	▪ 4.1 NP processes in reality ▪ 4.2 Data sources used for NP ▪ 4.3 IT tools used for network planning ▪ 4.4 Performance measurement of airline NP	▪ 5.1 Information needs for airline NP ▪ 5.2 Big data opportunities for airline NP ▪ 5.3 Evaluation of big data opportunity potential ▪ 6.1-6.3 Sizing the impact of big data for airline network planning	▪ All sub-chapters in chapters 4, 5 and 6
Key discussion topics	▪ Gap between scholarly and practical NP process ▪ Airline business model influence on NP processes ▪ Data used by scientists vs. practitioners	▪ Review of the 5 V's in terms of airline NP big data opportunities ▪ Relevance of airline big data literature for NP ▪ Corporate vs. department specific big data solutions	▪ Presence of BDA resources in airlines ▪ Outlook for an adaptive NP capability

Figure 7.1 – Structure of discussion in chapter 7[228]

Sub-chapter 7 discusses the consistency of the status quo of network planning in airlines with a scholarly perspective. Sub-chapter 7.2 analyzes how applicable the theoretical big data concepts are for the information needs and BDOs for airline network planning. Finally, sub-chapter 7.3 links the research back to the RBV and critically appraises the role of assets, resources, and capabilities in the context of airline NP.

---

[228] Source: Own illustration.

M. Schosser, *Big Data to Improve Strategic Network Planning in Airlines*,
Schriftenreihe der HHL Leipzig Graduate School of Management,
https://doi.org/10.1007/978-3-658-27582-2_7

7.1 Status quo of network planning in airlines

7.1.1 Airline business models and network planning

Many authors have noted the convergence of airline business models into hybrid business models (Daft & Albers, 2015; Shaw, 2016) that display the characteristics of two or more archetypical business models[229]. This observation is confirmed by the airlines of the case study. While the cargo airlines maintain their traditional business model due to their exclusive freight focus, the differentiation between the other airlines becomes blurred.

Both FSCs of the case study group have followed the dual-hybridization approach suggested by Klophaus et al. (2012), in which they debundle their service offering into an a-la-carte pricing model and maintain a low-cost spin-off as part of a larger airline group at the same time. On the contrary, one of the two LCCs is also moving towards a hybrid business model by bundling their a-la-carte services. Both SCAs have hybridized their business models and are complementing the traditional block capacity business with tour operators, which is described by Sterzenbach et al. (2013, p. 232) as one of the key aspects of the SCA business model, with direct single-seat distribution. SCA 1 also deploys a limited hub-and-spoke network with interline agreements[230] to feed its long-haul routes.

Scholars such as Sterzenbach et al. (2013), Shaw (2016), and Bieger and Wittmer (2011) have named the network type among others as the differentiating feature for airline business models. The length of the network planning cycle is strongly influenced by the airline business model. FSCs rely on complex network and schedule integration with their alliance

---

[229] FSC, LCC, SCA, REC, CAR.

[230] Interline agreements are commercial arrangements between airlines to handle passengers traveling on itineraries that require multiple flights on multiple airlines without re-checking of baggage.

partners and hence use longer planning cycles than airlines with other business models. Similarly, SCAs have to commit certain capacity to tour operators up to 18 months in advance and hence have limited short-term flexibility. In contrast, LCCs and CARs tend to have extremely short-term planning cycles, which reduce the time horizon between route selection until the inaugural flight to less than three months.

The automation of the NP process also depends on the business model. Scholars such as Grosche (2009) and Kölker and Lütjens (2015) have proposed a selection of concepts and mathematical optimization techniques for automating a large number of network optimization sub-problems. However, only FSCs have implemented a certain degree of automation of tactical network decisions and are working towards automating selected strategic network planning steps. All other business models rely on human decisions even for the purpose of tactical optimization. This difference between business models may change in the future due to advancing technology and increasing competitive pressure. Airlines moving towards dynamic scheduling inevitably need to automate large parts of the NP process in order to manage additional complexity (Jiang & Barnhart, 2009; Warburg et al., 2008). Until today, only FSCs were considering investments to build dynamic scheduling competences.

While different planning horizons and degrees of automation are distinctive characteristics of airline business models, other NP process aspects are not. There is no clear correlation in the case study group between business models and the use of specific data types. Furthermore, the organizational setup and anchoring of the NP departments cannot be derived from the chosen business model. Goedeking (2010, p. 99) assumed that NP departments are either profit centers or revenue centers that are integrated in the commercial function of an airline. In the case study group, both LCCs and CAR 3 consider their NP departments to be cost centers, which is also in line with their direct performance KPIs in case of LCC 2 and CAR 3. The

NP departments can hence also be a part of the operational function of the airline, which has not been mentioned in the literature so far.

7.1.2 The network planning process in literature and practice

Scholarly literature pertaining to network planning in airlines, which mostly originates from the operations research field, has focused predominantly on mathematical aspects of network optimization. Section 3.5.7 presented the derivation of a sequential network planning process based on 37 scholarly contributions. Due to the massive complexity of the NP process, the authors have focused on the sequential solution of sub-problems, which are similar to individual process steps (compare Grosche et al., 2001).

In practice, few of the process steps are currently automated with a mathematical optimizing algorithm. FSCs have deployed operation research models for automating tactical network planning; however, strategic network planning remains a manual task across the case study group. This means that scientific contributions to strategic NP process steps, such as network structure definition, route selection, flight frequency determination, and scheduling, have limited practical relevance for today's airline network planners.

This may have multiple reasons. Scholars focusing on network design, such as Lederer and Nambimadom (1998) and Carmona Benitez (2012), have assumed that an airline network is designed from scratch, and hence, important design problems evolve. In reality, most airlines have a legacy network that is gradually adjusted instead of being redesigned. This process step is hence only relevant for new or strongly growing airlines, which expand into new geographies. However, new airlines often do not have the financial resources for an automated network design tool. LCCs have been the fastest growing airlines in Europe in the previous two decades, but they are reluctant to invest in sophisticated decision-support systems, as their flexible NP process allows them to pursue a trial-and-error approach for strategic network planning[231].

Route selection plays a much more prominent role for airline network planners, as the addition of new routes and the discontinuation of existing routes are major network adjustment decisions. Operations research models require standardized and constant input data (e.g., a distance matrix for network nodes or historic demand data) that yield predictable and reproducible results (Grosche et al., 2001, pp. 260–262). However, the large number of possible routes makes the problem very difficult to generalize. The reasons to add or delete specific routes may require more information than a pure profit maximization function, as political and strategic reasons may also play a role (Goedeking, 2010, p. 119).

The case study group airlines follow different approaches for route selection and flight frequency determination. Both FSCs, CAR 1 and CAR 2, use an internal business case scheme to optimally allocate resources to routes and flight frequencies. Both LCCs and SCA 2 follow a trial-and-error approach, whereby a failing route or frequency decision is corrected after a test phase. SCA 1 has a joint decision board with the P&RM department for deciding on route and frequency decisions. None of the case study airlines uses one of the scientific route selection models (e.g., from Kölker & Lütjens, 2015 or Teodorović et al., 1994).

The tactical NP process steps are partly automated, where the FSCs are the most advanced airlines. Here, the sequential optimization models proposed in the literature are deployed within the NP optimization systems.

The generic NP process derived in section 3.5.7 is sequential and is based on the different network optimization models in the literature. In practice, however, the NP process steps are often overlapping and include multiple

[231] Both LCCs in the case study group use a "probation phase" approach for new routes. If a route does not perform during the probation phase, the route is cancelled immediately.

feedback loops. This is only possible due to the fact that the process steps are not fully automated yet and rely on human decision making. Feedback loops increase the complexity of optimization models and are hence not solvable with exact heuristics and current computation resources (Kölker & Lütjens, 2015). Non-exact heuristics could solve this issue, but they have not yet been implemented by any of the case study airlines.

7.1.3 Current data use in literature and practice

Airline NP scholars and practitioners have different access to data sources and hence differ in their use of data types. Figure 7.2 compares the use of 15 data types in the case study group and across a set of 72 scientific articles analyzed in section 1. Both practitioners and researchers most frequently use cost data, which is provided by airlines or can be derived from literature pertaining airline cost (e.g., Holloway, 2008 or Seristö & Vepsäläinen, 1997). However, there is no clear pattern indicating that data types used by airline NP practitioners are also used by academic scholars and vice versa. While market estimates (expressed as O&D demand), actually flown traffic data, fare data, and aircraft data are widely used in science and practice, many data types tend to be favored by one group only.

The differences in data types used can either originate from different access to data sources or from different data needs. Scholars mainly use publicly available data types, such as flown traffic and fare data, which are both included in the US Department of Transportation DB1B database. Similarly, aircraft data and economic data are publicly available from aircraft manufacturers and economic research reports (such as International Monetary Fund Economic outlook).

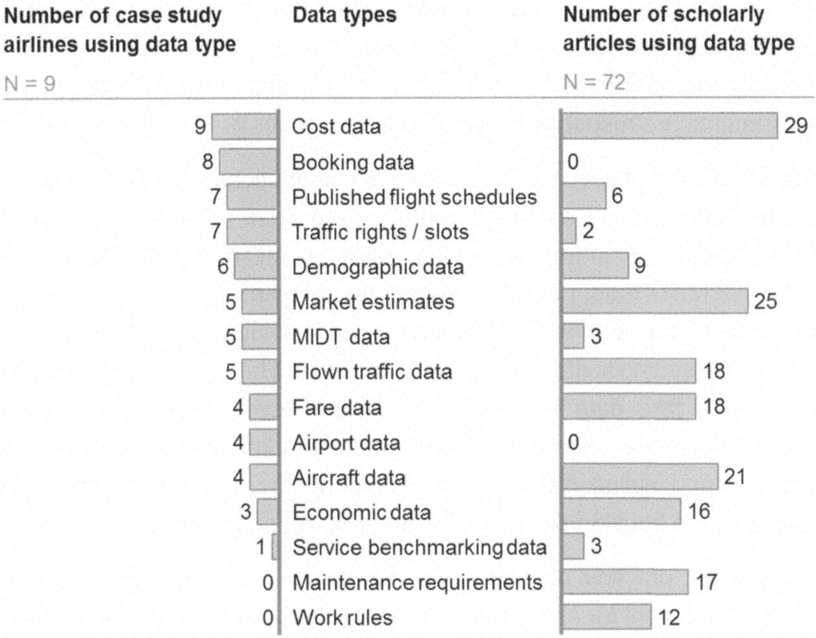

Figure 7.2 – Comparison of data types used by airlines and in NP literature[232]

Airline network planners can use internal data sources to access booking data, traffic rights, slots, and aircraft and airport data. Airlines are also willing to invest in external data such as MIDT data, fare analyses, and published flight schedules. These data are the most relevant for monitoring competitors and for informing market estimates with holistic input data. The data types are either rarely available for research or very expensive to access and hence not widely used in academic literature.

Maintenance requirements and work rules are common data types in literature pertaining to aircraft routing and crew planning (see Appendix

[232] Source: Own illustration.

15). There are, however, not used by airline network planners. The action task for maintenance planning and crew planning lies typically with the operations departments and not with airline NP departments, although NP departments are responsible for the final outcome.

Only nine[233] out of seventy-two academic contributions pertaining to airline network planning use competitor data – either from published schedules, MIDT data, or QSI index values. In contrast, all airlines of the case study group use MIDT data, published schedules, or both. Since many scholarly contributions focus on the optimization of an individual airline network, the competitive setting is often assumed to be static. Therefore, historic market shares and fare data are sufficient for the development of the static optimization model. In practice, however, the market environment is highly dynamic, and airline network planners depend on future-oriented data types such as booking data, MIDTs, and published schedules.

Furthermore, practical planning constraints such as traffic rights and slots are highly relevant for airline network planners. Except for Wei and Hansen (2006) and Yan et al. (2008), no academic contribution included a data type of slots and traffic rights that goes beyond a simple binary indicator of whether traffic rights and slots are present. Moreover, airport characteristics such as curfews, runway restrictions, or other operation-limiting factors have not been considered in any scholarly contribution.

One reason for the lacking application of scientific network design and optimization models in practice may be the misalignment of data sources. While scholars focus on static optimization parameters, airline network planners require dynamic optimization models that take into consideration competitive actions and a wide range of planning constraints. These

[233] Abrahams (1983), Carson et al. (2011), Cohn & Barnhart (2003), Hsiao & Hansen (2011), Kölker & Lütjens (2015), Teodorović & Krčmar-Nožić (1989), Valdes (2015), Weide et al. (2010), Yan et al. (2008).

requirements are especially relevant for strategic network planning, which must define the competitive positioning of an airline.

The emergence of big data opportunities may provide a chance for scholars to implement relevant information at little cost and without access to airline internal data. Google Trend data could, for example, estimate future booking intentions and be readily available for research, which has already been proven by scholars from the tourism research domain (Carrière-Swallow & Labbé, 2013; Önder & Gunter, 2016; Park et al., 2016; Rivera, 2016). In any case, current network design and optimization models must become more dynamic and adaptive, which may also be achieved by using non-exact optimization heuristics (Kölker & Lütjens, 2015).

7.2 Big data in airline network planning

7.2.1 Big data characteristics of BDOs for airline NP

While the functionality and business value of BDOs for airline network planning has been presented in the previous chapters, the actual importance of big data characteristics – the 5 Vs – for airline network planning has not yet been clarified. Five characteristics of big data were introduced in section 3.6.2, which are volume, velocity, variety, veracity, and value. Appendix 26 summarizes the big data characteristics for the long-list of BDOs for airline NP.

Since data volume is not explicitly defined in the literature (Gandomi & Haider, 2015, p. 138), the volume thresholds were defined for batch size and daily streaming volume respectively[234]. All but three BDOs produce at

---

[234] Data sets may be considered "big" if they exceed the maximum file size of common MS Office tools (Manyika et al., 2011, p. 1). So, the maximum MS Access file size of 2 GB (Microsoft, 2018) is used as the threshold between low and medium data volume. The upper threshold is set at 1 TB per batch or daily stream, which is the average hard drive size offered on Amazon Germany in September 2018.

least a medium data volume, and eleven BDOs are even expected to produce high data volumes. In many cases, it is not necessary for airlines to process the entire data volume associated with a BDO, as many data providers process or filter the data prior to the data transfer. However, the underlying pattern proves that volume is a highly significant characteristic for almost all BDOs for NP in airlines.

Data for 16 out of 23 BDOs could potentially be transmitted in real time, although a batch-aggregation may seem to be appropriate before transmission in some cases. Only one BDO relies on monthly batch data (exhibitor analysis of industry fairs). Six BDOs rely on a single source of data, while seenteen BDOs use two or more data sources. Nine BDOs include unstructured data, which contributes towards a larger data variety.

Data veracity has been evaluated qualitatively, depending on the expected data quality risk of each BDO. Seven BDOs are likely to incur high data quality risks, six BDOs show a medium level of veracity, and there are ten BDOs with high veracity level. The value analysis is based on the benefit potential assessment by the airline network planners[235], which is discussed in sub-chapter 5.3. The value distribution of BDOs is quite balanced, with 4 to 8 BDOs in each value level.

Figure 7.3 visualizes the aggregated big data characteristics from Appendix 26. Variety and veracity are the least dominant big data characteristics for the 23 analyzed BDOs. In contrast, volume, velocity, and value are the most defining attributes, with a large majority of BDOs being classified in the medium or high category of each big data characteristic. This finding is in line with the current discussion in the literature, which has not been conclusive regarding whether veracity should be considered a defining characteristic of big data (Günther et al., 2017, p. 200).

---

[235] Very high > 4.0; High 3.0–4.0; Medium 2.0–3.0; Low <2.0.

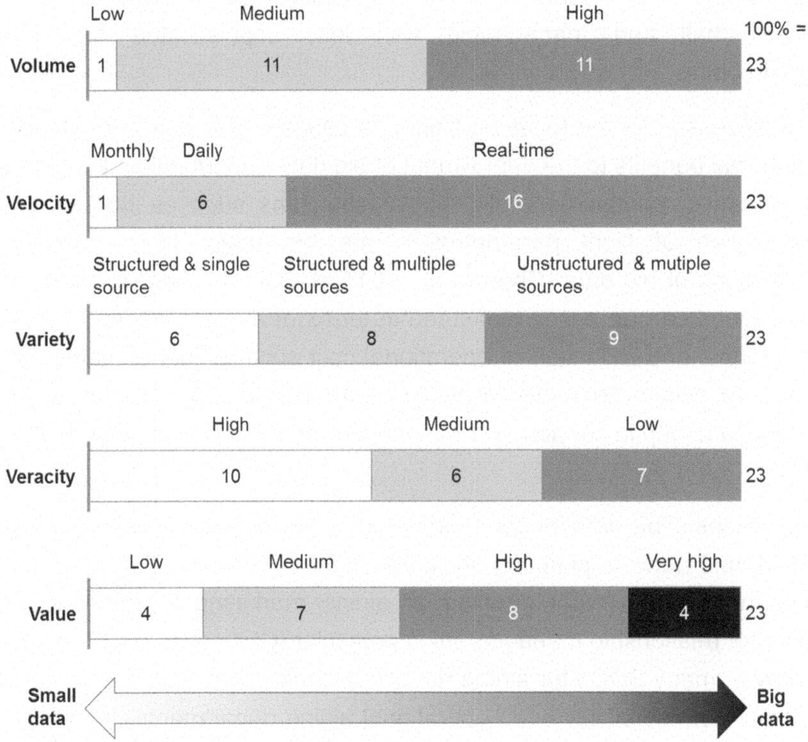

Figure 7.3 – Big data characteristics of 23 BDOs for airline NP[236]

7.2.2 Relevance of BDOs for other airline departments

The focus of airline big data researchers has been remaining on flight operation optimization by primarily using aircraft sensor data and meteorological data (Ayhan et al., 2013; Badea et al., 2018; Larsen, 2013). The focus on operational optimization might result from the extremely large

236 Source: Own illustration.

data volume of up to 20 TB per hour that can be produced on a single flight. Compared to this volume, all BDOs for airline network planning seem rather small and manageable with less sophisticated big data infrastructure.

Another reason for the focus on flight operations is the clear attributability of financial benefits to the deployment of big data opportunities. Predictive maintenance, containment of irregular situations such as delays, and optimization of flight parameters [237] are the major flight operation applications of big data (Chen et al., 2017, p. 22). The benefits of these applications can be easily measured in terms of avoided delays, aircraft groundings, and reduction of operational cost such as fuel consumption. Therefore, airlines are more willing to invest in big data pilot projects as did Lufthansa Group in cooperation with the University of Hawaii (Chen et al., 2017).

Applications of big data for commercial airline functions such as marketing, P&RM, and network planning are emerging only recently. The academic focus has been clearly directed at airline marketing in general and customer relationship management in particular (Chen et al., 2017, p. 25). However, many BDOs for airline network planning may also create value for other commercial or even operational airline departments. In order to follow a corporate-wide big data approach, the cross-functional applicability of BDOs should be considered and incorporated in any investment decision.

Appendix 27 evaluates the applicability of the 23 BDOs for six adjacent airline functions [238], namely strategic planning, finance, marketing and sales, P&RM, flight operations, and maintenance planning. As expected, the applicability of BDOs appears to be the highest for the commercial

[237] E.g., speed, routing, fuel consumption.

[238] Qualitative outside-in analysis to exemplify BDO applicability.

functions of P&RM and marketing and sales. The demand-based information needs of these two functions are similar to NP. Both these functions rely on accurate transportation demand forecasts, trend identification, and real movements to steer revenues and marketing campaigns. Especially economic forecast, BDOs (A1–A3, A7), and long-term trends also constitute valuable information for strategic planning and finance.

Competitor monitoring (C1 and C2) are relevant for both strategic and commercial departments, while real-time flight tracking also creates value for flight operations. Flight operations benefit from real-time location information on booked cargo shipments (D3) as well as on BDOs for planning constraints and early warning systems. Maintenance and finance are least likely to use airline NP-specific BDOs. However, there is not a single BDO that has no relevance for other airline departments.

7.2.3 Integration of BDOs in corporate big data ecosystems

This study has focused on describing big data opportunities that address very specific information needs for airline network planning. Chapter 6 developed a business case calculation framework that is purely based on airline NP-relevant KPIs. However, the last section revealed that many BDOs are also valuable for other airline functions. A single-handed approach by the NP department is, therefore, neither prudent nor desired from a corporate perspective.

Larsen (2013) recommended the implementation of an airline-wide big data ecosystem, where all data is accessible to the function in need. This idea is not new, as Wixom et al. (2008) described, prior to the "big data" age, the example of Continental Airlines, which managed to build a holistically accessible data warehouse to host all relevant structured data. In the big data era, however, a local and interconnected data warehouse might not be the optimal reference architecture anymore. Yaqoob et al.

(2016, p. 1232) argued in favor of a corporate-wide big data ecosystem that can host all relevant data sources and formats in a data lake model.

Legacy airlines often struggle with a multitude of IT systems that are used in parallel and are usually set up locally and function-specific (Wixom et al., 2008, p. 103). The move to a cloud-based big data ecosystem may open the opportunity to integrate different systems and data pools in order to overcome the data silos. Larsen (2013, p. 2) proposes four different cloud-based ecosystem models differentiated by privacy level and industry specificity. Referring to the big data value chain (see section 3.6.3), airlines could set up a corporate-wide storage and processing ecosystem that is fed by function-specific data requirements and can be accessed by function-specific analytics tools.

Figure 7.4 presents a simplified and exemplary corporate big data ecosystem for airlines. The big data storage and processing infrastructure that includes stream- and batch-specific processing clusters as well as the data lake can be shared across the corporation. Sensible data can be protected by function-specific and role-specific access rights. The data sources and the BDA layers can be customized for each function needs, although a common analytics layer for functions with very similar information needs appears to be possible (e.g., for all commercial functions). This shared ecosystem approach also reduces the implementation and configuration cost, as the main storage and processing system only required to be configured once.

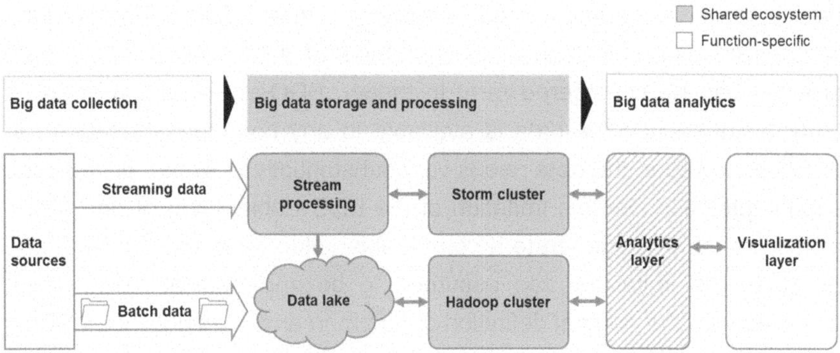

Figure 7.4 – Exemplary airline big data ecosystem[239]

7.3 Revisiting the RBV for big data in airline network planning

7.3.1 Review of the components of an adaptive NP capability

Chapter 5 developed 23 big data opportunities for airline NP, 12 of which were assessed to have high or very high potential. However, do these BDOs constitute a resource as defined by Grover et al. (2018, p. 391), which includes physical *data* assets that are complemented by analytics and processing technology?

Barney (1991, pp. 102–111) defined four resource characteristics to enable a sustainable competitive advantage, namely value, rarity, imperfect imitability, and non-substitutability. Chapter 6 discussed the value of the BDOs and discovered that most BDOs are likely to create substantial financial value for airline NP. However, not all BDOs are rare, as access to some data sources, such as Facebook Audience Insights or Google Trends is free and unrestricted. These BDOs are valuable but not rare. The same is true for data processing and analytics tools, which can

---

[239] Source: Own illustration following Heilig and Voß (2017, p. 32).

be licensed as standardized solutions. Other BDOs that require customized data collection or the purchase of data access from a data provider can be considered rare. In theory, BDOs could be imitated by other airlines since the data is available to any commercial acquirer. In practice, however, the data needs vary substantially between airlines (see sub-chapter 5.3). Simple imitation of the BDO deployment of one airline would probably not generate a comparable value for another airline, and as such, the imitability can assumed to be imperfect at least, which complies with the original definition of Lippman and Rumelt (1982). BDOs carry unique information based on their data set, which cannot be substituted easily. As every BDO targets a specific need for information of airline network planners (see sub-chapter 5.2), it can be assumed that these specific information needs cannot be satisfied without the BDO. In summary, BDOs are certainly valuable and non-substitutable and are most likely imperfectly imitable. However, some BDOs are not rare.

Given that rarity is a necessary condition to constitute a competitive advantage, the simplistic view of big data analytics provided by Grover et al. (2018) does not hold for BDOs in the airline NP context. Other scholars complement the physical big data assets with organizational assets. Organizational assets include the specific big data skills of employees (Erevelles et al., 2016, p. 899), managerial talent, and a data-driven company culture (Gupta & George, 2016, p. 1051).

These organizational factors are rare and are not imitable by other firms. BDOs and other technology components rely on these organizational factors to unravel their full potential. Therefore, BDOs are only a true resource if they include organizational assets such as culture, organizational structure, and employee skills.

A similar conclusion applies for the airline network resource, although the literature contains no prior discussion on this topic. Physical assets such as airport slots, traffic rights, aircrafts, and supporting infrastructure are all valuable, imperfectly imitable, and non-substitutable. Traffic rights are only rare if they involve countries without an open sky agreement. Traffic rights within the EU, for example, are not rare and are accessible to every market participant. However, the creation of a network also requires managerial skills and a dedicated organization to plan and maintain it. Thus, an asset called “NP organization” needs to complement the physical network assets, as it was discussed in section 3.7.5. Figure 7.5 displays the revised research concept.

During the research process, multiple airline network planners have commented on their perception of the challenges for airline NP in the coming 20 years. The replacement of the current seasonal planning cycles by a dynamic scheduling approach has been mentioned by almost all the interviewees. Low-cost and cargo airlines have already abandoned the strict seasonal scheduling periods.

The capability to adjust the airline network to micro-seasonal demand, real-time events, or competitor actions requires a much more granular information base for decision making than the static NP process. It strongly increases the importance of the outside-in perspective for airline network planners. The resulting capability is, therefore, an adaptive NP capability, as it aims to foresee these developments and prepare strategic responses accordingly (Day, 2011, p. 183). Big data opportunities support this process and constitute a necessary input for any adaptive NP capabilities in airlines.

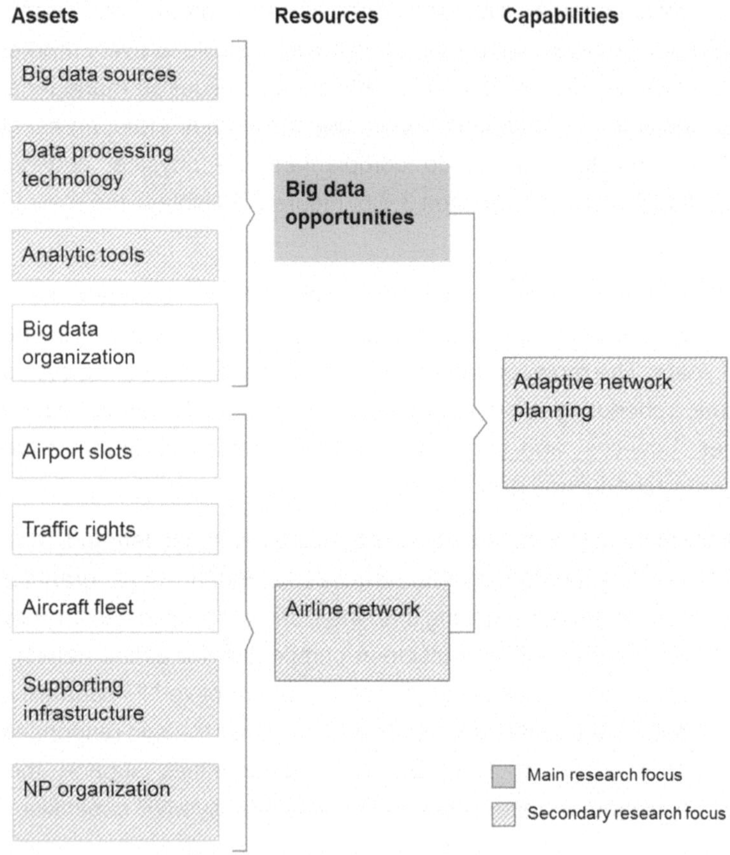

Figure 7.5 – Revised research concept based on RBV[240]

[240] Source: Own illustration.

7.3.2 *Organizational readiness of airlines*

The pivotal role of organizational factors must also be considered while evaluating the readiness of airlines to implement BDOs for NP. LaValle et al. (2011) noted early on that organizational factors such as managerial skills and corporate culture are the biggest challenges to big data adoption in large corporations. Information system scholars have developed a variety of maturity models to measure the adoption of BI&A (Cosic, Shanks, & Maynard, 2012; Muller & Hart, 2016) and later big data capabilities (Comuzzi & Patel, 2016) in organizations.

Most maturity models combine the technical dimension comprising data management, IT architecture, and IT tools with organizational and strategic dimensions. The latter includes strategic alignment (Cosic et al., 2012; Muller & Hart, 2016), culture (Comuzzi & Patel, 2016; Cosic et al., 2012; Muller & Hart, 2016), governance (Comuzzi & Patel, 2016; Cosic et al., 2012), and employee skills (Comuzzi & Patel, 2016; Cosic et al., 2012; Muller & Hart, 2016). However, none of these maturity models is industry- or process-specific. In a research paper independent from this study, an airline NP-specific maturity model for big data analytics was designed and tested with the same case study group (Hausladen & Schosser, 2018).

The maturity model for big data analytics in airline NP consists of four dimensions with two sub-dimensions each. The two technical dimensions (data and information technology) are complemented by two organizational dimensions (strategy alignment and organization). The scale of the maturity model reaches from level 0 (not existing) to level 5 (fully mature) for each sub-dimension. Eight airline network planners conducted a self-assessment with the maturity mode. The result is presented in Figure 7.6. The self-assessment scores are differentiated by the business model in order to highlight structural difference between airlines.

The range of the overall scores in the right column of Figure 7.6 is between 1.25 for employee skills and 2.28 for both information technology sub-domains. Since level 5 describes the highest theoretically possible stage of maturity, levels 2 and 3 can be assumed as medium-developed and level 1 as little developed. Overall, airline network planners assess their organizations' low-to-medium mature in big data analytics. While strategic alignment, data, and information technology appear to have a similar average maturity, the organizational dimension lags behind. Especially employee skills within the NP departments seem not yet ready to handle BDA applications, especially outside FSCs.

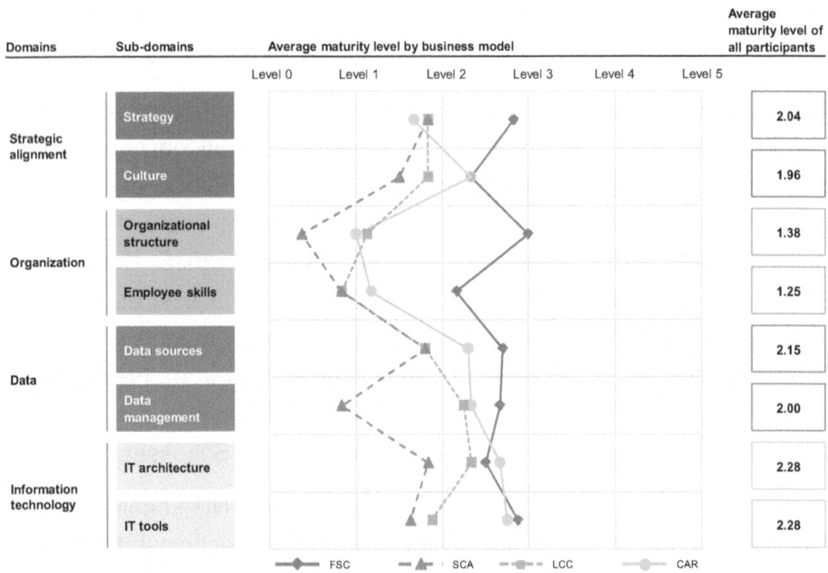

Figure 7.6 – Maturity model dimensions and maturity patterns by airline business model[241]

Looking at the airline business model patterns, it seems remarkable that FSCs assess themselves as the most mature in all but one sub-dimensions. The advantage is most pronounced in the organizational

---

[241] Source: Own illustration based on Hausladen and Schosser (2018).

structure, where both FSCs have dedicated cross-functional big data teams with clear responsibilities for BDA projects. They also conduct formal skill training for functional employees and develop a corporate big data strategy. In these circumstances, FSCs appear to be organizationally prepared to make use of big data opportunities. However, airlines with other business models might have to build an organizational structure for BDA and empower NP employees before they can successfully leverage the BDOs discussed in the previous chapters.

8 Conclusion and suggestions for further research

This final chapter concludes with the four research questions (sections 8.1.1 to 8.1.4) and provides general insights from across the study (section 8.1.5). The contribution to the scientific body of knowledge is summarized in section 8.1.6, which is followed by the second sub-chapter 8.2 suggesting methodological enhancements (section 8.2.1) and content extensions (section 8.2.2) for future research.

8.1 Conclusions on research outcome

8.1.1 How can "big data" be defined for network planning in airlines [RQ 1]?

The initial literature review revealed that big data can be differentiated from traditional data by five criteria, namely volume, variety, velocity, veracity, and value. For this study, data needs to meet at least two of these criteria in order to be considered big data. The analysis of 23 big data opportunities revealed that velocity is the most prominent characteristic of NP-related big data, followed by volume, value, variety, and veracity. All of the 23 analyzed BDOs fulfil at least two out of five big data characteristics (see Appendix 26).

The ingestion, processing, storage, and analysis of big data requires a big data ecosystem, parts of which may be set up on corporate scale and shared between departments. The parts of this ecosystem can be described using the value chain concept, where the big data sources represent only the very first step. Since network planning has very specific data and information needs, it requires specific data sources and customized analytics. The processing and storage of big data has the most potential to be shared across functional departments.

M. Schosser, *Big Data to Improve Strategic Network Planning in Airlines*,
Schriftenreihe der HHL Leipzig Graduate School of Management,
https://doi.org/10.1007/978-3-658-27582-2_8

8.1.2 What is the status quo of the business process, IT systems, and data use in airline network planning [RQ 2]?

In the first phase of a comparative case study including nine airlines with four different business models, a semi-structured interview was conducted to assess current business processes, IT systems, and data use. Prior to the data collection, a generic NP process was derived from the literature, which consists of nine distinct process steps. The long-term planning up to the initial schedule composition is called "strategic network planning"; the short-term network and schedule optimization is called "tactical network planning". Most components of the generic airline NP process derived in section 3.5.7 were found to be prevalent in practice. Only the network structure determination is obsolete for most airlines, as they already have a legacy network with a defined network type.

While the process steps in the literature are typically sequential due to the high degree of mathematical complexity, real-life NP processes feature iterative and parallel steps. Furthermore, different airline business models facilitate varying planning horizons. Low-cost carriers and cargo airlines have very short planning cycles, while full-service carriers and scheduled charter airlines follow long-term planning cycles. The main reasons for this discrepancy are less coordination needs with alliance partners and tour operators, the use of uncongested airports (which reduces dependency on slots), and shorter booking ramp-ups.

All airlines except for LCC 1 use standard NP software for tactical network planning, which is provided by the three system developers: AIMS, Lufthansa Systems, and Sabre. Only the full-service carriers use dedicated IT systems to support strategic network planning. All other airlines rely on individual, mostly Microsoft Excel-based tools. As a result, the degree of automation for strategic network planning is very low, while tactical network planning at least partly automated is in most airlines. The two low-cost carriers of the case study group deliberately decided against making investments in advanced NP systems, as network planning is decentralized for each individual base. The lack of coordination need with other airlines or transfer flights reduces complexity such that the entire NP process can be executed with standard Microsoft Excel functionality.

For the current data use, 22 data types were extracted from literature and the initial semi-structured interviews. The airline network planners were then asked to fill a structured survey that asked for data use and an assessment of usefulness and reliability of each data type. The use of the data types seems to be very specific to each airline, as there are no clear patterns across business models or other potential differentiation factors (e.g., fleet size, network type, route portfolio type).

Of the 22 data types, flight schedules, cost data, and traffic rights are the most frequently used (seven out of nine airlines). In contrast, meteorological data, real-time MIDT data, and clickstream data from flight search websites are the least frequently used. The latter two data types are also the only "big" data types that are currently employed by the airlines of the case study group.

Based on the usefulness and reliability assessment, the 22 data types can be classified in four groups. Half of all data types are "data essentials," which are highly reliable and highly useful. Seven data types are "unfulfilled data dreams," which are highly useful but unfortunately not reliable. The remaining classes of "hand-off data" (neither reliable nor useful) and "nice-to-have data" (reliable but not useful) contain two data types each. In summary, the large majority of currently used data types is highly useful but lacks reliability in some cases. Improving both usefulness and reliability of data types is one of the key purposes of BDOs for airline NP.

8.1.3 Which new "big data" opportunities are most suited to improve network planning for airlines or replace existing data types [RQ 3]?

Nine central information needs for airline network planners were defined based on the current data use. Subsequently, 23 big data opportunities were identified to satisfy the information requiremnets and to improve the usefulness and reliability of current data types. After introducing the 23 BDOs, the airline network planners of the case study group were asked to assess the potential of each BDO for their specific NP process.

Although the answer variance across all airlines was high, business model-specific assessment patterns could be identified. Five of the twenty-three BDOs bear only potential for cargo airlines, while six BDOs are relevant only for passenger airlines and 12 BDOs are relevant for both. On a more granular level, LCCs and CARs view most potential in BDOs that support short-term and mid-term demand forecasting as well as in real-time BDOs. On the contrary, FSCs and SCAs favor BDOs that improve reliability of long-term demand forecasts. Both are in line with the discovered differences in the network planning horizons of these business models.

Only the two BDOs addressing the planning constraints' need for information achieve consistent high potential assessment throughout all business models, namely a real-time traffic right information platform and a real-time slot trading platform. FSCs and SCAs view high potential in "trend identification" and "demand forecast" BDOs, which include clickstream data from meta-search websites, mobile location data, and general search engine data for detailed O&D demand. LCCs assign high potential to event analysis in social network and to a granular analysis of local hotel rates, which is also upheld by SCAs. All passenger airlines value demographic data from social networks.

Cargo airlines naturally assess cargo-specific BDOs with the highest potential, including location-transmitting sensors for cargo shipments, extended electronic air waybills with shipper addresses, shipping data from e-commerce platforms, and analysis of air cargo rates from online freight portals.

Subsequently, the feasibility of all BDOs was evaluated using five dimensions (feasibility of data acquisition, legal restrictions, data ownership, data variety, and availability of analytic tools). Six of the twelve

BDOs with the highest potential also showed a high feasibility and should be prioritized by airlines. The top priorities are cargo rate and hotel price analytics, search engine data, clickstream data from meta-search websites, mobile location data, and shipping data from e-commerce platforms.

Another six BDOs showed high potential but also had significant implementation challenges. These "long-term value creators" include demographic profiling and event analysis from social networks, real-time cargo tracking with location sensors, extended electronic AWBs with individual shipping addresses, a real-time traffic right information platform, and a real-time slot trading platform.

The remaining 11 BDOs were split in two categories. Six "data add-on" BDOs that are rather easy to implement but lack consistent high potential across airline business models. Five BDOs feature low potential and low feasibility and are hence possible "value traps" for airlines.

Current IT systems for airline NP are not capable of processing and analyzing BDOs, but they can partially integrate the analytic results. Considering the 12 high-potential BDOs, one large system developer views potential in integrating results from search-engine data analysis, event analysis from social media, and from both "planning constraint" BDOs. However, the need for a big data processing and analytics ecosystem is evident, as the current IT system cannot perform this task.

8.1.4 How can the impact of big data opportunities for airline network planning be quantified [RQ 4]?

In order to receive acceptance within the organization, any BDO must contribute towards the financial targets of the NP department. Otherwise, investments in BDOs are difficult to justify and may be de-prioritized against other investment opportunities with a clearer financial impact. The financial targets are typically derived from the role of the NP department within the airline organization and the associated KPIs.

The roles and responsibilities of NP departments vary widely across the case study group. Five out of nine airlines consider the NP department as a profit center (including both FSCs, two CARs, and SCA 1), which has a coordinating function between the commercial revenue centers and the operational cost centers. All these airlines use a profit KPI as primary target for NP. The two low-cost airlines and CAR 3 view the NP department as cost center with the mission to maximize aircraft utilization and operating cost. SCA 2 attaches NP to the commercial revenue center but imposes conflicting cost KPIs.

As the roles and responsibilities of the NP departments differ across airlines, so do the KPIs. Airlines use a broad selection of primary and secondary KPIs to measure NP performance. At the same time, different BDOs influence different KPIs. The same BDO may thus have a very different impact on the financial targets of different airline NP organizations.

The airline network planners of the case study group were asked to assess the financial impact of the 12 high-potential BDOs on their specific set of KPIs. Based on the results obtained, an impact profile could be created for each KPI and vice versa for each BDO. It appears that none of the 12 BDOs impacts all the KPIs that are currently used in the case study group. Nevertheless, every BDO had a high or a very high impact on at least one KPI. As a result, airline network planners should define a suitable set of BDOs based on their individual KPI set for NP.

In order to measure the impact of a BDO, airline network planners should rely on dynamic metrics that are in the remit of NP. Static and global metrics, such as load factor or total network profit, require superficial assumptions and are influenced by many factors outside NP control. Specific and dynamic metrics, however, can be associated directly with individual BDOs and are thus well suited to motivate BDO investments. Examples of specific and dynamic metrics include increased profitability of new flights or profit from additional flights that are enabled through increased asset utilization.

KPIs also differ in their value generation potential. Forecast accuracy, for example, is difficult to associate with financial performance metrics and is hence not suited as a primary justification for an NP investment. FTE reduction due to automation will only generate sufficient financial benefit to motivate BDO investment in very large NP departments. Airline network planners should rather rely on KPIs such as route profitability, asset utilization, and schedule robustness, all of which have a large value generation potential and suitable metrics for impact measurement.

The costs of BDO implementation are not generalizable but depend mainly on the data volume, data variety, and analytical complexity of the BDO. BDOs that provide not only raw data but also the processing and analytics platform (e.g., hotel price and cargo rate analysis tools) require little additional investment in the big data ecosystem. Similarly, BDOs that provide filtered and structured data are likely to be very cost efficient in terms of storage, processing, and analytics. In contrast, BDOs such as a real-time traffic right information platform, which combines large volumes of structured and unstructured data that need to be matched and analyzed, will require significant investments.

Investments in individual BDOs are likely to range from a few 10,000 USD to multi-million-dollar amounts. An example of a fictive full-service carrier showed that even mid-sized projects with a total investment volume of about 1 million USD over five years can break even with marginal performance improvements[242]. Five out of twelve high potential BDOs combine a high financial benefit potential with a very limited cost risk[243].

---

[242] E.g., 40 USD profit increase of every new flight, 0.5% delay reduction, or 0.5 flight per day due to increased asset utilization.

[243] Detailed demographic profiling with social media data, general search engine data for detailed O&D demand, analysis of air cargo rates from online freight portals, shipping data from e-commerce platforms, analysis of local hotel prices.

8.1.5 Overall conclusion

Network planning in airlines is much more diverse in practice than it is recorded in academic research. While scholars studying network planning typically assume a "standard" airline, there are no standard airlines in reality. Airlines differ according to business model, size, network, and organizational structure. This is also transferred to the NP departments, which have different roles, responsibilities, and organizational setups.

The plurality of NP approaches inhibits 'one-size-fits-all' solutions for NP optimization in the context of BDOs as well. Although there is a multitude of BDOs for airline NP, airline network planners must decide which BDOs are beneficial for their airline on the basis of their very specific department and process setup. Guidelines for selecting suitable BDO candidates as well as a potential calculation methodology have been described in this study.

Several BDOs are likely to be very cost efficient, as data is either available for free or at a monthly subscription, which includes critical big data value chain steps such as processing and analytics. Furthermore, many BDOs are also relevant for other airline departments, and as such, a joint procurement could even enhance the expected impact. The use of big data should not create additional data and IT silos within the airline. Therefore, a company-wide big data strategy is advisable. A shared big data ecosystem does not only lower costs for individual BDO adoption but creates a shared data and knowledge pool from which all airline departments could benefit.

Finally, the implementation and use of BDOs is only one dimension of a big data analytics capability. A parallel research project (Hausladen & Schosser, 2018) found that the organizational dimension is still very immature, especially outside the FSCs. Airlines and especially NP departments must actively invest in skill development and adjust their organizational structures to the big data age (e.g., by introducing formal top-executive project sponsorships and establishing cross-functional big data teams). A big data-friendly culture within the NP departments could immensely benefit any future BDO investment.

8.1.6 Contribution to the scientific body of knowledge

Besides addressing an exigent practical problem, this study contributes to the scientific body of knowledge in various aspects. First, to the best of my knowledge, it is the first academic contribution in the intersection between big data and strategic airline network planning. It combines insights from the information system perspective on big data with the operations research-dominated research domain concerning airline network planning. The resource-based view serves as a theoretical bridge to enable a joint perspective.

Second, this study is the first scientific contribution that describes and compares airline NP processes across a sample of airlines with different business models. The comparative case study approach allows for contrasting individual aspects of airline NP, such as the organizational setup, performance measurement, data use, and the NP process components.

Third, the study contributes a dedicated approach towards the development and evaluation big data opportunities. BDOs are developed to satisfy concrete information needs, which, in turn, have been derived from the literature and practice in parallel. A multi-step evaluation process embedded in the comparative case study approach considers both value creation potential and implementation feasibility.

Finally, the discussion highlighted misalignments between academic research concerning network planning and airline NP in practice. The network design problem is only a subsidiary concern for airline network planners, while it constitutes a major research object within the domain of operations research. By contrast, demand forecasting plays a much more important role in practice than in academia where demand is often seen as a simple input parameter. Furthermore, many scientific network optimization models lack strategic and political decision-making factors, which may lead to economically irrational competitor decisions. Finally, future network planning models must incorporate dynamic scheduling functionality in order to reflect the requirement profile of practical airline NP.

8.2 Suggestions for further research

8.2.1 Methodological enhancements

As discussed in chapter 2, a qualitative-dominant multi-phase research setup has been chosen, with a literature review and a comparative case study as the main research methods. This choice was motivated by the exploratory character of the research topic, which is characterized by its recency and the lack of preceding literature. The exploratory research has been concluded with the publication of this study, which opens the opportunity for investigating big data in airline NP from different research perspectives.

The main weak point of the chosen research setup is the limited external validity due to the small number of case study airlines. A *quantitative research setup* could test and validate the hypotheses derived in this research project. The airline sample could be broadened to a statistically meaningful sample size (preferably 30 or more airlines). Airlines from other continents should be included to overcome the Europe bias of the current case study group. The inclusion of regional airlines could also strengthen the explanatory power of the results.

The quantitative elements in this research project, such as the surveys, can serve as starting points for a quantitative follow-up study. The use and evaluation of current data types could easily be extended to a larger airline sample. The results of the semi-structured interviews in this study, such as the organizational structure, performance measurement, process steps, and used IT systems, could eventually also be transformed into a structured questionnaire. This would yield a broader dataset on NP process characteristics, which could also be used to develop and test hypotheses concerning the use and evaluation of current data types. The second survey concerning the value creation potential of the 23 BDOs could be applied to a broader airline sample as well.

A second weak point of the chosen methodology is that some KPIs are not used at all by the case study group, and other KPIs such as load factor and schedule robustness are utilized only by a small number of airlines. Including 30 or more airlines would potentially yield a broader coverage of KPIs, which makes the KPI-specific benefit estimate for BDOs more valid. The preliminary hypotheses formulated in sub-chapter 6.5 could hence be refined.

A second complementary research approach could be a design science study, which has its roots in action research (Hevner et al., 2004). One or more BDOs could be implemented with a research partner airline. An IT artefact for the relevant big data value chain steps could be developed. This research approach could reveal the implementation obstacles and assist in refining the feasibility assessment framework developed in section 5.3.4. The real-life implementation of one or more BDOs could also inform future cost and benefit estimates with actual costs and financial impact data.

8.2.2 Content suggestions for further research

A similar research approach could be employed for researching topic extensions of this study. Topic extensions could extend the process, industry, and scope of the research.

A process extension could target other airline processes that could bear the potential for the application of big data. Commercial processes, such as pricing and revenue management, marketing and sales, as well as operational processes, which include flight operations and maintenance, are worth mentioning. Section 7.2.2 noted that many BDOs are also applicable to some of the abovementioned processes. A similar explorative comparative case study may identify the primary information needs of this business process and develop additional BDOs for fulfiling these needs. A benefit potential assessment from other department perspectives could provide a more holistic view of big data opportunities for the entire airline organization.

An industry extension will examine the information needs and the data use of NP departments in other transportation industries, such as railways, shipping, and trucking. The basic function of network planning and management should be present in all of these industries, although the information needs may differ significantly. A similar methodology could be employed to evaluate information needs and data use in order to derive and evaluate industry-specific BDOs. The results could be aggregated in a comparative study across different transportation modes.

Finally, a research object extension could focus on the different components of the big data value chain. A promising research field involves the applicability of different analytics techniques for the BDOs of network planning, particularly more complex analytics techniques such as advanced machine learning could lead to new BDOs. The in-depth study of the symbiosis between advanced big data analytics and individual BDOs could also sharpen the cost and benefit estimates.

A last suggestion concerns the role of NP system developers. In the research setup of this study, the role of the system developers and data providers was to provide their perspective on the data use and the applicability of BDOs in airline network planning. A more prominent role, and especially the addition of more NP system developers, could improve the likelihood that some BDOs may be integrated directly in current or newly developed NP IT systems. Especially the action research approach suggested in the previous section would provide a superb opportunity for increased involvement of system developers.

List of Appendices

M. Schosser, *Big Data to Improve Strategic Network Planning in Airlines*,
Schriftenreihe der HHL Leipzig Graduate School of Management,
https://doi.org/10.1007/978-3-658-27582-2

Appendix 1 – Literature review typology proposed by Paré et al. (2015, p. 186)

Overarching goal	Theoretical review types	Scope of questions	Search strategy	Nature of primary sources	Explicit study selection	Quality appraisal	Methods for synthesizing/ analyzing findings
Summarization of prior knowledge	Narrative review	Broad	Usually selective	Conceptual and empirical	No	No	Narrative summary
	Descriptive review	Broad	Representative	Empirical	Yes	No	Content analysis/ frequency analysis
	Scoping review	Broad	Comprehensive	Conceptual and empirical	Yes	Not essential	Content or thematic analysis
Data aggregation or integration	Meta-analysis	Narrow	Comprehensive	Empirical (quantitative only)	Yes	Yes	Statistical methods (meta-analytic techniques)
	Qualitative systematic review	Narrow	Comprehensive	Empirical (quantitative only)	Yes	Yes	Narrative synthesis
	Umbrella review	Narrow	Comprehensive	Systematic reviews	Yes	Yes	Narrative synthesis
Explanation building	Theoretical review	Broad	Comprehensive	Conceptual and empirical	Yes	No	Content analysis or interpretive methods
	Realist review	Narrow	Iterative and purposive	Conceptual and empirical	Yes	Yes	Mixed-methods approach
Critical assessment of extant literature	Critical review	Broad	Selective or representative	Conceptual and empirical	Yes or no	Not essential	Content analysis or critical interpretive methods

Appendix 2 – Keyword category combinations for literature search

Level	Combination	Object	Industry	Process	Theory
4	4	✓	✓	✓	✓
3	3a	✓	✓	✓	
	3b	✓	✓		✓
	3c	✓		✓	✓
	3d		✓	✓	✓
2	2a	✓	✓		
	2b	✓		✓	
	2c	✓			✓
	2d		✓	✓	
	2e		✓		✓
	2f			✓	✓
1	1a	✓			
	1b		✓		
	1c			✓	
	1d				✓

Appendix 3 – Evaluation of relevant research domains for the study

Research domain	Airlines	Big Data	Strategic network planning	Combined score	Overall relevance	Included?
General management science (GM)	2	3	2	7	medium	yes
Finance (FIN)	2	2	0	4	low	no
Accounting (ACC)	2	2	0	4	low	no
University management (UM)	0	0	0	0	none	no
International management (INT)	3	1	2	6	medium	yes
Logistics (LOG)	4	3	4	11	high	yes
Marketing (MARK)	2	4	2	8	medium	yes
Sustainability management (SUS)	2	1	1	4	low	no
Public administration (PAM)	1	2	1	4	low	no
Operations research (OR)	4	3	3	10	high	yes
Organization science (ORG)	2	2	3	7	medium	yes
Production management (PROD)	1	4	3	8	medium	yes
Tax management (TAX)	2	1	0	3	low	no
Strategic management (SM)	3	2	4	9	high	yes
Technology, innovation & entrepreneurship (TIE)	2	4	1	7	medium	yes
Business ethics (BETH)	1	2	0	3	low	no
Information systems (IS)	3	4	2	9	high	yes
Service & retail management (SRM)	1	2	2	5	low	no
Entrepreneurship (ENT)	1	4	2	7	medium	yes

Research domain	Airlines	Big Data	Strategic network planning	Combined score	Overall relevance	Included?
Healthcare management (HM)	0	2	1	3	low	no
Small & midsized enterprises (SME)	1	2	1	3	low	no
Insurance management (IM)	1	3	0	4	low	no

Legend:

Individual scores: *4 – > 75% of maximum hit number, 3 – 50-75 %, 2 – 25-50%, 1 – 5-25%, 0 – <5%*

Aggregate scores: *9-12 –high relevance, 6-8 – medium relevance, 3-5 – low relevance, 0-2 – no relevance*

Appendix 4 – A+ and A-rated journals from relevant research domains

Journal name	Rating	Corresponding research domains	Databases
Academy of Management Journal (AMJ)	A+	GM	Business Source Complete
Academy of Management Review	A+	GM	Business Source Complete
Administrative Science Quarterly	A+	GM	Business Source Complete
American Economic Review	A+	GM	Business Source Complete
Discrete Applied Mathematics	A	LOG, OR	Elsevier/ScienceDirect
Econometrica	A+	GM	JSTOR, Wiley Online
European Journal of Information Systems	A	IS	SpringerLINK
European Journal of Operational Research (EJOR)	A	OR	Elsevier/ScienceDirect
IIE Transactions	A	OR	Business Source Complete

Journal name	Rating	Corresponding research domains	Databases
Information Systems Journal	A	IS	Business Source Complete
Information Systems Research (ISR)	A+	OR, IS	Business Source Complete
INFORMS Journal on Computing	A	OR, IS	Business Source Complete
Journal of Consumer Research	A+	MARK	JSTOR
Journal of Economic Dynamics & Control	A	OR	Elsevier/ScienceDirect
Journal of Economics & Management Strategy	A	SM	Business Source Complete
Journal of Information Technology	A	IS	SpringerLINK, Taylor & Francis
Journal of Management Information Systems	A	IS	Business Source Complete
Journal of Marketing	A+	MARK	Business Source Complete
Journal of Marketing Research	A+	MARK	Business Source Complete
Journal of Operations Management	A	LOG, OR	Elsevier/ScienceDirect
Journal of Political Economy	A+	GM	Business Source Complete
Journal of Scheduling	A	OR	SpringerLINK
Journal of the Association for Information Systems (JAIS)	A	IS	Business Source Complete
Management Information Systems Quarterly (MISQ)	A+	OR, PROD, IS	Business Source Complete
Management Science	A+	GM	Business Source Complete
Manufacturing & Service Operations Management	A	OR	Business Source Complete
Marketing Science	A+	MARK	Business Source Complete
Mathematical Programming	A	OR, IS	SpringerLINK, Business Source Complete
Mathematics of Operations Research	A	OR	Business Source Complete

Journal name	Rating	Corresponding research domains	Databases
Operations Research	A+	OR	Business Source Complete
OR Spectrum	A	OR	SpringerLINK, Business Source Complete
Organization Science	A+	ORG	Business Source Complete
Proceedings of the International Conference on Information Systems (ICIS)	A	IS	AISeL, SpringerLINK
Science	A+	GM	JSTOR
SIAM Journal on Computing	A	OR, IS	Business Source Complete
Strategic Entrepreneurship Journal	A	SM, TIE	Wiley Online
Strategic Management Journal (SMJ)	A	SM	JSTOR, Wiley Online
The Journal of Strategic Information Systems	A	IS	Elsevier/ScienceDirect
Transportation Science	A	LOG, OR	Business Source Complete

Appendix 5 – Number of relevant journals per database and search engine

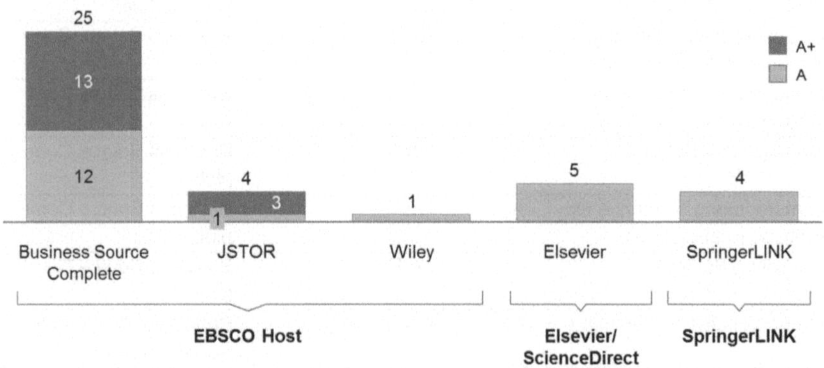

Appendix 6 – Results of the initial structured keyword search

Combination code	"big data"	"airline"	"strategic network planning" OR "strategic planning" OR "network planning"	"resource-based view" OR "network theory"	Hits per access point (relevant contributions): Ebsco-Host	Science Direct	Springer LINK	Google Scholar
4a	yes	yes	yes	yes	2 (0)	4 (0)	5 (0)	76 (2)
3a	yes	yes	yes	no	79 (2)	34 (5)	37 (3)	713 (9)
3b	yes	yes	no	yes	8 (2)	29 (5)	24 (1)	525 (9)
3c	yes	no	yes	yes	20 (1)	34 (8)	25 (0)	795 (9)
3d	no	yes	yes	yes	235 (9)	115 (24)	73 (1)	2'030 (14)
2a	yes	yes	no	no	825 (19)	424 (23)	443 (3)	8'930 (16)
2b	yes	no	yes	no	1'292 (21)	739 (23)	446 (2)	11'800 (19)
2c	yes	no	no	yes	161 (7)	370 (14)	295 (5)	9'650 (13)
2d	no	yes	yes	no	5'550 (19)	2'486 (21)	952 (4)	17'300 (11)
2e	no	yes	no	yes	727 (5)	701 (18)	451 (2)	11'600 (15)
2f	no	no	yes	yes	3'291 (25)	1'194 (36)	834 (2)	17'400 (15)
1a	yes	no	no	no	38'596 (6)	20'311 (11)	16'159 (2)	304'000 (9)
1b	no	yes	no	no	236'127 (5)	43'680 (12)	17'856 (4)	753'000 (24)
1c	no	no	yes	no	186'982 (10)	51'883 (16)	24'215 (3)	184'400 (8)
1d	no	no	no	yes	21'839 (7)	26'604 (15)	15'003 (2)	179'000 (20)
Number of unique relevant contributions:					**138**	**232**	**35**	**205**

Appendix 7 – Most frequent publications as per VHB-rank

VHB rank	Number of contributions	Most frequent publications	Relevance
No journals	53	N/A	
A+	52	MIS Quarterly (13), Operations Research (8), Management Science (8)	Literature from **highly acknowledged scholarly journals ensuring the scientific relevance** of the used literature body
A	64	Transportation Science (20), European Journal of Operations Research (16), Strategic Management Journal (9)	
B	76	Transportation Research (22), Computers & Operations Research (7), Information & Management (6)	
C	15	International Journal of Forecasting (3), MIT Sloan Management Review (3), Harvard Business Review (3)	Literature from **industry and practitioner journals ensuring the practical relevance** of the used literature body
Not VHB ranked	83	Journal of Air Transport Management (17), Transportation Planning and Technology (5), Journal of Transport Geography (4)	

Appendix 8 – Set of questions for first interview round

Interview guide – Status Quo Interview

A. Introduction to research project

See presentation

B. Strategic network planning in practice

a. NP process

Ba1 – Please describe the concrete steps of the NP process in your airline.

Ba2 - What is the chronological sequence of the NP process in your airline?

Ba3 - Which departments are involved in the individual steps of the NP process?

Ba4 - What are the principal optimization factors in your NP process (e.g. cost minimization, revenue maximization, operational performance)?

b. IT systems for network planning

Bb1 - Which IT systems do you use currently for network planning?

Bb2 - Which decisions in the NP process are currently automatized or heavily supported by IT systems?

Bb3 - Which are in your opinion limiting factors for further automation of the NP process?

c. Data sources for network planning

Bc1 - Which data sources do you currently use for the individual steps of the NP process?

Bc2 - Do you collect these data internally or are these data acquired from third party providers?

Bc3 - Do you receive any data directly from (potential) destination airports?

Bc4 - How satisfied are you with the currently used data sources?

d. Organizational set-up and performance management

Bd1 - Please describe the organizational structure of the NP department.

Bd2 - What are the key roles and responsibilities of the NP department?

Bd3 - What are the primary and secondary key performance indicators for network planning in your airline?

Bd4 - Is the NP department a cost, revenue or profit center?

Appendix 9 – Set of questions of the first-round online questionnaire

Big data in airline network planning - status-quo follow up

After the semi-structured interview, we need to finalize the status-quo assessment with a short survey featuring the most common current data sources.

1. **Email address** *

____

Which of these data types do you currently use for network planning?

Please tick the boxes for all data types that you use for network planning

2. **Demand forecasts**
Check all that apply.

- [ ] Ready-made market forecasts (e.g., from IATA, ICAO, Airbus, Boeing, Seabury or national aviation authorities)
- [ ] Economic forecasts (from international organizations , e.g., World Bank or IMF, or private research institutes, e.g., Oxford Economics)
- [ ] Demographic data (e.g., from national statistic bureaus)
- [ ] Information on unconstrained demand (e.g., "unserved route of the week" using booking portal search data)
- [ ] Real-time booking curves (from internal booking data)
- [ ] Real-time booking data from Global Distribution Systems (GDS)
- [ ] Other: ____________________

3. **Cost forecasts**
Check all that apply.

- [ ] Oil price forcasts
- [ ] Airport and traffic fees (e.g., from AirPas, RDC Aviation, etc.)
- [ ] Other direct operating cost (e.g., crew, direct maintenance, depreciation)
- [ ] Other: ____________________

4. **Information on scheduled (flown) flights**
Check all that apply.

- [ ] Flight schedules (e.g., from OAG, Innovata, Amadeus, etc.)
- [ ] MIDT data (e.g., from Sabre, TravelPort, Amadeus, etc.)
- [ ] Flight event data on actually flown flights (e.g., from National statistic bureaus, FiPlan, flightaware, etc.)
- [ ] Fare data (e.g., from Infare, IATA PaxIS and CASS, WorldACD)
- [ ] Airport traffic statistics (from individual airports or from ACI)
- [ ] Other: ____________________

5. **Transparency on planning constraints**
Check all that apply.

- [ ] Airport slot allocation (e.g., from IATA SlotLink, ACL or individual airports)
- [ ] Real-time slot availability (e.g., from OCS, e-Airportslots or individual airports)
- [ ] Traffic rights including overflight rights (from national authorities)
- [ ] Aircraft specifications (from manufacturers or internal database)
- [ ] Airport characteristics (e.g., from Jeppesen, Eurocontrol, Amadeus, etc.)
- [ ] Other: ______________________

6. **Political and environmental events**
Check all that apply.

- [ ] Meteorological events such as storms, floodings, heat waves, etc. (from meteorological services)
- [ ] Political events such as terror attacks, overflight risks, travel bans, additional security regulations, etc. (from risk consulting firms, insurances, ICAO, etc.)
- [ ] Competitor-related events such as bankruptcies, accidents, strikes, etc. (from industry monitors and news providers)
- [ ] Other: ______________________

Big data in airline network planning - reliability of used data sources

How reliable are the data sources you are using?

If you use multiple data sources for a data item (e.g., Airbus and IATA market forecasts), please state an average degree of satisfaction

7. **Demand forecasts**
Mark only one oval per row.

	Highly unreliable	Rather unreliable	Rather reliable	Completely reliable	Data type not used
Ready-made market forecasts	◯	◯	◯	◯	◯
Economic forecasts	◯	◯	◯	◯	◯
Demographic data	◯	◯	◯	◯	◯
Information on unconstrained demand	◯	◯	◯	◯	◯
Real-time booking curves	◯	◯	◯	◯	◯
Real-time booking data from GDS	◯	◯	◯	◯	◯

8. **Cost forecasts**
Mark only one oval per row.

	Highly unreliable	Rather unreliable	Rather reliable	Completely reliable	Data type not used
Oil price forcasts	◯	◯	◯	◯	◯
Airport and traffic fees	◯	◯	◯	◯	◯
Other direct operating cost	◯	◯	◯	◯	◯

9. **Information on scheduled (flown) flights**
Mark only one oval per row.

	Highly unreliable	Rather unreliable	Rather reliable	Completely reliable	Data type not used
Flight schedules	◯	◯	◯	◯	◯
MIDT data	◯	◯	◯	◯	◯
Flight event data on actually flown flights	◯	◯	◯	◯	◯
Fare data	◯	◯	◯	◯	◯
Airport traffic statistics	◯	◯	◯	◯	◯

10. **Transparency on planning constraints**
Mark only one oval per row.

	Highly unreliable	Rather unreliable	Rather reliable	Completely reliable	Data type not used
Airport slot allocation	◯	◯	◯	◯	◯
Real-time slot availability	◯	◯	◯	◯	◯
Traffic rights including overflight rights	◯	◯	◯	◯	◯
Aircraft specifications	◯	◯	◯	◯	◯
Airport characteristics	◯	◯	◯	◯	◯

11. **Political and environmental events**
Mark only one oval per row.

	Highly unreliable	Rather unreliable	Rather reliable	Completely reliable	Data type not used
Meteorological events	◯	◯	◯	◯	◯
Political events	◯	◯	◯	◯	◯
Competitor-related events	◯	◯	◯	◯	◯

Big data in airline network planning - usefulness of traditional data sources

How useful are these data types for your current network planning process?

You can also indicate your perceived usefulness for data types that you are not currently using. Please consider a data type to be useful if it improves your decision-making process for any decisions related to network planning.

12. **Demand forecasts**
Mark only one oval per row.

	Completely useless	Rather useless	Rather useful	Very useful	I don't know
Ready-made market forecasts	⬭	⬭	⬭	⬭	⬭
Economic forecasts	⬭	⬭	⬭	⬭	⬭
Demographic data	⬭	⬭	⬭	⬭	⬭
Information on unconstrained demand	⬭	⬭	⬭	⬭	⬭
Real-time booking curves	⬭	⬭	⬭	⬭	⬭
Real-time booking data from GDS	⬭	⬭	⬭	⬭	⬭

13. **Cost forecasts**
Mark only one oval per row.

	Completely useless	Rather useless	Rather useful	Very useful	I don't know
Oil price forcasts	⬭	⬭	⬭	⬭	⬭
Airport and traffic fees	⬭	⬭	⬭	⬭	⬭
Other direct operating cost	⬭	⬭	⬭	⬭	⬭

14. **Information on scheduled (flown) flights**
Mark only one oval per row.

	Completely useless	Rather useless	Rather useful	Very useful	I don't know
Flight schedules	⬭	⬭	⬭	⬭	⬭
MIDT data	⬭	⬭	⬭	⬭	⬭
Flight event data on actually flown flights	⬭	⬭	⬭	⬭	⬭
Fare data	⬭	⬭	⬭	⬭	⬭
Airport traffic statistics	⬭	⬭	⬭	⬭	⬭

15. **Transparency on planning constraints**
Mark only one oval per row.

	Completely useless	Rather useless	Rather useful	Very useful	I don't know
Airport slot allocation	⬭	⬭	⬭	⬭	⬭
Real-time slot availability	⬭	⬭	⬭	⬭	⬭
Traffic rights including overflight rights	⬭	⬭	⬭	⬭	⬭
Aircraft specifications	⬭	⬭	⬭	⬭	⬭
Airport characteristics	⬭	⬭	⬭	⬭	⬭

16. **Political and environmental events**
Mark only one oval per row.

	Completely useless	Rather useless	Rather useful	Very useful	I don't know
Meteorological events	⬭	⬭	⬭	⬭	⬭
Political events	⬭	⬭	⬭	⬭	⬭
Competitor-related events	⬭	⬭	⬭	⬭	⬭

Appendix 10 – Survey for qualitative big data opportunity evaluation

Ca1 - For each of the described potential big data opportunities, state the potential to improve decision-making for your network planning process

Code	Big data opportunity	No potential	Very small	Small	Medium	High	Very high	Comments
A1	Geo-spatial image analysis	□	□	□	□	□	□	
A2	Real-time inflation forecasts	□	□	□	□	□	□	
A3	Consumer confidence measurement with social media	□	□	□	□	□	□	
A4	Detailed demographic profiling with social networks	□	□	□	□	□	□	
A5	General search engine data for detailed O&D demand	□	□	□	□	□	□	
A6	Click-stream data of meta-search websites for flights	□	□	□	□	□	□	
A7	Social media mining to determine price elasticity	□	□	□	□	□	□	
A8	Analysis of air cargo rates from online freight portals	□	□	□	□	□	□	
A9	Analysis of exhibitor data of industry fairs	□	□	□	□	□	□	
AB	Shipping data from e-commerce platforms	□	□	□	□	□	□	
B1	Analysis of reviews in travel rating communities	□	□	□	□	□	□	
B2	Click-stream data from travel platforms	□	□	□	□	□	□	
B3	Analysis of local hotel prices	□	□	□	□	□	□	
B4	Analysis of events in social networks	□	□	□	□	□	□	
C1	Real-time flight tracking with transponder data	□	□	□	□	□	□	
C2	Network-relevant competitor news monitoring	□	□	□	□	□	□	
D1	Mobile location data from smartphones	□	□	□	□	□	□	
D2	Extended electronic AWB with shipper address	□	□	□	□	□	□	
D3	Location-transmitting sensors for cargo shipments	□	□	□	□	□	□	
H1	Real-time slot trading platform	□	□	□	□	□	□	
H2	Real-time traffic right information platform	□	□	□	□	□	□	
I1	Global meteorological warning platform	□	□	□	□	□	□	
I2	Global political risk assessments	□	□	□	□	□	□	

Appendix 11 – Literature definitions of big data characteristics

Author	Volume	Velocity	Variety	Veracity	Value
Laney, 2001	*"E-commerce channels increase the depth/breadth of data available about a transaction (or any point of interaction). The lower cost of e-channels enables an enterprise to offer its goods or services to more individuals or trading partners, and up to 10x the quantity of data about an individual transaction may be collected - thereby increasing the overall volume of data to be managed."*	*"E-commerce has also increased point-of-interaction (POI) speed and, consequently, the pace data used to support interactions and generated by interactions. As POI performance is increasingly perceived as a competitive differentiator (e.g., Web site response, inventory availability analysis, transaction execution, order tracking update, product/service delivery), so too is an organization's abil-*	*"[…] no greater barrier to effective data management will exist than the variety of incompatible data formats, non-aligned data structures, and inconsistent data semantics"*		

Author	Volume	Velocity	Variety	Veracity	Value
		ity to manage data velocity."			
Manyika et al., 2011	*"Big data" refers to datasets whose size is beyond the ability of typical database software tools to capture, store, manage, and analyze. This definition is intentionally subjective and incorporates a moving definition of how big a dataset needs to be in order to be considered big data—i.e., we don't define big data in terms of being larger than a certain number of terabytes (thousands of gigabytes).*				*Creating transparency Enabling experimentation to discover needs, expose variability, and improve performance Segmenting populations to customize actions Replacing/supporting human decision making with automated algorithms Innovating new business models, products, and services*
Russom, 2011	*"[…] data volume is the primary attribute of big data. With that in mind, most people define big data in terabytes—sometimes petabytes"*	*"Big data can be described by its velocity or speed. You may prefer to think of it as the frequency of data generation or the frequency of*	*"One of the things that makes big data really big is that it's coming from a greater variety of sources than ever before. Many of the newer ones*		

Author	Volume	Velocity	Variety	Veracity	Value
		data delivery.”	*are Web sources, including logs, clickstreams, and social media”*		
McAfee & Brynjolfsson, 2012	*“[…] More data cross the internet every second than were stored in the entire internet just 20 years ago. This gives companies an opportunity to work with many petabytes of data in a single data set—and not just from the internet.”*	*“For many applications, the speed of data creation is even more important than the volume. Real-time or nearly real-time information makes it possible for a company to be much more agile than its competitors.”*	*“Big data takes the form of messages, updates, and images posted to social networks; readings from sensors; GPS signals from cell phones, and more. Many of the most important sources of big data are relatively new."*		
Schroeck et al., 2012	*“The amount of data. Perhaps the characteristic most associated with big data, volume refers to the mass quantities of data that organizations are trying to harness to improve decision making across the enterprise”*	*“Data in motion. The speed at which data is created, processed and analyzed continues to accelerate. Contributing to higher velocity is the real-time nature of*	*“Different types of data and data sources. Variety is about managing the complexity of multiple data types, including structured, semi-structured and unstructured data”*	*“Data uncertainty. Veracity refers to the level of reliability associated with certain types of data”*	

Author	Volume	Velocity	Variety	Veracity	Value
		data creation, as well as the need to incorporate streaming data into business processes and decision making."			
Chen et al., 2014	*"Volume means, with the generation and collection of masses of data, data scale becomes increasingly big"*	*"Velocity means the timeliness of big data, specifically, data collection and analysis, etc. must be rapidly and timely conducted, so as to maximally utilize the commercial value of big data"*	*"Variety indicates the various types of data, which include semi-structured and unstructured data such as audio, video, webpage, and text, as well as traditional structured data."*		*"[…] big data technologies describe a new generation of technologies and architectures, designed to economically extract value from very large volumes of a wide variety of data, by enabling the high-velocity capture, discovery, and/or analysis."*
Gandomi & Haider, 2015	*"Volume refers to the magnitude of data. Big data sizes are reported in multiple terabytes and petabytes. […] Definitions of big data vol-*	*"Velocity refers to the rate at which data are generated and the speed at which it should be analyzed*	*"Variety refers to the structural heterogeneity in a dataset. Technological advances allow firms to use various*	*"Veracity. IBM coined Veracity as the fourth V, which represents the unreliability inherent in*	*"[…] big data are often characterized by relatively "low value density". That is, the data received in the original*

Author	Volume	Velocity	Variety	Veracity	Value
	umes are relative and vary by factors, such as time and the type of data."	*and acted upon."*	*types of structured, semi-structured, and unstructured data."*	*some sources of data. […] Thus, the need to deal with imprecise and uncertain data is another facet of big data, which is addressed using tools and analytics developed for management and mining of uncertain data."*	*form usually has a low value relative to its volume. However, a high value can be obtained by analyzing large volumes of such data."*
Wamba et al., 2015	*"Large volume of data that either consume huge storage or consist of large number of records"*	*"Frequency of data generation and/or frequency of data delivery"*	*"Data generated from greater variety of sources and formats, and contain multidimensional data fields"*	*"Inherent unpredictability of some data requires analysis of big data to gain reliable prediction"*	*"The extent to which big data generates economically worthy insights and or benefits through extraction and transformation."*

Appendix 12 – Big data analytics techniques

Context	Field	Technique	Description	Sources
Mathematical techniques	Statistics	**A/B testing**	▪ Comparison of a variety of test groups with control groups in order to determine the efficacy of a certain treatment or action	▪ Manyika et al. (2011)
		Time-series analysis	▪ Extraction of meaningful patterns and trends from a sequence of data points	▪ Manyika et al. (2011) ▪ Yaqoob et al. (2016)
		Regression models	▪ Detection of correlations through a description of how an independent variable changes if one or multiple dependent variables are altered	▪ Manyika et al. (2011) ▪ Wang et al. (2016)
	Data mining	**Association rule learning**	▪ Discovery of relevant relationships ("associations") in a big data set	▪ Ngai, Xiu & Chau (2009)
		Cluster analysis	▪ Unsupervised method (i.e. without training group) to identify groups of similar observations in a large and diverse dataset	▪ Manyika et al. (2011) ▪ Chen et al. (2014)
		Classification	▪ Supervised data mining technique to identify homogeneous groups by assigning new data points to existing groups which were derived from a "training group"	▪ Manyika et al. (2011) ▪ Chen et al. (2014) ▪ Yaqoob et al. (2016)
	Simulations		▪ Modeling of the behavior of complex systems used for scenario planning and as a theoretical concept for predictive modelling	▪ Wang et al. (2016)
	Optimization	**Annealing**	▪ Controlled loosening of rigidity criteria in order to find a better optimum	▪ Yaqoob et al. (2016)
		Swarm Optimization	▪ Emulation of swarm behavior to probe the solution space of an objective function and efficiently find the location where the optimal solution resides	▪ Torres (2012)
		Genetic algorithms	▪ Modelling of an evolutionary environment where potential solutions are encoded as genes which are then combined in a structured way and the "survival of the fittest" is calculated given the optimization objectives and constraints	▪ Manyika et al. (2011) ▪ Kölker & Lütjens (2015)
	Forecasting	**Predictive modelling**	▪ Mathematical combination one or more statistical and data mining techniques to predict observations in the future	▪ Manyika et al. (2011)
Unstructured data analytics	Text analytics / Natural language processing (NLP)	**Information summarization**	▪ Extraction of specific attributes and keywords from a written text	▪ Gandomi & Haider (2015)
		Text summarization	▪ Algorithms summarize a written text by searching for specific combinations of keywords	▪ Gandomi & Haider (2015)
		Question answering	▪ Highly advanced NLP technique requiring a certain degree of machine learning (see below) ability to fully develop	▪ Gandomi & Haider (2015)
		Sentiment analysis	▪ Identification of features, aspects and objects on which sentiments are expressed	▪ Manyika et al. (2011) ▪ Gandomi & Haider (2015)
	Speech analytics	**Large vocabulary continuous speech recognition**	▪ Direct matching of sounds to words in order to transcribe a text	▪ Gandomi & Haider (2015)
		Phonetic speech recognition	▪ Creation of strings of phonemes which are translated to entire sentences	▪ Gandomi & Haider (2015)
	Video content analysis		▪ Still not well developed and currently subject to further research	▪ Gandomi & Haider (2015)
AI	Machine learning	**Artificial neural networks**	▪ Modelling of brain structure of axons and to solve non-linear and complex models	▪ Yaqoob et al. (2016)

Appendix 13 – Overview of application of RBV to logistics

Authors	Definition of logistic capability	Operationalization of logistics capability	Relevant resources for logistics capability	Role of logistic networks
Morash et al. (1996)	"Logistic attributes, abilities, organizational processes, knowledge, and skills that allow a firm to achieve superior performance and sustained competitive advantage over competitors" (p. 1)	Demand-oriented capabilities: Pre-sale customer service Post-sale customer service Delivery speed Delivery reliability Responsiveness to target markets Supply-oriented capabilities: Widespread distribution coverage Selective distribution coverage Low total distribution cost	No specific resources mentioned	Not explicitly mentioned, network aspects implicitly present in capabilities
Closs et al. (1997)	Capabilities are subcomponents of logistic competence, which leads to superior logistic performance	17 capabilities form part of 4 *competences*: *Positioning:* Strategy Supply chain Network Organization *Integration:* Supply chain unification Information technology Information sharing Connectivity Standardization Simplification Discipline *Agility:* Relevance Accommodation Flexibility	Information are defined as logistics resource	Network considered a distinct capability within logistics competence framework

Authors	Definition of logistic capability	Operationalization of logistics capability	Relevant resources for logistics capability	Role of logistic networks
		Measurement Functional assessment Process assessment Benchmarking		
Olavarrieta and Ellinger (1997)	Logistics distinctive capability can be instrumental in the creation of time, place, quantity, form and possession utilities within and among firms and individuals through strategic management, infrastructure management and resource management with the goal of creating products/services that satisfy the customer through the attainment of value	No operationalization of logistics capability	Logistics capability defined as a resource itself	No specific mentioning of logistic networks
Fawcett et al. (1997)	"logistics practices are transformed into a strategic capability as the firm develops and focuses the appropriate logistics-related human and technological resources to deliver world-class services that support operations and meet the real needs of customers" (p. 102)	Operationalization in 5 constructs: **Delivery:** Ability to deliver expedited shipments **Quality:** Customer satisfaction provided by logistics services **Flexibility:** Logistics system's ability to accommodate special or non-routine requests **Cost:** Inventory costs (raw materials, finished goods, and pipeline)	Strategic planning and information support system considered key resources	Operating a network seen as a boundary condition for a logistical system, hence NP process at the focus of strategic planning

Authors	Definition of logistic capability	Operationalization of logistics capability	Relevant resources for logistics capability	Role of logistic networks
		Innovation: Aggressiveness in increasing the value-added content of logistics services		
Zhao et al. (2001)	No formal definition of logistics capability, only serving as wrapper term for consumer-focused and information-focused capabilities	Customer-Focused Capabilities: Segmental focus Relevancy Responsiveness Flexibility Information-focused capabilities: Information sharing Information technology Connectivity	No specific resources defined	No specific mentioning of logistic networks
Lai (2004)	Capability to "shape the ability of logistic service providers to create and deploy resources to satisfy the logistics needs of their customers in pursuit of better service performance" (p. 387)	14 activities: Assembling/reassembling Repackaging/relabeling Purchasing/procurement Cross-docking Order processing Customer-specific label printing Fleet management L/C compliance and negotiation Warehousing Information systems management Tracking and tracing shipment information	"Resources and capabilities interchangeably used" (p. 386)	No specific mentioning of logistic networks, but implicit presence in 14 activities

Authors	Definition of logistic capability	Operationalization of logistics capability	Relevant resources for logistics capability	Role of logistic networks
		Web-based linkages Receiving/sending shipment notices, advanced ship notices (ASN) through EDI Freight forwarding		
Cho et al. (2008)	"Logistics capability is that part of a firm's resources – including all assets, competencies, organizational processes, firm attributes, information, knowledge, etc. – which allow it to conceive of and implement strategies that improve efficiency and effectiveness" (p. 337)	Capability set adopted from Morash et al. (1996) and 3 e-commerce-specific capabilities added: Delivery information communication Web-based order handling Global distribution coverage	No specific resources defined	Not explicitly mentioned, network aspects implicitly present in capabilities
Yew Wong and Karia (2010)	Following Theory of resource management by Sirmon, Hitt, and Ireland (2007) : "The theory includes comprehensive processes in structuring a firm's resource portfolio, bundling the resources to build capabilities, and leveraging those capabilities to realize a competitive advantage." (p. 53)	Operationalization as bundle of resources (see right)	5 types of resources: **Physical** - hubs, bases, road vehicles, aircraft, etc. **Information** — information system capability **Human** — no. of skilled employees **Knowledge** - expertise & know-how **Relational** — long-term contracts with customers	Mentioning of network coverage as capability requiring physical, human, information and knowledge resources

Authors	Definition of logistic capability	Operationalization of logistics capability	Relevant resources for logistics capability	Role of logistic networks
Cui and Hertz (2011)	Capability definition from Amit and Schoemaker (1993)	2 forms of network capabilities: *Networks of actors:* Consolidating products and connecting carriers and clients Coordinating clients, logistics intermediary firms and carriers in order to provide an integrated service *Networks of logistics service systems:* Moving products from point A to point B in the most efficient way	Physical, human and organizational resources	Explicit focus on network with 2 types of networks: (1) *logistics service networks* and (2) *networks of actors*
Gligor and Holcomb (2012)	"The term "capabilities" reflects the major role of strategic management in adapting, integrating and reconfiguring resources, organizational skills and functional competencies to respond to the challenges of the external environment. Capabilities, which are complex bundles of skills and accumulated knowledge, determine a company's capacity of general efficiency and ability" (p. 445)	5 meta-capabilities derived from literature: Demand-management capability Supply-management capability Integration capability Measurement capability Information exchange capability	No explicit definition of resources	Supply chain management can be viewed as a network of logistics systems and related activities of the individual supply chain members

Appendix 14 – Overview of literature on air travel demand estimation

Author	Model focus	Perspective	Data focus	Time horizon	Model type	Methodology used
Ippolito (1981)	Market Size	Microscopic	Service-related data	None	Causal	2-staged least square regression
Abrahams (1983)	Market Size	Microscopic	Service-related data	None	Causal	Linear regression model
Fleming and Ghobrial (1994)	Market Size	Macroscopic	Geo-economic	None	Causal	Log linear regression model
Jorge-Calderón (1997)	Market Size	Macroscopic	both	None	Causal	Linear regression model
Hsu and Wen (1998)	Market Size	Macroscopic	Historic time series	10 years	Time-series	Gray model
Profillidis (2000)	Market Size	Macroscopic	Geo-economic	12 years	Mixed	Fuzzy regression model
Abed, Ba-Fail, and Jasimuddin (2001)	Market Size	Macroscopic	Geo-economic	None	Causal	Linear regression model
Saab and Zouein (2001)	Market Size	Microscopic (flight level)	Actual booking data	2 weeks to several months	Time-series	Autoregressive model
Grubb and Mason (2001)	Market Size	Macroscopic	Geo-economic	15 years	Mixed	Damped Holt-Winters forecast (univariate)
Wei and Hansen (2006)	Market Size	Microscopic	both	None	Causal	Linear regression model

Author	Model focus	Per-spec-tive	Data focus	Time horizon	Model type	Methodology used
Dobruszkes and van Hamme (2011)	Market Size	Macro-scopic	Geo-eco-nomic	None	Causal	Linear regression model
Carson et al. (2011)	Market size	Micro and Macro	Geo-eco-nomic	1 year (comparing methods)	Mixed	OLS linear regression model & Aggregating individual markets (AIM) approach
Fildes, Wei, and Ismail (2011)	Market size	Macro-scopic	Geo-eco-nomic	1-3 year (comparing methods)	Mixed	Comparison of various econometric models: • Autoregressive distributed lag (ADL) model • Pooled ADL model • PcGive automatic econometric model • Time Varying Parameter modelling (TVP) • Vector autoregressive (VAR) model • Naïve models • Exponential smoothening model
Chen (2012)	Market Size	Macro-scopic	Geo-eco-nomic data	10 years	Mixed	Fuzzy neural network
Carmona Benítez et al. (2013)	Market Size	Micro-scopic	Historic time series	40 years	Time-series	Damp trend Gray model

Author	Model focus	Per-spec-tive	Data focus	Time horizon	Model type	Methodology used
Sismanidou et al. (2013)	Market Size	Micro-scopic	Actual traffic data	none	QSI model	Linear estimation model
Itani et al. (2014)	Market Size	Macro-scopic	Geo-eco-nomic	none	Causal	Structured Equation Modelling
Valdes (2015)	Market Size	Macro-scopic	Geo-eco-nomic	none	Causal	Linear regression model
Hsiao and Hansen (2011)	Inte-grated model	Micro-scopic	Ser-vice-re-lated factors	None	Causal & discrete choice	Aggregated multinomial logit (MNL) and aggregated nested logit (NL) model
Coldren et al. (2003)	Market share	Micro-scopic	Ser-vice-re-lated data	None	Discrete choice	Aggregated multinomial logit (MNL)
Wei and Hansen (2005)	Market Share	Micro-scopic	none	none	Discrete choice	Log-linear demand model

Appendix 15 – Data use in network planning literature

Method: T - Theoretical; E – Empirical; T/E – Mixed approach

Data types: I – Data used as input data; O – Data produced as output data

Author	Method	Actually flown flights (incl. LF)	Published schedules	Economic data	Demographic data	Fare data	Set of airports/destinations	Competitor information	Operating cost	Aircraft specifications	Slots	Maintenance requirements	Work rules	Crew resources	O&D demand	Market share	Network structure	Routes	Fleet information	flight frequencies	Schedule	Fleet assignment	Aircraft routing	Crew roster
Levin, 1971	T						I											I	O					
Rubin, 1973	T												I	I							I			O
Chan, 1974	T						I		I	I					I		O	O	O	O		O		
Ippolito, 1981	E	I			I	I									O									
Abrahams, 1983	E	I	I	I	I	I									O									
O'Kelly, 1987	T / E	I					I		I								O							
Abara, 1989	T / E								I	I		I							I		I	O		
Daskin & Pa-nayotopou-los, 1989	T									I									I		I	O		
Feo & Bard, 1989	T / E											I							I		I	I	O	
Gershkoff, 1989	T / E								I				I	I							I			O
Teodorović & Krčmar-Nožić, 1989	T					I		I	I						I			I		O				
Balakrish-nan et al., 1990	T					I	I		I	I					I		O	O	I					
Campbell, 1992	T						I		I						I		O							
Ghobrial et al., 1992	T						I		I	I					I		O	O		O	O		O	
Berge & Hopper-stad, 1993	T / E								I				I	I							I			O

Author	Method	Actually flown flights (incl. LF)	Published schedules	Economic data	Demographic data	Fare data	Set of airports/destinations	Competitor information	Operating cost	Aircraft specifications	Slots	Maintenance requirements	Work rules	Crew resources	O&D demand	Market share	Network structure	Routes	Fleet information	flight frequencies	Schedule	Fleet assignment	Aircraft routing	Crew roster
Graves et al., 1993	E	I		I	I	I									O									
Fleming & Ghobrial, 1994	T					I	I		I						I			O		O				
Teodorović et al., 1994	T						I		I						I		O							
Aykin, 1995	T / E											I	I						I		I	O		
Clarke et al., 1996	T / E						I								I		O		I					
Jaillet et al., 1996	T / E																		I		I	O	O	
Yan & Young, 1996	T / E											I									I	I	O	
Clarke et al., 1997	T / E											I									I	I	O	
Desaulniers et al., 1997	E			I	I	I	I			I					O					I				
Jorge-Calderón, 1997	T / E											I		I					I		I	O		
Rushmeier & Kontogiorgis, 1997	T								I	I		I							I		I	O	O	
Barnhart et al., 1998	T											I									I	I	O	
Gopalan & Talluri, 1998	T / E	I		I											O									
Hsu & Wen, 1998	T						I		I	I					I		O			O				
Lederer & Nambimadom, 1998	T								I			I							I		I	O	O	
Ioachim et al., 1999	T					I			I						I		O							

Author	Method	Actually flown flights (incl. LF)	Published schedules	Economic data	Demographic data	Fare data	Set of airports/destinations	Competitor information	Operating cost	Aircraft specifications	Slots	Maintenance requirements	Work rules	Crew resources	O&D demand	Market share	Network structure	Routes	Fleet information	flight frequencies	Schedule	Fleet assignment	Aircraft routing	Crew roster
Barla & Constantatos, 2000	T / E	I		I					I	I					O		O	O	I	O		O		
Hsu & Wen, 2000	T / E	I		I											O									
Profillidis, 2000	E	I		I	I										O									
Abed et al., 2001	T / E	I				I	I		I	I					I		O							
Adler & Berechman, 2001	T / E											I	I	I					I		I		O	O
Cordeau et al., 2001	T / E						I			I					I			O	I	O	O			
Erdmann et al., 2001	E	I													O									
Grubb & Mason, 2001	T					I									I			O			O			
Mashford & Marksjö, 2001	T						I		I						I									
Wojahn, 2001a	T												I	I									I	O
Klabjan et al., 2002	T / E								I						I			I	I		O		O	
Yan & Tseng, 2002	T											I		I							I		O	O
Cohn & Barnhart, 2003	T / E		I			I	I			I					I	O								
Coldren et al., 2003	T			I		I	I		I						I		O							
Brueckner, 2004	T					I			I	I					I			I	I	I	O	O		
Lohatepanont & Barnhart, 2004	T / E	I				I				I					O	O				I				

Author	Method	Actually flown flights (incl. LF)	Published schedules	Economic data	Demographic data	Fare data	Set of airports/destinations	Competitor information	Operating cost	Aircraft specifications	Slots	Maintenance requirements	Work rules	Crew resources	O&D demand	Market share	Network structure	Routes	Fleet information	flight frequencies	Schedule	Fleet assignment	Aircraft routing	Crew roster
Wei & Hansen, 2005	T								I			I			I				I		I	O	O	
Bélanger et al., 2006	T / E												I	I							I	I		O
Guo et al., 2006	T	I		I		I	I			I					O					I				
Wei & Hansen, 2006	T / E										I		I	I					I	I	O		I	O
Mercier and Soumis 2007	T / E								I			I	I	I							I	I	O	O
Sandhu & Klabjan, 2007	T					I			I						I			I	I			O		
Sherali & Zhu, 2008	T / E								I	I					I			I	I	I	O			
Yan et al., 2008	T		I				I	I	I	I	I	I			I		O	O	I	O	O	O	O	
Grosche, 2009	T / E									I					I			I	I		I	O	O	
Haouari et al., 2009	T / E								I			I			I			I	I		O	O	O	O
Papadakos, 2009	T / E												I	I							I			O
Souai & Teghem, 2009	T / E																I	I		I	O			
Burke et al., 2010	T / E											I	I	I							I		O	O
Weide et al., 2010	T / E		I	I	I										O									
Carson et al., 2011	E		I	I											O									
Dobruszkes & van Hamme, 2011	E	I		I											O									

Author	Method	Actually flown flights (incl. LF)	Published schedules	Economic data	Demographic data	Fare data	Set of airports/destinations	Competitor information	Operating cost	Aircraft specifications	Slots	Maintenance requirements	Work rules	Crew resources	O&D demand	Market share	Network structure	Routes	Fleet information	flight frequencies	Schedule	Fleet assignment	Aircraft routing	Crew roster
Fildes et al., 2011	T / E	I		I	I										O	I								
Hsiao & Hansen, 2011	T / E	I		I	I	I	I	I	I	I					O	O	O	O	I	O				
Carmona Benitez, 2012	T / E									I								I	I	I	O			
Jiang & Barnhart, 2013; Sis-manidou et al., 2013	E	I				I	I								O	I								
Sismanidou et al., 2013	E	I		I	I										O									
Itani et al., 2014	T / E									I		I	I	I					I		I	O	O	O
Salazar-González, 2014	T / E						I										I	O						
Wei et al., 2014	T / E						I		I						I			I	I	O	O	O	O	
Kölker & Lütjens, 2015	E	I	I	I											O									
Valdes, 2015	I	I	I											O										

Appendix 16 – Data sources used by scientific network planning literature

Author	Major data sources used
Levin, 1971	-
Rubin, 1973	-
Chan, 1974	-
Ippolito, 1981	Public authorities
Abrahams, 1983	Public authorities
O'Kelly, 1987	Public authorities
Abara, 1989	Airline internal data
Daskin & Panayotopoulos, 1989	-
Feo & Bard, 1989	Airline internal data
Gershkoff, 1989	Airline internal data
Teodorović & Krčmar-Nožić, 1989	-
Balakrishnan et al., 1990	-
Campbell, 1992	-
Ghobrial et al., 1992	-
Berge & Hopperstad, 1993	Airline internal data
Graves et al., 1993	-
Fleming & Ghobrial, 1994	-
Teodorović et al., 1994	-
Aykin, 1995	Airline internal data
Clarke et al., 1996	Public authorities
Jaillet et al., 1996	Airline internal data
Yan & Young, 1996	Airline internal data
Clarke et al., 1997	Unknown
Desaulniers et al., 1997	Public authorities, private data provider, statistical bureau
Jorge-Calderón, 1997	Airline internal data
Rushmeier & Kontogiorgis, 1997	-
Barnhart et al., 1998	-
Gopalan & Talluri, 1998	Aircraft OEM

Author	Major data sources used
Hsu & Wen, 1998	-
Lederer & Nambimadom, 1998	-
Ioachim et al., 1999	-
Barla & Constantatos, 2000	Aircraft OEM, airline internal data
Hsu & Wen, 2000	Public authorities
Profillidis, 2000	Public authorities, private data provider,
Abed et al., 2001	Public authorities, private data provider, statistical bureau
Adler & Berechman, 2001	Airline internal data
Cordeau et al., 2001	Airline internal data
Erdmann et al., 2001	Public authorities
Grubb & Mason, 2001	-
Mashford & Marksjö, 2001	-
Wojahn, 2001a	-
Klabjan et al., 2002	Airline internal data
Yan & Tseng, 2002	-
Cohn & Barnhart, 2003	Airline internal data
Coldren et al., 2003	-
Brueckner, 2004	-
Lohatepanont & Barnhart, 2004	Private data providers
Wei & Hansen, 2005	-
Bélanger et al., 2006	Airline internal data
Guo et al., 2006	-
Wei & Hansen, 2006	Airline internal data
Mercier and Soumis 2007	-
Sandhu & Klabjan, 2007	-
Sherali & Zhu, 2008	Airline internal data
Yan et al., 2008	-
Grosche, 2009	Airline internal data
Haouari et al., 2009	Airline internal data

Author	Major data sources used
Papadakos, 2009	Airline internal data
Souai & Teghem, 2009	Airline internal data
Burke et al., 2010	Private data provider
Weide et al., 2010	Public authorities, Statistic bureaus
Carson et al., 2011	Public authorities, Private data providers
Dobruszkes & van Hamme, 2011	Public authorities, Statistic bureaus
Fildes et al., 2011	Public authorities, private data provider, statistical bureau
Hsiao & Hansen, 2011	Public authorities, OEMs, Private data provider
Carmona Benitez, 2012	Airline internal data
Jiang & Barnhart, 2013; Sismanidou et al., 2013	Private data provider
Sismanidou et al., 2013	Public authorities, Private data providers
Itani et al., 2014	Airline internal data
Salazar-González, 2014	Airline internal data
Wei et al., 2014	Airline internal data
Kölker & Lütjens, 2015	Public authorities, Private data providers
Valdes, 2015	-

Appendix 17 – Impact of BDOs on the NP process steps

		Strategic network planning			Tactical network planning				
Big data opportunities	Demand forecast	Network structure	Route selection	Flight frequency	Flight scheduling	Fleet assignment	Aircraft routing	Crew assignment	Disruption management
A1 Geo-spatial image analysis	☑		☑						
A2 Real-time inflation forecasts	☑		☑	☑					
A3 Consumer confidence measurement with social media	☑								
A4 Detailed demographic profiling with social networks	☑		☑						
A5 General search engine data for detailed O&D demand	☑		☑	☑		☑			
A6 Click-stream data of meta-search websites for flights	☑		☑	☑	☑	☑			
A7 Social media mining to determine price elasticity	☑								
A8 Analysis of air cargo rates from online freight portals	☑		☑	☑	☑	☑	☑		
A9 Analysis of exhibitor data of industry fairs	☑		☑	☑	☑	☑	☑		
A10 Shipping data from e-commerce platforms	☑	☑	☑	☑	☑	☑	☑		
B1 Analysis of reviews in travel rating communities	☑		☑	☑					
B2 Click-stream data from travel platforms	☑		☑	☑					
B3 Analysis of local hotel prices	☑		☑	☑	☑	☑			
B4 Analysis of events in social networks	☑			☑	☑	☑			
C1 Real-time flight tracking with transponder data				☑	☑	☑	☑		☑
C2 Network-relevant competitor news monitoring	☑	☑	☑	☑	☑	☑			
D1 Mobile location data from smartphones	☑	☑	☑	☑	☑	☑			
D2 Extended electronic AWB with shipper address	☑	☑	☑	☑					
D3 Location-transmitting sensors for cargo shipments	☑	☑	☑	☑	☑	☑	☑		
H1 Real-time slot trading platform			☑	☑	☑				
H2 Real-time traffic right information platform			☑	☑	☑	☑	☑		
I1 Global meteorological warning platform	☑		☑	☑	☑				☑
I2 Global political risk assessments	☑		☑	☑					

Appendix 18 – Overview of properties of BDOs

General information					Supply			Use	
Code	**BD opportunity**	**Data type**	**Data volume**	**Data velocity**	**Data provider**	**BDA used**	**Data cost**	**Addressed information needs**	**Major NP process steps impacted**
A1	Geo-spatial satellite image analysis	Unstructured (Pictures)	Medium	Daily	• SpaceKnow • Orbital Insight • Nowcast	Supervised machine learning	Depending on volume and analytical intensity	• Primary: TDF • Secondary: CM, TI, RM, EWS	Demand forecast Route selection
A2	Real-time inflation forecast	Structured	Medium	Daily	• The Billion Prices Project • PriceStats	Econometrics	Not available	• Primary: TDF • Secondary: TI, EWS	Demand forecast Route selection Flight frequencies
A3	Consumer confidence measurement with social media	Unstructured (Text)	High	Real-time	No commercial provider yet	NLP (sentiment analysis)	Depending on scraped volume	• Primary: TDF • Secondary: TI	Demand forecast
A4	Detailed demographic profiling with social networks	Structured	High	Real-time	• Facebook (Audience Insight) • LinkedIn (potentially) • SproutSocial (potentially)	Statistics	Free access to Facebook Audience Insight, no commercialization of other data yet	• Primary: TDF	Demand forecast Route selection
A5	General search engine data for detailed O&D demand	Structured	Low to high	Real-time	• Google Trends	Statistics	Free	• Primary: TDF • Secondary: CM, TI, IBS, EWS	Demand forecast Route selection Flight frequencies Fleet assignment
A6	Clickstream data of metasearch websites for flights	Structured	Medium	Daily	• Skyscanner • Kayak (potentially) • Expedia (potentially)	Statistics	Yearly subscriptions between 1'000 and 10'000 USD	• Primary: TDF • Secondary: CM, TI, RM, IBS	Demand forecast Route selection Scheduling Flight frequencies Fleet assignment
A7	Social media mining to determine price elasticity	Unstructured (all data formats)	High	Real-time	• Facebook • Instagram • Other social media channels	Data mining, machine learning, statistics	Not available	• Primary: TDF • Secondary: IBS	Demand forecast
A8	Analysis of air cargo rates from online flight portals	Structured	Medium	Daily	• Cargoguide • Freightos • Xeneta	Statistics	Not available	• Primary: TDF • Secondary: CM, TI, IBS	Demand forecast Route selection Flight frequencies Scheduling Fleet assignment Aircraft routing
A9	Analysis of exhibitor data of industry fairs	Unstructured (Text)	Medium to high	Monthly	• Data scraping providers	Data mining, Text	Depending on scraped volume	• Primary: TDF	Demand forecast Route selection

General information					Supply			Use	
Code	BD opportunity	Data type	Data volume	Data velocity	Data provider	BDA used	Data cost	Addressed information needs	Major NP process steps impacted
						analytics		• Secondary: RM, TI	Flight frequencies Scheduling Fleet assignment Aircraft routing
A10	Shipping data from e-commerce platforms	Structured	Low to medium	Daily	• Alibaba (potentially) • Amazon (potentially)	Statistics	Not available	• Primary: TDF • Secondary: CM, TI, RM, IBS	Demand forecast Network structure Route selection Flight frequencies Fleet assignment Aircraft routing
B1	Analysis of reviews in travel rating communities	Unstructured (text) and structured (review score)	High	Real-time	• TripAdvisor • Foursquare • Yelp	NLP (semantic analytics) and statistics	Not available	• Primary: TI	Demand forecast Route selection Flight frequencies
B2	Clickstream data from travel websites	Structured	Medium	Daily	• TripAdvisor	Statistics	Not available	• Primary: TI • Secondary: TDF	Demand forecast Route selection Flight frequencies
B3	Analysis of local hotel prices	Structured	Medium	Real-time	• RateGain • TravelClick • Octorate • DataCrops	Statistics	Depending on scraped volume	• Primary: TI • Secondary: TDF, IBS	Demand forecast Route selection Flight frequencies Scheduling Fleet assignment
B4	Analysis of events on social media platforms	Structured	High	Real-time	• Facebook • MeetUp	Statistics	Depending on scraped volume	• Primary: TI	Demand forecast Flight frequencies Scheduling Fleet assignment
C1	Real-time tracking with transponder data	Structured	Medium	Real-time	• FlightRadar24 • FlightAware • OAG	None	<100k per year	• Primary: CM • Secondary: CF, PC, EWS	Flight frequencies Fleet assignment Aircraft routing Flight Ops
C2	Network-relevant competitor news monitoring	Unstructured (Text)	High	Real-time	• Meltwater • Universal Information	NLP & machine learning	Not available	• Primary: CM • Secondary: EWS	Demand forecast Network structure Route selection Flight frequencies Fleet assignment

General information					Supply			Use	
Code	**BD opportunity**	**Data type**	**Data volume**	**Data velocity**	**Data provider**	**BDA used**	**Data cost**	**Addressed information needs**	**Major NP process steps impacted**
D1	Mobile location data from smartphones	Structured	High	Potentially real-time	• Motionlogic • Telefónica NEXT • AirSage • Streetlight Data	Data mining and large-scale statistics	Depending on subscribed volume	• Primary: RM • Secondary: TDF, TI, CM	Demand forecast Network structure Route selection Flight frequencies Scheduling Fleet assignment
D2	Extended electronic air waybill with shipper address	Structured	Medium	Real-time	• Forwarders and shippers	None	None	• Primary: RM • Secondary: TI	Demand forecast Network structure Route selection Flight frequencies
D3	Location-transmitting sensors for cargo shipments	Structured	High	Real-time	• Sendum • Sensitech • Cargo Signal	None	Depending on sensor type; Currently >10 USD per shipment	• Primary: RM • Secondary: IBS, PC	Demand forecast Network structure Route selection Flight frequencies Scheduling Fleet assignment Aircraft routing
H1	Real-time slot trading platform	Structured	Low	Real-time	• ACL (for UK)	None	Currently 3000 USD per trade	• Primary: PC	Route selection Flight frequencies Scheduling
H2	Real-time traffic right information platform	Unstructured (law texts) and structured (Transponder data)	High	Real-time	• ICAO (traffic rights) • WTO (bilateral agreements) • Flightradar24 (Transponder data)	Text mining and NLP	Not available	Primary: PC Secondary: CF	Route selection Flight frequencies Scheduling Fleet assignment Aircraft routing
I1	Global meteorological warning platform	Unstructured (all types) and structured (weather data)	High	Real-time	• All social media • Weather services • IBM	Artificial intelligence, data mining	Not available	Primary: EWS Secondary: TDF, CF	Demand forecast Route selection Flight frequencies Scheduling Flight Ops
I2	Global political risk assessments	Unstructured (all types)	High	Real-time	• GeoQuant • Grisk	Data mining, artificial intelligence	Not available	Primary: EWS Secondary: TDF	Demand forecast Route selection Flight frequencies

Legend:
Data volume: *High > 1TB per day ; Medium 1 GB – 1 TB per day ; Small <1 GB per day*
Information needs:

General information					Supply			Use	
Code	**BD opportunity**	**Data type**	**Data volume**	**Data velocity**	**Data provider**	**BDA used**	**Data cost**	**Addressed information needs**	**Major NP process steps impacted**
NP process steps:	*TDF – Transportation demand forecast; TI – Trend identification; CM – competitor monitoring; RM – real movements of passengers and goods; IBS – Internal booking situation; CF – Cost forecasts; PC – planning constraints; EWS – early warning systems;* *DF – Demand forecast; FP – Fleet planning; NS – Network structure definition; RS – Route selection; FF – Flight frequency definition; SC – Scheduling; FA – Fleet assignment; AR – Aircraft routing; CA – Crew assignment; FO – Flight operations*								

Appendix 19 – Qualitative potential scores and variances, by need for information clusters

	BDO qualitative potential score					Answer variance
	Global	FSC	CAR	LCC	SCA	
Transportation demand forecast	1.9	2.3	2.2	1.3	1.8	2.06
Trend identification	2.3	2.8	0.3	3.4	2.6	2.38
Competitor monitoring	2.3	1.5	3.5	2.0	2.0	1.05
Real movements	2.0	2.5	3.2	1.0	1.2	4.83
Planning constraints	3.6	3.3	4.0	4.3	2.8	1.17
Incident warnings	2.3	1.8	2.8	2.3	2.3	1.63

Appendix 20 – Recalculated qualitative evaluation scored for BDOs, sorted by average score

Code	Big data opportunity	Recalculated mean	FSC	CAR	LCC	SCA
D3	Location-transmitting sensors for cargo shipments	5.0	-	5.0	-	-
A10	Shipping data from e-commerce platforms	4.5	-	4.5	-	-
D2	Extended electronic AWB with shipper address	4.5	-	4.5	-	-
A8	Analysis of air cargo rates from online freight portals	4.0	-	4.0	-	-
H1	Real-time slot trading platform	3.9	3.5	5.0	4.5	2.5
D1	Mobile location data from smartphones	3.7	4.5	-	3.0	3.5
A4	Detailed demographic profiling with social networks	3.5	3.5	-	3.5	3.5
A5	General search engine data for detailed O&D demand	3.4	4.0	3.0	3.0	3.5
A6	Clickstream data of meta-search websites for flights	3.4	5.0	2.0	2.5	4.0
H2	Real-time traffic right information platform	3.3	3.0	3.0	4.0	3.0
B3	Analysis of local hotel prices	3.2	2.5	0.5	3.5	3.5
B4	Analysis of events in social networks	3.0	3.5	0.5	4.0	1.5
B1	Analysis of reviews in travel rating communities	2.8	2.5	-	3.0	3.0
B2	Clickstream data from travel platforms	2.7	2.5	-	3.0	2.5
C2	Network-relevant competitor news monitoring	2.4	1.5	3.5	2.0	2.5
I1	Global meteorological warning platform	2.4	2.0	3.5	2.5	1.5

Code	Big data opportunity	Recalculated mean	FSC	CAR	LCC	SCA
C1	Real-time flight tracking with transponder data	2.1	1.5	3.5	2.0	1.5
I2	Global political risk assessments	2.1	1.5	2.0	2.0	3.0
A9	Analysis of exhibitor data of industry fairs	2.0	-	2.0	-	-
A3	Consumer confidence measurement with social media	1.9	2.0	1.5	1.5	2.5
A1	Geo-spatial image analysis	1.8	2.0	2.5	1.0	1.5
A2	Real-time inflation forecasts	1.6	3.0	1.5	0.5	1.5
A7	Social media mining to determine price elasticity	1.3	3.0	0.5	0.5	1.0

Appendix 21 – Cost drivers for short-listed BDOs

Code	BDO	BD acquisition				BD storage		BD processing	BD analytics	
		Type of data	*Data velocity*	*Pricing*	*Scraping*	*Data volume*	*Data structure*	*Data sources*	*Analytical complexity*	*Tool availability*
A4	Detailed demographic profiling with social media data	Query results	Batch	Free	No	Low	Structured	Single	Low	Available
A5	General search engine data for detailed O&D demand	Query results	Batch	Free	No	Low	Structured	Single	Low	Available
A6	Clickstream data of meta-search websites for flights	Processed data	Batch	Subscription	No	Medium	Structured	Multiple	Low	Available
A8	Analysis of air cargo rates from online freight portals	Query results	Batch or stream	Subscription	No	Low	Structured	Single	Low	Integrated
A10	Shipping data from e-commerce platforms	Processed data	Batch	Subscription	No	Medium	Structured	Multiple	Low	Available
B3	Analysis of local hotel prices	Query results	Batch or stream	Subscription	Yes / No	Medium	Structured	Single	Low	Integrated
B4	Analysis of events in social networks	Raw data	Stream	Volume dependent	Yes	High	Structured	Multiple	Low	Development need
D1	Mobile location data from smartphones	Processed data	Batch	Volume dependent	No	High	Structured	Multiple	Medium	Available
D2	Extended electronic AWB with shipper address	Raw data	Stream	Free	No	Medium	Structured	Multiple	Low	Available
D3	Location-transmitting sensors for cargo shipments	Processed data	Batch or stream	Volume dependent	No	High	Structured	Multiple	Medium	Development need
H1	Real-time slot trading platform	Query results	Stream	Subscription	No	Medium	Structured	Multiple	Low	Development need
H2	Real-time traffic right information platform	Raw data	Batch and stream	Subscription	No	High	Unstructured (law texts) and structured (Transponder data)	Multiple	High	Development need

Appendix 22 – Scoring model for cost risks of cost drivers

Code	BDO	BD acquisition				BD storage		BD processing	BD analytics		
		Type of data	*Data velocity*	*Pricing*	*Scraping*	*Data volume*	*Data structure*	*Data sources*	*Analytical complexity*	*Tool availability*	*Overall score*
A4	Detailed demographic profiling with social media data	2	2	2	2	2	2	2	2	1	17
A5	General search engine data for detailed O&D demand	2	2	2	2	2	2	2	2	1	17
A6	Clickstream data of meta-search websites for flights	1	2	1	2	1	2	1	2	1	13
A8	Analysis of air cargo rates from online freight portals	2	1	1	2	2	2	2	2	2	16
A10	Shipping data from e-commerce platforms	1	2	1	2	1	2	1	2	1	13
B3	Analysis of local hotel prices	2	1	1	2	1	2	2	2	2	15
B4	Analysis of events in social networks	0	1	0	0	0	2	1	2	0	6
D1	Mobile location data from smartphones	1	2	0	2	0	2	1	1	1	10
D2	Extended electronic AWB with shipper address	0	1	2	2	1	2	0	2	1	11
D3	Location-transmitting sensors for cargo shipments	1	1	0	2	0	2	0	1	0	9
H1	Real-time slot trading platform	2	1	1	2	1	2	0	2	0	11
H2	Real-time traffic right information platform	0	0	1	2	0	0	0	0	0	3

Overall score: 14-18 Low cost risk; 9-13 Medium cost risk; below 9 High cost risk;

Appendix 23 – Net present value calculation for investment scenarios

	One-time implementation cost	Recurring yearly cost
Small project	20'000	50'000
Medium Project	200'000	200'000
Large project	1'000'000	500'000
Mega Project	5'000'000	1'000'000

Discount rate 10%

	Small project				
	Year 1	*Year 2*	*Year 3*	*Year 4*	*Year 5*
BD project cost	-70'000	-50'000	-50'000	-50'000	-50'000
Required benefit	**54'796**	54'796	54'796	54'796	54'796
Free-cash-flow (FCF)	-15'204	4'796	4'796	4'796	4'796
Discounted FCF	-13'822	3'964	3'604	3'276	2'978
Terminal value (TV)					47'963
NPV with TV	47'963				
NPV no TV	**0**				

	Medium project				
	Year 1	*Year 2*	*Year 3*	*Year 4*	*Year 5*
BD project cost	-400'000	-200'000	-200'000	-200'000	-200'000
Required benefit	247'963	247'963	247'963	247'963	247'963
Free-cash-flow (FCF)	-152'037	47'963	47'963	47'963	47'963
Discounted FCF	-138'215	39'639	36'035	32'759	29'781
Terminal value (TV)					479'632
NPV with TV	479'632				
NPV no TV	**0**				

	Large project				
	Year 1	*Year 2*	*Year 3*	*Year 4*	*Year 5*
BD project cost	-1'500'000	-500'000	-500'000	-500'000	-500'000
Required benefit	739'816	739'816	739'816	739'816	739'816
Free-cash-flow (FCF)	-760'184	239'816	239'816	239'816	239'816
Discounted FCF	-691'076	198'195	180'177	163'797	148'907
Terminal value (TV)					2'398'159
NPV with TV	2'398'159				
NPV no TV	**0**				

	Mega project				
	Year 1	*Year 2*	*Year 3*	*Year 4*	*Year 5*
BD project cost	-6'000'000	-1'000'000	-1'000'000	-1'000'000	-1'000'000
Required benefit	2'199'079	2'199'079	2'199'079	2'199'079	2'199'079
Free-cash-flow (FCF)	-3'800'921	1'199'079	1'199'079	1'199'079	1'199'079
Discounted FCF	-3'455'382	990'975	900'886	818'987	744'534
Terminal value (TV)					11'990'795
NPV with TV	11'990'795				
NPV no TV	**0**				

Appendix 24 – Required yearly benefit calculation for different scenarios

		Required yearly benefit			
		Small project	Medium project	Large project	Mega project
		54'796	247'963	739'816	2'199'079
Profit delta from flight portfolio changes					
Number of yearly changed flight events	7'800				
Required BDO profit impact per flight event		**7.03 €**	**31.79 €**	**94.85 €**	**281.93 €**
Total network profit					
Network profit	500'000'000				
Required percent increase		**0.01%**	**0.05%**	**0.15%**	**0.44%**
Load factor					
EBIT margin	8.3%				
Required Revenue increase		660'197 €	2'987'508 €	8'913'445 €	26'494'933 €
Yield per ASK	€ 0.10				
Required RSK increase		6'601'966	29'875'082	89'134'446	264'949'332
Available Capacity in ASK	70'000'000'000				
Old RSK	60'000'000'000				
New RSK		60'006'601'966	60'029'875'082	60'089'134'446	60'264'949'332
Old load factor	85.7%				
New load factor		85.7%	85.8%	85.8%	86.1%
Required load factor increase in percentage points		**0.01**	**0.04**	**0.13**	**0.38**
Idle hours per aircraft type					
Average flight event profit	1'500 €				
Additional flight events needed		37	165	493	1466
Daily additional flight events needed		**0.10**	**0.45**	**1.35**	**4.02**
Percent increase of idle base		0.20%	0.91%	2.70%	8.03%
On-time performance					
Total delay cost	51'813'360				
Percent delay reduction needed		**0.11%**	**0.48%**	**1.43%**	**4.24%**
FTE per process step					
FTE gross cost	200'000				
FTE reduction needed		**0.3**	**1.2**	**3.7**	**11.0**
In percent of total FTEs		1.8%	8.3%	24.7%	73.3%
Operational cost reduction					
Operational cost in remit of NPM	500'000'000				
Operational cost reduction required		**0.01%**	**0.05%**	**0.15%**	**0.44%**

Appendix 25 – Scoring of BDO benefit impact on KPIs

Code	Big data opportunities	*Route profitability*	*FTE efficiency*	*Aircraft utilization*	*Forecast accuracy*	*Schedule robustness*	*Load factor*	*Direct cost*	**Total weighted benefit score**
	KPI weight	2	0	2	0	1	1	1	
A4	Detailed demographic profiling with social media mining	6.0	-	5.0	-	3.0	-	-	**14.0**
A5	General search engine data for detailed O&D demand	7.0	-	5.0	-	-	2.0	-	**14.0**
A6	Click-stream data of meta-search websites for flights	6.5	-	4.0	-	-	2.0	-	**12.5**
A8	Scraping of published rates of cargo shipping portals	8.0	-	8.0	-	-	2.0	-	**18.0**
A10	Shipping data from e-commerce platforms	8.0	-	8.0	-	-	4.0	-	**20.0**
B3	Scraping of regional hotel prices	8.0	-	7.0	-	-	-	1.0	**16.0**
B4	Analysis of events on social media platforms	5.3	-	5.0	-	-	-	-	**10.3**
D1	Mobile location data	7.3	-	5.0	-	-	-	2.0	**14.3**
D2	Extended electronic AWB with shipper address	8.0	-	-	-	2.0	2.0	-	**12.0**
D3	Location-transmitting sensors for cargo shipments	8.0	-	-	-	4.0	3.0	1.0	**16.0**
H1	Real-time slot trading platform	4.5	-	4.7	-	2.0	-	4.0	**15.2**
H2	Real-time traffic right information platform	3.0	-	3.3	-	1.5	-	3.5	**11.3**

Appendix 26 – Big data characteristics of BDOs for airline NP

Code	BD opportunity	Data type	Data volume	Update velocity	Variety of sources	Data veracity	Value for airline NP
A1	Geo-spatial satellite image analysis	Unstructured (Pictures)	Medium	Daily	Multi-source	Low	Low
A2	Real-time inflation forecast	Structured	Medium	Daily	Multi-source	Medium	Low
A3	Consumer confidence measurement with social media	Unstructured (Text)	High	Real-time	Multi-source	Low	Low
A4	Detailed demographic profiling with social networks	Structured	High	Real-time	Multi-source	Medium	High
A5	General search engine data for detailed O&D demand	Structured	Low to high	Real-time	Single-source	Low	High
A6	Clickstream data of meta-search websites for flights	Structured	Medium	Daily	Multi-source	High	High
A7	Social media mining to determine price elasticity	Unstructured (all data formats)	High	Real-time	Multi-source	Low	Low
A8	Analysis of air cargo rates from online flight portals	Structured	Medium	Daily	Single-source	High	Very high
A9	Analysis of exhibitor data of industry fairs	Unstructured (Text)	Medium to high	Monthly	Multi-source	Low	Medium
A10	Shipping data from e-commerce platforms	Structured	Low to medium	Daily	Multi-source	High	Very high
B1	Analysis of reviews in travel rating communities	Unstructured (text) and struc-	High	Real-time	Multi-source	Medium	Medium

Code	BD opportunity	Data type	Data volume	Update velocity	Variety of sources	Data veracity	Value for airline NP
		tured (review score)					
B2	Clickstream data from travel websites	Structured	Medium	Daily	Multi-source	High	Medium
B3	Analysis of local hotel prices	Structured	Medium	Real-time	Single-source	High	High
B4	Analysis of events on social media platforms	Structured	High	Real-time	Multi-source	Medium	High
C1	Real-time tracking with transponder data	Structured	Medium	Real-time	Single-source	High	Medium
C2	Network-relevant competitor news monitoring	Unstructured (Text)	High	Real-time	Multi-source	Medium	Medium
D1	Mobile location data from smartphones	Structured	High	Potentially real-time	Multi-source	High	High
D2	Extended electronic air waybill with shipper address	Structured	Medium	Real-time	Single-source	High	Very high
D3	Location-transmitting sensors for cargo shipments	Structured	High	Real-time	Multi-source	High	Very high
H1	Real-time slot trading platform	Structured	Low	Real-time	Single-source	High	High
H2	Real-time traffic right information platform	Unstructured (law texts) and structured (Transponder data)	High	Real-time	Multi-source	Medium	High
I1	Global meteorological warning platform	Unstructured (all types) and structured	High	Real-time	Multi-source	Low	Medium

Code	BD opportunity	Data type	Data volume	Update velocity	Variety of sources	Data veracity	Value for airline NP
		(weather data)					
I2	Global political risk assessments	Unstructured (all types)	High	Real-time	Multi-source	Low	Medium
Legend	*Volume: High > 1TB per day ; Medium 2 GB – 1 TB per day ; Small <2 GB per day* *Veracity: Qualitatively evaluated* *Value: Potential score >4 = very high; Potential score 3-4 = high; Potential score 2-3 = medium; Potential score 1-2 = Low; Potential score <1 Very low*						

Appendix 27 – Applicability of NP BDOs to other airline functions

Code	BD opportunity	Administrative functions		Commercial functions		Operational functions	
		Strategic planning	Finance	Marketing & sales	Pricing & revenue management	Flight operations	Engineering & maintenance
A1	Geo-spatial satellite image analysis	High	Low	High	High	Medium	Low
A2	Real-time inflation forecast	High	High	Medium	High	Low	Low
A3	Consumer confidence measurement with social media	Medium	Low	Medium	Medium	Low	Low
A4	Detailed demographic profiling with social networks	Low	Low	High	Medium	Medium	Low
A5	General search engine data for detailed O&D demand	Low	Low	Medium	High	Low	Low
A6	Clickstream data of metasearch websites for flights	Low	Low	High	High	Low	Low
A7	Social media mining to determine price elasticity	Low	Low	High	High	Low	Low
A8	Analysis of air cargo rates from online flight portals	Medium	Medium	High	High	Low	Low
A9	Analysis of exhibitor data of industry fairs	Low	Low	High	High	Low	Low
A10	Shipping data from e-commerce platforms	Medium	Medium	High	High	Low	Low
B1	Analysis of reviews in travel rating communities	Medium	Low	High	Medium	Low	Low

Code	BD opportunity	Administrative functions		Commercial functions		Operational functions	
		Strategic planning	Finance	Marketing & sales	Pricing & revenue management	Flight operations	Engineering & maintenance
B2	Clickstream data from travel websites	Medium	Low	High	High	Low	Low
B3	Analysis of local hotel prices	Medium	Low	High	High	Low	Low
B4	Analysis of events on social media platforms	Medium	Low	High	High	Low	Low
C1	Real-time tracking with transponder data	Low	Low	Low	Low	High	Low
C2	Network-relevant competitor news monitoring	High	Medium	Medium	High	High	Low
D1	Mobile location data from smartphones	Medium	Low	High	Medium	Low	Low
D2	Extended electronic air waybill with shipper address	Medium	Low	High	High	Low	Low
D3	Location-transmitting sensors for cargo shipments	Low	Low	Low	Low	High	Low
H1	Real-time slot trading platform	Low	Low	Low	Low	High	Low
H2	Real-time traffic right information platform	Low	Low	Low	Low	High	Low
I1	Global meteorological warning platform	Low	Low	Low	Low	High	Medium
I2	Global political risk assessments	Medium	Medium	Medium	Medium	Low	Medium

References

Abara, J. (1989). Applying Integer Linear Programming to the Fleet Assignment Problem. *Interfaces*, *19*(4), 20–28.

Abbasi, A., Sarker, S., & Chiang, R. H. L. (2016). Big Data Research in Information Systems: Toward an Inclusive Research Agenda. *Journal of the Association for Information Systems*, *17*(2), i–xxxii.

Abdelghany, A., & Abdelghany, K. (2009). *Modeling Applications in the Airline Industry*. Burlington: Ashgate Publishing Limited.

Abed, S. Y., Ba-Fail, A. O., & Jasimuddin, S. M. (2001). An econometric analysis of international air travel demand in Saudi Arabia. *Journal of Air Transport Management*, *7*(3), 143–148.

Abrahams, M. (1983). A service quality model of air travel demand: An empirical study. *Transportation Research Part A: General*, *17*(5), 385–393.

Ackoff, R. L. (1989). From data to wisdom. *Journal of Applied Systems Analysis*, *16*, 3–9.

Addo-Tenkorang, R., & Helo, P. T. (2016). Big Data Applications in Operations/Supply-Chain Management: A Literature Review. *Computers & Industrial Engineering*, *101*, 528-543.

Adler, N., & Berechman, J. (2001). Evaluating optimal multi-hub networks in a deregulated aviation market with an application to Western Europe. *Transportation Research Part A: Policy and Practice*, *35*(5), 373–390.

Agarwal, D. (2017). Announcing the Economic Graph Research Program. Retrieved August 30, 2018, from LinkedIn: https://engineering.linkedin.com/blog/2017/03/announcing-the-economic-graph-research-program.

Ahuja, R., Magnanti, T., & Orlin, J. (1991). Some Recent Advances in Network Flows. *SIAM Review*, *33*(2), 175–219.

M. Schosser, *Big Data to Improve Strategic Network Planning in Airlines*,
Schriftenreihe der HHL Leipzig Graduate School of Management,
https://doi.org/10.1007/978-3-658-27582-2

Ahuja, R. K., Magnanti, T. L., & Orlin, J. B. (1993). *Network flows: theory, algorithms, and applications*. London: Pearson.

AIMS. (2017). Commercial Planning - Flight Scheduling. Retrieved October 01, 2017, from AIMS Airline Software: http://www.aims.aero/commercial-planning.html.

Air Cargo News. (2017). Ocean rate platform Xeneta targets air cargo. Retrieved September 03, 2018, from Air Cargo News: https://www.aircargonews.net/news/freight-forwarder/single-view/news/ocean-rate-platform-xeneta-targets-air-cargo.html.

Air Cargo News. (2018). Cathay Pacific homes in on real-time cargo tracking. Retrieved September 03, 2018, from Air Cargo News: https://www.aircargonews.net/news/single-view/news/cathay-pacific-homes-in-on-real-time-cargo-tracking.html.

Airbus. (2017). Orders & Deliveries. Retrieved December 12, 2017, from http://www.aircraft.airbus.com/market/orders-deliveries/.

airfleets.net. (2016). Airfleets database. Retrieved October 04, 2016, from http://www.airfleets.net/home/.

Airline Software. (2017). Digital Solution Directory: Planning & scheduling. Retrieved October 01, 2017, from https://www.airlinesoftware.net/products/15/planning--scheduling.

Airport Coordination Limited. (2018a). Completed Trades. Retrieved September 03, 2018, from Airport Coordination Limited: https://www.acl-uk.org/completed-trades/.

Airport Coordination Limited. (2018b). Slot trading. Retrieved September 03, 2018, from Airport Coordination Limited: https://www.acl-uk.org/slot-trading/.

Airportzentrale. (2014). Lufthansa: 80 Jahre Luftpostverbindung über den Südatlantik. Retrieved November 28, 2017, from http://www.airportzentrale.de/lufthansa-80-jahre-luftpostverbindung-zum-suedatlantik/30564/.

Akartunalı, K., Boland, N., Evans, I., Wallace, M., & Waterer, H. (2013). Airline planning benchmark problems—Part II: Passenger groups, utility and demand allocation. *Computers & Operations Research*, *40*(3), 793–804.

Akoka, J., Comyn-Wattiau, I., & Laoufi, N. (2017). Research on Big Data – A systematic mapping study. *Computer Standards & Interfaces*, *54*, 105–115.

Akter, S., & Wamba, S. F. (2017). Big data and disaster management: A systematic review and agenda for future research. *Annals of Operations Research*, *4*(9), 95.

Akter, S., Wamba, S. F., Gunasekaran, A., Dubey, R., & Childe, S. J. (2016). How to improve firm performance using big data analytics capability and business strategy alignment? *International Journal of Production Economics*, *182*, 113–131.

Albert, R., & Barabási, A.-L. (2002). Statistical mechanics of complex networks. *Reviews of Modern Physics*, *74*(1), 47–97.

Alderighi, M., Cento, A., Nijkamp, P., & Rietveld, P. (2007). Assessment of New Hub-and-Spoke and Point-to-Point Airline Network Configurations. *Transport Reviews*, *27*(5), 529–549.

Allan, G., & Ito, K. (2016). This Startup Uses Night Lights to Forecast GDP. Retrieved August 30, 2018, from Bloomberg: https://www.bloomberg.com/news/articles/2016-12-13/startup-to-forecast-gdp-using-satellite-images-of-night-lights.

Alumur, S., & Kara, B. Y. (2009). A Hub Covering Network Design Problem for Cargo Applications in Turkey. *Journal of the Operational Research Society*, *60*(10), 1349–1359.

Alumur, S., & Kara, B. Y. (2008). Network hub location problems: The state of the art. *European Journal of Operational Research*, *190*(1), 1–21.

Amit, R., & Schoemaker, P. J. (1993). Strategic Assets and Organizational Rent. *Strategic Management Journal*, *14*(1), 33–46.

Andrews, K. R. (1971). *Concept of corporate strategy*. New York: Dow Jones-Irwin.

Angelini, E., Camba-Mendez, G., Giannone, D., Reichlin, L., & Rünstler, G. (2011). Short-term forecasts of euro area GDP growth. *Econometrics Journal*, *14*(1), C25-C44.

Anna.aero. (2017). Opportunity to take flight: looking back at a year of anna.aero-Skyscanner Unserved Route of the Week. Retrieved September 05, 2018, from Anna.aero: https://www.anna.aero/2017/04/27/opportunity-take-flight-looking-back-year-skyscanner-anna-aero-unserved-route-week/.

Antes, J., Derigs, U., & Zils, M. (1997). Flugroutenplanung im Cargo Sektor. In U. Zimmermann, U. Derigs, W. Gaul, R. H. Möhring, & K.-P. Schuster (Eds.), *Operations Research Proceedings 1996: Selected Papers of the Symposium on Operations Research (SOR 96), Braunschweig, September 3 - 6, 1996* (pp. 359–362). Berlin, Heidelberg: Springer.

Antwi, S. K., & Hamza, K. (2015). Qualitative and quantitative research paradigms in business research: A philosophical reflection. *European Journal of Business and Management*, *7*(3), 217–225.

APM Technologies. (2017). For scheduling and slot management. Retrieved October 01, 2017, from APM Technologies: http://www.apmtechnologies.com/software/scheduling/.

Asay, M. (2014). 8 Reasons Big Data Projects Fail. Retrieved September 05, 2017, from InformationWeek: https://www.informationweek.com/big-data/big-data-analytics/8-reasons-big-data-projects-fail/a/d-id/1297842.

AVES - Flight Operations Management Systems. (2017). AVES Solutions. Retrieved October 01, 2017, from http://www.aves.eu/aves-solution/.

Aviation Research Technologies. (2017). NetworkPlanner. Retrieved October 01, 2017, from Aviation Research Technologies: http://network-planningit.com/networkplanner.htm.

Aviolinx. (2017). RAIDO. Retrieved October 01, 2017, from Aviolinx: http://aviolinx.com/product/raido.

Ayhan, S., Pesce, J., Comitz, P., Sweet, D., Bliesner, S., & Gerberick, G. (2013). Predictive analytics with aviation big data. In *Integrated Communications, Navigation and Surveillance Conference (ICNS), 2013* (pp. 1–13).

Aykin, T. (1995). The hub location and routing problem. *European Journal of Operational Research*, *83*(1), 200–219.

Azadian, F., Murat, A. E., & Chinnam, R. B. (2012). Dynamic routing of time-sensitive air cargo using real-time information. *Transportation Research Part E: Logistics and Transportation Review*, *48*(1), 355–372.

Badea, V. E., Zamfiroiu, A., & Boncea, R. (2018). Big Data in the Aerospace Industry. *Informatica Economica*, *22*(1), 16–24.

Bakhtyar, S., & Henesey, L. (2014). Freight transport prediction using electronic waybills and machine learning. In *ICCSS 2014. Proceedings of the 2014 International Conference on Informative and Cybernetics for Computational Social Systems : October 9-10, 2014, Qingdao, Shandong, China* (pp. 128–133). Piscataway, NJ: IEEE.

Bakhtyar, S., Holmgren, J., & Persson, J. A. (2013). Analysis of information synergy between e-Waybill solutions and intelligent transport system services. *World Review of Intermodal Transportation Research*, *4*(2/3), 123.

Balakrishnan, A., Chien, T., & Wong, R. T. (1990). Selecting aircraft routes for long-haul operations: A formulation and solution method. *Transportation Research Part B: Methodological*, *24*(1), 57–72.

Baltagi, B. H., Griffin, J. M., & Rich, D. P. (1995). Airline Deregulation: The Cost Pieces of the Puzzle. *International Economic Review*, *36*(1), 245–258.

Barla, P., & Constantatos, C. (2000). Airline network structure under demand uncertainty. *Transportation Research Part E: Logistics and Transportation Review*, *36*(3), 173–180.

Barney, J. (1991). Firm Resources and Sustained Competitive Advantage. *Journal of Management*, *17*(1), 99–120.

Barney, J., Wright, M., & Ketchen, D. J., JR. (2001). The resource-based view of the firm: Ten years after 1991. *Journal of Management*, *27*(6), 625–641.

Barney, J. B., Ketchen, D. J., & Wright, M. (2011). The Future of Resource-Based Theory. *Journal of Management*, *37*(5), 1299–1315.

Barnhart, C., Boland, N. L., Clarke, L. W., Johnson, E. L., Nemhauser, G. L., & Shenot, R. G. (1998). Flight String Models for Aircraft Fleeting and Routing. *Transportation Science*, *32*(3), 208.

Barton, D., & Court, D. (2012). Making Advanced Analytics Work For You. *Harvard Business Review*, *90*(10), 78–83.

Batrinca, B., & Treleaven, P. C. (2015). Social media analytics: a survey of techniques, tools and platforms. *AI & Society*, *30*(1), 89–116.

Baxter, P., & Jack, S. (2008). Qualitative Case Study Methodology: Study Design and Implementation for Novice Researchers. *The Qualitative Report*, *13*(4), 544–559.

Bazargan, M. (2016). *Airline operations and scheduling*. Abingdon-on-Thames: Routledge.

Bel, G., & Fageda, X. (2010). Intercontinental Flights From European Airports: Towards Hub Concentration Or Not? *International Journal of Transport Economics*, *37*(2), 133–153.

Bélanger, N., Desaulniers, G., Soumis, F., & Desrosiers, J. (2006). Periodic airline fleet assignment with time windows, spacing constraints, and time dependent revenues. *European Journal of Operational Research*, *175*(3), 1754–1766.

Bell, M. G. H., & Iida, Y. (1997). *Transportation Network Analysis*. Chichester: John Wiley & Sons, Ltd.

Berg, B. L. (2004). *Qualitative research methods for the social sciences* (Vol. 5). Boston, MA: Pearson.

Berge, M. E., & Hopperstad, C. A. (1993). Demand Driven Dispatch: A Method for Dynamic Aircraft Capacity Assignment, Models and Algorithms. *Operations Research*, *41*(1), 153–168.

Bertram, T. (2017). *Breaking Down Big Data: Analyzing Big Data For More Precise Commercial Planning.* Sabre Inc. (Ascend for airlines No. Issue 1). Retrieved from Sabre Inc. website: http://www.ascendforairlines.com/sites/default/files/Breaking_Data_0.pdf

Bharadwaj, A., El Sawy, O. A., Pavlou, P. A., & Venkatraman, N. (2013). Digital Business Strategy: Toward A Next Generation Of Insights. *MIS Quarterly*, *37*(2), 471–482.

Bharadwaj, A. S. (2000). A Resource-Based Perspective On Information Technology Capability And Firm Performance: An Empirical Investigation. *MIS Quarterly*, *24*(1), 169–196.

Bhatt, G. D., & Grover, V. (2005). Types of Information Technology Capabilities and Their Role in Competitive Advantage: An Empirical Study. *Journal of Management Information Systems*, *22*(2), 253–277.

Bieger, T., & Wittmer, A. (2006). Air transport and tourism—Perspectives and challenges for destinations, airlines and governments. *Journal of Air Transport Management*, *12*(1), 40–46.

Bieger, T., & Wittmer, A. (2011). Airline Strategy: From Network Management to Business Models. In A. Wittmer, T. Bieger, & R. Müller (Eds.), *Aviation Systems: Management of the Integrated Aviation Value Chain* (pp. 77–102). Berlin, Heidelberg: Springer.

Bley, K., & Büermann, T. (2016). Business Processes and IT Solutions in the Low Fare Environment. In S. Gross & A. Schröder (Eds.), *Handbook of Low Cost Airlines. Strategies, Business Processes and Market Environment* (2nd ed., pp. 45–66). Elmshorn: IDT-Verlag.

Boin, R., Coleman, W., Delfassy, D., & Palombo, G. (2017). *How airlines can gain a competitive edge through pricing*. McKinsey. Retrieved from McKinsey website: https://www.mckinsey.com/~/media/McKinsey/Industries/Travel%20Transport%20and%20Logistics/Our%20Insights/How%20airlines%20can%20gain%20a%20competitive%20edge%20through%20pricing/How-airlines-can-gain-a-competitive-edge-through-pricing.ashx

Bonnel, P., Hombourger, E., Olteanu-Raimond, A.-M., & Smoreda, Z. (2015). Passive Mobile Phone Dataset to Construct Origin-destination Matrix: Potentials and Limitations. *Transportation Research Procedia*, *11*, 381–398.

Boonekamp, T., & Burghouwt, G. (2017). Measuring connectivity in the air freight industry. *Journal of Air Transport Management*, *61*, 81–94.

Borgatti, S. P., & Halgin, D. S. (2011). On Network Theory. *Organization Science*, *22*(5), 1168–1181.

Borgatti, S. P., Mehra, A., Brass, D. J., & Labianca, G. (2009). Network Analysis in the Social Sciences. *Science*, *323*(5916), 892.

Bowcott, H., & Dichter, A. (2014). The clairvoyant airline. Retrieved October 26, 2018, from McKinsey: https://www.mckinsey.com/industries/travel-transport-and-logistics/our-insights/the-clairvoyant-airline.

Bowen, J. (2015). Trends affecting social media: implications for practitioners and researchers. *WW Hospitality Tourism Themes*, *7*(3), 221–228.

Bowen, J. T. (2012). A spatial analysis of FedEx and UPS: hubs, spokes, and network structure. *Journal of Transport Geography*, *24*, 419–431.

Boylan, P. (2016). How Real-Time Monitoring Has Altered the Air Cargo Landscape. Retrieved September 03, 2018, from Acceyla: https://w3.accelya.com/blog/how-real-time-monitoring-has-altered-the-air-cargo-landscape.

Bradbury, D. (2018). How Big Data in Aviation Is Transforming the Industry. Retrieved March 26, 2018, from Hortonworks: https://de.hortonworks.com/article/how-big-data-in-aviation-is-transforming-the-industry/.

Brass, D. J., Galaskiewicz, J., Greve, H. R., & Tsai, W. (2004). Taking Stock of Networks and Organizations: A Multilevel Perspective. *Academy of Management Journal*, *47*(6), 795–817.

Brons, M., Pels, E., Nijkamp, P., & Rietveld, P. (2002). Price elasticities of demand for passenger air travel: A meta-analysis. *Journal of Air Transport Management*, *8*(3), 165–175.

Brueckner, J. K. (2004). Network Structure and Airline Scheduling. *The Journal of Industrial Economics*, *52*(2), 291–312.

Brueckner, J. K. (2009). Price vs. quantity-based approaches to airport congestion management. *Journal of Public Economics*, *93*(5-6), 681–690.

Brueckner, J. K., & Spiller, P. T. (1991). Competition and mergers in airline networks. *International Journal of Industrial Organization*, *9*(3), 323–342.

Buneman, P. (1997). Semistructured data. *Sixteenth ACM SIGACT-SIGMOD-SIGART symposium on Principles of database systems*, 117–121.

Burgess, M. (2018). Facebook fixed a massive data scraping issue it said wasn't a problem. Retrieved September 03, 2018, from Wired: https://www.wired.co.uk/article/facebook-news-data-scraping-mark-zuckerburg.

Burghouwt, G. (2007). *Airline network development in Europe and its implications for airport planning*. Burlington: Ashgate Publishing, Ltd.

Burghouwt, G., & Redondi, R. (2013). Connectivity in Air Transport Networks: An Assessment of Models and Applications. *Journal of Transport Economics and Policy*, *47*(1), 35–53.

Burghouwt, G., & Wit, J. de. (2005). Temporal configurations of European airline networks. *Journal of Air Transport Management*, *11*(3), 185–198.

Burke, E. K., Causmaecker, P. de, Maere, G. de, Mulder, J., Paelinck, M., & Vanden Berghe, G. (2010). A multi-objective approach for robust airline scheduling. *Computers & Operations Research*, *37*(5), 822–832.

Button, K. J., & Stough, R. (2000). *Air transport networks: Theory and policy implications*. Cheltenham: Edward Elgar Publishing.

Buyck, C. (2018). EC Aviation Official Urges Slot Allocation Review. Retrieved September 10, 2018, from AIN Online: https://www.ainonline.com/aviation-news/air-transport/2018-03-19/ec-aviation-official-urges-slot-allocation-review.

Cacchiani, V., & Salazar-González, J.-J. (2016). Optimal Solutions to a Real-World Integrated Airline Scheduling Problem. *Transportation Science*, *51*(1), 250–268.

Calabrese, F., Di Lorenzo, G., Liu, L., & Ratti, C. (2011). Estimating Origin-Destination Flows Using Mobile Phone Location Data. *IEEE Pervasive Computing*, *10*(4), 36–44.

Campbell, J. F. (1992). Location and allocation for distribution systems with transshipments and transportation economies of scale. *Annals of Operations Research*, *40*(1), 77–99.

Carey, S. (2017). Meet Freightos: The Israeli Startup Aiming to be Expedia for Freight. Retrieved September 03, 2018, from Techworld: https://www.techworld.com/startups/meet-freightos-israeli-startup-aiming-be-expedia-for-freight-3663131/.

Cargo Signal. (2018). Cargo Signal Solutions. Retrieved September 03, 2018, from Cargo Signal: https://cargosignal.com/.

Cargoguide. (2018). Online freight rates. Retrieved September 03, 2018, from Cargoguide: https://www.cargoguide.com/air/.

Carmona Benitez, R. B. (2012). *The Design of a Large Scale Airline Network*. TU Delft: Delft University of Technology.

Carmona Benítez, R. B., Carmona Paredes, R. B., Lodewijks, G., & Nabais, J. L. (2013). Damp trend Grey Model forecasting method for airline industry. *Expert Systems with Applications*, *40*(12), 4915–4921.

Carrière-Swallow, Y., & Labbé, F. (2013). Nowcasting with Google Trends in an Emerging Market. *Journal of Forecasting*, *32*(4), 289–298.

Carson, R. T., Cenesizoglu, T., & Parker, R. (2011). Forecasting (aggregate) demand for US commercial air travel. *International Journal of Forecasting*, *27*(3), 923–941.

Casanueva, C., Gallego, Á., Castro, I., & Sancho, M. (2014). Airline alliances: Mobilizing network resources. *Tourism Management*, *44*, 88–98.

Casti, J. L. (1995). The Theory of Networks. In D. Batten, J. Casti, & R. Thord (Eds.), *Networks in Action: Communication, Economics and Human Knowledge* (pp. 3–24). Berlin, Heidelberg: Springer.

Cavallo, A., & Rigobon, R. (2016). The Billion Prices Project: Using Online Prices for Measurement and Research. *Journal of Economic Perspectives*, *30*(2), 151–178.

Caves, D. W., Christensen, L. R., & Tretheway, M. W. (1984). Economies of Density versus Economies of Scale: Why Trunk and Local Service Airline Costs Differ. *The RAND Journal of Economics*, *15*(4), 471–489.

Chae, B., Yang, C., Olson, D., & Sheu, C. (2014). The impact of advanced analytics and data accuracy on operational performance: A contingent resource based theory (RBT) perspective. *Decision Support Systems*, *59*, 119–126.

Chamlou, N. (2018). Amazon Air confirms 767 delivery schedule for 2018. Retrieved September 06, 2018, from Air Cargo World: http://aircargoworld.com/allposts/amazon-air-confirms-767-delivery-schedule-for-2018/.

Chan, Y. (1974). Configuring a transportation route network via the method of successive approximation. *Computers & Operations Research*, *1*(3), 385–420.

Chang, Y.-H., & Chang, Y.-W. (2009). Air cargo expansion and economic growth: Finding the empirical link. *Journal of Air Transport Management*, *15*(5), 264–265.

Chen, C.-J. (2012). A self-organized neuro-fuzzy system for air cargo and airline passenger dynamics modeling and forecasting. *International Journal of Fuzzy System Applications (IJFSA)*, *2*(2), 36–49.

Chen, H.-M., Schütz, R., Kazman, R., & Matthes, F. (2017). How Lufthansa Capitalized on Big Data for Business Model Renovation. *MIS Quarterly Executive*, *16*(1), 19–34.

Chen, H., Chiang, R. H. L., & Storey, V. C. (2012). Business Intelligence and Analytics: From Big Data to Big Impact. *MIS Quarterly*, *36*(4), 1165–1188.

Chen, M., Mao, S., & Liu, Y. (2014). Big data: a survey. *Mobile Networks and Applications*, *19*(2), 171–209.

Chen, Y., Wang, Y., Nevo, S., Benitez-Amado, J., & Kou, G. (2015). IT capabilities and product innovation performance: The roles of corporate entrepreneurship and competitive intensity. *Information & Management*, *52*(6), 643–657.

Cho, J. J., Ozment, J., & Sink, H. (2008). Logistics capability, logistics outsourcing and firm performance in an e-commerce market. *International Journal of Physical Distribution & Logistics Management*, *38*(5), 336–359.

Choi, H., & Varian, H. (2012). Predicting the Present with Google Trends. *Economic Record*, *88*, 2–9.

Choi, S., Kim, Y. J., Briceno, S., & Mavris, D. (2016). Prediction of weather-induced airline delays based on machine learning algorithms. In *35th DASC - Digital Avionics Systems Conference. 2016 proceedings papers : Sacramento California, USA* (pp. 1–6). Piscataway, NJ: IEEE.

Chou, Y. (1990). The hierarchical-hub model for airline networks. *Transportation Planning and Technology*, *14*(4), 243–258.

Clark, P. (2017). *Buying the big jets: fleet planning for airlines*. New York: Routledge.

Clarke, L. W., Hane, C. A., Johnson, E. L., & Nemhauser, G. L. (1996). Maintenance and Crew Considerations in Fleet Assignment. *Transportation Science*, *30*(3), 249–260.

Clarke, L., Johnson, E., Nemhauser, G., & Zhu, Z. (1997). The aircraft rotation problem. *Annals of Operations Research*, *69*(1-4), 33–46.

Closs, D. J., Goldsby, T. J., & Clinton, S. R. (1997). Information technology influences on world class logistics capability. *International Journal of Physical Distribution & Logistics Management*, *27*(1), 4–17.

Cohen, D. (2016). LinkedIn Rolls Out Audience Insights. Retrieved August 30, 2018, from Adweek: https://www.adweek.com/digital/linkedin-audience-insights/.

Cohn, A. M., & Barnhart, C. (2003). Improving Crew Scheduling By Incorporating Key Maintenance Routing Decisions. *Operations Research*, *51*(3), 387.

Çolak, S., Alexander, L. P., Alvim, B. G., Mehndiratta, S. R., & González, M. C. (2015). Analyzing Cell Phone Location Data for Urban Travel. *Transportation Research Record: Journal of the Transportation Research Board*, *2526*, 126–135.

Coldren, G. M., Koppelman, F. S., Kasturirangan, K., & Mukherjee, A. (2003). Modeling aggregate air-travel itinerary shares: logit model development at a major US airline. *Journal of Air Transport Management*, *9*(6), 361–369.

Comuzzi, M., & Patel, A. (2016). How organisations leverage Big Data: a maturity model. *Industrial Management & Data Systems*, *116*(8), 1468–1492.

Cook, A., Tanner, G., & Anderson, S. (2004). *Evaluating the true cost to airlines of one minute of airborne or ground delay.* Transport Studies Group of the University of Westminster. London.

Cook, A., Tanner, G., Williams, V., & Meise, G. (2009). Dynamic cost indexing – Managing airline delay costs. *Journal of Air Transport Management*, *15*(1), 26–35.

Cooper, B. L., Watson, H. J., Wixom, B. H., & Goodhue, D. L. (2000). Data Warehousing Supports Corporate Strategy At First American Corporation. *MIS Quarterly*, *24*(4), 547–567.

Cooper, D. R., & Schindler, P. S. (2000). *Business Research Methods* (7th). New York: McGraw-Hill.

Cordeau, J.-F., Stojković, G., Soumis, F., & Desrosiers, J. (2001). Benders Decomposition for Simultaneous Aircraft Routing and Crew Scheduling. *Transportation Science*, *35*(4), 375.

Cosic, R., Shanks, G., & Maynard, S. (2012). Towards a business analytics capability maturity model. In *ACIS 2012: Location, location, location: Proceedings of the 23rd Australasian Conference on Information Systems 2012* (pp. 1–11).

Crainic, T. G., & Laporte, G. (1997). Planning models for freight transportation. *European Journal of Operational Research*, *97*(3), 409–438.

Creswell, J. W. (2013). *Research design: Qualitative, quantitative, and mixed methods approaches*. Thousand Oaks: SAGE Publications.

Cui, L., & Hertz, S. (2011). Networks and capabilities as characteristics of logistics firms. *Industrial Marketing Management*, *40*(6), 1004–1011.

Daas, P. J. H., & Puts, M. (2014). *Social media sentiment and consumer confidence. Statistics paper series / European Central Bank: no 5 (September 2014)*. Frankfurt am Main, Germany: European Central Bank.

Retrieved from https://www.ecb.europa.eu/pub/pdf/scpsps/ecbsp5.en.pdf

Daft, J., & Albers, S. (2013). A conceptual framework for measuring airline business model convergence. *Journal of Air Transport Management, 28*, 47–54.

Daft, J., & Albers, S. (2015). An empirical analysis of airline business model convergence. *Journal of Air Transport Management*, *46*, 3–11.

Daskin, M. S., & Panayotopoulos, N. D. (1989). A Lagrangian Relaxation Approach to Assigning Aircraft to Routes in Hub and Spoke Networks. *Transportation Science*, *23*(2), 91.

DataCrops. (2018a). Hotel Pricing Intelligence. Retrieved September 03, 2018, from DataCrops: https://datacrops.com/hotel-pricing-intelligence/.

DataCrops. (2018b). Web Data Extraction Software. Retrieved September 03, 2018, from https://datacrops.com/web-data-extraction-software/.

Davenport, T. H., Barth, P., & Bean, R. (2012). How big data is different. *MIT sloan management review*, *54*(1), 43.

Day, G. S. (2011). Closing the Marketing Capabilities Gap. *Journal of Marketing*, *75*(4), 183–195.

Defee, C. C., Williams, B., Randall, W. S., & Thomas, R. (2010). An inventory of theory in logistics and SCM research. *International Journal of Logistics Management*, *21*(3), 404–489.

Deo, N., & Pang, C.-Y. (1984). Shortest-path algorithms: Taxonomy and annotation. *Networks*, *14*(2), 275–323.

Derigs, U., & Friederichs, S. (2013). Air cargo scheduling: integrated models and solution procedures. *OR Spectrum*, *35*(2), 325–362.

Derigs, U., Friederichs, S., & Schäfer, S. (2009). A New Approach for Air Cargo Network Planning. *Transportation Science*, *43*(3), 370–380.

Desaulniers, G., Desrosiers, J., Dumas, Y., Solomon, M. M., & Soumis, F. (1997). Daily aircraft routing and scheduling. *Management Science, 43*(6), 841.

Dijkstra, E. W. (1959). A note on two problems in connexion with graphs. *Numerische Mathematik, 1*(1), 269–271.

Dobruszkes, F., & van Hamme, G. (2011). The impact of the current economic crisis on the geography of air traffic volumes: an empirical analysis. *Journal of Transport Geography, 19*(6), 1387–1398.

Doganis, R. (2010). *Flying off Course* (4th ed.). Abingdon-on-Thames: Routledge.

Dominitz, J., & Manski, C. F. (2004). How Should We Measure Consumer Confidence? *Journal of Economic Perspectives, 18*(2), 51–66.

Döring, T. (1999). *Airline-Netzwerkmanagement aus kybernetischer Perspektive: ein Gestaltungsmodell*. Bern: Haupt.

Dožić, S., & Kalić, M. (2015). Three-stage airline fleet planning model. *Journal of Air Transport Management, 46*(Supplement C), 30–39.

Dreyfus, S. E. (1969). An Appraisal Of Some Shortest-Path Algorithms. *Operations Research, 17*(3), 395–412.

e-Airportslots.aero. (2018). Our Services. Retrieved September 03, 2018, from e-Airportslots.aero: https://e-airportslots.aero/flight-slot-portal-webui/Login.do;jsessionid=389CD8777DC86E603BB3DA249CB58875.

Echenique, M. (2018). Venezuela's Biggest Airport Is in Free Fall. Retrieved September 04, 2018, from Citylab: https://www.citylab.com/transportation/2018/06/venezuela-biggest-airport-is-in-free-fall/561875/.

Ehie, I. C., & Madsen, M. (2005). Identifying critical issues in enterprise resource planning (ERP) implementation. *Computers in Industry*, *56*(6), 545–557.

Eisenhardt, K. M. (1989). Building Theories from Case Study Research. *Academy of Management Review*, *14*(4), 532–550.

Eisenhardt, K. M., & Graebner, M. E. (2007). Theory Building from Cases: Opportunities and Challenges. *Academy of Management Journal*, *50*(1), 25–32.

Elbashir, M. Z., Collier, P. A., Sutton, S. G., Davern, M. J., & Leech, S. A. (2013). Enhancing the Business Value of Business Intelligence: The Role of Shared Knowledge and Assimilation. *Journal of Information Systems*, *27*(2), 87–105.

Emirates Sky Cargo. (2018). Online quotes. Retrieved September 05, 2018, from Emirates Sky Cargo: http://www.skycargo.com/english/?AspxAutoDetectCookieSupport=1.

Erdmann, A., Nolte, A., Noltemeier, A., & Schrader, R. (2001). Modeling and Solving an Airline Schedule Generation Problem. *Annals of Operations Research*, *107*(1), 117–142.

Erevelles, S., Fukawa, N., & Swayne, L. (2016). Big Data consumer analytics and the transformation of marketing. *Journal of Business Research*, *69*(2), 897–904.

Etschmaier, M. M., & Mathaisel, D. F. X. (1985). Airline Scheduling: An Overview. *Transportation Science*, *19*(2), 127.

Existek. (2018). Big Data Solutions: Example of The Development Cost. Retrieved August 28, 2018, from Existek: https://existek.com/blog/big-data-solutions-development-cost-example-software/.

Expedia Group. (2018). Media Solution Products. Retrieved August 30, 2018, from https://advertising.expedia.com/solutions/products.

Facebook. (2018a). Audience Insights. Retrieved August 30, 2018, from https://www.facebook.com/ads/audience-insights/.

Facebook. (2018b). Export API. Retrieved September 03, 2018, from Facebook: https://developers.facebook.com/docs/analytics/export.

Fan, J., Han, F., & Liu, H. (2014). Challenges of big data analysis. *National Science Review*, *1*(2), 293–314.

Farahani, R. Z., Miandoabchi, E., Szeto, W. Y., & Rashidi, H. (2013). A review of urban transportation network design problems. *European Journal of Operational Research*, *229*(2), 281–302.

Fawcett, S. E., Stanley, L. L., & Smith, S. R. (1997). Developing a logistics capability to improve the performance of international operations. *Journal of Business Logistics*, *18*(2), 101.

Federal Aviation Authority. (2015). Slot Management and Transparency for LaGuardia Airport, John F. Kennedy International Airport, and Newark Liberty International Airport. *Federal Register*, *80*(5), 1274–1306.

Feng, B., Li, Y., & Shen, Z.-J. M. (2015). Air cargo operations: Literature review and comparison with practices. *Transportation Research Part C: Emerging Technologies*, *56*, 263–280.

Feo, T. A., & Bard, J. F. (1989). Flight Scheduling And Maintenance Base Planning. *Management Science*, *35*(12), 1415–1432.

Fildes, R., Wei, Y., & Ismail, S. (2011). Evaluating the forecasting performance of econometric models of air passenger traffic flows using multiple error measures. *International Journal of Forecasting*, *27*(3), 902–922.

Filippova, K. (2012). User demographics and language in an implicit social network. *Proceedings of the 2012 Joint Conference on Empirical Methods in Natural Language Processing and Computational Natural Language Learning*, 1478–1488.

Fitzgerald, E. P. (1993). Success measures for information systems strategic planning. *The Journal of Strategic Information Systems*, *2*(4), 335–350.

Fleming, K., & Ghobrial, A. (1994). An analysis of the determinants of regional air travel demand. *Transportation Planning and Technology*, *18*(1), 37–44.

Flightradar24. (2018). Data services. Retrieved September 03, 2018, from Flightradar24: https://www.flightradar24.com/business/data-services.

Ford, J. L. R., & Fulkerson, D. R. (1956). Maximal flow through a network. *Canadian Journal of Mathematics*, *8*(3), 399–404.

Forster, P., & Regan, A. (2001). Electronic Integration in the Air Cargo Industry: An Information Processing Model of On-Time Performance. *Transportation Journal*, *40*(4), 46.

Foursquare, I. (2018). Foursquare Location Intelligence for Enterprise: The Future of Location Technology. Retrieved September 03, 2018, from Foursquare: https://enterprise.foursquare.com/.

Friederichs, S. (2010). *Air cargo schedule planning: integrated models and solution procedures. Wirtschaftsinformatik und Operations Research: Vol. 15*. Aachen: Shaker Verlag.

Frybourg, M., & Nijkamp, P. (1998). Assessing Changes in Integrated European Transport Network Operations. In K. Button, P. Nijkamp, & H. Priemus (Eds.), *Transport Networks in Europe* (pp. 15–34). Edward Elgar Publishing.

Fukui, H. (2010). An empirical analysis of airport slot trading in the United States. *Transportation Research Part B: Methodological*, *44*(3), 330–357.

Gandomi, A., & Haider, M. (2015). Beyond the hype: Big data concepts, methods, and analytics. *International Journal of Information Management*, *35*(2), 137–144.

Garlaschelli, D., & Loffredo, M. I. (2004). Patterns of Link Reciprocity in Directed Networks. *Physical Review Letters*, *93*(26), 268701.

Gennaioli, N., La Porta, R., Lopez De Silanes, F., & Shleifer, A. (2014). Growth in regions. *Journal of Economic Growth*, *19*(3), 259–309.

Geoquant. (2018). Real Time Political Risk Management. Retrieved September 04, 2018, from Geoquant: https://www.geoquant.io/.

Gershkoff, I. (1989). Optimizing Flight Crew Schedules. *Interfaces*, *19*(4), 29–43.

Gersuni, R. (2016). How Artificial Intelligence Is Affecting Media Monitoring. Retrieved September 03, 2018, from pressrelations: https://www.pressrelations.de/blog/interview-how-artificial-intelligence-is-affecting-media-monitoring/.

Ghobrial, A., Balakrishnan, N., & Kanafani, A. (1992). A heuristic model for frequency planning and aircraft routing in small size airlines. *Transportation Planning and Technology*, *16*(4), 235–249.

Ghose, A., Ipeirotis, P. G., & Li, B. (2018). Modeling Consumer Footprints on Search Engines: An Interplay with Social Media. *Management Science*.

Gillen, D. (2005). The Evolution of Networks with Changes in Industry Structure and Strategy: Connectivity, Hub-and-Spoke and Alliances. *Research in Transportation Economics*, *13*, 49–73.

Gillen, D. (2006). Airline Business Models and Networks: Regulation, Competition and Evolution in Aviation Markets. *Review of Network Economics*, *5*(4), 366–385.

Gillen, D., & Morrison, W. G. (2005). Regulation, competition and network evolution in aviation. *Journal of Air Transport Management*, *11*(3), 161–174.

Gligor, D. M., & Holcomb, M. C. (2012). Understanding the role of logistics capabilities in achieving supply chain agility: a systematic literature review. *Supply Chain Management*, *17*(4), 438–453.

Goedeking, P. (2010). *Networks in aviation: strategies and structures*. Berlin, Heidelberg: Springer.

Goetschalckx, M., & Fleischmann, B. (2005). Strategic network planning. In H. Stadtler & C. Kilger (Eds.), *Supply chain management and advanced planning* (pp. 117–137). Springer.

Goldman, A. J., & Nemhauser, G. L. (1967). A Transport Improvement Problem Transformable to a Best-Path Problem. *Transportation Science*, *1*(4), 295.

Goodhue, D. L., Quillard, J. A., & Rockart, J. F. (1988). Managing The Data Resource: A Contingency Perspective. *MIS Quarterly*, *12*(3), 373–392.

Google. (2018). Google Trends: Explore what the world is searching. Retrieved August 30, 2018, from Google: https://trends.google.com/trends/?geo=DE.

Gopalan, R., & Talluri, K. T. (1998). The Aircraft Maintenance Routing Problem. *Operations Research*, *46*(2), 260–271.

Govindan, K., Cheng, T., Mishra, N., & Shukla, N. (2018). Big data analytics and application for logistics and supply chain management. *Transportation Research Part E: Logistics and Transportation Review*, *114*, 343–349.

Granados, N., Kauffman, R. J., Lai, H., & Lin, H.-c. (2012). À la carte pricing and price elasticity of demand in air travel. *Decision Support Systems*, *53*(2), 381–394.

Granovetter, M. S. (1973). The strength of weak ties. *American Journal of Sociology*, *78*(6), 1360–1380.

Grant, R. M. (1996). Toward a knowledge-based theory of the firm. *Strategic Management Journal*, *17*(S2), 109–122.

Graves, G. W., McBride, R. D., Gershkoff, I., Anderson, D., & Mahidhara, D. (1993). Flight Crew Scheduling. *Management Science*, *39*(6), 736–745.

Grisk. (2018). Political Risk Analysis meets Big Data. Retrieved September 04, 2018, from Grisk: https://www.grisk.cn/en/.

Grosche, T. (2009). *Computational Intelligence in Integrated Airline Scheduling* (Studies in Computational Intelligence). Berlin, Heidelberg: Springer.

Grosche, T., Heinzl, A., & Rothlauf, F. (2001). A conceptual approach for simultaneous flight schedule construction with genetic algorithms. *Applications of Evolutionary Computing*, *1*(1), 257–267.

Grover, V., Chiang, R. H., Liang, T.-P., & Zhang, D. (2018). Creating Strategic Business Value from Big Data Analytics: A Research Framework. *Journal of Management Information Systems*, *35*(2), 388–423.

Grubb, H., & Mason, A. (2001). Long lead-time forecasting of UK air passengers by Holt–Winters methods with damped trend. *International Journal of Forecasting*, *17*(1), 71–82.

Guihaire, V., & Hao, J.-K. (2008). Transit network design and scheduling: A global review. *Transportation Research Part A: Policy and Practice*, *42*(10), 1251–1273.

Guimerà, R., Mossa, S., Turtschi, A., & Amaral, L. A. N. (2005). The worldwide air transportation network: Anomalous centrality, community structure, and cities' global roles. *Proceedings of the national academy of sciences*, *102*(22), 7794–7799.

Gulati, R., Nohria, N., & Zaheer, A. (2000). Strategic networks. *Strategic Management Journal, 21*(3), 203.

Gundecha, P., & Liu, H. (2012). Mining social media: a brief introduction. *Tutorials in Operations Research, 1*(4), 1–17.

Günther, W. A., Rezazade Mehrizi, M. H., Huysman, M., & Feldberg, F. (2017). Debating big data: A literature review on realizing value from big data. *The Journal of Strategic Information Systems, 26*(3), 191–209.

Guo, Y., Mellouli, T., Suhl, L., & Thiel, M. P. (2006). A partially integrated airline crew scheduling approach with time-dependent crew capacities and multiple home bases. *European Journal of Operational Research, 171*(3), 1169–1181.

Gupta, M., & George, J. F. (2016). Toward the development of a big data analytics capability. *Information & Management, 53*(8), 1049-1064.

Haouari, M., Aissaoui, N., & Mansour, F. Z. (2009). Network flow-based approaches for integrated aircraft fleeting and routing. *European Journal of Operational Research, 193*(2), 591–599.

Hausladen, I., & Schosser, M. (2018). Towards a maturity model for big data analytics in airline network planning. In Air Transport Research Society (Ed.), *Proceedings of the 22nd ATRS World Conference* (Forthcoming).

Heilig, L., & Voß, S. (2017). Managing Cloud-Based Big Data Platforms: A Reference Architecture and Cost Perspective. In F. P. García Márquez & B. Lev (Eds.), *Big Data Management* (pp. 29–45). Cham: Springer.

Henderson, J. V., Storeygard, A., & Weil, D. N. (2012). Measuring Economic Growth from Outer Space. *American Economic Review, 102*(2), 994–1028.

Herrmann, R., & Herrmann, O. (2014). Hotel roomrates under the influence of a large event: The Oktoberfest in Munich 2012. *International Journal of Hospitality Management*, *39*, 21–28.

Hevner, A. R., March, S. T., Park, J., & Ram, S. (2004). Design science in information systems research. *MIS Quarterly*, *28*(1), 75–105.

HITIT. (2017). Schedule Planning Overview. Retrieved October 01, 2017, from HITIT: https://crane.aero/solutions-services/operations-planning/schedule-planning.

Hodgson, C., & Waldmeir, P. (2018). How airlines aim to use big data to boost profits. Retrieved October 26, 2018, from Financial Times: https://www.ft.com/content/f3a931be-47aa-11e8-8ae9-4b5ddcca99b3.

Holloway, S. (2008). *Straight and level: Practical airline economics*. Aldershot: Ashgate Publishing, Ltd.

Hsiao, C.-Y., & Hansen, M. (2011). A passenger demand model for air transportation in a hub-and-spoke network. *Transportation Research Part E: Logistics and Transportation Review*, *47*(6), 1112–1125.

Hsu, C.-I., & Wen, Y.-H. (2000). Application of Grey theory and multiobjective programming towards airline network design. *European Journal of Operational Research*, *127*(1), 44–68.

Hsu, C.-I., & Wen, Y.-H. (2002). Reliability evaluation for airline network design in response to fluctuation in passenger demand. *Omega*, *30*(3), 197–213.

Hsu, C.-I., & Wen, Y.-H. (2003). Determining flight frequencies on an airline network with demand–supply interactions. *Transportation Research Part E: Logistics and Transportation Review*, *39*(6), 417–441.

Hsu, C., & Wen, Y. (1998). Improved grey prediction models for the transpacific air passenger market. *Transportation Planning and Technology*, *22*(2), 87–107.

IATA. (2017a). *Annual Review 2017.* IATA. Montreal. Retrieved from IATA website: https://www.iata.org/publications/Documents/iata-annual-review-2017.pdf

IATA. (2017b). *Air cargo serving e-commerce.* IATA (IATA Cargo white paper). Montreal. Retrieved from IATA website: https://www.iata.org/whatwedo/cargo/stb/Documents/StB-Cargo-White-Paper-e-commerce.pdf

IATA. (2018a). e-AWB. Retrieved September 03, 2018, from IATA: https://www.iata.org/whatwedo/cargo/e/eawb/Pages/index.aspx.

IATA. (2018b). *IATA Cargo Strategy.* IATA. Montreal. Retrieved from IATA website: http://www.iata.org/whatwedo/cargo/Documents/cargo-strategy.pdf

ICAO. (2018a). Database of World's Air Services Agreements. Retrieved September 04, 2018, from ICAO: https://www.icao.int/sustainability/Pages/Doc9511.aspx.

ICAO. (2018b). Freedoms of the Air. Retrieved September 10, 2018, from ICAO: https://www.icao.int/Pages/freedomsAir.aspx.

ICF. (2017). NetWorks: Network and Schedule Analysis/Systems and Software. Retrieved October 01, 2017, from ICF Inc.: https://www.icf.com/resources/solutions-and-apps/networks.

Ioachim, I., Desrosiers, J., Soumis, F., & Bélanger, N. (1999). Fleet assignment and routing with schedule synchronization constraints. *European Journal of Operational Research*, *119*(1), 75–90.

Ippolito, R. A. (1981). Estimating Airline Demand with Quality of Service Variables. *Journal of Transport Economics and Policy*, *15*(1), 7–15.

Iqbal, M. S., Choudhury, C. F., Wang, P., & González, M. C. (2014). Development of origin–destination matrices using mobile phone call data. *Transportation Research Part C: Emerging Technologies*, *40*, 63–74.

Itani, N. (2017). How Migration is Reshaping Air Transport. Retrieved September 05, 2018, from New Airport Insider: https://newairport-insider.com/this-is-how-migration-is-reshaping-air-transport/.

Itani, N., O'Connell, J. F., & Mason, K. (2014). A macro-environment approach to civil aviation strategic planning. *Transport Policy*, *33*, 125–135.

Jacobs, T. L., Garrow, L. A., Lohatepanont, M., Koppelman, F. S., Coldren, G. M., & Purnomo, H. (2012). Airline Planning and Schedule Development. In C. Barnhart & B. Smith (Eds.), *Quantitative Problem Solving Methods in the Airline Industry: A Modeling Methodology Handbook* (pp. 35–99). Boston, MA: Springer.

Jacquemin, M. (2007). *Netzmanagement im Luftverkehr: Statische und dynamische Planungsmodelle zur Gestaltung von Hub&Spoke-Flugnetzwerken*. Berlin, Heidelberg: Springer.

Jaillet, P., Song, G., & Yu, G. (1996). Airline network design and hub location problems. *Location Science*, *4*(3), 195–212.

Jalles, J. T. (2017). Inflation Forecasts' Performance in Latin America. *Review of Development Finance*, *7*(2), 157–168.

Jarillo, J. C. (1988). On strategic networks. *Strategic Management Journal*, *9*(1), 31–41.

Jarrah, A. I., Goodstein, J., & Narasimhan, R. (2000). An Efficient Airline Re-Fleeting Model for the Incremental Modification of Planned Fleet Assignments. *Transportation Science*, *34*(4), 349–363.

Jean, N., Burke, M., Xie, M., Davis, W. M., Lobell, D. B., & Ermon, S. (2016). Combining satellite imagery and machine learning to predict poverty. *Science*, *353*(6301), 790–794.

Jiang, H., & Barnhart, C. (2009). Dynamic Airline Scheduling. *Transportation Science*, *43*(3), 336–354.

Jiang, H., & Barnhart, C. (2013). Robust airline schedule design in a dynamic scheduling environment. *Transport Scheduling*, *40*(3), 831–840.

Johnson, L. (2017). Facebook Is Shutting Down Its API That Marketers Lean on for Research. Retrieved September 05, 2018, from Adweek: https://www.adweek.com/digital/facebook-is-shutting-down-its-api-that-marketers-lean-on-for-research/.

Jorge-Calderón, J. D. (1997). A demand model for scheduled airline services on international European routes. *Journal of Air Transport Management*, *3*(1), 23–35.

Kauder, S., & Meyr, H. (2009). Strategic network planning for an international automotive manufacturer. *OR Spectrum*, *31*(3), 507–532.

Kauffman, C. (2018). ASL Airlines launches first freighter flight to Europe from Urumqi. Retrieved September 06, 2018, from Air Cargo World: http://aircargoworld.com/allposts/asl-airlines-launches-first-freighter-flight-to-europe-from-urumqi/.

KAYAK. (2018). Travel Trends. Retrieved August 30, 2018, from https://www.kayak.com/trends.

Keola, S., Andersson, M., & Hall, O. (2015). Monitoring Economic Development from Space: Using Nighttime Light and Land Cover Data to Measure Economic Growth. *World Development*, *66*, 322–334.

Keuning, K., & Balkir, H. (2013). The Keys to Calculating Big Data Costs. Retrieved August 28, 2018, from Forsythe Focus: https://focus.forsythe.com/articles/270/The-Keys-to-Calculating-Big-Data-Costs.

Kim, G., Shin, B., Kim, K. K., & Lee, H. G. (2011). IT Capabilities, Process-Oriented Dynamic Capabilities, and Firm Financial Performance. *Journal of the Association for Information Systems*, *12*(7), 487–517.

King, W. R. (1983). Editor's Comment: Information as a Strategic Resource. *MIS Quarterly*, *7*(3), iii–iv.

King, W. R., Grover, V., & Hufnagel, E. H. (1989). Using information and information technology for sustainable competitive advantage: Some empirical evidence. *Information & Management*, *17*(2), 87–93.

Klabjan, D., Johnson, E. L., Nemhauser, G. L., Gelman, E., & Ramaswamy, S. (2002). Airline Crew Scheduling with Time Windows and Plane-Count Constraints. *Transportation Science*, *36*(3), 337.

Kladou, S., & Mavragani, E. (2015). Assessing destination image: An online marketing approach and the case of TripAdvisor. *Journal of Destination Marketing & Management*, *4*(3), 187–193.

Klein, L. R. (2001). An Essay On The Accuracy Of Economic Prediction. *International Journal of Applied Economics & Econometrics*, *9*(1), 29–69.

Klophaus, R., Conrady, R., & Fichert, F. (2012). Low cost carriers going hybrid: Evidence from Europe. *Journal of Air Transport Management*, *23*, 54–58.

Kölker, K., & Lütjens, K. (2015). Using Genetic Algorithms to Solve Large-scale Airline Network Planning Problems. *Procedia Transportation Research*, *10*, 900–909.

Komissarov, V. (2017). AI Applications for Satellite Imagery and Satellite Data. Retrieved August 30, 2018, from techemergence: https://www.techemergence.com/ai-applications-for-satellite-imagery-and-data/.

Korpela, J., & Tuominen, M. (1996). A decision support system for strategic issues management of logistics. *International Journal of Production Economics*, *46*, 605–620.

Kruskal, J. B. (1956). On the Shortest Spanning Subtree of a Graph and the Traveling Salesman Problem. *Proceedings of the American Mathematical Society*, *7*(1), 48–50.

L.E.K. Consulting. (2017). Network Planning. Retrieved October 01, 2017, from L.E.K. Consulting: https://www.lek.com/industries/travel-transport/services/network-planning.

Lai, K.-h. (2004). Service capability and performance of logistics service providers. *Transportation Research Part E: Logistics and Transportation Review*, *40*(5), 385–399.

Laney, D. (2001). 3D data management: Controlling data volume, velocity and variety. *META Group Research Note*, *6*, 70–74.

Larsen, T. (2013). Cross-platform aviation analytics using big-data methods. In *Integrated Communications, Navigation and Surveillance Conference (ICNS), 2013* (pp. 1–9).

LaValle, S., Lesser, E., Shockley, R., Hopkins, M. S., & Kruschwitz, N. (2011). Big data, analytics and the path from insights to value. *MIT sloan management review*, *52*(2), 21–31.

Lavie, D. (2006). The Competitive Advantage of Interconnected Firms: An Extension of the Resource-Based View. *Academy of Management Review*, *31*(3), 638–658.

Lavie, D. (2008). Network Resources: Toward a New Social Network Perspective. *Academy of Management Review*, *33*(2), 546–550.

Lazer, D., Kennedy, R., King, G., & Vespignani, A. (2014). The parable of Google flu: traps in big data analysis. *Science*, *343*(6176), 1203–1205.

Lederer, A. L., & Hannu, S. (1996). Toward a theory of strategic information systems planning. *The Journal of Strategic Information Systems*, *5*(3), 237–253.

Lederer, A. L., & Sethi, V. (1988). The implementation of strategic information systems planning methodologies. *MIS Quarterly*, 445–461.

Lederer, P. J., & Nambimadom, R. S. (1998). Airline Network Design. *Operations Research*, *46*(6), 785–804.

Leibold, K. (2001). *Optimierung von Flugplänen: Anwendung quantitativer Methoden im Luftverkehr*. Berlin, Heidelberg: Springer.

Levin, A. (1971). Scheduling and Fleet Routing Models for Transportation Systems. *Transportation Science*, *5*(3), 232.

Levitin, A. V., & Redman, T. C. (1998). Data as a Resource: Properties, Implications, and Prescriptions. *Sloan Management Review*, *40*(1), 89–101.

Li, D., Huang, H.-C., Morton, A., & Chew, E.-P. (2006). Simultaneous fleet assignment and cargo routing using benders decomposition. *OR Spectrum*, *28*(3), 319–335.

Li, J., Xu, L., Tang, L., Wang, S., & Li, L. (2018). Big data in tourism research: A literature review. *Tourism Management*, *68*, 301–323.

Lift - airline planning solutions. (2017). LiftPlan. Retrieved October 01, 2017, from Lift - airline planning solutions: https://www.liftaps.com/?avada_portfolio=liftplan.

Lin, C.-C., Lin, J.-Y., & Chen, Y.-C. (2012). The capacitated p-hub median problem with integral constraints: An application to a Chinese air cargo network. *Applied Mathematical Modelling*, *36*(6), 2777–2787.

Lippman, S. A., & Rumelt, R. P. (1982). Uncertain Imitability: An Analysis of Interfirm Differences in Efficiency under Competition. *The Bell Journal of Economics*, *13*(2), 418–438.

Liu, H., Ke, W., Wei, K. K., & Hua, Z. (2013). The impact of IT capabilities on firm performance: The mediating roles of absorptive capacity and supply chain agility. *Decision Support Systems*, *54*(3), 1452–1462.

Liu, X., Wang, M., & Huet, B. (2016). Event analysis in social multimedia: A survey. *Frontiers of Computer Science*, *10*(3), 433–446.

Lohatepanont, M., & Barnhart, C. (2004). Airline Schedule Planning: Integrated Models and Algorithms for Schedule Design and Fleet Assignment. *Transportation Science*, *38*(1), 19–32.

Lohmann, G., & Koo, T. T. (2013). The airline business model spectrum. *Journal of Air Transport Management*, *31*, 7–9.

Lönnqvist, A., & Pirttimäki, V. (2006). The Measurement of Business Intelligence. *Information Systems Management*, *23*(1), 32–40.

LoRa Alliance. (2018). Home page. Retrieved September 10, 2018, from LoRa Alliance: https://lora-alliance.org/.

Lordan, O. (2014). Study of the full-service and low-cost carriers network configuration. *Journal of Industrial Engineering and Management*, *7*(5), 1112–1123.

Lufthansa Cargo. (2018a). eServices & eBooking. Retrieved September 05, 2018, from Lufthansa Cargo: https://lufthansa-cargo.com/eservices/eservices-ebooking.

Lufthansa Cargo. (2018b). liveSensor - Our Add-on Service for real-time tracking. Retrieved September 03, 2018, from Lufthansa Cargo: https://lufthansa-cargo.com/aos-livesensor.

Lufthansa Systems. (2017). NetLine Suite. Retrieved October 01, 2017, from Lufthansa Systems: https://www.lhsystems.de/netline-suite.

Madas, M. A., & Zografos, K. G. (2006). Airport slot allocation: From instruments to strategies. *Journal of Air Transport Management*, *12*(2), 53–62.

Magnanti, T. L., & Wong, R. T. (1984). Network Design and Transportation Planning: Models and Algorithms. *Transportation Science*, *18*(1), 1–56.

Malighetti, P., Paleari, S., & Redondi, R. (2008). Connectivity of the European airport network: “Self-help hubbing” and business implications. *Journal of Air Transport Management*, *14*(2), 53–65.

Manyika, J., Chui, M., Brown, B., Bughin, J., Dobbs, R.,. . . Byers, A. H. (2011). *Big data: The next frontier for innovation, competition, and productivity.* McKinsey Global Institute.

Mareels, I. (2018). Data in Disasters: Coding our way to improved disaster resilience. Retrieved September 10, 2018, from IBM: https://www.ibm.com/blogs/ibm-anz/data-in-disasters/.

Marr, B. (2018). How Much Data Do We Create Every Day? The Mind-Blowing Stats Everyone Should Read. Retrieved October 11, 2018, from Forbes: https://www.forbes.com/sites/bernardmarr/2018/05/21/how-much-data-do-we-create-every-day-the-mind-blowing-stats-everyone-should-read/#f3e89ff60ba9.

Marsten, R. E., & Muller, M. R. (1980). A Mixed-Integer Programming Approach to Air Cargo Fleet Planning. *Management Science, 26*(11), 1096–1107.

Mashford, J. S., & Marksjö, B. S. (2001). Airline Base Schedule Optimisation by Flight Network Annealing. *Annals of Operations Research, 108*(1), 293–313.

Mata, F. J., Fuerst, W. L., & Barney, J. B. (1995). Information Technology and Sustained Competitive Advantage: A Resource-Based Analysis. *MIS Quarterly, 19*(4), 487–505.

Mauro, A. de, Greco, M., & Grimaldi, M. (2015). What is big data? A consensual definition and a review of key research topics. In *AIP Conference Proceedings* (Vol. 1644, pp. 97–104).

McAfee, A., & Brynjolfsson, E. (2012). Big data: The management revolution. *Harvard Business Review, 90*(10), 61–67.

McCallie, D., Butts, J., & Mills, R. (2011). Security analysis of the ADS-B implementation in the next generation air transportation system. *International Journal of Critical Infrastructure Protection, 4*(2), 78–87.

McGovern, A., Elmore, K. L., Gagne, D. J., Haupt, S. E., Karstens, C. D.,. . . Williams, J. K. (2017). Using Artificial Intelligence to Improve Real-Time Decision-Making for High-Impact Weather. *Bulletin of the American Meteorological Society*, *98*(10), 2073–2090.

MeetUp. (2018). Meet the API. Retrieved September 06, 2018, from MeetUp: https://www.meetup.com/de-DE/meetup_api/.

Meixell, M. J., & Gargeya, V. B. (2005). Global supply chain design: A literature review and critique. *Global Logistics*, *41*(6), 531–550.

Meltwater. (2018). Meltwater Products — AI-driven Deep Media and Social Insights. Retrieved September 03, 2018, from Meltwater: https://www.meltwater.com/products/#executives.

Melville, N., Kraemer, K., & Gurbaxani, V. (2004). Information Technology And Organizational Performance: An Integrative Model Of It Business Value. *MIS Quarterly*, *28*(2), 283–322.

Mercier, A., & Soumis, F. (2007). An integrated aircraft routing, crew scheduling and flight retiming model. *Computers & Operations Research*, *34*(8), 2251–2265.

Merkert, R., & Morrell, P. S. (2012). Mergers and acquisitions in aviation – Management and economic perspectives on the size of airlines. *Transportation Research Part E: Logistics and Transportation Review*, *48*(4), 853–862.

Miah, S. J., Vu, H. Q., Gammack, J., & McGrath, M. (2017). A Big Data Analytics Method for Tourist Behaviour Analysis. *Information & Management*, *54*(6), 771–785.

Microsoft. (2018). MS Access specifications. Retrieved October 17, 2018, from Microsoft: https://support.office.com/en-us/article/access-specifications-0cf3c66f-9cf2-4e32-9568-98c1025bb47c.

Milgram, S. (1967). The small world problem. *Psychology Today*, *1*(1), 61–67.

Milis, K., & Mercken, R. (2004). The use of the balanced scorecard for the evaluation of Information and Communication Technology projects. *International Journal of Project Management*, *22*(2), 87–97.

Minges, M., Fredriksson, T., Korka, D., Fondeur, S., Donohoe, P., & Ansón, J. (2016). *In Search of Cross-border E-commerce Trade Data.* United Nations Conference on Trade And Development (UNCTAD Technical Notes on ICT for Development No. 6). Retrieved from United Nations Conference on Trade And Development website: http://unctad.org/en/PublicationsLibrary/tn_unctad_ict4d06_en.pdf

Mintzberg, H. (1994). The fall and rise of strategic planning. *Harvard Business Review*, *72*(1), 107–114.

Moore, N. C. (2014). How big data could reduce weather-related flight delays. Retrieved September 04, 2018, from University of Michigan News: https://news.umich.edu/how-big-data-could-reduce-weather-related-flight-delays/.

Morash, E. A., Droge, C. L. M., & Vickery, S. K. (1996). Strategic logistics capabilities for competitive advantage and firm success. *Journal of Business Logistics*, *17*(1), 1–22.

Motionlogic. (2018). Motionlogic Solutions. Retrieved September 03, 2018, from Motionlogic GmbH: https://www.motionlogic.de/blog/ en/solutions/.

Muller, L., & Hart, M. (2016). Updating business intelligence and analytics maturity models for new developments. In *International Conference on Decision Support System Technology* (pp. 137–151).

Mumbower, S., Garrow, L. A., & Higgins, M. J. (2014). Estimating flight-level price elasticities using online airline data: A first step toward integrating pricing, demand, and revenue optimization. *Transportation Research Part A: Policy and Practice*, *66*, 196–212.

Muñoz, K. (2016). The Case for Big Data Analysis in Predicting Political Risks. Retrieved September 04, 2018, from LinkedIn: https://www.linkedin.com/pulse/case-big-data-analysis-predicting-political-risks-dr-katja-mu%C3%B1oz/.

Nakicenovic, N. (1995). Overland Transportation Networks: History of Development and Future Prospects. In D. Batten, J. Casti, & R. Thord (Eds.), *Networks in Action: Communication, Economics and Human Knowledge* (pp. 195–228). Berlin, Heidelberg: Springer.

Nešetřil, J., Milková, E., & Nešetřilová, H. (2001). Otakar Borůvka on minimum spanning tree problem translation of both the 1926 papers, comments, history. *Discrete Mathematics*, *233*(1-3), 3–36.

Newman, M. (2003). The Structure and Function of Complex Networks. *SIAM Review*, *45*(2), 167–256.

Newman, M., Barabasi, A.-L., & Watts, D. J. (2011). *The structure and dynamics of networks*. Princeton, NJ: Princeton University Press.

Niehaus, T., Ruehle, J., & Knigge, A. (2009). Relevance of route and network profitability analysis for the network management process of network carriers. *Journal of Air Transport Management*, *15*(4), 175–183.

Noyes, K. (2014). For the airline industry, big data is cleared for take-off. Retrieved May 12, 2017, from http://fortune.com/2014/06/19/big-data-airline-industry/.

npm Inc. (2018). Google Trends Api. Retrieved August 30, 2018, from https://www.npmjs.com/package/google-trends-api.

Octorate. (2018). Rate Intelligence - The Best Rated for your Hotel, BnB, apartment. Retrieved September 03, 2018, from Octorate: https://www.octorate.com/en/rate-intelligence/.

O'Kelly, M. E. (1987). A quadratic integer program for the location of interacting hub facilities. *European Journal of Operational Research*, *32*(3), 393–404.

O'Kelly, M. E., & Miller, H. J. (1994). The hub network design problem: A review and synthesis. *Journal of Transport Geography*, *2*(1), 31–40.

Olavarrieta, S., & Ellinger, A. E. (1997). Resource-based theory and strategic logistics research. *International Journal of Physical Distribution & Logistics Management*, *27*(9/10), 559–587.

Önder, I., & Gunter, U. (2016). Forecasting Tourism Demand with Google Trends For a Major European City Destination. *Tourism Analysis*, *21*(2-3), 203–220.

O'Neill, S. (2018). Amadeus Buys Hotel Tech Firm TravelClick for $1.5 Billion. Retrieved September 03, 2018, from Skift: https://skift.com/2018/08/10/amadeus-buys-travelclick/.

Optym. (2017). Amadeus SkyMax by Optym. Retrieved October 01, 2017, from Optym: https://www.optym.com/sky/skymax/.

Orbital Insight. (2018). Public Sector. Retrieved August 30, 2018, from Orbital Insight: https://orbitalinsight.com/industries/public-sector/.

Oum, T. H., Zhang, A., & Zhang, Y. (1995). Airline Network Rivalry. *The Canadian Journal of Economics*, *28*(4a), 836–857.

Oxford University Press. (2017). English Oxford Dictionnary: Network. Retrieved October 12, 2017, from Oxford University Press: https://en.oxforddictionaries.com/definition/network.

Pan, B., Chenguang Wu, D., & Song, H. (2012). Forecasting hotel room demand using search engine data. *Journal of Hospitality and Tourism Technology*, *3*(3), 196–210.

Papadakos, N. (2009). Integrated airline scheduling. *Computers & Operations Research*, *36*(1), 176–195.

Paré, G., Trudel, M.-C., Jaana, M., & Kitsiou, S. (2015). Synthesizing information systems knowledge: A typology of literature reviews. *Information & Management*, *52*(2), 183–199.

Park, S., Lee, J., & Song, W. (2016). Short-term forecasting of Japanese tourist inflow to South Korea using Google trends data. *Journal of Travel & Tourism Marketing*, *34*(3), 357–368.

Park, S. Y., & Pan, B. (2018). Identifying the next non-stop flying market with a big data approach. *Tourism Management*, *66*, 411–421.

PDC Aviation. (2017). Flight Planning Software. Retrieved October 01, 2017, from https://www.pdc.com/aviation/aviation_solutions/flight time-reduce-costs-fleet-management.html.

Pels, E. (2008). Airline network competition: Full-service airlines, low-cost airlines and long-haul markets. *Research in Transportation Economics*, *24*(1), 68–74.

Pels, E. (2009). Network competition in the open aviation area. *Journal of Air Transport Management*, *15*(2), 83–89.

Pels, E., Nijkamp, P., & Rietveld, P. (2000). A note on the optimality of airline networks. *Economics Letters*, *69*(3), 429–434.

Penrose, E. T. (1959). *The theory of the growth of the firm.* New York: Wiley.

Peteraf, M. A. (1993). The Cornerstones of Competitive Advantage: A Resource-Based View. *Strategic Management Journal*, *14*(3), 179–191.

Pita, J. P., Barnhart, C., & Antunes, A. P. (2013). Integrated Flight Scheduling and Fleet Assignment Under Airport Congestion. *Transportation Science*, *47*(4), 477–492.

Poenicke, O., Kirch, M., Richter, K., & Schwarz, S. (Eds.) 2018. *LoRaWAN for IoT Applications in Air Cargo - Development of a GSE Tracking System for DHL Air Cargo Hub Leipzig*. Smart SysTech 2018; European Conference on Smart Objects, Systems and Technologies.

Pompl, W. (2007). *Luftverkehr: Eine ökonomische und politische Einführung*. Berlin, Heidelberg: Springer.

Popescu, A., Keskinocak, P., Johnson, E., LaDue, M., & Kasilingam, R. (2006). Estimating Air-Cargo Overbooking Based on a Discrete Show-Up-Rate Distribution. *Interfaces*, *36*(3), 248–258.

PriceStats. (2018). Inflation Series. Retrieved September 04, 2018, from PriceStats: https://www.pricestats.com/inflation-series?chart=1836.

Profillidis, V. (2000). Econometric and fuzzy models for the forecast of demand in the airport of Rhodes. *Journal of Air Transport Management*, *6*(2), 95–100.

Provan, K. G., Fish, A., & Sydow, J. (2007). Interorganizational Networks at the Network Level: A Review of the Empirical Literature on Whole Networks. *Journal of Management*, *33*(3), 479–516.

Raghupathi, W., & Raghupathi, V. (2014). Big data analytics in healthcare: Promise and potential. *Health Information Science and Systems*, *2*(3), 1–10.

Raguseo, E. (2018). Big data technologies: An empirical investigation on their adoption, benefits and risks for companies. *International Journal of Information Management*, *38*(1), 187–195.

RateGain. (2018). Competitive Pricing Intelligence and Monitoring for Travel Companies. Retrieved September 03, 2018, from RateGain: https://rategain.com/travel-software/competitor-pricing/.

Reals, K., & Hadwick, A. (2015). *The Future of Metasearch 2015.* Eye-fortravel. Retrieved from Eyefortravel website: https://www.eye-fortravel.com/sites/default/files/1570_eft_metasearch_report_v6.pdf

Recklies, B. (2018). Aktuelle Streckenmeldungen - Das sind die Änderungen im ersten Sommerflugplan ohne Air Berlin. Retrieved September 07, 2018, from Airliners.de: http://www.airliners.de/das-aenderungen-sommerflugplan-air-berlin/44242.

Redman, T. C. (1995). Improve data quality for competitive advantage. *Sloan Management Review*, *36*(2), 99.

Reichert, I. (2018). Chaos bei der Lufthansa-Tochter: Was läuft schief bei Eurowings? Retrieved September 07, 2018, from SPIEGEL Online: http://www.spiegel.de/wirtschaft/unternehmen/eurowings-flugausfa-elle-verzehnfacht-was-laeuft-schief-a-1214942.html.

Rivera, R. (2016). A dynamic linear model to forecast hotel registrations in Puerto Rico using Google Trends data. *Tourism Management*, *57*, 12–20.

Rodriguez, J. I., & King, W. R. (1977). Competitive information systems. *Long Range Planning*, *10*(6), 45–50.

Ross, J. W., Beath, C. M., & Goodhue, D. L. (1996). Develop Long-Term Competitiveness Through It Assets. *Sloan Management Review*, *38*(1), 31.

Ross-Smith, M. (2016). How Big Data is Changing The Way We Fly: A journey into predictive analytics and how big data will drive up airline ticket prices. Retrieved June 26, 2017, from https://www.traveldata-daily.com/how-big-data-is-changing-the-way-we-fly/.

Rouda, N. (2014). *Getting Real About Big Data: Build Versus Buy.* Enterprise Strategy Group (ESG White Papers).

Rubin, J. (1973). A Technique for the Solution of Massive Set Covering Problems, with Application to Airline Crew Scheduling. *Transportation Science*, *7*(1), 34–48.

Rushmeier, R. A., & Kontogiorgis, S. A. (1997). Advances in the Optimization of Airline Fleet Assignment. *Transportation Science*, *31*(2), 159.

Russom, P. (2011). *Big data analytics.* TDWI.

Saab, S. S., & Zouein, P. P. (2001). Forecasting passenger load for a fixed planning horizon. *Journal of Air Transport Management*, *7*(6), 361–372.

Sabherwal, R., & King, W. R. (1991). Towards a theory of strategic use of information resources. *Information & Management*, *20*(3), 191–212.

Sabre. (2017). Planning & Scheduling: Optimize Your Network Planning. Retrieved October 01, 2017, from Sabre, Inc.: https://www.sabreairlinesolutions.com/home/software_solutions/product/airline_planning_and_scheduling/.

Salazar-González, J.-J. (2014). Approaches to solve the fleet-assignment, aircraft-routing, crew-pairing and crew-rostering problems of a regional carrier. *Omega*, *43*(Supplement C), 71–82.

Saldaña, J. (2016). *The Coding Manual for Qualitative Researchers* (2nd). London: SAGE Publications.

Sandhu, R., & Klabjan, D. (2007). Integrated Airline Fleeting and Crew-Pairing Decisions. *Operations Research*, *55*(3), 439–456.

Schäfer, M., Strohmeier, M., Lenders, V., Martinovic, I., & Wilhelm, M. (2014). Bringing Up OpenSky: A Large-scale ADS-B Sensor Network for Research. In : *IPSN '14, Proceedings of the 13th International Symposium on Information Processing in Sensor Networks* (pp. 83–94). Piscataway, NJ, USA: IEEE Press.

Schmidt, G., & Wilhelm, W. E. (2000). Strategic, tactical and operational decisions in multi-national logistics networks: a review and discussion of modelling issues. *International Journal of Production Research*, *38*(7), 1501–1523.

Schosser, M., & Wittmer, A. (2015). Cost and revenue synergies in airline mergers – Examining geographical differences. *Journal of Air Transport Management*, *47*, 142–153.

Schroeck, M., Shockley, R., Smart, J., Romero-Morales, D., & Tufano, P. (2012). Analytics: The real-world use of big data. *IBM Global Business Services*, 1–20.

Seabury Consulting. (2017). Network, Fleet, Alliance Optimization & Tools. Retrieved October 01, 2017, from Seabury Consulting (Accenture): https://www.accenture.com/t20170421T024045Z__w__/hu-en/_acnmedia/PDF-49/Accenture-Network-Fleet-Alliance-Optimization-Tools.pdf.

Seddon, P. B., Constantinidis, D., & Dod, H. (2012). How does business analytics contribute to business value? *Proceedings of the 33rd International Conference on Information Systems (ICIS)*.

Sendum. (2018). PT300 Package Tracker. Retrieved September 03, 2018, from Sendum: https://sendum.com/pt300-package-tracker/.

Sensitech. (2018). Tracking Devices. Retrieved September 03, 2018, from Sensitech: http://www.sensitech.com/en/supply-chain-security/sensiguard-technology/tracking-devices/.

Seristö, H., & Vepsäläinen, A. P. (1997). Airline cost drivers: cost implications of fleet, routes, and personnel policies. *Journal of Air Transport Management*, *3*(1), 11–22.

Shaw, S. (2016). *Airline marketing and management*. Farmham: Ashgate Publishing Limited.

Sheivachman, A. (2017). Channel Shock: The Future of Travel Distribution. Retrieved September 06, 2018, from Skift: https://skift.com/2017/08/07/channel-shock-the-future-of-travel-distribution/.

Sherali, H. D., & Zhu, X. (2008). Two-Stage Fleet Assignment Model Considering Stochastic Passenger Demands. *Operations Research*, *56*(2), 383–399.

Shieber, J. (2017). Global risk analysis gets an artificial intelligence upgrade with GeoQuant. Retrieved September 04, 2018, from Techcrunch: https://techcrunch.com/2017/06/20/global-risk-analysis-gets-an-artificial-intelligence-upgrade-with-geoquant/.

Sirmon, D. G., Hitt, M. A., & Ireland, R. D. (2007). Managing Firm Resources in Dynamic Environments to Create Value: Looking inside the Black Box. *Academy of Management Review*, *32*(1), 273–292.

Sismanidou, A., Tarradellas, J., Bel, G., & Fageda, X. (2013). Estimating potential long-haul air passenger traffic in national networks containing two or more dominant cities. *Journal of Transport Geography*, *26*, 108–116.

Skyscanner. (2018). Travel Insight. Retrieved August 30, 2018, from Skyscanner: https://partners.skyscanner.net/insights/travel-insight/.

Sloan, L., Morgan, J., Burnap, P., & Williams, M. (2015). Who tweets? Deriving the demographic characteristics of age, occupation and social class from twitter user meta-data. *PloS one*, *10*(3), e0115545.

Souai, N., & Teghem, J. (2009). Genetic algorithm based approach for the integrated airline crew-pairing and rostering problem. *European Journal of Operational Research*, *199*(3), 674–683.

SpaceKnow. (2018). Artificial Intelligence Detections. Retrieved August 30, 2018, from SpaceKnow: https://www.spaceknow.com/.

Stadtler, H. (2005). Supply chain management and advanced planning—basics, overview and challenges. *European Journal of Operational Research*, *163*(3), 575–588.

StatCounter. (2018). Search Engine Market Share Worldwide. Retrieved September 05, 2018, from StatCounter: http://gs.statcounter.com /search-engine-market-share.

Statista. (2018). *Airline alliances.* Statista. Retrieved from Statista website: https://www.statista.com/study/47501/airline-alliances/

Statistisches Bundesamt (DESTATIS). (2017). *Bevölkerung mit Migrationshintergrund - Ergebnisse des Mikrozensus* (Fachserie 1 Reihe 2.2). Retrieved from https://www.destatis.de/DE/Publikationen/Thematisch/Bevoelkerung/MigrationIntegration/Migrationshintergrund2010220177004.pdf?__blob=publicationFile

Sterzenbach, R., Conrady, R., & Fichert, F. (2013). *Luftverkehr: Betriebswirtschaftliches Lehr- und Handbuch*. München: Oldenbourg Wissenschaftsverlag.

Stieglitz, S., Mirbabaie, M., Ross, B., & Neuberger, C. (2018). Social media analytics – Challenges in topic discovery, data collection, and data preparation. *International Journal of Information Management*, *39*, 156–168.

Stinchcombe, A. L. (1965). Social structure and organizations. In J. G. March (Ed.), *Handbook of Organizations* (pp. 142–193). Chicago: Rand-McNally.

Stoel, D. M., & Muhanna, W. A. (2009). IT capabilities and firm performance: A contingency analysis of the role of industry and IT capability type. *Information & Management*, *46*(3), 181–189.

Stojković, G., Soumis, F., Desrosiers, J., & Solomon, M. M. (2002). An optimization model for a real-time flight scheduling problem. *Transportation Research Part A: Policy and Practice*, *36*(9), 779–788.

Storey, V. C., Firth, C. P., & Wang, R. Y. (1995). A Framework for Analysis of Data Quality Research. *IEEE Transactions on Knowledge & Data Engineering*, *7*, 623–640.

StreetLight Data. (2018). Big Data Technology for Transportation. Retrieved September 03, 2018, from StreetLight Data: https:// www.streetlightdata.com/population-mobility-technology/.

Strohmeier, M., Schafer, M., Lenders, V., & Martinovic, I. (2014). Realities and challenges of nextgen air traffic management: The case of ADS-B. *IEEE Communications Magazine*, *52*(5), 111–118.

Suryani, E., Chou, S.-Y., & Chen, C.-H. (2012). Dynamic simulation model of air cargo demand forecast and terminal capacity planning. *Simulation Modelling Practice and Theory*, *28*(Supplement C), 27–41.

Takebayashi, M. (2013). Network competition and the difference in operating cost: Model analysis. *Transportation Research Part E: Logistics and Transportation Review*, *57*(Supplement C), 85–94.

Tang, C.-H., Yan, S., & Chen, Y.-H. (2008). An integrated model and solution algorithms for passenger, cargo, and combi flight scheduling. *Transportation Research Part E: Logistics and Transportation Review*, *44*(6), 1004–1024.

Tecnoshow Comigo. (2018). Tecnoshow Comigo Home. Retrieved September 06, 2018, from Tecnoshow Comigo: undefined.

Teece, D. J., Pisano, G., & Shuen, A. (1997). Dynamic Capabilities and Strategic Management. *Strategic Management Journal*, *18*(7), 509–533.

Telefónica Next. (2018). Transport Analytics - Bewegungsdaten verstehen. Retrieved September 03, 2018, from Telefónica Next: https://next.telefonica.de/loesungen/transport-analytics.

Teodorović, D., & Guberinić, S. (1984). Optimal dispatching strategy on an airline network after a schedule perturbation. *European Journal of Operational Research*, *15*(2), 178–182.

Teodorović, D., Kalić, M., & Pavković, G. (1994). The potential for using fuzzy set theory in airline network design. *Transportation Research Part B: Methodological*, *28*(2), 103–121.

Teodorović, D., & Krčmar-Nožić, E. (1989). Multicriteria Model to Determine Flight Frequencies on an Airline Network under Competitive Conditions. *Transportation Science*, *23*(1), 14–25.

The Billion Prices Project. (2018). The Billion Prices Project. Retrieved August 30, 2018, from MIT Sloan School of Business: http:// www.thebillionpricesproject.com/.

The Weather Company. (2018). Aviation Weather Forecast Solutions. Retrieved September 04, 2018, from IBM: https://business.weather.com/industry-solutions/aviation.

Tolouei, R., Psarras, S., & Prince, R. (2017). Origin-Destination Trip Matrix Development: Conventional Methods versus Mobile Phone Data. *Transportation Research Procedia*, *26*, 39–52.

Totamane, R., Dasgupta, A., & Rao, S. (2012). Air Cargo Demand Modeling and Prediction. *IEEE Systems Journal*, *8*(1), 52–62.

Tripadvisor. (2018a). Tripadvisor Business Advantage - Better Data Means Better Business Decisions. Retrieved September 03, 2018, from Tripadvisor, Inc.: https://www.tripadvisor.com/BusinessAdvantage#/analytics?_k=hsrht7.

Tripadvisor. (2018b). TripBarometer. Retrieved September 03, 2018, from Tripadvisor, Inc.: https://www.tripadvisor.com/TripAdvisorInsights/tripbarometer.

Trkman, P., McCormack, K., Oliveira, M. P. V. d., & Ladeira, M. B. (2010). The impact of business analytics on supply chain performance. *Decision Support Systems*, *49*(3), 318–327.

Tuckett, D., Nyman, R., Ormerod, P., & Smith, R. (2014). Big data and economic forecasting: a top-down approach using directed algorithmic text analysis. *ECB Workshop on Big Data for Forecasting and Statistics*, *1*.

Universal Information. (2018). Media Monitoring Service. Retrieved September 03, 2018, from Universal Information: https://universal-info.com/media-monitoring/.

Valdes, V. (2015). Determinants of air travel demand in Middle Income Countries. *Journal of Air Transport Management*, *42*(Supplement C), 75–84.

Vaske, H. (2017). Loadfox, FreightHub, Cargonnex & Co.: Online-Speditionen wirbeln Logistikmarkt durcheinander. Retrieved September 03, 2018, from Computerwoche: https://www.computerwoche.de/a/online-speditionen-wirbeln-logistikmarkt-durcheinander,3329617.

Verhoef, E. T. (2010). Congestion pricing, slot sales and slot trading in aviation. *Transportation Research Part B: Methodological*, *44*(3), 320–329.

VHB. (2015). VHB-JOURQUAL3. Retrieved October 10, 2016, from Verband der Hochschullehrer für Betriebswirtschaftslehre e.V.: http://vhbonline.org/vhb4you/jourqual/vhb-jourqual-3/.

Vom Brocke, J., Simons, A., Niehaves, B., Riemer, K., Plattfaut, R.,. . . others (2009). Reconstructing the giant: On the importance of rigour in documenting the literature search process. In *17th European Conference on Information Systems (ECIS 2009), Verona, Italy* (pp. 2206–2217).

Waal-Montgomery, M. de. (2015). World's data volume to grow 40% per year & 50 times by 2020: Aureus. Retrieved November 18, 2016, from Aureus Analytics: https://e27.co/worlds-data-volume-to-grow-40-per-year-50-times-by-2020-aureus-20150115-2/.

Wade, M., & Hulland, J. (2004). The Resource-Based View and Information Systems Research: Review, Extension, and Suggestions for Future Research. *MIS Quarterly*, *28*(1), 107–142.

Wadud, Z. (2014). The asymmetric effects of income and fuel price on air transport demand. *Transportation Research Part A: Policy and Practice*, *65*, 92–102.

Wamba, S. F., Akter, S., Edwards, A., Chopin, G., & Gnanzou, D. (2015). How 'big data' can make big impact: Findings from a systematic review and a longitudinal case study. *International Journal of Production Economics*, *165*, 234–246.

Wamba, S. F., Gunasekaran, A., Akter, S., Ren, S. J.-f., Dubey, R., & Childe, S. J. (2016). Big data analytics and firm performance: Effects of dynamic capabilities. *Journal of Business Research*, -.

Wang, R. Y., & Strong, D. M. (1996). Beyond accuracy: What data quality means to data consumers. *Journal of Management Information Systems*, *12*(4), 5–33.

Warburg, V., Gotsæd Hansen, T., Larsen, A., Norman, H., & Andersson, E. (2008). Dynamic airline scheduling: An analysis of the potentials of refleeting and retiming. *Journal of Air Transport Management*, *14*(4), 163–167.

Wasserman, S., & Faust, K. (1994). *Social network analysis: Methods and applications*. Cambridge: Cambridge University Press.

Watson, H. J., & Wixom, B. H. (2007). The current state of business intelligence. *Computer*, *40*(9).

Wei, P., Chen, L., & Sun, D. (2014). Algebraic connectivity maximization of an air transportation network: The flight routes' addition/deletion problem. *Transportation Research Part E: Logistics and Transportation Review*, *61*, 13–27.

Wei, W., & Hansen, M. (2005). Impact of aircraft size and seat availability on airlines' demand and market share in duopoly markets. *Transportation Research Part E: Logistics and Transportation Review*, *41*(4), 315–327.

Wei, W., & Hansen, M. (2006). An aggregate demand model for air passenger traffic in the hub-and-spoke network. *Transportation Research Part A: Policy and Practice*, *40*(10), 841–851.

Weide, O., Ryan, D., & Ehrgott, M. (2010). An iterative approach to robust and integrated aircraft routing and crew scheduling. *Computers & Operations Research*, *37*(5), 833–844.

Wensveen, J. G. (2015). *Air Transportation: A Management Perspective* (8th). Burlington: Ashgate Publishing Limited.

Wernerfelt, B. (1984). A resource-based view of the firm. *Strategic Management Journal*, *5*(2), 171–180.

Whitefield, M. (2017). After frequent price hikes, cost of visiting Cuba coming down. Retrieved September 06, 2018, from Miami Herald: https://www.miamiherald.com/news/nation-world/world/americas/cuba/article134586559.html.

Whyte, R., & Lohmann, G. (2017). Airline business models. In L. Budd & S. Ison (Eds.), *Air Transport Management* (pp. 107–122). London: Routledge.

Willcocks, L. P. (2009). 9 Evaluating the Outcomes of Information Systems Plans Managing information technology evaluation—techniques and processes". In R. Galliers & D. E. Leidner (Eds.), *Strategic information management. Challenges and strategies in managing information systems / edited by Robert D. Galliers and Dorothy E. Leidner* (4th ed., pp. 239–259). London: Routledge.

Williams, J. K. (2014). Using random forests to diagnose aviation turbulence. *Machine Learning*, *95*(1), 51–70.

Wittmer, A., & Bieger, T. (2011). Fundamentals and Structure of Aviation Systems. In A. Wittmer, T. Bieger, & R. Müller (Eds.), *Aviation Systems: Management of the Integrated Aviation Value Chain* (pp. 5–38). Berlin, Heidelberg: Springer.

Wittmer, A., & Vespermann, J. (2011). The Environment of Aviation. In A. Wittmer, T. Bieger, & R. Müller (Eds.), *Aviation Systems: Management of the Integrated Aviation Value Chain* (pp. 39–57). Berlin, Heidelberg: Springer.

Wixom, B. H., Watson, H. J., Reynolds, A. M., & Hoffer, J. A. (2008). Continental Airlines Continues to Soar with Business Intelligence. *Information Systems Management*, *25*(2), 102–112.

Wixom, B. H., Yen, B., & Relich, M. (2013). Maximizing Value from Business Analytics. *MIS Quarterly Executive*, *12*(2).

Wojahn, O. W. (2001a). Airline network structure and the gravity model. *Transportation Research Part E: Logistics and Transportation Review*, *37*(4), 267–279.

Wojahn, O. W. (2001b). *Airline networks*. Bern: Lang.

WTO. (2013). Air Service Agreements Projector (ASAP). Retrieved September 04, 2018, from WTO: https://www.wto.org/asap/index.html.

Wynn, J. D., & Williams, C. K. (2012). Principles for Conducting Critical Realist Case Study Research in Information Systems. *MIS Quarterly*, *36*(3), 787–810.

Xu, Y. (2011). Competitive Network And Competitive Behavior: A Study Of The U.S. Airline Industry. *Academy of Strategic Management Journal, 10*(1), 45–63.

Yan, S., & Chen, C.-H. (2008). Optimal flight scheduling models for cargo airlines under alliances. *Journal of Scheduling, 11*(3), 175–186.

Yan, S., Chen, S.-C., & Chen, C.-H. (2006). Air cargo fleet routing and timetable setting with multiple on-time demands. *Transportation Research Part E: Logistics and Transportation Review, 42*(5), 409–430.

Yan, S., Tang, C.-H., & Fu, T.-C. (2008). An airline scheduling model and solution algorithms under stochastic demands. *European Journal of Operational Research, 190*(1), 22–39.

Yan, S., & Tseng, C.-H. (2002). A passenger demand model for airline flight scheduling and fleet routing. *Computers & Operations Research, 29*(11), 1559–1581.

Yan, S., & Young, H.-F. (1996). A decision support framework for multi-fleet routing and multi-stop flight scheduling. *Transportation Research Part A: Policy and Practice, 30*(5), 379–398.

Yang, H., & H. Bell, M. G. (1998). Models and algorithms for road network design: a review and some new developments. *Transport Reviews, 18*(3), 257–278.

Yang, X., Pan, B., Evans, J. A., & Lv, B. (2015). Forecasting Chinese tourist volume with search engine data. *Tourism Management, 46*, 386–397.

Yaqoob, I., Hashem, I. A. T., Gani, A., Mokhtar, S., Ahmed, E.,. . . Vasilakos, A. V. (2016). Big data: From beginning to future. *International Journal of Information Management, 36*(6, Part B), 1231–1247.

Yelp. (2018). Yelp Knowledge - Local Analytics & Insights. Retrieved September 03, 2018, from Yelp: https://www.yelp.com/knowledge.

Yew Wong, C., & Karia, N. (2010). Explaining the competitive advantage of logistics service providers: A resource-based view approach. *International Journal of Production Economics*, *128*(1), 51–67.

Yin, R. K. (2017). *Case study research and applications: Design and methods*. Thousand Oaks: SAGE Publications.

York, A. (2018). Social Media Demographics to Inform a Better Segmentation Strategy. Retrieved August 30, 2018, from SproutSocial Inc.: https://sproutsocial.com/insights/new-social-media-demographics/.

Zhan, F. B., & Noon, C. E. (1998). Shortest Path Algorithms: An Evaluation using Real Road Networks. *Transportation Science*, *32*(1), 65.

Zhao, M., Dröge, C., & Stank, T. P. (2001). The Effects of Logistics Capabilities on Firm Performance: Customer-Focused versus Information-Focuses Capabilities. *Journal of Business Logistics*, *22*(2), 91–107.

The manufacturer's authorised representative in the EU is Springer Nature Customer Service Centre GmbH, Europaplatz 3, 69115 Heidelberg, Germany. If you have any concerns regarding our products, please contact ProductSafety@springernature.com

Printed and bound by CPI Group (UK) Ltd, Croydon, CR0 4YY
23/09/2026
02221733-0003